2 419650 001

CW00854293

CENTRAL LIBRARY, WESTGATE

To renew, please quote these details

If you wish to renew this loan without bringing the book to the library, please quote number from label at top of this page. Books can be renewed **once only** in this way.

CENTRAL LIBRARY OXFORD
RENEWALS OXFORD 241718
ENQUIRIES OXFORD 815509

This book is due for return on or before the last date shown above. It may be renewed at the Library or by post or telephone.

OXFORDSHIRE COUNTY LIBRARIES

Fiji
Coups in
Paradise

Race, Politics
and Military
Intervention

Victor Lal

Victor Lal

Oxford

Zed Books Ltd
London and New Jersey

Fiji: Coups in Paradise was first published by
Zed Books Ltd, 57 Caledonian Road, London N1 9BU, UK, and
171 First Avenue, Atlantic Highlands, New Jersey 07716, USA,
in 1990. Edition for India published by Allied Publishers
Private Ltd, PO Box No 155, 13/14 Asaf Ali Road,
New Delhi 110 002, India.

Copyright © Victor Lal, 1990

Cover designed by Andrew Corbett.
Typeset by Allied Publishers (Pvt) Ltd, New Delhi.
Printed and bound in the United Kingdom
by Biddles Ltd, Guildford and King's Lynn.

British Library Cataloguing in Publication Data

Lal, Victor
Fiji : coups in paradise : race, politics and
military intervention.
1. Fiji. Political events
I. Title
996'.11

ISBN 0-86232-776-8
ISBN 0-86232-777-6 pbk

Library of Congress Cataloging-in-Publication Data

Lal, Victor.
Fiji : coups in paradise.

Includes index.
1. Fiji—History.   2. Fiji—Race relations.
1. Title.
DU600.L293   1990   996'.11   88-14217
ISBN 0-86232-776-8
ISBN 0-86232-777-6 (pbk.)

This book is dedicated to my late father

Contents

'I have a dream that one day on the red hills of Georgia, sons of former slaves and the sons of former slave-owners will be able to sit down together at the table of brotherhood. I have a dream that one day the state of Missippippi, a state sweltering with the heat of injustice, sweltering with the heat of oppression, will be transformed into an oasis of freedom and justice. I have a dream that my four little children will one one day live in a nation where they will not be judged by the colour of their skin but by the content of the character...'

Martin Luther King, Washington, 28 August, 1963

PREFACE

The tragedy of societies divided along ethnic or religious lines has always existed. But in the second half of the twentieth century much of the bloodshed in the world has been between peoples who find it difficult to coexist in a single polity. Catholic and Protestant in Northern Ireland, Jew and Arab in Palestine, Sikh and Hindu in Punjab, Tamil and Sinhalese in Sri Lanka, Malay and Chinese in Malaysia all provide examples of the failure of political institutions to contain conflicting loyalties, in a way that avoids violence.

Fiji looked for a while like a model for the rest of the world to admire. A dangerously equal balance existed between a traditional indigenous people and an implanted workforce four generations away from their roots. But electoral rules and other devices seemed to offer a formula for civilised co-existence. At the time of writing, the racial strains inherent in the Fijian situation have not led to loss of life in the way that has happened elsewhere.

But democracy depends on trust and in 1987 the world learnt that some Fijians were not prepared to accept the outcome when a properly conducted election produced a predominantly Indian government.

Victor Lal, an experienced journalist in his native Fijian Islands, was awarded a Fellowship to Queen Elizabeth House at Oxford University by the Reuter Foundation in 1984. As he began to study the politics of other ethnically divided states he reconized that the ingredients which had elsewhere led to conflict existed in his own country, and he decided to extend his time at Oxford to write a study of Fiji's racial politics. From the beginning he foresaw, with notable prescience, what the outcome would be—military intervention on behalf of the political supremacy of the indigenous community. The events he had anticipated occurred just as he was completing this study.

Victor Lal's account, which I have had the fortune to watch him working on over the past two years, is a sad but riveting story—and an uncompleted one. It offers insights not just into one South Pacific polity but into the worldwide dilemma of preserving democracy and harmony when fundamental racial divisions exist.

Dr David Butler
Nuffield College
Oxford
September 1987

ACKNOWLEDGEMENTS

I owe thanks to numerous people for assistance in writing this book. My greatest debt is to the Reuter Foundation which in 1984, awarded me a Fellowship to Queen Elizabeth House, thus making it possible for me to relinquish my journalistic work in Fiji and to benefit from the immense resources at Oxford University.

First among individuals to whom I am most grateful is the late Professor Hedley Bull, Balliol College, Oxford, who provided helpful criticism, particularly with regard to Australia's role in the South pacific.

After Professor Bull's death in 1985 Dr David Butler of Nuffield College, Oxford, took over the supervision of my work. His knowledge of electoral politics, his close, detailed and constructive criticisms of the draft were invaluable. Thanks also to Neville Maxwell, the founder and Director of the Journalists' Fellowship Programme at Queen Elizabeth House, who not only interested himself in the project but also helped me in many other ways.

Others at Queen Elizabeth House to whom I owe thanks are Penny Edmeades, Shirley Ardener, Albertha King, Enid Joseph, James (Jimmy) Gordon, Norman Coates and the hospitable and friendly domestic staff who helped me adjust with pleasure to life in Great Britain. Special thanks, too, to Alison Nicol, Angela Milne, and Roy and Thelma Edmeades of Oxford; Anton Hemerijck of Holland; Yakubu Aliyu and Alhaji Mahmood Yakubu of Nigeria; Ben Acquaah of Ghana; and Beathe Skoglie. My gratitude to Joanna Bartlett is deep and personal. Other Journalist Fellows at QEH, notably my contemporary, Michael Overmeyer, were always stimulating and encouraging.

I would also like to thank Professor Lawrence Ziring of Western Michigan University for his helpful suggestions. Other scholars for whose help I am grateful are Professor Ralph Premdas of the University of the West Indies, Trinidad; Professor Arend Lijphart of the University of California, San Diego; Brian Keith-Lucas (the only surviving member of the three-man team which reviewed Fiji's electoral system in 1975); Dr Peter Lyon of the Institute of Commonwealth Studies, University of

London; Professor Yash Ghai of Warwick University; and Professor David Murray of the Open University, England. Sir Zelman Cowen, former Governor-General of Australia and Provost of Oriel College, Oxford, made helpful comments after reading Chapter Four on the 1977 Fiji constitutional crisis.

Several scholars in the field of ethnic politics have also been of great help; among them R.S. Milne, Professor Emeritus of Political Science at the University of British Columbia, Canada; Dr R.K. Vasil of Victoria University, Wellington, New Zealand; and Dr K.L. Gillion, whose writings on Fiji have been stimulating and who helped me evaluate and understand pluralism.

My thanks also to the former Commander of the Royal Fiji Military Forces, Ratu Epeli Nailatikau, for granting me an interview on the role of the army in Fiji politics. To those people in Fiji, too many to name, who contributed their time, knowledge and advice during the preparation of this book, and especially to the political leaders and candidates of diverse experiences, ideologies and activities who granted me lengthy interviews, I wish to express my gratitude.

I proffer special thanks to Dr Cheddi Jagan, the leader of the opposition People's Progressive Party (PPP) and former Prime Minister of Guyana; the former US Ambassador to Fiji, Carl Edward Dillery, who in 1985 granted me an in-depth interview on the role of the US in the South Pacific, especially in Fiji; and to Rosemarie Gillespie, the Australian market researcher who exposed the 'Carroll Team' during the 1982 Fiji general elections.

I would also like to record my debt to the staff of Rhodes House, and of the Social Studies and the Commonwealth Studies libraries. In particular, I wish to acknowledge the help and patience of the Commonwealth Studies librarians Bob Townsend and his assistant Gill Short. The close and careful reading of the final draft by Anna Gourlay of Zed Books greatly helped the clarity of my writing.

The views expressed in this book and the responsibility for any errors are exclusively my own.

Victor Lal
Queen Elizabeth House
Oxford 1988

ABBREVIATIONS

AAFLI	Asian-American Free Labor Institute
ABC	Australian Broadcasting Commission
ACP-EEC	Afro/Caribbean/Pacific-European Economic Community
ACTU	Australian Council of Trade Unions
ALP	Australian Labor Party
ALTA	Agricultural Landlord and Tenants Act
ALTO	Agricultural Landlord and Tenants Ordinance
ASIO	Australian Security and Intelligence Organisation
ASIS	Australian Security and Intelligence Service
BI	Business International
BP	British Petroleum
CEDA	Committee for Economic Development of Australia
CHOGM	Commonwealth Heads of Government Meeting
CIA	Central Intelligence Agency
CMA	Central Monetary Authority
CSR	Colonial Sugar Refining Company
FAB	Fijian Affairs Board
FANG	Fiji Anti-Nuclear Group
FCTU	Fiji Council of Trade Unions
FDFB	Fijian Development Fund Board
FEA	Fiji Electricity Authority
FLP	Fiji Labour Party
FML	Fiji Muslim League
FMPO	Fiji Muslim Political Organisation
FMWO	Fiji Muslim Welfare Organisation
FNP	Fijian Nationalist Party
FPC	Fiji Pine Commission
FPSA	Fiji Public Service Association
FPSC	Fiji Public Service Commission
FTUC	Fiji Trade Union Congress
GEA	General Electors' Association

ICFTU	International Confederation of Free Trade Unions
IMET	International Military Education and Training Programme
LPCA	Labour Committee for Pacific Affairs
NCC	National Civic Council
NED	National Endowment for Democracy
NLC	Native Lands Commission
NLDC	Native Land Development Corporation
NLTB	Native Land Trust Board
NLTO	Native Land Trust Ordinance
PAMS	Pacific Armies Management Seminar
PDU	Pacific Democratic Union
PTUF	Pacific Trade Union Forum
RFMF	Royal Fiji Military Forces
UMC	United Marketing Corporation
USAID	United States Agency for International Development
USP	University of the South Pacific
WUF	Western United Front

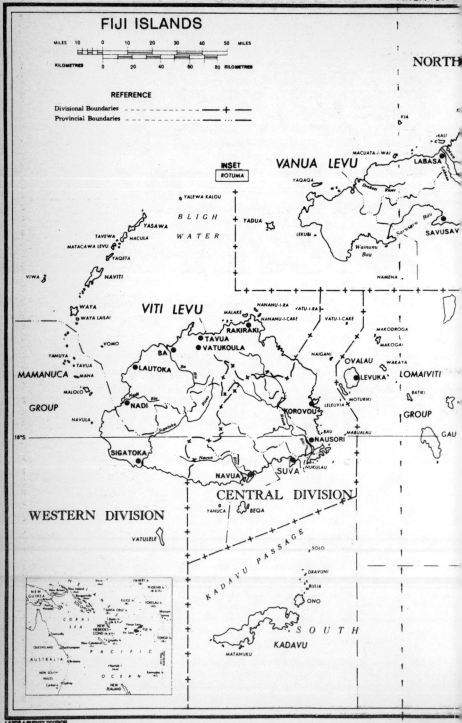

FIJI ISLANDS

MILES 10   0   10   20   30   40   50   MILES

KILOMETRES   0   20   40   60   80   KILOMETRES

REFERENCE

Divisional Boundaries   — — — — — — + — —
Provincial Boundaries   — — — — — — ··· — —

INSET
ROTUMA

NORTH

VANUA LEVU

MACUATA-I-WAI

LABASA

KIA

MALI

YAQAGA

Drakeli River

LEKUBI

Savusavu Bay

SAVUSAV

Wainunu Bay

NAMENA

YALEWA KALOU

BLIGH

WATER

YADUA

YASAWA

TAVEWA

NACULA

MATACAWA LEVU

YAQETA

VIWA

NAVITI

WAYA

WAYA LAILAI

VITI LEVU

MALAKE

NANANU-I-RA

NANANU-I-CAKE

VATU-I-RA

VATU-I-CAKE

MAKODROGA

MAKOGAI

RAKIRAKI

TAVUA

VATUKOULA

NAIGANI

OVALAU

WAKAYA

LOMAIVITI

YANUYA

VOMO

BA

Ba Riv

LAUTOKA

TAVUA

MANA

LEVUKA

BATIKI

MAMANUCA

MALOLO

Nadi Riv

LELEUVIA

MOTURIKI

GROUP

NADI

Sigatoka River

Riv

KOROVOU

BAU

MABUALAU

GROUP

NAVULA

GAU

18°S

NAUSORI

SIGATOKA

Navua

RIV

SUVA

NUKULAU

NAVUA

CENTRAL DIVISION

WESTERN DIVISION

YANUCA

BEQA

VATULELE

KADAVU PASSAGE

SOLO

DRAVUNI

BULIA

ONO

SOUTH

KADAVU

MATANUKU

E180°W

CIKOBIA

NORTHERN DIVISION

VETAVUUA

QELE LEVU

KAVEWA   DRUA DRUA
TUTU
HAALI
Udu Pt

NUKUBASAGA
NUKUBALATE

LABASA
COBIA
YAVU YANUCA
RABI

NANUKU PASSAGE

KIOA

LAUCALA
QAMEA

SAVUSAVU

TAVEUNI

WAILAGI LALA

NAITAUBA

MALIMA
AVEA   SOVU
VANUA BALAVU
CIKOBIA-I-LAU

KORO

NUKUTOLU   YACATA
KAIBU
KANACEA
SUSUI   MUNIA

VATU VARA
MAGO

KATAFAGA

KORO

TUVUCA

MAIVITI
ATIKI
NAIRAI
CICIA
LAU
AROUA

OUP

LATE I VITI
LATE I TOGA
18°S

GAU
SEA
NAYAU
VANUA MASI

LAKEBA PASSAGE

EASTERN DIVISION

LAKEBA

AIWA

VANUA VATU   GROUP
ONEATA

ONEATA PASSAGE

MOALA
OLORUA   MOCE
KOMO   KARONI

TAVU NA SICI
BOUNTY BOAT PASSAGE
VUAQAVA   NAMUKA-I-LAU

TOTOYA
NAVUTU-RA AGASA LEVU
KABARA
NAVUTU-I-LOMA
MARABO

PACIFIC   OCEAN
FULAGA
OGEA LEVU

MATUKU
OGEA DRIKI

INSET

VATOA
ONO-I-LAU
TUVANA-I-COLO
TUVANA-I-RA

MRS. S. NAND

CHAPTER ONE

FIJI: A NEW NATION IS BORN

Fiji has developed stable political institutions, a thriving healthy
economy and high social and educational standards. The peoples
of Fiji are thus fitted to take the next important step in their progress among the nations.
— *Lord Shepherd* (then British Minister of State for Foreign and
Commonwealth Affairs, 1970).

The tenth of October is a memorable date in Fiji's historical and political
calendar. In 1874 it recorded the surrender of the islands' sovereignty to
Great Britain, and in 1970 the end of British rule and Fiji's entry into the
Commonwealth of Nations as an independent state. In the 96 years between these two dates astonishing political, social and economic changes
took place.
    The history of British rule in Fiji is, broadly speaking, one of benevo-
lent apartheid. It had kept apart the settler Europeans, the indigenous
Fijians, and the Indians who had been brought from British India to
work on the sugar plantations as 'coolie labourers'. Later, at independence, the Constitution of Fiji codified these vestiges of racialism. Today
in Fiji, with a population of 714,000 in which Fiji Indians (48.6%)
slightly outnumber ethnic Fijians (46.2%) and the minority European,
part-European, Chinese and other groups (normally referred to as
General Electors), politics is race and race is politics.
    Fiji is a prime example of J.S. Furnivall's definition of the plural socie-
ty as 'comprising two or more elements or social orders which live side
by side, yet without mingling, in one political unit'.[1] The ethnic groups
have preserved many of the social customs and the language, religion
and etiquette of their forbears, but for the most part have adopted the
English language and aspects of English manners. Nevertheless, ethnic
affiliation remains the main basis of identity.

The Colonial Era

The unity with Great Britain was forged on 10 October 1874 when a
group of Fijian chiefs, led by the self-styled 'King of Fiji', Ratu Seru
Cakobau, signed the Deed of Cession whereby Fiji became a possession
and dependency of the British Crown. In Cakobau's words, the British
were called upon to 'exercise a watchful control over the welfare of his
children and people; and who, having survived the barbaric law and age,
are now submitting themselves under Her Majesty's rule to civilization.'[2]

Of the several factors that had compelled the Fijian chiefs to pass their country to the British Crown, one was the menacing threat from the restless white settlers. Soon after the Deed of Cession the British government appointed Sir Arthur Hamilton Gordon (later Lord Stanmore), as the first resident Governor of Fiji. The youngest son of the fourth Earl of Aberdeen, Gordon, who had earlier ruled Trinidad (1866-70) and Mauritius (1870-74), arrived in Fiji with a reputation—although his true intentions have since been closely questioned—as 'an uncompromising guardian of native rights', and his influence can still be found in the land policies in Fiji.

But by providing that land not yet alienated to Europeans, consisting of nearly 90 per cent of the country, was to remain under Fijian ownership Gordon left a most bitter and intractable legacy. He also introduced a new ethnic group into Fiji—the indentured Indian labourers—in order to provide a work force for the colony's cane-fields, while simultaneously safeguarding Fijian culture.

Consequently, the chiefs—Fiji's traditional rulers from time immemorial—were also recognized by the British colonial government. Through the system of indirect rule, evolved by Lord Lugard[3] and applied by his successors elsewhere, separate Fijian institutions were established to facilitate ruling them. These institutions, while creating a 'state within a state', gave the Fijian chiefs limited powers to rule their people, and to deeply influence the subsequent history of the colony. The objectives underlying Gordon's policies were similar to those which had given rise to colonial practices elsewhere: a divide and rule policy whereby the colonial government divided in order to rule what it integrated in order to exploit. The partnership between the chiefs and Gordon not only enabled 'the domination of the eastern chiefs particularly over the west, but it also resulted in the rise of a new type of bureaucratic chief, aware of the need to adjust to the demands of the colonial state if they were to achieve their class aims'.[4]

Meanwhile, for 90 years, Fiji was provided with the usual British colonial type government: a Governor, responsible to the Queen through the Secretary for Colonies; an Executive Council, to advise the Governor on policy; and a Legislative Council, to help him make laws.

In the early days the white planters' attitudes also underwent many changes leading to a clear shift in their outlook. They demanded democratic rights and self-government and condemned the Crown colony authorities and their native policy: 'One of the most powerful chiefs in Fiji was seen as only fit to be a white man's gardener.'[5] In 1883 and 1885 they had tried unsuccessfully to oust the colonial government by federation with Australia and New Zealand.

When they took stock of the racial and political future, however, they began to demand separate representation in the Legislative Council; this was granted to them in 1904. After securing political paramountcy in the affairs of the colony, the Europeans gradually developed strong ties with the Fijians. The special relationship between the British and the Fijian chiefs, which was to remain intact even after independence, further strengthened the European position in the colony.

The Indian 'Coolies'

Meanwhile, the Indians continued to labour for the Australian commercial giant, the Colonial Sugar Refining (CSR) company which virtually financed the colony. The inhumane treatment the indentured Indians suffered at the hands of their white masters on the plantations, between 1879 and 1916 (a period remembered in Indo-Fijian folklore as *narak* (hell)) when the indenture system was stopped, permanently embittered the relationship between the Indians and the Europeans. Memories of the harsh indenture days still linger on, as one labourer who arrived in 1911 recalled:

> When we arrived in Fiji we were herded into a punt like pigs and taken to Nukulau where we stayed for a fortnight. We were given rice ... full of worms [and] kept and fed like animals. Later we were separated into groups for various employers to choose who they wanted.... We got to Navua and were given a three-legged pot, a large spoon, a bucket and a billycan, and some rice. We then went to Nakaulevu where we saw the lines.[6]

Even the Indian women did not escape the yoke of indenture. According to Miss Hannah Dudley of the Methodist Mission:

> They arrive in this country timid, fearful women, not knowing where they are to be sent. They are allotted to plantations like so many dumb animals. If they do not perform [their work] satisfactorily they are struck or fined, or ... sent to gaol. The life on the plantations alters their demeanour and even their very faces. Some look crushed and broken-hearted, others sullen, others hard and evil. I shall never forget the first time I saw "indentured" women when they were returning from their day's work. The look on those women's faces haunts me.[7]

The 'free' and politically conscious Indians' clamour in the 1920s for a common voters' roll and for economic rights aroused strong political feeling among the whites. As European politician Henry Marks remarked in a speech in 1929: 'We have the Indians here and we must make the best of it and teach them we are the colony and not the Indians.'[8] Indians in Fiji were to be no more than domesticated serfs. But they continued their struggle, especially after 1920, when unexpired contracts of indenture were cancelled and the Indian population settled down as farmers and cane growers. Convinced that political activity held the key to further progress, they attempted with increased determination to make inroads into the political system, and in 1929 were finally granted communal franchise.

This chance to use the ballot box, as Ahmed Ali puts it, 'contributed to their political advancement; it increased their political awareness, taught them to make political judgements; accustomed them to the hurly-burly of elections, and having tasted the fruits of democracy, albeit very limited, their appetite for political growth and power increased.'[9] For the next 30 years the Indians continued to fight for political emancipation, culminating in the formation of their own political party, the Federation Party, in the 1960s. This party subsequently merged with a small but predominantly Fijian Western Democratic Party, led by a militant trade unionist Apisai Tora, to form the National Federation Party (NFP).

The Indians also became formidable rivals to the Europeans in many spheres of life but, although they were becoming a force to be reckoned with, they became isolated from the running of the country because of their demand for common roll; their repeated strikes in the cane fields; their refusal to support the war effort and the fact that by 1946 they had become the majority ethnic group.

Thus in the intervening years the relationship between the different communities greatly deteriorated. Political arguments became transformed into racial quarrels. The races drifted apart. The Fijians were not going to give up on common roll and the land question. Despite the Indian pressure and a walkout from the Legislative Council in 1929, the Fijians were in no mood to be conciliatory and the differences became temporarily irreconcilable.

The first political change came in 1904 when the composition of the Legislative Council was amended to comprise ten officials, six elected (European) members and two Fijian members, selected by the Governor, from a list submitted by the Fijian Council of Chiefs. In 1916, provision was made for an Indian nominated member, and in 1929 further changes included provision for elected Indian representation.

The franchise was limited to British subjects of European or Indian descent, with certain income or property qualifications and, in the case of Indians, able to read and write in English or an Indian language. In 1937, further changes introduced into the Constitution increased the number of official members of the legislature to 16 (including three *ex officio*) and of unofficial members to 15, comprising: five Europeans (three elected, two nominated); five Fijians (at first selected by the Governor, later elected by the Council of Chiefs); five Indians (three elected, two nominated).

The Legislative Council remained unchanged for 25 years. While Fijians were securely on the side of the British, the Europeans continued as the dominant force in the country. Their sense of superiority, developed through years of privilege, was all too often demonstrated by the arrogance and rudeness that characterized their dealings with the Indians. This, combined with a number of other interrelated factors, served to encourage and provoke a new and more aggressive expression of Indian demands.

The Fijians' displeasure over the granting of franchise to the Indians was counterbalanced by the appointment of an eminent Oxford-educated Fijian high chief, Ratu Sir Lala Sukuna, as the first Speaker of the Legislative Council to preside in the Governor's absence. This appointment, in 1956, has been described as a major landmark in Fijian political development.

As the British moved to divest themselves of their colonies the pace of constitutional development accelerated. Early in 1961 the government presented a plan for constitutional advancement for Fiji, including a membership system, designed as the first step towards a full ministerial system, with unofficial members of the Executive Council taking responsibility for government departments.

The Politics of Communalism

This proposal was shelved after both the Fijian and European unofficial members opposed it. In an atmosphere of mistrust and hostility, a new plan was announced, representing the greatest measure of agreement that could be reached among the unofficial members. This plan was approved by the Secretary for Colonies and came into force by a February 1963 Order of Council.

The sudden discernible change in the pace of political development aroused grave concern for the country's future. Many thought it could ultimately lead to an open conflict between the Fijian population and Indian interests.[10]

Britain, however, provided an interim respite. In July 1964 it was found possible to introduce the 'membership' system, but attempts to introduce further constitutional changes were viewed with apprehension by the Fijian leaders, mainly chiefs. One of a handful of Fijians, concerned with a sense of self-preservation, was Ratu George Cakobau, great-grandson of Ratu Seru Cakobau and the first local Governor-General after independence, who warned: 'I have nothing against independence. Let [it] come. But when [it] comes, I should like this recorded in this House—Let the British government return Fiji to Fijians in the state and in the same spirit with which Fijians gave Fiji to Great Britain.'[11] Other Fijian politicians expressed similar views. Ratu Penaia Ganilau, another leading chief who replaced Ratu George as Governor-General, had also declared that when the composition of the Legislative Council was changed, 'the running of this colony must be handed over [to] the Fijians—by that, I mean administratively, and politically.'[12] These statements demonstrated the determination of the great majority of Chiefs to maintain effective control over the country's affairs.

In November 1933, the Council of Chiefs in its resolution, which still stands to this day, had categorically rejected the possibility that Fiji would one day be ruled by the 'immigrant' Indians:

That this Council records its strong and unanimous opinion that Fiji, having been ceded to Her Majesty the Queen of Great Britain and Ireland, Her Heirs and Successors, the immigrant Indian population should neither directly or indirectly have any part in the control of direction of matters affecting the interests of the Fijian race.[13]

Meanwhile, under the membership system, six unofficial members of the Legislative Council were invited to become members of the Executive Council: three of which, a Fijian (Ratu Mara), an Indian (Ambalal Dahyabhai Patel) and a European (John Falvey), were given the portfolios of Natural Resources, Social Services and Works and Communications, respectively.

Thus, in accordance with Article 73(b) of the UN Charter, Britain was preparing 'to develop self-government, to take due account of the political aspirations of the people, and to assist them in the progressive development of their free political institutions, according to the particular circumstances of each territory and its people'.[14] As one colonial territory after another sought and won independence, the UN Committee on Colonialism was also putting pressure on Britain to end colonial rule in Fiji.

The 'winds of change' sweeping across Africa and Asia were now approaching Fiji, prompting the different groups to consolidate their own positions. In 1956, Fijians had formed the Fijian Association primarily to check the political aspirations of the Indians. But as the reality of independence dawned upon them, the Association was reorganized to involve itself fully in the future constitutional talks. The granting of the franchise to the Fijians in 1963 and the Fijian Association's victory in the general elections that same year encouraged the chiefly leaders to appeal directly to the Fijian community for unity and support.

The events and elections of 1963 strengthened the politics of communalism. Ethnic groups began to view each other in terms of 'us' and 'them'. For example, the part-Europeans, an ethnically mixed group, became aware of their latent power in Fiji politics. As Norman Meller and James Anthony wrote: 'As this segment of the population continues to grow, so that its vote becomes even more decisive in the European contests, the support of the part-European will undoubtedly be cultivated with greater assiduity.'[15] The Indian leaders, spurred by political events in Kenya and the tacit support of emissaries from India, responded similarly, with the Federation Party under A.D. Patel's leadership appealing to the Indian community for support and unity.

Predictably the Europeans too voiced their views, bitterly condemning Indian demands for common roll and openly siding with the Fijians on any proposals for a political arrangement to deny the Indians any effective leverage. As far back as 1922 they were asserting that '99% of the Europeans and Fijians are loyalists and the handing over of

Fiji to evil-smelling, treacherous, non-educated, garlic eating Indians would be one of the greatest crimes in the history of the British Empire'.[16]

The Indian stereotype of the Fijian as an 'irresponsible, childish, uncivilised fellow, or *jungli*', while the Fijian learned to avoid 'the heathen and undersized Indian coolie, brought to work as a plantation slave',[17] also proved advantageous for the Europeans. In order to remain masters, the Europeans had imposed their own racial segregation with separate halls, churches, voluntary associations, tennis clubs and Sunday schools.[18]

Official British Crown colony policies also failed to bring the races together, especially the Indians and the Fijians. Separate political representation and separate associations were largely designed to protect Fijian interests. In response, the Fijians sought refuge and protection from the British, even during the height of independence negotiations. 'We demand ... to know whether our bond with the Crown is the same as when the high chiefs of Fiji handed over their land and people to Her late Majesty, Queen Victoria ... the Fijian people must be informed of what is going on behind the scenes.'[19]

Fear of the unknown troubled the Fijians. In the words of Ratu Mara, later to become the first Prime Minister of independent Fiji: 'undefined constitutional changes conjure up all sorts of political perils in the minds of Fijians', and, 'it can throw up on the screen of one's mind the Congo, Algeria, Cyprus, Cuba or even the partition of India and Pakistan.'[20] Ratu Mara stressed that the Fijians should be pitied rather than condemned for preferring the known to the unknown devil.

Despite the phobias and suspicions; animosity and ill-will between the different groups; gross economic disparities, with the Fijians at the bottom of the ladder, and a political system based on premises of racial segregation, British officialdom found itself required to satisfy simultaneously three divergent requests: 'to safeguard Fijian paramountcy; to preserve the privileges of the European minority, who were resentful of any attempt to erode their special position, and to grant Indians political rights which did not emphasize inequality and discrimination against them.'[21]

Against this background, in early January 1963 the then Under-Secretary of State for Colonies, Nigel Fisher, visited Fiji on a fact-finding mission; the trip was designed to calm the inflamed feelings of both Indians and Fijians and to explore the possibility of self-government or even independence. 1963 also saw the introduction of universal franchise to Fijians; elections to the new Legislative Council in April; and granting of the franchise to women for the first time. Income and property qualifications were abolished and only a simple literacy qualification retained. In 1964, the Governor, Sir Derek Jakeway, convened a meeting of the unofficial members of the Legislative Council to discuss the constitutional conference to be held in London.

Political changes were on the way. In February 1965 it was decided to hold the London Conference in July, and in April of the same year the then Parliamentary Under-Secretary of State, Mrs Eirene White, made a short visit to Fiji. The prevailing opinion in official circles in London was that intercommunal talks alone could bring a peaceful constitutional change. The Constitutional Conference to be held in London, from 26 July to 9 August 1965, was to construct a framework that would preserve Fiji's continuing association with Britain and within which further progress towards self-government could be made.

Even before the group went to London, however, controversy broke out between the two parties over common franchise and land issues, and the strained atmosphere was later transferred to London.

Common Roll

Since the issue of common roll would resurface again and again, it would be useful at this point to put it in its true perspective. The roots of the Indian demand for common roll reach deep into history. Common franchise had been idealized by Indians as 'the panacea that would provide them with security by ensuring them a permanent place in the Fijian sun', and equality they saw as 'a matter of *izzat* (self-respect) and communal franchise as their stigma of inferiority'.[22] The plight of Indians in other British ex-colonies had further heightened their fears. In desperation, they sometimes sought help from India, insisting that 'the Government of India must do something to protect the rights of the Indians settled here as otherwise Fiji will become in all respects South Africa.'[23]

The response they received was encouraging in the main. Mahatma Gandhi, for example, advised: 'United effort and agitation will surely bring about relief at an early or late period but whether it comes early or late it is perfectly useless to go to the [Legislative] Council unless this elementary thing [common franchise] is done.'[24] Other concerned groups, such as the Imperial Indian Citizenship Association in Bombay and the Indians Overseas Association in London, were always available to advise the Indo-Fijian leaders.

Thus the Indian leaders in Fiji made the issue of common roll a rallying cry for any political agreement. Even the founder of the NFP, A.D. Patel, the India-born lawyer turned politician, was to assert in 1965 that common franchise was the only genuine method of democratic representation. 'It is the only way to bring about political integration and change a multi-racial society into one nation. It should precede and not follow racial integration.'[25] For several reasons the NFP was against a communal franchise.[26]

Meanwhile, when the respective parties finally met in London for the 1965 constitutional talks, the growing power struggle for the country came into the open. The Indian delegation contended that the proper course was to proceed at once to elections by single-member constituencies, on a common roll, with neither communal qualifications for electors nor communal reservations of seats for candidates. They made clear their view that as the Indians constituted the majority of the population, they were entitled to at least parity of representation with the Fijians; and they considered that full internal self-government should be introduced forthwith. The Fijians and their European allies disagreed, insisting that a common franchise was a desirable but long-term objective.

In sum, a by-product of the debate was the introduction of a partial communal roll and the new cross-voting system. The British government decided that common roll was not practicable until the communities had achieved a greater degree of integration. Most important, the communal roll chosen by the British was the kind of franchise that had already proved to be unworkable in many parts of the British Empire.[27]

One outcome of the 1965 constitutional talks was that the British had washed their hands of the affair by 'imposing' a racial constitution that left the Indian delegation bitter and frustrated. 'The error we all made', one delegate claimed, 'was in thinking that the Fijian would be treated like any ordinary colonial—however, he had found a special place in the hearts of the British people.'[28] The Fijians and the Europeans ruthlessly used their minority positions as a psychological weapon for maximum political advantage. European over-representation in the new Constitution was justified on the grounds of their contribution of capital and skill to the well-being of the colony.

Another feature of the new Constitution was the enfranchisement of minority groups, such as the Chinese (who had hitherto had no vote) and immigrants from other Pacific islands. The principal new Constitutional provisions were for an elected majority in the Legislative Council (36 elected members with not more than four official members nominated by the Governor); enfranchisement of minority groups; a Bill of Rights; and the provision for a ministerial system.

The cross-voting system was designed to protect the rights of different racial groups. Overall, the voting system was such that for a communal seat, the voters of a particular race only should vote for a candidate of that race; in cross-voting for a national seat, voters of all races vote for a candidate of a particular race.

In this case, of the 36 elected members of the Legislative Council, nine Fijians (including Rotumans and other Pacific Islanders), nine Indians and seven general members (a term introduced to include Chinese and other races as well as Europeans) were to be elected on three communal rolls; two Fijians were to be elected by the Council of Chiefs, and a further nine members were to be elected under the new system, in which people of all races would vote together but seats would be reserved in equal propositions for members of the three groups. The 1966 Constitution also reflected the ethnic markers of Fiji's society.

Party Politics

Following the introduction of universal adult franchise and a system that combined communal with cross-voting, the stage was set for general elections to be held in September-October 1966, the first to be fought on party lines. In the early 1960s, while the Fijians saw their future in the Fijian Association, the Indians, mostly farmers, pinned their hopes on the various cane unions, notably the Maha Sangh and the Kisan Sangh. They found it hard, however, to reconcile their differences between 'sugar politics' and politics in general. While the Fiji Kisan Sangh was led by a school-teacher, Ayodhya Prasad, the Maha Sangh comprised activists like A.D. Patel (a Gujarati), S.M. Koya (a South Indian Muslim), and James Madhavan (a Christian) who also represented the Indian community in the Legislative Council.

Towards the end of the 1960s the Kisan Sangh broke ranks after a dispute about sugar-cane prices and signed an agreement with the CSR company. The deal also split the Indian community, giving rise to the Indian National Congress, a political wing of the Kisan Sangh. In early 1965 Ayodhya Prasad made private approaches to the president of the Fijian Association, Ratu Mara, for political association; Ratu Mara, who 'had begun to view politics from a larger new perception',[29] agreed. He had come to realize that Indian participation in the political life of Fiji was inevitable and in an attempt to provide an alternative to Indian majority rule propounded the idea of building Fiji as a multiracial society. On 12 March 1966, therefore, the Fijian Association, the General Electors' Association, Fiji Minority Party, Rotuman Convention, Tongan Organizations and Suva Rotuman Association, convened in Suva to form 'an all-races political alliance'.

The end result was the birth of the Alliance Party which encompassed the various groups in a coalition of three major constituents: the Fijian Association; the National Congress of Fiji (Indian Alliance); and the General Electors' Association. The Alliance, sporting a multiracial image, like that of its counterpart in Malaysia, was, in Ratu Mara's words, 'the outstanding achievement of the decade, if not of the century', because 'all races are coming together to find areas of agreement'.[30] In some respects this was true, but the Indian representatives did not have the blessing of the Indian community.[31] Some Indians saw the formation of the Alliance as another example of political opportunism to exploit them for Fijian political ends.

The principal issue in the 1966 election was the Constitution. The Federation Party condemned it and called for its abolition, claiming that it provided nothing tangible and immediate for the Indian people and left everything to the future. European over-representation was again condemned and the common roll issue regained widespread currency. The appearance of ethnically based politics also gave rise to political entrepreneurs, the growth of extremist parties and the polarization of voters.

Each side accused the other of fanning the flames of communal hatred. Ratu Mara denounced the policies of the Federation Party, accusing them of concentrating on 'personal abuse and vilification of other candidates and their supporters, and [having] made racial hatred and ill-will a dominant feature of their campaign'.[32] He said there was no place for such instigators and warned of the evils of racial politics as exemplified by British Guiana (later to become Guyana), which 'was a peaceful country till one politician and his followers ... told his supporters to vote only for candidates of their own race.'[33] The dramatic events that occurred in British Guiana as a result of racial politics were not repeated in Fiji, but the ethnic nature of support for the parties was clear. The Alliance won 23 seats but, joined by the two victorious Independents and the two Council of Chiefs' members, its final total was 27. The Federation Party won the remaining nine, but these were the nine Indian communal seats. The Alliance won nine Fijian and six out of seven General Elector communal seats, the remaining General Elector seat went to one of the Independents who had joined with the Alliance.

The nine seats in the three-man cross-voting constituencies were taken by the Alliance because of a significant percentage of Indian votes while hardly any Fijians supported the Federation Party. The Alliance polled 67.6 per cent of Fijian votes for its nine communal seats; the Federation Party polled 65.3 per cent of the Indian votes.[34]

In a deeply divided society each ethnic community has its own party, and in 1966 the Indians clearly identified themselves with the Federation Party which was founded as a political organization to champion their causes and aspirations. The Alliance, on the other hand, revealed itself as a predominantly, though not exclusively Fijian party. The 1966 elections were simply another form of ethnic struggle. There was also a qualitative change in the attitude of Indian leaders soon after the resumption of business in the Legislative Council.

On 1 September 1967 the Executive Council, despite much controversy, was replaced by a Council of Ministers, and Ratu Mara became Chief Minister. The opposition Federation Party again condemned the Constitution as iniquitous and undemocratic and walked out—all reminiscent of 1929.[35] They stayed out but resigned only some months later, causing a set of by-elections.

The walkout was bitterly denounced. Some observers, however, saw it as an inevitable response to the compulsions of a political climate. A small minority of Indians in the Alliance were openly forthright in their condemnations. But the walkout failed to disrupt the running of the colony. Shortly after assuming office, Ratu Mara set out on a study tour of some of the new multiracial countries to acquaint himself with the workings of the ministerial system and these countries' methods of economic development. He had useful discussions with Forbes Burnham of Guyana, Dr Eric Williams of Trinidad, Hugh Shearer of Jamaica, Lee Kwan Yew of Singapore, and Tunku Abdul Rahman of Malaysia.

In the 1968 by-elections, the Federation Party again returned to the political arena and convincingly trounced the Alliance candidates to win the nine Indian communal seats that had become vacant after the 1967 walkout. Although the Indian voter turnout was lower than in 1966, Indian votes rose from 65.3 per cent in 1966 to 78.6.[36] The expected results coupled with the Eatanswill style of campaigning by the Federation Party offended the Fijians. Indignantly interpreting the election results as 'ingratitude' and as part of an Indian plan for domination, the Fijians went on the offensive.

The 'political insults' heaped on the Fijian chiefs by the Indian leaders caused ill-feeling. The Fijians felt that the Indian voters had let down Ratu Mara. Tension heightened when one Indian speaker openly boasted that if the Fijians offered any violence, it would be met by violence. One commentator noted that:

> In this tense situation, the Chief Minister decreed that there should not be any demonstrations by the Alliance Party and that the defeat at the polls should be accepted. But ... some of the younger and more aggressive Fijian backbenchers in the Legislative Council ... organised massive demonstrations ... in Indian dominated areas. In their tens of thousands, Fijians paraded grimly, massively, but quietly—through townships with streets lined with Indian owned shops. Not a blow was struck, not a stone was thrown, not a threat was made—but for the first time Indians felt the shock of seeing their normally friendly Fijian neighbours carrying banners with the words, 'Indians Go Home'.[37]

The demonstrations and events of 1968 proved useful in revealing that the fears of each community would become the problems of the other unless there was a bold move towards a settlement in the near future. The ethnic leaders had to abandon their protective stances if they were to avoid communal mayhem. 'If anything affected our decision to seek independence', Ratu Mara said, 'it was the animosity which arose during the by-elections for Indian communal seats in 1968. This generated greater efforts to find agreement between the races because we realised that we were right on the brink of disaster if we were not careful.'[38]

The Road to Independence

In addition, despite militant leadership, leaders were emerging within the Federation Party who enjoined caution, reason, constitutionalism, and the politics of compromise. The lessons of other strife-torn countries helped convince Fiji's political leaders that moderation and understanding were essential for political stability. For example, the bloody racial riots that convulsed Malaysia in May 1969 stunned Fiji's political leaders who were accustomed to admire that country's record of multiracialism.

In August 1969 a series of discussions took place between the Alliance and the NFP to consider further constitutional changes and, on 3 November 1969, the two major parties agreed that Fiji should become independent by way of Dominion status. This sudden, amicable agreement was possible because in October 1969, during the negotiations, the leader of the NFP, A.D. Patel, had died. His successor, Koya, a lawyer by profession, proved flexible and conciliatory towards the Alliance and Ratu Mara; also, the gesture on the part of the Fijians temporarily forced the Indians to shelve their demand for common roll.

During the series of discussions in August 1969 the Alliance favoured Dominion status, with the Queen as constitutional monarch, represented in Fiji by a Governor-General. The NFP envisaged Fiji as an independent state, with an elected President of Fijian origin as its Head, but Fiji should be a member of the Commonwealth. Both parties agreed on Commonwealth membership and that Fiji should proceed to independence. Events abroad had again influenced their decision; this time it was the violence in Mauritius, on 12 March 1968, the day of Independence.[39]

Following the broad agreement between the two parties, Lord Shepherd, the British Minister of State for Foreign and Commonwealth Affairs, visited Fiji from 26 January to 2 February 1970, 'to acquaint himself at first hand with the position reached in the talks'. The parties agreed on most issues except on the composition of the Legislature and method of election. The Constitutional Conference was subsequently held at Marlborough House in London from 20 April to 5 May 1970.

On 30 April, in the course of the Conference, Ratu Mara announced that agreement had been reached on an interim solution. He told the Conference, in plenary session, that he had discussed the matter further with the Leader of the Opposition, Koya, and they had agreed that he should make the following statement to the Conference:

> The Alliance Party stated that as in 1965 they recognised that election on a common roll basis was a desirable long-term objective but they could not not agree to its introduction at the present stage. On the other hand the National Federation Party reiterated its stand that common roll could be introduced immediately in Fiji and could form the basis of the next general elections without in any way one race dominating others but resulting in a justly representative national Parliament.
>
> The two parties having regard to the national good and for peace, order and good government of independent Fiji reached the following conclusions ... that the democratic processes of Fiji should be through political parties, each with its own political philosophy and programme for the economic and social advancement of the people of Fiji cutting across race, colour and creed, and that all should work to this end. The Conference called upon the Government of Fiji to see to the immediate completion of the extension of common roll to all

towns and township elections, in particular, Lautoka and Suva. The Conference also agreed that at some time after the next election and before the second election the Prime Minister, after consultation with the Leader of the Opposition, should arrange that a Royal Commission should be set up to study and make recommendations for the most appropriate method of election and representation for Fiji and that the terms of reference should be agreed by the Prime Minister with the Leader of the Opposition. The Conference further agreed that the Lower House should be composed as follows:

	Communal	National Roll
Fijian	12	10
Indian	12	10
General	3	5

In agreeing to this composition for the Lower House the parties acknowledged that this is an *interim solution* and provides for the first House of Representatives elected after Independence, and the Parliament would, after considering the Royal Commission Report, provide through legislation for the composition and method of election of a new House of Representatives, and that such legislation so passed would be regarded as an *entrenched* part of the Constitution.[40]

It was also agreed that a Senate comprising 22 members be appointed by the Governor-General on the basis of nominations distributed as follows: Prime Minister, seven; Leader of the Opposition, six; Great Council of Chiefs, eight; and Council of Rotuma, one. Nevertheless, the Senate, which was created at the suggestion of the Indian delegates, was designed to serve as a protector of the land rights and customs of the native Fijians. Any legislation that affected these rights could be vetoed by the representatives of the Great Council of Chiefs. It may be noted that, while the Indian leaders opted for a small piece of the political pie rather than none, the 1970 Marlborough House Conference was a solid victory for Fijians. The Fijians were a minority and the Constitution went out of its way to safeguard their interests.

On 10 October 1970 Fiji became independent, ending all the social and political tensions of over three-quarters of a century of British rule. The country moved into an equable political climate of a parliamentary democracy in which rival communal parties were to compete for power. The political leaders signed the Constitution, which assumed the operation of representative and responsible government using the Westminster model, but future political conflicts were by no means unlikely.

That the British had devolved upon the two major communities the responsibility of reaching an agreement provoked severe criticism, and the Indian leaders did not hesitate to raise the issue. The following exchange between R.D. Patel (who became the first Speaker of the House of Representatives after independence) and Lord Shepherd, exemplifies the situation:[41]

> *R.D. Patel:* Surely, Britain had kept the races apart for the last 90 years, and now it must take some responsibility to bring them together. It cannot just leave us to our own devices.
>
> *Lord Shepherd:* My dear chap, if I had to assume responsibility for the sins of my British forefathers for the past 300 years, I would hardly be sitting here as a Minister of the Crown. Indeed, I would be in sackcloth and ashes doing penance in some monastery.

Power Politics

Politics is about power. During the London talks the principal issue was about who was losing power and who was gaining it. In Ahmed Ali's words:

> Colonial rule on its departure left Fiji in Fijian hands and might thereby be deemed to have fulfilled, at least in a political sense, its promise of the paramountcy of indigenous interests. By permitting European over-representation and facilitating an alliance of European and Fijian communities, it substantially secured the European position. As for Indians, who had been brought in initially as indentured labourers but with the promises of "employment of rights" and a large majority of whom in 1970 supported the opposition National Federation Party, the care of their future was transferred, without any special legal provisions, from the British to the new rulers of Fiji.[42]

As mentioned earlier, whenever the question of constitutional reform was considered during the period of British rule, all the minority communities, including the Fijians, showed no hesitation in emphasizing the need for adequate safeguards for their rights to be inscribed in the Constitution. The principal aim of the Fijian and European leaders was the prevention of the 'Indianization' of Fiji. Racialism was thus to become the key to future policies in the country. The problem of minorities, wherever it exists, is usually a sensitive one. Throughout Fiji's history this problem has been one of the most fundamental issues in its government and politics. The political demands of the Fijians were sharpened further by their special status as a minority fighting for a separate identity. In similar situations elsewhere Arend Lijphard argues that

> the key to the fair treatment of minorities is the combined application of power-sharing and autonomy. The ideal is a democratic regime in which minorities can participate fully in decision-making at all levels and in which they have exclusive power in those areas which can be defined as regarding only their own interests. When this ideal cannot be attained because of political or numerical considerations, the second best solution is to try to approximate power-sharing and minority autonomy as closely as possible.[43]

Fiji's Constitution did just that; it is the final depository of a Fijian's Charter of Rights. The possibility of domination by the Indians was, and is, the nightmare of many Fijians and other ethnic groups. While the Fijians did not, and do not attempt to justify their domination, nevertheless the very idea of equality alarms them and their traditional chiefs. They offered political representation to the Indians without in any way diminishing their own hegemony.

A deeper study of the decision reached at the London constitutional talks, however, shows that fear of Fijians being swamped by the majority Indians, because the two races were 'equally numerous racial groups, effectively two "majority" communities, each large enough to view itself as capable of assuming a majority role, giving it the right to rule'[44] was an oversimplification. Apparently no consideration had been given to future population trends which could result in Indians becoming a minority in Fiji. In fact, in 1976, for the first time since censuses had been conducted, the number of persons of Indian origin had declined as a percentage of the total population, once more constituting just under 50 per cent of the total population. There were also projections that by 1988 the Fijian population would overtake the Indians as the largest racial group in the country. Apart from the far-reaching implications, this trend also raises a fundamental question: which group is to be treated as a minority in need of constitutional and political safeguards?

All the current indicators suggest that the Indians are on their way to becoming a minority. The latest population figures released in 1986 reveal that the Fijian percentage increased from 44.2 in 1976 to 46.2 in 1986, while the Indian percentage had decreased from 49.8 to 48.6 over the same period. The gap between the Indian and the Fijian populations has dropped from 5.6 to 2.4 per cent.[45]

Ironically, the brief explosion of joy which marked the ushering in of independence, the political honeymoon between Ratu Mara and Koya, and the rapprochement between the Alliance and the NFP during the constitutional talks, came to a close after the first general election in 1972. The Alliance, led by Ratu Mara, easily won 33 out of the 52 seats in the House of Representatives; the NFP won 19 seats. By the time of the 1972 general elections communal polarization between the different racial groups was complete. The Fijians, by now securely ensconced in power, immediately set about trying to consolidate their political hold of the country.

Among the Indian community there is a general consensus that their leaders had failed to ensure their security. There have been charges of a 'sell-out' of the community. The infighting amongst the Indians leaders; the Fijians' perception that despite their ownership of land, they are an endangered species; and competition in education and business fields continue to provide tinder for communal warfare.

If there were any losers in the long, tortuous, and complex struggle for political power, it was not the chosen *petit-bourgeois* Indian leaders but the ordinary Indian who had placed faith and hope in the London constitutional talks. The Constitution, as succeeding chapters show, left a legacy of hatred and mistrust amongst the different races. Although the predominantly Fijian Alliance government promised to carve out 'unity in diversity', the euphoria of independence was only the beginning of a long journey for the Indians who had marched from plantation to politics.

In his 1971 New Year message, Ratu Mara, as Prime Minister of independent Fiji, described 1970 as the 'year of hope fulfilled'. The peaceful transition from colony to independence for him was 'a pearl of great pride which can perhaps be shared with the world at large'.[46]

But how far his fellow Fijians would go in sharing political power with the Indians was to be revealed after the 1972 general elections.[47]

Notes

1. J.S. Furnivall, 1948.
2. Quoted in Sir Alan Burns, 1963, p. 99.
3. On indirect rule, see Lugard, *The Dual Mandate in British Tropical Africa*, (4th ed.), Edinburgh, 1929.
4. R.T. Robertson, *The Journal of Pacific Studies (JPS)*, Vol. 12, 1986.
5. Wadan Narsey, *JPS*, Vol. 5, 1979, p. 74.
6. Quoted in Ahmed Ali, 1980, p. 6.
7. Quoted in K.L. Gillion, 1962, p. 107.
8. Quoted in Ali, 1980, p. 143.
9. Ibid., p. 139.
10. Adrian Mayer, 1963, p. 135.
11. Quoted in N. Meller and J. Anthony, 1968, p. 103.
12. Quoted in R.F. Watters, 1969, p. 24.
13. Quoted in Ali, 1980, p.143.
14. *Fiji*, 1970, Central Office of Information, London.
15. Meller and Anthony, 1968, p. 100.
16. *Fiji Times*, 1 March 1922.
17. Gillion, 1977, pp. 14-15.
18. See Alexander Mamak, 1978, p. 26.
19. Quoted in Ali, 1977, p. 45.
20. Ibid.
21. Ibid., p. 17.
22. Ibid., p. 19.
23. Quoted in Gillion, 1977, p. 155.
24. Quoted in Ali, 1977, p. 19.
25. Quoted in R.K. Vasil, 1984, p. 115.
26. Ibid., p. 116.
27. See *Report of the Special Commission on the Constitution of Ceylon*, Cmd. 3131, 1928, London.

28. K.C. Ramrakha, 'The Great Constitution Chaos', *Fiji Sun*, 11 July 1978, p. 8.
29. Vasil, 1984, p. 262.
30. Quoted in Mamak, 1978, p. 147.
31. Vasil, 1984, p. 263.
32. *Fiji Times*, 24 September 1966.
33. Ibid.
34. This background on the 1966 general election is largely drawn from Ahmed Ali, 1976, p. 68.
35. Ibid., p. 69.
36. Ibid.
37. 'Bright Future for Independent Fiji, *Commonwealth*, Vol. XIV, No. 5, October 1970, p. 174.
38. Ibid.
39. Ramrakha, 1978, p. 9.
40. Legislative Council of Fiji, *Report of the Fiji Constitutional Conference 1970*, Council Paper No. 5, 1970, p. 1.
41. Quoted in Ramrakha, 1978, p. 9.
42. Ali, 1980, pp. 163-64.
43. Arend Lijphart in Georgina Ashworth (ed.), *World Minorities in the Eighties*, London, 1980, Preface, xvii.
44. Vasil, 1984, p. 357.
45. *Fiji Sun*, 3 October 1986, p. 1.
46. *Fiji: Report for the Year 1970*, London, 1972.
47. For a discussion of this 1972 general election, see Ahmed Ali, *Journal of Pacific History*, Vol. 8, 1973, pp. 171-80, and J.D. Chick, *Pacific Perspective*, Vol. 1, No. 2, 1973, pp. 54-61.

CHAPTER TWO

INDIANS GO HOME

The time has arrived when Indians or people of Indian origin in this country be repatriated back to India and that their travelling expenses back home and compensation for their properties in the country be met by the British Government.

Sakeasi Butadroka, 1975 (Leader of the Fijian Nationalist Party).

The political, social and economic history of the overseas Indians in former British colonies has been one of discrimination, restriction and non-acceptance. Historically, it was the needs of the British Empire that prompted the recruitment of thousands of Indians from British India to work in various parts of the Empire as 'coolie labourers'. Table 2.1 shows indentured Indian immigration to seven countries between 1834 and 1916:

Table 2.1

Indentured Indian Immigration

Country	Dates	Numbers
Mauritius	1834-1910	453,063
British Guiana	1838-1916	238,909
Trinidad	1845-1916	143,939
Jamaica	1845-1916	36,412
Natal	1860-1911	152,184
Surinam	1873-1916	34,000
Fiji	1879-1916	60,969

Source: Brij V. Lal, 'Fiji Girmitiyas: The Background to Banishment', in Vijay Mishra (ed.), *Rama's Banishment* (Auckland: Heinemann Educational Books, 1979), p. 18.

The Fiji Indians, as has already been noted, were accommodated as members of independent Fiji and their rights protected under a Bill of Rights incorporated in the Constitution. This, however, was not a sufficient guarantee. Many Indians believed that over time their vulnerability would increase, and for example they turned to the fate of overseas Indians.

The problems and hardships of many of these overseas Indians ranged from subjection and humiliation to persecution and even mass explusion. In East and Central Africa the Asian community, which had unified in its resolve to free itself from the shackles of European domination and exploitation, found itself in the post-independence era prey to the politics or Africanization policies of the new governments. In South Africa they had been stripped of their basic rights and their fate placed in the hands of a white minority.

In Malaysia and Sri Lanka, the Indians remain predominantly a rural, plantation-based population, cut off from the mainstream of national politics. In the West Indies and Mauritius, their struggle for political power gave rise to violent clashes with those of African descent. Racial tensions run high, especially during election times. V.S. Naipaul observes that his country, Trinidad, 'teeters on the brink of a racial war'. To him the African 'has a deep contempt for all that is not white; his values are the values of white imperialism at its most bigoted', while the Indian 'despises the Negro for not being an Indian'.[1] In Guyana the East Indians suffered most under the despotic leadership of the late Forbes Burnham. The former Dutch colony of Surinam, which has a large East Indian (Hindustani) population, has not been free of racial troubles; and in Madagascar the Indians and Pakistanis were beaten up for 'getting too rich'.

Overseas Indians had hoped that India's independence and the end of the indenture system would bring a change of attitude. Instead, however, they were advised to identify themselves with the colonies in which they had settled. Nationalist Indian leaders vigorously campaigned on behalf of the overseas Indians, but stressed repeatedly that 'integration' was the key to their salvation in the foreign lands. This point was clearly emphasized by the first Prime Minister of India, Pandit Jawaharlal Nehru, when he raised the issue of citizenship, including that of Fiji Indians, in the Lok Sabha on 8 March 1948:

> Now these Indians abroad. . . . Are they Indian citizens . . . or not? If . . . not, then our interest in them becomes cultural and humanitarian, not political. . . . Take the Indians of Fiji or Mauritius: are they going to retain their nationality, or will they become Fiji nationals or Mauritians? The same question arises in regard to Burma and Ceylon. . . . This House . . . wants to treat them as Indians, and with the same breath it wants a complete franchise for them in the countries where they are living. Of course, the two things do not go together. Either they get the franchise as nationals of the other country, or treat them as Indians minus the franchise and ask for them the most favourable treatment given to an alien.[2]

But reality was different. Many overseas Indians earnestly supported integration, yet circumstances would not permit it. In South Africa, for example, their growing capacity to compete in the economic field led not to integration but segregation.

The Durban riots of 1949, in which many Asians were killed and their homes pillaged and plundered, also alarmed South Africa's already oppressed Asian community. The riots increased anxiety among other overseas Indians in British colonies. They also stood as a warning that full-scale racial violence could erupt anywhere. Indians' fears were compounded further when in 1954 Africans 'staged a boycott of Asian business in Uganda, accompanied by much violence and intimidation. This was followed by another boycott campaign in 1959, causing many Asians to flee Uganda in the pre-independence years.'³ Further, in Kenya, the Asians' problems increased when, after gaining independence in 1963, the Kenyan government instituted a policy of Africanization, reserving top positions in business and government for those of African origin, and requiring Kenyan Asians to renounce British citizenship if they wished to enjoy privileges in Kenya. All these developments gave Indian leaders in Fiji a greater cause for concern. The British government's hastily legislated Special Immigration Act in 1968 to curtail the inflow of Kenyan Asians during the 'Kenya Exodus', when thousands of Kenyan Asians holding British citizenship fled to Britain, brought the hidden fears of Fiji's Indian community to the surface.

A wave of hysteria launched by the actions of British MP, Enoch Powell, and a former Commonwealth and Colonial Secretary, Duncan Sandys, to keep the Kenyan Asians out, forced some radical Fiji Indian leaders to press for specific rights for their fellow Indians during the 1970 constitutional talks in London. But they were not surprised by Sandys' actions; East Indians in Guyana had accused him of conniving with the Americans to prevent their leader Cheddi Jagan from coming to power.

Against this grim international backdrop the Indian leaders negotiated for Fiji's independence. And on 10 October 1970 more then 98 per cent of Fiji-born Indians accepted Fijian citizenship. It was felt that it would not be in the national interest to permit the people of Fiji to have dual citizenship, or indeed any other citizenship rights which would be inconsistent with Fiji's sovereignty; neither did the leaders wish to see another Kenya in the South Pacific.

In the wake of Fiji's independence in 1970, as already noted, Fiji's Indians were fearful for their security in the country, and there was a corresponding fear among the Fijians of the superior economic abilities and political aspirations of the settler Indian community. While outwardly the Indians displayed solidarity with the Fijians in securing a peaceful and bloodless transition to independence, they knew that the outcome for them had yet to be seen. Nevertheless they joined in the independence celebration hoping that common sense and fair play would prevail in the near future. The cordial relationship between Ratu Mara and Koya, culminating in them travelling together to India and the United Nations, held bright prospects for race relations in Fiji. Ratu Mara's public admission regarding the lack of Indian participation in running the country and his advocacy for a coalition government also portended hopes of political stability.

The first major post-independence test came shortly after the 1972 general elections. The Alliance's overwhelming success at the polls on the slogan 'peace, progress and prosperity' gave the party a clear opportunity to fulfil its promises. Furthermore, the Alliance's 24 per cent Indian support reflected the strong appeal that party's doctrine of multiracialism had for some Indians, especially those with influential financial clout. The appointment of a successful NFP candidate, R.D. Patel, as the first Speaker of the Alliance-controlled House of Representatives provided at least temporary assurance to the beleaguered Indian community.

Meanwhile, events in Uganda increased the concern and sense of insecurity of Fiji Indians. In 1972 President Idi Amin ordered the expulsion of thousands of British Asians from Uganda. The events that followed frightened the Indians in Fiji. Worldwide shock and dismay had been expressed over the expulsions, but many countries' unwillingness to provide sanctuary to the expelled Asians; the Indian government's 'cool response' that all Asians in East Africa holding British passports were Britain's responsibility; and mass demonstrations in London against the 'invasion of Britain',[4] all combined to heighten rumours among Fiji Indians that they would be next. They argued, with justification, that no one had either foreseen or even thought that the Asians would be expelled *en masse* from Africa.

The Fijian Association, the predominant arm of the Alliance Party, made it clear that it was not prepared to accept any Ugandan Asians into Fiji. Ratu Mara, who was out of the country at the time, later expressed regret at this decision and admitted that nothing had set back his efforts towards creating a multiracial state in Fiji more than Amin's action in Uganda. But the Indians concluded that there were elements in the Fijian community, including some in the Alliance government, likely to follow in Amin's footsteps.

The origins of the anti-Indian crusade can be traced back to 1877, two years before the first batch of indentured Indians were introduced to Fiji. Reflecting the voice of the planters over the proposed Indian immigration, the *Fiji Times* in an editorial on 27 October 1877 proclaimed: 'The interests of the country are better served by the immigration of Polynesians than the introduction of a class whose lives, traditions, habits, and thoughts are so widely opposed to those of the people amongst who they have to reside. . . . "India for the Indians, Fiji for the Fijians".'[5]

In later years the Fijians themselves began to make similar statements, and in 1888, as more labourers were introduced, the chiefs questioned the colonial governor about the Indians' future position. The most 'notorious agitator in the early days of the indenture was a Fijian carpenter, Apolosi Nawai [described as the 'Rasputin of the Pacific'], who was three times banished to the island of Rotuma, in 1917, 1930 and 1940, for his semi-religious anti-white and anti-Indian propaganda, promising a new era of prosperity for the Fijians, with himself as their Messiah.'[6]

The demise of Nawai, however, failed to discourage other Fijians from taking up the 'Fiji for the Fijians' slogan. As the Indian population increased and prospered on Fijian soil, the slogan gained widespread support among the Fijians. Many chose to ignore the contributions of the Indians, and especially the tribute paid by their own Fijian leader, Ratu Sukuna, who in 1936 told the Council of Chiefs:

> Let us not ignore the fact that there is another community settled here in our midst. I refer to the Indians. They have increased more rapidly than we. They have become producers on our soil. They are continuously striving to better themselves. Although they are a different race, yet we are each a unit in the British Empire. They have shouldered many burdens that have helped Fiji onward. We have derived much money from them by way of rents. A large proportion of our prosperity is derived from their labour.[7]

Between the 1940s and the 1960s Fijian nationalism intensified, culminating in 1973 when an assistant Fijian minister in the Alliance government, Sakeasi Butadroka, challenged the party's multiracial policies, claiming that they neglected the welfare and economic needs of the Fijians. Although there was some truth in Butadroka's claims, the Alliance felt it smacked of racism and endangered the party's 'pluralistic ideology' at a time when one of the most crucial problems facing the Alliance Party, under the leadership of Ratu Mara, was the question of national integration.

Butadroka was summarily expelled from the party, but continued to sit in Parliament as an independent member, until on 10 January 1974 he formed his own Fijian Nationalist Party (FNP), adopting a 'Fiji for the Fijians' stance. He focussed his assault on the Indians and the Fijian chiefs in the Alliance Party.

To analyse the rise of the FNP and its implications for future race relations a brief examination of Butadroka and the Fijian society is necessary. The Fijians are essentially a traditional-minded people living in their villages under the chiefs. The distinction between the chiefs and the commoners is marked. Structurally, fijian society is

> traditionally hierarchical. . . . The essential social strata to which every Fijian belongs are the *i tokatoka* (extended family), the *mataqali* (family group), and the *yavusa* (clan). In any locality a number of *yavusa* group together to form a *vanua*, which is in fact a socio-political association, cemented by social and economic ties, with common allegiance to a chief.
>
> A number of *vanua* group together through kinship links, or conquest to form a *matanitu* (state). Fijian society is largely patrilineal, and the direct agnatic descendants of a legendary founder (the *kalou vu* or ancestor god) formed the *yavusa*.
>
> Below and descended from this founder are the senior male relatives who form the *mataqali*; below this are the *i tokatoka* which are subdivisions based on the same principle of patrilineal agnatic descent. This pattern of social organization is repeated throughout the

Fijian countryside. . . . These groupings are universally recognised by Fijians: they are the units under which Fijians are registered as land-owners, and quite distinct from other communities in Fiji. . . . Basically unchanged for generations their codification and maintenance through the registration of all Fijian births ensure their permanence.[8]

Any intrusion from outside the traditional Fijian system is thus viewed with apprehension. But in 1973 the legitimacy of the chiefly rule, based upon traditional norms, faced an internal challenge. Butadroka declared an all-out verbal war on Ratu Mara. Butadroka himself was from a non-chiefly background and hailed from Reva province whose paramount chief is Adi Lady Lala, Ratu Mara's wife. But Butadroka described his dispute with Ratu Mara as a political one claiming that 'European politics and traditional matters are two different things'.[9] He went on to state that 'in traditional matters I greatly respect this man of noble birth and I also have reverence and try at all times to do what is right'.[10]

Henceforth the FNP was to portray itself as an ethno-nationalist movement formed to help and protect Fijians. Thus Butadroka (a man who had 'lost his senses', according to Ratu Mara) permanently revolutionized Fiji's politics, paving the way for other disgruntled Fijians to follow suit in the future. He had finally broken the tenuous thread of tolerance for the chiefs, and the effects were to be felt in the subsequent elections.

Butadroka had now achieved a new political base. His involvement with the rural Fijians had placed him at a crossroads. He launched a great popular campaign for the betterment of the Fijian way of life, claiming that the Alliance Party 'drowns all the objectives of the Fijian Association. . . . It is their ticket that got the government into power. Yet the government itself turns around and brands any issue for the Fijian interests "racist".'

The FNP leadership, meanwhile, continued to emphasize its cultural and political control of the country, successfully penetrating the consciousness of the Fijian masses. In its 1977 submission to the then Governor-General, Ratu George Cakobau, the FNP claimed to be an independence movement. It regarded the Deed of Cession—interpreted by the Fijians as their Magna Carta—and the Independence Constitution as documents designed to serve foreign interests.

The FNP also charged that: the Alliance has sold out Fijian rights; the Alliance is a tool of European and Indian businessmen; and Ratu Mara has been running a Lauan administration—claiming that the people of Ratu Mara's home province, Lau, were reaping most benefit from the government's rural development programme, and that the Lauans received the best jobs and government opportunities.[11] In short, the FNP wanted the Fijianization of the country. This was clearly spelled out in their party's programme adopted at its convention in December 1976,[12] which stated:

1. The interests of the Fijians will be paramount at all times.
2. The Fijians must always hold the positions of Governor-General, Prime Minister, Minister for Fijian Affairs and Rural Development, Minister for Lands, Minister for Education, Minister for Agriculture, Minister for Home Affairs and Minister for Commerce, Industry and Co-operatives.
3. More opportunities should be given for Fijians to enter business and commerce.
4. Total opposition to common roll.
5. Strengthen Fijian Administration and the Government should give it financial backing and support.
6. Establishment of a Fijian institute to teach Fijians business skills.
7. Pensions for ex-servicemen.
8. Indians should be repatriated to India after Fiji gains full independence.
9. More Government development projects should be concentrated in rural areas.
10. Expansion of the Royal Fiji Military Forces' trade section to help ease unemployment.
11. The return to Fijians of all land that was illegally sold.

In these demands the nationalists not only displayed their 'racialist nationalism' but explained publicly the whole of their vision. They also served notice that the FNP was to stay on the political stage and not disappear as rapidly as it had emerged. The nationalists were, in fact, fulfilling the fears expressed by the Fijian Association during the pre-constitutional talks in 1970: that if the Fijians were pushed too far, the time would come 'when it would dawn on them that probably the only outlet would be to take things into their own hands'.[13] In 1977 the FNP did not rule out using violence to attain its end.

What circumstances and conditions have led to the present state of affairs? And why, in 1977, after seven years of independence, did Fiji still have a divided polity experiencing acute ethno-nationalist conflict between the Fijians and the Indians?

The erroneous and often repeated notion that the Fijians hold the political power while the Indians hold the economic power must also be put into perspective.

The origins of the contemporary state of affairs must be sought elsewhere. The economic imbalances among the ethnic groups can be traced to the period of British rule. Jai Narayan, in his book, *The Political Economy of Fiji*, has shown how the colonial government's native policy was responsible for the post-war gap in resource distribution between the Fijians and those of other racial/ethnic groups.[14] In recent years some students of Fijian politics have blamed this situation on the present Fijian institutions, in-built customs and traditions, and the role of the chiefs, which they claim hinders Fijian commecial enterprises.[15] The Indians, on the other hand, had learnt their lessons from their indentured experiences, which, as Ahmed Ali notes, had 'left the labourers and their descendants convinced that they alone were able to help themselves, charity in a strange land they could not expect'.[16]

The economic disparities and occupational distribution of the different racial/ethnic groups have been thoroughly documented in detailed studies of the period under review, notably in 1970, by the Australian economist E.K. Fisk.[17] In assessing the relative economic position of the Indians *vis-à-vis* others, Fisk noted that in 1969 approximately 75 per cent of the new investments in all industries were accounted for by overseas companies. The Indians were engaged in medium- to small-scale enterprises, including most of the commercial farming, while the European/ Chinese group managed and operated the large corporations and institutions, often for foreign owners; and the Fijians were in non-monetary, but affluent, subsistence sector. This then, as Ali comments, 'is hardly a picture of Indian prosperity; in fact it signifies a very inequitable distribution of wealth'.[18]

He further notes that prosperity among the Indians is largely in the hands of 'free migrants': the Gujerati merchants who dominate commerce. Among the non-Gujerati Indians, wealth lies in the hands of the few who own large construction firms, monopolize the transport industry or have other large business interests.[19] The Royal Commission on Voting made a similar observation in 1975:

> The ordinary men, seeing the extent to which shops and other commercial activities are in Indian hands, believe that the economic power of the Indian population as a whole is very great. In fact, it is not so significant when compared with the international companies in Fiji.[20]

Over the years the income disparity between the two major races has narrowed as is evident from the World Bank Report, which disclosed that the income gap between the two groups was, in fact, relatively moderate. The difference was really $F5 a household in 1977 with the average yearly income of an Indian family being $4,003, a Fijian family $3,398, while that of a family of other races averaged $6,228. Furthermore, the position of employed Indians was better than that of Fijians, but when it came to unemployment the situation was reversed. A nationwide unemployment survey in 1973 reported that of all those unemployed 37 per cent were Fijian, 58 per cent Indian and only 5 per cent from among other races. Of the employed Indians 35.9 per cent were engaged in agriculture, predominantly in sugar-cane cultivation.[21] Indians fared better in the professional, top-, middle- and lower-management levels including skilled and semi-skilled work, while the Fijians dominated the technical, semi-professional and the unskilled levels.

The Indians swiftly countered Butadroka's charges about their 'economic dominance' by pointing out the Fijian dominance in the Civil Service, government, and the law and order institutions. The complaint of racial imbalance, however, is an Indian one: that Fijians are excessively represented in crucial Civil Service posts. The Fijians, on the other hand, claim that such Indian complaints are purely political and not racial. It is, therefore, not surprising, as Myron Weiner and Mary Katzenstein state about preferential policies in India, that where employment preferences are implemented they produce 'angry responses on the part of other ethnic groups'.[22] Accordingly, the Indo-Fijian leaders are quick to raise a battle cry on behalf of their community and some often charged the Alliance government with taking a pro-Fijian stance, which in their opinion is 'reflected in much of what it says and does'.[23] While multiracialism is still espoused, and was a matter of slogans, very little multiracialism was at work. One Indian political leader, Jai Ram Reddy, even alleged that in almost 'all aspects of government work and activities, from its composition, its development work and appointment to boards, promotion in the Civil Service, its Crown land policy, everywhere",[24] the Alliance government had practised discrimination.

The motive, claimed Reddy, was purely racial, and he charged that Fiji was implementing a policy designed to ensure that all strategic levels of government were staffed by 'loyal personnel', which in effect meant that Fijians were placed in positions of command in order to deliberately create an 'out group', namely the Indians. Indian indignation is further fuelled by the fact that many candidates of Indian extraction are better qualified and that the percentage of Indian passes in internal examinations conducted by the FPSC are significantly higher than those of their Fijian counterparts.

The government could not escape the discrimination charges, as the following figures in some crucial ministries and institutions in mid-1975 clearly reveal: The Ministry of Fijian Affairs and Rural Development: Fijians 51; Indians 4; Others 1. The Ministry of Home Affairs (responsible for the country's security): Fijians 35; Indians and Others nil. The Royal Fiji Police Force: Fijians 638; Indians 457; Europeans 21; Others 12.[25]

By taking Reddy's charges further and examining the racial composition of the police force it can be seen that there has been no significant change in the recruitment pattern (see Table 2.2), the one exception being that in 1974 the force was led by a European, while in 1984 it was led by an Indian.

Table 2.2

Racial Composition of Fiji's Police Force

Year	Total	Fijians	Europeans	Indians	Others
1970	85	25	10	46	4
1972	114	36	16	62	—
1975	1,128	638	21	457	12
1977	No figures available				

Year	Total	Fijians	Europeans	Indians	Others
1979	1,459	779	1	621	58
1980	No figures available				
1981	1,506	775	—	651	80
1982	1,518	774	3	678	63
1983	1,540	774	—	700	66
1984	1,502	755	—	684	63

Source: Fiji Public Service Commission, 1985.

The racial disparity in the composition of Fiji's armed forces—the key instrument of power and an essential feature of any multi-party system, particularly in an ethnically divided society—is even sharper. In 1975 the armed forces were and still are the exclusive domain of the Fijians—Indian representation is insignificant.

The four most sensitive issues, however, are: the electoral system; land ownership; education; and that Fijians, compared to other racial groups, are minimally integrated into a money economy. The most intense debate, however, centres upon land and education, particularly during election times, with the issue of land ownership as the single most divisive one. The Fijians regard it as the crucial axis of both economic and political power; to them 'the land is the people; break up the land and you break the people'.[26] As the Governor-General, Ratu Sir Penaia Ganilau, put it: 'Ownership of land is to the Fijians an extension of themselves. It represents culture, identity, and security.'[27]

Conversely, education is to Indians what land is to Fijians—the source of their existence. During colonial days the planters were totally opposed to educating Indians, and the Christian missions were already committed to the education of the Fijians.[28] Today Indians contend that:

> Without education, their children will grow up untrained and will be fit only for manual labour ... just as their ancestors had to indenture themselves to labour abroad, so their children would be destined to do likewise ... they would not even be able to emigrate from Fiji, and if evicted, what would they do abroad but become slaves of someone else, like their forefathers.[29]

The history of the land in Fiji has been thoroughly covered elsewhere. Briefly, to own land is a natural ambition of the Indians. But the realization of this ambition has been circumscribed everywhere by different land ordinances. Most of the land, as already stated, is Fijian owned; the freehold land is in European hands, and Indians own barely 1.7 per cent; but over 80 per cent of Indians work as cane farmers on land leased from the Fijians. Consequently, they feel insecure and vulnerable because, as Reddy has noted, 'many of them, particularly farmers, are mere tenants with very limited security of tenure—and they realise that it is in the nature of a lease that it will expire one day, be it 20 or 30 years' and that while 'the tenant knows that he has a place to live, he is not sure that his dependant will when he is gone'.[30]

The Indian dilemma is exacerbated because (1) the largest group of unemployed are Indians with no material security; (2) they are generally squatters, their mobility is severely limited; (3) they have no social security system; (4) they cannot fall back on land because they have none; (5) the greatest degree of undernourishment and poverty exists within this group.

Above all, the Indians have nothing similar to the Fijian Administration through which to articulate their problems and marshal their opinions and grievances. Neither the British nor the Alliance government made any effort to establish a Ministry of Indian Affairs, even as a symbolic gesture, to indicate that they are not, as some claim, deliberately treated as second-class citizens. Inevitably, the Indians could not but make empty protests.[31]

Fijians, on the other hand, have the protection of the Fijian Administration, reorganized in its modern form on 1 January 1945. Its chief architect, Ratu Sukuna, saw the Administration as a body 'to train chiefs and people in orderly, sound and progressive government, the better to fit them eventually for the give and take of democratic institutions'.[32] The Fijian Administration may be regarded 'as a system of local government for Fijians ... a system empowered by law to organise some of the activities of the Fijian people for their own social, economic and political development as well as for the preservation of their traditional way of life.'[33]

Fijians are further protected by other statutory boards and councils: the Fijian Affairs Board (FAB); the Council of Chiefs; the Provincial Councils; the Fijian Development Fund Board (FDFB); the Native Land Trust Board (NLTB); and the Native Land Development Corporation (NLDC). The Fijian Administration system functions under the authority of the FAB, which comprises the Minister for Fijian Affairs and Rural Development, eight members elected by the Fijian members of the House of Representatives, and two members of the Great Council of Chiefs. It also has several expert advisers. One of its main functions is to make recommendations to the government on proposals it considers of benefit to the Fijian people. It also expresses opinion on legislation that affects Fijians before it is submitted to Parliament.

But it is the NLTB which has frequently attracted widespread Indian criticism, both from the cane farmers and from the politicians. The Native Land Trust Ordinance (NLTO) of 1940 established the NLTB to: administer all native land 'for the benefit of the Fijian owner'; protect the interest of the native owners by reserving sufficient lands for their present and future needs; provide suitable land for settlement; and secure continuity of policy and security of tenure.

The highly politicized issue, however, is the nature of land tenure in Fiji. Since the majority of Indian cane farmers depend on the leased land for their livelihood, any attempt by the Fijian landowners or the NLTB (which has from time to time threatened to evict farmers who renege on their debts) to tamper with the conditions of a lease attracts passionate outbursts.

As already stated, with the exception of Crown land, most land was declared inalienable to non-Fijians. In the 1930s, competition for land between the Indians and the Fijians increased, with Fijians refusing to renew old leases or to offer new ones. The typical Fijian assertion was that 'the Indian community, having shown us the way and given us the example, can hardly expect to continue to hold all the agricultural land in the sugar districts . . . where the plough mints money'.[34] In some instances, when Fijians did agree to lease out their land, prices were exorbitant.

The Fijian Administration finally decided to grant 30-year leases to Indian tenants, but to safeguard future Fijian interests a policy of reserve land—that is, no longer available to non-Fijians—was formulated in 1940. Additionally, under the Native Lands Commission, during the colonial government, claims to the native lands were established, as was a Reserve Commission, chaired by Ratu Sukuna who, in that capacity, personally approved and endorsed a large part of the reserves.

According to the Spate Reports,[35] however, the policy of reserves was 'over-protective' and, contrary to intentions, harmful to Fijian interests. The Burns Commission of 1959, while reaffirming British commitment to the Fijians, maintained that 'we do not consider that this implies the right of the Fijians to use (or neglect) all this land without regard to the other sections of the population, and, indeed, to the long-term interests of the Fijian peoples themselves'.[36]

The Commission advocated the abolition of reserves if Fijians could be persuaded to agree; but the policy was not abandoned. The Council of Chiefs rejected it, and the demarcation of reserves continued until its completion in 1967. The Commission had also recommended the provision of greater security to Indian settlers; an Agricultural Landlord and Tenants Ordinance (ALTO), granting Indians a 30-year lease consisting of three 10-year periods (10+10+10), was thus passed in 1967. The majority of Indians, however, found this gesture on the part of the Fijians unsatisfactory.

In 1976, to allay Indian fears, the Alliance government passed the Agricultural Landlords and Tenants Act (ALTA) which guaranteed Indians 30-year leases but, unlike the specification of the 1967 ALTO's three 10-year periods, the 1976 Act specified an uninterrupted 20-year lease period, plus 10 years. This Act split the NFP: a group of NFP parliamentarians, defying their colleagues' demands for 99-year leases, supported the Alliance which, constitutionally, needed 39 votes, including that of the Speaker, to push the Act through Parliament.

Many Indians thought this spelt the end of their fight for long-term security. The opposing faction charged the NFP 'ALTO Gang' with selling out the community while the Alliance faced similar charges from the FNP, which claimed that the extension of the leases robbed the Fijians of their land rights. And once again the land issue emerged as a source of conflict. As K.C. Ramrakha put it: 'No matter what Mrs Jai Narayan would have said on the ALTO, Koya was determined to oppose her and the party broke into two pieces over this bill. Please do not forget, it was not Karam Ramrakha who broke the party, it was an issue, the ALTO bill.'[37]

Similarly, an attack by Ramrakha on the NLTB provoked the Minister of Fijian Affairs, Ratu William Toganivalu, into stating that the Board would lease no more land to the Indians. But it was Prime Minister Ratu Mara's statement on land matters that took the Indian community by storm. On 1 March 1978, while the House of Representatives was debating a government sponsored motion to grant $1,270,000 to the NLTB, Ratu Mara warned the country of the Fijians' response if their land rights were trampled upon. In his statement to the House, claiming that he had been provoked by an Indain MP's 'malicious, insulting and provocative statement on the NLTB', Ratu Mara said:

> Why do the Fijians feel so emotional when questions of their land is discussed in this House? ... if people, the citizens of this nation, do not understand the deep emotional feeling of the Fijians, they should know now because if they tread on it and hurt it, blood will flow in this country.[38]

Others, notably Butadroka, saw a peaceful and bloodless solution: the deportation of the people of Indian origin at the expense of the British government. The FNP maintained that 'in the trichotomy that existed during the colonial period, the Indians played the economic go-between role for the benefit of the white settlers and to the detriment of the native Fijians' and that 'the Indians were the catalyst for the transformation of traditional Fiji into a semi-European style one'.[39] Butadroka, who claims to have been influenced by Gandhi's struggle against British rule in India, also questioned the legitimacy of Indian citizenship accorded to them in the Fiji Constitution. He claimed that realization of the essence of the slogan 'Fiji for the Fijians', as Gandhi and Nehru had achieved in India with the slogan 'India for the Indians', had failed because the Fijians had been sold out at the London constitutional talks.

Butadroka pointed out that the Constitution gave the Fijians only 22 seats in the House of Representatives whereas other races had a total of 30. Therefore, he maintained, Fijians had no power in Parliament, and that foreigners actually ruled Fiji. On 9 October 1975, Butadroka introduced a motion in Parliament which read:

> That this House agrees that the time has arrived when Indians or people of Indian origin in this country be repatriated back to India and that their travelling expenses back home and compensation for their properties in the country be met by the British government.[40]

Reactions varied. An Indian member of the Alliance seconded the motion to ensure that it received a proper response. All MPs were united in their condemnation of the motion but opinions were divided regarding how to formulate their criticisms. The Alliance was extremely cautious on this point. The Indians thought that Butadroka was virtually reiterating what Fijian leaders had said before and during independence talks. Ratu Mara described the motion as 'a pernicious doctrine, a despicable doctrine that a politician resorts to only after he has known that he is a hopeless case as a politician',[41] and moved an amendment seeking

> to reaffirm the credit due to Indians [and] Europeans, Chinese and Pacific Islanders for [their] role ... in the development of Fiji, and in particular their concern and willingness to support government's policy in helping the Fijian people to improve their economic situation as quickly as possible.[42]

But the NFP contended that Ratu Mara's amendment was unacceptable to them because it was too weak. Koya, as Opposition leader, proposed the following amendment to Ratu Mara's:

> to reaffirm that Indians along with other races who settled permanently, and their descendants, are full and first-class citizens, that Fiji is their homeland, that they are here to stay permanently. And having regard to the spirit and the letter of the London Constitutional Agreement, this House calls upon every citizen and every organisation in Fiji, regardless of its ethnic background, to denounce publicly any person or organisation which interferes with or disrupts the multi-racial harmony in Fiji.[43]

Butadroka's motion was lost and Ratu Mara's amendment was accepted by acclamation, but the fact that the motion had been introduced at all multiplied Indians' fears about their future in Fiji. Hence political tension and complexity intensified and the Alliance was increasingly seen as approaching Fiji's political problems in terms of the importance of maintaining Fijian privilege, in so far as the new government policies included: (a) reserving 50 per cent of places at the University of the South Pacific for Fijians; (b) granting soft loans to ethnic Fijians to help them in commerce; (c) gearing much of the rural development towards an effort to help the Fijians improve their living standards; (d) the establishment of the Seaqaqa Sugar Scheme to bring Fijians into the sugar industry, and the planting of pine in Fijian land areas to provide extra jobs to them and to cut dependency on sugar to sustain the economy.

In 1976 a Fijian nominee of the Great Council of Chiefs, Senator Inoke Tabua, suggested that 100,000 Fiji Indians should be deported to relieve the 'population pressure'. The Council of Chiefs had raised the issue of potential overpopulation during the Burns Commission in 1959, and had expressed that it was 'a clear moral duty of those who contribute to this growth to display a sense of responsibility in controlling their birth rate'.[44]

The Indians needed no further assurance, even from Ratu Mara who strongly condemned Tabua's remarks and offered to resign from the Alliance if he found proof of any plan afoot within his party to deport the Indians. But both Butadroka's and Tabua's statements revealed the pivotal role played by ethnicity in the country's politics.

Under these circumstances relations between the two communities began to sour. The Fijian population, which regarded Butadroka as a true nationalist, evinced substantial support for the FNP, and anti-Indian propaganda began to find a sympathetic ear amongst certain sections.

The Indians, already deeply disturbed, eagerly awaited the outcome of the findings of the Royal Commission's examination of the country's electoral system to determine their political and constitutional fate. Many, however, feared that another Uganda or South Africa was in the making in the South Pacific.

Notes

1. V.S. Naipaul, 1962, p. 80.
2. Quoted by Hugh Tinker, in Michael Twaddle (ed.), 1975, p. 25.
3. F.R. Metrowich, 1971, p. 71.
4. See William G. Kuepper et al. (1975).
5. Cited in K.L. Gillion, 1962, p. 15.
6. Sir Alan Burns, 1963, p. 184.
7. Quoted in Legislative Council of Fiji, 1960, p. 10.
8. Isireli Lasaqa, 1983, pp. 18-19.
9. Quoted in John Nation, 1978, p. 137.
10. Ibid.
11. Ralph Premdas, *Pacific Perspective*, Vol. 9, No. 2, 1980, p. 34.
12. Quoted in Ahmed Ali, *The Journal of Pacific History*, Vol. 7, 1977, p. 190.
13. R.K. Vasil, 1984, p. 118.
14. Jai Narayan, 1984, p. 91.
15. Aporosa Rakoto, *Pacific Perspective*, Vol. 2, No. 2, 1973, p. 32.
16. Ahmed Ali, 1973, p. 1665.
17. E.K. Fisk, 1970, p. 42.
18. Ali, 1973, p. 1658.
19. Ibid.
20. Quoted in ibid.
21. Alexander Mamak and Ahmed Ali, 1979, p. 193.
22. See Myron Weiner and Mary Fanisod Katzenstein (1981)
23. Jai Ram Reddy, 1980.
24. Ibid., p. 11.
25. Ahmed Ali, 1976, p. 420.
26. O.H.K. Spate, 1959 (subsequently referred to as the *Spate Report*).
27. 'G.G. opens chiefly meeting', *Fiji Department of Information*, No. 454, 1986.
28. On Indian education see K.L. Gillion, 1977, pp. 102-129.
29. Ali, 1980, p. 203.
30. Reddy, 1980, p. 7.
31. As K.C. Ramrakha, quoted in R.S. Milne, 1981, p. 210, stated: 'We do not enjoy any basic say in the centre of power, nor are we ever likely to do so. No com-

munity, no, not even a heavy-duty one like the Indians, can continue to nourish itself on the politics of protest; no community which contributes so much to the life-blood of the country can tolerate such isolation, or can be so forgotten. We must not be placed in a corner, but in the centre.'

32. See F.J. West, 1961, p. 25.
33. R.R. Nayacakaloy, 1975.
34. Quoted in Deryck Scarr (ed.), 1983, p. 147.
35. The *Sapte Report* on Fiji was written by O.H.K. Spate. Professor Spate was summoned to enquire into the economic disparities between the Fijians and the Indians, and to determine whether the traditional structure was responsible for the Fijians' economic position.
36. Quoted in Sir Alan Burns, 1963, p. 204.
37. *Fiji Sun*, 4 July 1978, p. 7.
38. Ibid., 30 March 1978.
39. Ralph Premdas, 1980, p. 34.
40. *Fiji Times*, 10 October 1975.
41. Ibid.
42. Ibid.
43. *Fiji Times*, 14 October 1975.
44. See R.G. Ward, 1965.

CHAPTER THREE

THE ELECTORAL SYSTEM

If Fiji is to take its place in the international world of today it cannot afford to maintain an electoral system which can be represented as racialism

Royal Commission on Fiji's Electoral System, 1975

In Vernon Bogdanor's words 'Electoral systems are the practical instruments through which notions such as consent and representation are translated into reality. For an electoral system is above all a method of converting votes cast by electors into seats in a legislature.'[1] This can be achieved through *plurality, majority*, and *proportional* electoral systems.

The 1970 Fiji Constitution, characterized as a Westminster export model, sought to ensure the rules of the political game. As already noted, however, the basis of franchise on which to elect Members of the House of Representatives has been the most controversial issue in Fiji's politics. It was agreed that elections of 1972 should be conducted on a system of separate communal rolls and cross-voting. Thus, in one way or the other, these elections were based on racial distinctions, and were conducted in single-member constituencies on the British majority or 'first-past-the-post' pattern. But the general consensus was that this system of voting was unsuitable for Fiji because it generated fear among different ethnic groups and encouraged the politics of communalism. In the words of British psephologist David Butler:

> [T]he consequences of first-past-the-post voting are full of paradox. . . . sometimes predictable, sometimes unpredictable, sometimes stabilising, sometimes destabilising. They are certainly not uniform. First-past-the post voting was the instrument that ended Mrs Gandhi's emergency in 1977, and two years later . . . restored her to full power. It . . . brought in apartheid in South Africa in 1948 on a mere 40% of white vote and . . . in the postwar period in Britain, gave full power to government after government without one of them receiving 50% of the ballots cast. . . .[2]

As we shall see later, the first-past-the-post system ended 17 years of Alliance rule in Fiji in 1987 and provoked the violent overthrow of a democratically elected new coalition government by the Fijian military.

During the constitutional talks in 1970 it had been agreed that the basis and mode of representation in Parliament were only 'interim' and that after the 1972 general elections 'a Royal Commission should be set up to study and make recommendations for the most appropriate method of election and representation for Fiji', the terms of reference to be agreed by the Prime Minister and the Leader of the Opposition.

In March 1975, the Governor-General, Ratu George Cakobau, appointed a Royal Commission composed of Professor Harry Street (Chairman), Sir William Hart, and Professor Bryan Keith-Lucas, all British citizens, none of whom had any previous connection with Fiji. In August-September 1975, the Commission toured Fiji extensively and discussed the issue of parliamentary representation with the different political parties, notably individuals and organizations. In all, it received more than 200 oral or written submissions. As Keith-Lucas was to write, 'never again, in all probability, would it be possible for these problems to be looked at in a dispassionate way by uncommitted visitors from the far side of the world.'[3] In the same article he also spelled out the central questions the Commission asked themselves.

Although the Alliance Párty had previously said that the composition of the Lower House was 'an interim solution', it was scornful of the final findings of the Royal Commission. The Alliance's formal written submission to the Commission asserted that it 'is unanimous that the present system is the most appropriate ... for Fiji's political problems and the country's political process'.[4] Displaying 'little enthusiasm for the Commission' and 'little willingness to discuss other possibilities',[5] the party submitted the following arguments in favour of the retention of the existing system:

(a) [It] ensured parliamentary representation to most ethnic groups irrespective of their size while the common roll method of election would give them little chance of having their own representatives in the Lower House as was the case in Britain.

(b) The ... cross-voting [system] 'provides incentive for ethnically-based political groups to align themselves with other ethnic groups and to work together on a platform designed to appeal across ethnic divisions'.

(c) [It] had been tested and had proved itself successful in restraining political groups and leaders from exploiting racial prejudices, especially during elections.

(d) [It] 'recognizes [indigenous Fijian] claims for what many of them consider as their rightful status in their country' and in so doing it had restrained and contained nationalism in the form of indigenous communalism.

(e) As [it] was acceptable to the Alliance Party and its allies, which commanded the greatest support of the voters in the country, it could be asserted that a majority of the people in the country did not wish to see any change in the system.

(f) The combination of communal and cross-voting allowed for the expression of both communal-oriented views and interests based on common good.

(h) The Europeans, part-Europeans, and the Chinese, who constituted less than 5 per cent of the population, felt secure as they had guaranteed seats in Parliament.

(i) [It] ensured a strong Government and a strong Opposition.

(j) The prnciple of communal representation on which the existing system was based 'has contributed substantially to constructive race relations'.

(k) Finally, it would generate a strong sense of insecurity if a system of election was introduced under which no race would know how many of its members would eventually be seated in Parliament until after the votes had been counted.[6]

Moreover, in their submission the Alliance strongly defended the eight seats allocated to the general electors who have traditionally supported the Fijians in their fight against the 'Indianization' of Fiji.

It further asserted that the Fijians perceived 'the desire and agitation for change in the present system by some non-indigenous, whose motivation leans towards greater political power as an attempt to gain political dominance in Fiji'.[7] It also stressed that whatever constitutional changes were introduced, it was essential for all ethnic groups to have maximum participation, especially the minority groups, who should retain their present guaranteed seats in Parliament.

The most startling statement in the Alliance submission was that 'the idea expressed in some quarters that the present Constitution is interim is an *erroneous* one'[8] (my emphasis). This implied that there was no compulsion on Parliament to change the electoral system when it received the Royal Commission's Report. Many political observers therefore concluded that the Alliance leaders were unlikely to accept any proposals for electoral reform.

Despite the mood of pessimism among many, the NFP wholeheartedly welcomed the Commission, and its supporters in their submissions favoured the common roll and the abolition of communal voting. In a surprising move, the NFP flew in an eminent Queen's Counsel, Tom Kellock, the former Director, Legal Division, at the Commonwealth Secretariat, to present its submission to the Commission. And even to the Commission's surprise, Kellock, who had been briefed to present the Opposition's evidence in private, cogently argued for the introduction of proportional representation and the concept of a Government of National Unity and Concord. The NFP had invited an acknowledged expert on multiracial politics in the Third World, Dr. R.K. Vasil of Victoria University, New Zealand, to act as a consultant and prepare its submission to the Royal Commission. It was he who had strongly recommended proportional representation as the most suitable electoral system for the bi-racial society of Fiji.

In another submission the NFP had taken a markedly different view about the object and status of the Royal Commission's Report. It maintained that 'the understanding of 1970 clearly visualised that the Royal Commission would be the instrument to establish fully the fundamental principles of democracy and representative government in this country'; the contemporary constitutional arrangement was only an interim one and was 'the penultimate step in the direction of a fully representative and popular democracy'. It went on to state that 'this is how the arrangement was offered to us and we accepted it in good faith even though in our view it was in many important respects contrary to the very principles of democracy and justice.'[9]

Koya, in his capacity as president of NFP, had taken an active role in the constitutional talks, and in his oral submission had paraphrased the 1970 agreement as a 'package deal', tacitly assuming that 'both sides . . . would accept the recommendations of the Royal Commission on moral grounds if nothing else'.[10] To buttress the Opposition's case, Kellock quoted Ratu Mara's 13th Plenary Session speech in the 1970 London Conference, in which he had stated that the report the Royal Commission might make 'would be taken into consideration, and then become part of the Constitution, otherwise its recommendations could be subject to the whims and fancies of any Parliament'.[11] This, Kellock asserted, amounted to 'an undertaking by the present government that the recommendations you make shall be inserted into the Constitution and become entrenched.'[12]

The NFP also pointed out that Fijian interests were constitutionally protected, and that the maintenance of an undemocratic election system to achieve that objective was, therefore, unnecessary. As already noted, the NFP, during the constitutional talks, had readily conceded that any bill regarding Fijian and other institutions could be neither revoked nor amended without the consent of six of the eight nominees of the Council of Chiefs in the Senate and the supporting votes of three-quarters of the members of each of the two Houses of Parliament. During the constitutional talks Ramrakha had categorically stated:

> We are quite sympathetic to the idea of a weightage for the Fijians. I think you will have to spell it out because too much is bad; again too little is just as worse. I think the upper house would be the best place to do it; even if you want the Council of Chiefs as a base . . . I think it is inevitable that somewhere you will have to give Fijians a weightage, for particular legislation and for power of veto. You can assume for that purpose that upper house is agreed to.[13]

Ratu Mara, in response, had said:

> I think this is most significant in dealing with the Council of Chiefs, the fact that I should indicate to them the sympathy of the Opposition particularly in the safeguard of their interests which will be affected by the change in the Constitution. . . . I want to repeat that so that I can indicate to them that the [Opposition] message is the most sympa-

thetic how Fijian interest could be safeguarded as it has been in the past.[14]

In view of past concessions, the NFP did not hesitate to draw the Commission's attention to these significant statements. As the party's submission put it: 'We readily agreed to this important provision, even though it may hinder social and economic progress in this country, especially with regard to the Fijian community, to reassure our Fijian compatriots that in no way we would want to threaten their interests.'[15] The party reiterated its opposition to communal and cross-voting and communal representation. In its view, given the Fijians' political grasp on the country, land and the armed forces, to argue that any changes to the electoral system might jeopardize their rights was unreal.

The NFP maintained that if any ethnic group had reason to fear future consequences it was the Indians. The Indian birthrate was falling and was now below that of the Fijians; a significant number of Indians had emigrated to such countries as North America, Australia and New Zealand. In a few years' time the Fijian population would exceed the Indian population. The NFP also contended that to reserve eight seats for the General Electors was excessive and disproportionate to the distribution of the population of the country. It also stressed that if Fiji wanted to retain the skilled Indians seeking better opportunities elsewhere, 'the only way ... is by giving the people a stake in the society and the recognition that they are citizens of equal worth'.[16]

Finally, the NFP claimed that the first-past-the-post system as practised in Fiji was 'crude, undependable and undemocratic'. The party thus called upon the Royal Commission to introduce proportional representation in Fiji. It also insisted, as Professor Mackenzie had stated, that the first-past-the-post system was found in many Anglo-Saxon countries 'because the system is justified by history rather than logic'. It had no historical roots in Fiji.

The democratic problem in a plural society 'is to create political institutions which give all the various groups the opportunity to participate in the decision-making, since only thus can they feel that they are full members of a nation, respected by their numerous brethren, and owing equal respect to the national bond which holds them together'.[17]

In Fiji, the quota system of communal representation was entrenched in the country's Constitution to guarantee such membership for all the racial and ethnic groups. In 1975, however, the NFP considered that the electoral system had failed to provide that satisfaction, and in its Royal Commission submission stated:

> The present electoral system in Fiji normally produces a two-party system ... [which] is fine in milti-racial societies where there are a large number of ethnic groups. However, in bi-racial societies such as Fiji, a system of elections more favourable to the growth of a two-party system would tend to maintain parties on the basis of the ethnic

divide. A multi-party system emerging through the operation of proportional representation would inevitably cut across ethnic divisions
and in the process promote ethnic harmony and make the political
system and processes viable and workable.

[Noting further that] In multi-racial societies it is of special significance as in such societies by-elections often create the greatest amount
of ethnic disharmony and conflict. In such elections the attention of
the whole country is focused on them.[18]

Mackenzie stated that communal elections strengthen communal
feelings because in public debate appeals are made principally to the
interests of each community, and within each community the more
violent and selfish spokesmen of special interests outbid the 'moderates
and public-spirited', and further asserted that, 'people entering public
life learn first to talk the language of communal politics, not that of
national politics; communalism may thus defeat nationalism and destory
the possibility of national self-government'[19] Therefore, the NFP
maintained, in order to unite the diverse ethnic groups the best system
for Fiji was proportional representation.

This system is designed to ensure the representation of all contending
political parties in proportion to the number of votes each receives. The
NFP submitted that the method by which this system should be operated
was that of the single transferable vote with multi-member constituencies. This method has been successfully operated in, for example, Ireland,
Australia (Upper House), Malta and Tasmania. Electors are required to
number the candidates in order of preference; surplus votes are reallo-
cated according to second preferences; candidates with the lowest
number of votes are successively eliminated and their preferences
redistributed until all the seats are filled.

To support its case for recommending proportional representation the
NFP spelt out the system's main virtues as:

(a) [It] did not allow for gerrymandering in the delimitation of electoral
constituencies.

(b) No election contest would be between one candidate of one race
and the other of another race.

(c) It encouraged the emergence of a multi-party system which probably was the most workable in a bi-racial society.

(d) No votes were wasted and all votes secured representation in the
legislature.

(e) The system had been devised primarily to provide adequate and
equitable representation to minorities.

(f) It ensured majority rule.

(g) It encouraged continuity of leadership by responsible and reasonable men and women and the system ensured that such leaders would
not be under undue pressure to give in to popular prejudices and extremist ideas.

(i) It would tend to focus attention more on the vital and larger political, economic and social issues during elections than on local, sectarian and religious issues.

(j) Locally powerful extremists and opportunists would in general find it more difficult to get elected than under the first-past-the-post system; and

(k) Bye-elections would be dispensed with.[20]

The NFP's submission finally added that, if its proposals for the introduction of proportional representation were accepted and implemented before the next elections, they believed that a start could be made towards defeating communalism, before the elections, by forming a government of national unity and concord which would include all political parties, but was not to be confused with a coalition government. It gave the following reasons for suggesting a government of national unity and concord: (a) The two-party system was not viable in fragmented societies ... [because] it essentially amounted to one ethnic group in power and the other completely excluded. ... This naturally was a source of ethnic disharmony and conflict. A government of national unity and concord would avoid this problem. (b) Under the existing system, one racial group alone was in power and it also enjoyed complete control over the armed and security forces. Experience of other countries showed that in such conditions if its monopoly of political power was threatened through the ballot box, there was a temptation to use security and armed forces to maintain itself in power. (c) It would substantially improve the international image of Fiji and thereby enable it to attract greater amounts of external aid.[21]

The NFP submissions reiterated the demands spelled out in the previous chapter. It asserted that the Fijians should dominate the House of Representatives. Accordingly, either all, or 75 per cent, of the seats in the House should be reserved for Fijians, with voting open to electors of all races. One or two witnesses suggested that more power should be conferred upon the chiefs. The most extreme view was that voting should be abolished and the Council of Chiefs should appoint the Government.

Submissions from other minority groups, not surprisingly, sought special representation, usually in the form of seats reserved for election by their members. The Rotuma Association, representing Rotumans living in Fiji, requested for a separate constituency in which all Rotumans would be eligible to vote whether living in Rotuma or elsewhere in Fiji. The Association of the Tongan Community called for two members to be elected by the Pacific islanders residing in Fiji, one for the Polynesians and one for the Melanesians. They claimed that because culturally and socially they differed from other communities in Fiji they should be entitled to their own representatives in Parliament.

The submissions of two Muslim groups—the Fiji Muslim Welfare Organization and the Fiji Muslim Political Organization—surprised many

Indians. Muslims, who arrived in Fiji under the indenture system and constituted only 14.6% of the indenture workforce, have retained their distinct sense of religious identity to a much greater extent than have the Hindus. Dispersed throughout Fiji, plus their distinct religious identity and fear of Hindu domination, it was expected that a segment of the Muslim population would opt for separate representation, a desire they had first expressed in January 1930 in a petition addressed to the colonial governor requesting for the creation of a constituency for all Muslims in Fiji in order that they might have one representative in the Legislative Council.[22] In recent years many Muslims have openly supported the Alliance, reaping benefits in terms of political appointments and patronage. But a questionnaire, administered at random in 1980, found that of the 373 Muslims questioned 62 per cent favoured separate seats in Parliament for Muslim representatives elected by Muslims.[23]

Under the Fiji Constitution Muslims are classified as Indians, but, in their submission, the two Muslim groups claimed that this classification was illogical and unjust; and that the different cultural, social and political backgrounds of Muslims and Hindus justified considering each as a separate community. Muslims should, therefore, have separate representation. Their spokesmen stated that there were approximately 50,000 to 60,000 Muslims in Fiji, comprising about 10 per cent of the total population.

The FMWO proposed that the Muslim community should have five seats, to be facilitated by taking three from the Indian and two from the General Electors' present seats. They also proposed the reduction of the total number of seats in the House of Representatives to 50, with 23 for the Fijian community; 18 for the Indians; Europeans and part-Europeans two; and Chinese and Rotumans one each. They also suggested the abolition of national rolls and elections to be based on the common roll principle.

The FMPO proposed that three Indian seats (two from the communal and one from the national roll) should be transferred to the Muslims. But a division within the Muslim community, and the fact that the Hindu-dominated Indian community had chosen a Muslim, Koya, to lead them, indicated that the two groups were unlikely to succeed in their communal demands.[24]

On 10 December 1975 the Commission finally released its report, with certain specific and definitive proposals. Addressing the pivotal aspect of Fiji's politics—race—the Commission noted that 'race must remain a significant factor in the electoral system for some time to come.'[25] It also considered that in terms of their social and economic development the Fijians were still at a transitional stage; and the breakdown of their traditional culture under the impact of modern conditions was likely to promote strong resentment against the Indians. The sharp contrast between urban Indians and new migrant urban Fijians, and the increasing perception of economic disparity, even if such perceptions were inaccurate, 'can seem to the Fijian to be to his disadvantage' and thus 'can result in frustration and a feeling of having been dispossessed in their own country'.[26]

On the issue of common roll, the Commission clearly doubted that its introduction would lead to the 'Indianization' of Fiji. It pointed out the Fijian control of the Senate, the factors outlined by the NFP during the Commission's hearing, and noted that an analysis of the 1972 general elections in Fiji showed that Indians were less inclined to vote on racial lines than were Fijians.

With the sole exception of the Rotumans, the Commission rejected minority groups' claims for separate representation. It recommended that Rotuma should form a single-member constituency in which all those who ordinarily reside in Rotuma and are duly registered as voters in that constituency would be eligible to vote and that such persons should cease to be registered on either the communal rolls or the national roll.

The Commission was of the opinion that 'it would be a mistake to fragment the electoral system by adding a further racial element at a time when a beginning ought to be made in reducing racial distinctions.'[27] In outlining the fundamentals of a democratic model that would provide for national integration, the Commission emphasized that 'if Fiji is to take its place in the international world of today it cannot afford to maintain an electoral system which can be represented as racialist'.[28]

Regarding the Westminster system of democracy, the Commission considered it to be unsuitable for Fiji because 'it is an unfair and inexact system, which is increasingly coming under criticism. It distorts the result. It is not a system which we could recommend for Fiji.'[29] The country needed a fair and equitable system, which neither encouraged nor perpetuated communal thinking or communal politics. The Commission, however, recommended that the existing arrangement, which allocated communal seats (12 Fijian, 12 Indian and three General Electors), be 'retained for the present', but called for the abolition of the first-past-the-post electoral system. In view of the close contact between the MP and his constituents in comparatively small constituencies, the retention of the single-member constituencies was recommended. To avoid the possibility of a candidate being elected by a minority vote, the Commission also recommended that, instead of the first-past-the-post system, the 27 members on the communal rolls should be elected on the single transferable vote system.

The major changes, however, were proposed in the 'national' or cross-voting seats. In the Commission's opinion, election to these should be on an inter-communal basis, with both voting and candidature open to all citizens of Fiji. In the language of the Commission: 'This will be a [limited] step ... away from the divisions of the people into separate racial groups, and towards the ideal of inter-racial co-operation. But if this is to be done, it must be done on a basis which is fair and just, and which does not dramatically change the present political pattern. Any sudden and extensive change might have disastrous consequences for the country.'[30] It, therefore, recommended:

> Having thus preserved a sufficient element to counter racial fears and provide reassurance and a sense of security, we recommend that the further step towards a fully democratic system should be taken by removing the present racial reservations from the remaining 25 seats (10 Fijian, 10 Indian and 5 General Electors).[31]

Elections to these 25 national seats could, then, be replaced by open elections (that is, a common electoral roll without any racial reservations) which should be organized on the basis of proportional representation, with five constituencies each returning five members. The General Electors, who would clearly lose out, were assured that they would be adequately compensated by the introduction of proportional representation and 'by the opportunities they would have to secure representation by appealing to the electorate as an important minority group'.[32] In short, the Commission recommended proportional representation by the STV method.

The Commission was careful to defend its recommendations and to answer possible criticisms. For example, it stated that some people might object that the new system would upset the political balance of the country and thus lead to unrest, and noted further the possible argument that as the Indian population 'now outnumbers the Fijian it would lead to political domination by the Indians, with unforeseeable results'.[33] The Commission was of the opnion that this would not be the case, and pointed out that although at that time the Indian population substantially outnumbered the Fijian, all the factors indicated that 'in a few years' time, if present trends continue, the Fijian population will outnumber the Indian'. The relevant question, the Commission stated, was not the balance of *races* but the balance of *parties*.

After the report was finally presented to the Governor-General, there was a period of speculation and delay until, in January 1976, the *Fiji Times* 'leaked' the recommendations. Ratu Mara reacted immediately, rejecting the findings of the report in a strongly-worded statement. He stated that Fijians had nothing to fear because he would oppose common roll for the rest of his political life. His government was, therefore, bound to reject the recommendation for a partial introduction of common roll. He was convinced that its introduction would cause bloodshed, citing the sectarian war in Northern Ireland, and the troubles in Cyprus and Africa.

Predictably, his rejection drew criticism from Koya and the members of the Indian community who had favoured common roll since 1929. But once again, Ratu Mara surrendered to the wishes of the Fijians, primarily to counter the rise of the FNP. He effectively retracted his 1961 statement on the issue of common roll: 'I do not believe that constitutional reforms at the present stage will develop properly without the common roll which at present is something that the Fijians will not accept. I think it is for the Government to create the environment in which all the people of the Colony would be able to accept the common roll.'[34]

In 1965 he had stated that he and his party believed that the common roll 'is our ultimate goal just as to Christians heaven is our ultimate goal'.[35] His outright rejection of the Commission's report raised important questions, as a *Fiji Times* editorial put it: 'The Prime Minister has long been a leading advocate of the politics of compromise. It is a pity that by his strong statement on the Commission's report he seems to have virtually shut the door on dialogue and compromise with the Opposition. . . . It is pertinent to ask: where do we go now?'[36]

But many thought that Ratu Mara's statement was not a final declaration of intent and they were vindicated when, in 1980, he floated the idea of the establishment of a government of national unity, a system presumably based on a realistic sharing of power. This system of government, he asserted, would open vistas of hope and progress for all the people. He was inspired by Prime Minister Robert Mugabe's 'statesman-like solution to the problem of Zimbabwe'.

Ratu Mara subsequently explained his position in 1980 when he released a statement[37] in which he argued against coalition and singled out the inherent dangers in the system. Coalition, he said, was always a temporary measure and solutions to Fiji's problems did not lie in resorting to compromises. In his opinion 'modification and bargaining for the sake of keeping power will not do—they will become ends in themselves, exhibiting social and economic disparities which might in the end polarise to a degree of intransigency which conflict alone might thaw'.[38]

While rejecting compromise, he went on to state that the answer lay in one ethnic group agreeing to help another. For this to materialize, the process of consensus and not compromise was chosen. According to Ratu Mara, the magnitude of problems confronting Fiji and the need to solve these with justice to all made imperative a national effort based on consensus. In sum, a government of national unity was deemed the most appropriate to tackle the nation's ills.

The thrust of his concern was clearly centred on the Indian community who have continued to demand more land rights, more key positions in the civil service, greater access to better education and a greater say in the running of the country. In the face of these demands, Ratu Mara asked 'whether the country can afford to continue adhering to a mode of government wherein at present Indians comprising 49.8 per cent of the total population do not possess in national policy a voice commensurate with their size, talents and commitment'.[39]

A problem avoided becomes a crisis and unresolved crises can breed disaster. The exclusion of Fiji's Indians from national policy-making was one problem that demanded urgent attention, even if it meant over-hauling the political system.

In a parliamentary democracy the key institutions which set the pattern and pace of development are Parliament and the Cabinet. The future of the country depends upon the successful functioning of these institutions. In his quest to forge a new more powerful national identity Ratu Mara chose the Cabinet system as the ideal institution to experiment with the concept of a government of national unity; it was also to be employed to unite the two deeply divided and estranged communities. A government of national unity in Ratu Mara's words was 'to be reflected in a Cabinet which drew upon the best talents in the country'.[40]

In other words, a government of national unity was to comprise statesmen working for the welfare of the nation and not politicians engaged in petty, parochial interests. To ensure adequate representation of the various groups, particularly the ethnic proportional representation in the Cabinet, Ratu Mara proposed to solve the Indian/Fijian ratio by: (1) relative ethnic population size in the country; and (2) percentage control by the various parties in Parliament and of the majority party as a result of the previous 1977 election.

The aim of the experiment was to ensure adequate participation in the decision-making process by all communities. The NFP, however, now led by an Indian lawyer, Reddy, rejected the proposal claiming that the offer of a government of national unity was 'a public relations gimmick' on Ratu Mara's part. It was also seen as politically infeasible because 'the underlying principles for sharing power and the machinery of operations left a yawning gap in the proposal'.[41] Reddy, however, agreed with Ratu Mara that communal politics and the existing institutionalized and political structures spelled disaster for Fiji. But, he charged, having put people into racial compartments, it was only natural that people should behave that way. Far from cutting across race, the political parties in Fiji had polarized the population along racial lines.

The Alliance was also reminded of NFP's concern, in 1975, about racial polarization, and the party's submission to the Royal Commission that Fiji should opt for a government of national unity and concord. Thus Reddy claimed that 'consistent with the proposals and when the opportunity presented itself in April 1977, we offered to go into a coalition ... but our pleas were rejected'.[42] The reference to the Alliance's reaction in 1977 suggested that NFP would not be intimidated into supporting a coalition on Ratu Mara's terms and conditions. The major confrontation was over power-sharing. In Reddy's opinion, a coalition government was not necessarily a matter of political compulsion. In support he cited the National Country Party coalition in Australia, and others in Europe.

In Reddy's opinion Ratu Mara's assertion of 'no compromise' was the most fatal item in his case for a government of national unity: 'If the Prime Minister's no compromise formula presupposes that one group alone must lay down the policies and the other must join merely in implementing them by becoming part of a broadly based multi-racial

Cabinet, then such a system is doomed to failure.'[43] Compromise, by definition, requires concessions producing a mutually acceptable outcome that changes the position of the bargainers: in short, it is successful bargaining. While admitting that true compromise on crucial issues may be difficult to achieve, it was, he maintained, absolutely essential.

In any form of government of national unity, the leaders must continue to command the trust and confidence of their respective followers or racial groups. That confidence can be retained only if such government is seen to be acting in the interests of all the people. Consensus, Reddy insisted, was its common denominator, whether one called it coalition, government of national unity, or consociational politics. In short, Reddy rejected the idea of a government of national unity as long as the racial disparities weighted against the Indians, notably the land issue and the electoral system, continued to exist. He felt national unity could not be built on slogans and expressions of goodwill alone.

But if Reddy was genuinely pursuing the Indian cause Ratu Mara, in his reply had to strongly defend the Fijian interests. He again reiterated his initial reasoning behind the proposal which he saw was vital for upgrading the country's political system to provide the guaranteed peace and stability. He further maintained that a government of consensus provided one solution that was rooted in traditional Fijian society. He then turned to specific issues vital to the Fijians and to a great degree for his own political survival, stating that:

> We are not unmindful of the fact that the price for the establishment of dialogue on the government of national unity demanded by the Leader of Opposition—the undermining of the constitutional protection afforded to Fijian interests—is too much for any Fijian leader to entertain.[44]

The forceful and contrasting attitudes of the two leaders thus provides us a broad overall institutionalized political and emotive climate of ethnic animosity, the prevention of compromise and a negotiated settlement of ethnic differences, and the increasing rigidity of the political leadership of both the communities. Their responses raise other questions: was there an immediate need for a government of national unity?

Ralph Premdas, in his analysis of the political context of the proposals, singled out two immediate sets of Alliance interests which were likely to be fulfilled. Firstly, by forming a government of national unity, the Alliance (as we shall shortly see) would have weathered a challenge from the Fijian nationalists who were poised to repeat their March/April 1977 performance at the next general election. The Alliance could not afford to risk another defeat.

Secondly, it also seemed to capitalize on NFP's weak position in Parliament. 'In his paper', Premdas said, 'Mara indicated that the relative parliamentary strength of the Alliance and the NFP would feature as a criterion in forging power sharing formula for a new government', which would have meant that 'the Federation Party, with only 15 seats out of the 52, would be a junior partner to a joint arrangement dominated by the Alliance'. Further, the timing of the proposal 'coincided with the fact that the Alliance was at its most powerful parliamentary level in its history, while the Federation Party, plagued by dissension, was at its weakest parliamentary level in its existence.'[45] Reddy's speech was perhaps the most bitter delivered by any Indian leader in recent times. He seemed openly to espouse the Indian cause thus challenging Ratu Mara's Alliance government to respond. He spoke publicly of the problems that many Indians had been complaining about only in private. Was his speech an election ploy? Was it designed to boost NFP's sagging image, or was he consolidating his own position as party leader to counter Ratu Mara's image as the national leader most capable of providing peace and stability in Fiji? Premdas thought that Reddy emerged at least 'as large as his formidable communal rival, Siddiq Koya, who is known as a tough, straight-talking politician'.[46] Reddy also transformed his image from 'a moderate compromiser unable to stand firm to Ratu Mara's political and personal strength'.

Meanwhile, whatever posture the two leaders tried to adopt, it was the events and results of the two general elections in 1977 that impaired the foundation of trust and goodwill between them, and largely reflected the opinions of their respective communities.

Notes

1. Vernon Bogdanor and David Butler (eds.), 1983, p. 1.
2. Ibid., p. 46.
3. Bryan Keith-Lucas, 1976, p. 330.
4. Alliance Party, *Submissions to the Royal Electoral Commission*, Suva, 8 August 1975, p. 10, quoted in R.K. Vasil, 1984, p. 128.
5. Keith-Lucas, 1976, p. 329.
6. Quoted in Vasil, 1984, p. 129.
7. Ibid.
8. Parliament of Fiji, *Report of the Royal Commission*, Parliamentary Paper No. 24 of 1975, p. 3.
9. National Federation Party, *Submissions to the Royal Commission on Fiji's Electoral Systems*, 5 August 1975, quoted in *Report of the Royal Commission*, 1975, p. 3.
10. Quoted in *Report of the Royal Commission*, 1975, p. 3.
11. Quoted in Vasil, 1984, p. 130.
12. Quoted in ibid.
13. Quoted in ibid., pp. 119-20.
14. Ibid., p. 120.
15. Quoted in ibid., p. 131.
16. See *Report of the Royal Commission*, p. 5; Vasil, p. 133.
17. W. Arthur Lewis, 1965.
18. Quoted in Vasil, 1984, p. 135.
19. W.J.M. Mackenzie, 1958, p. 35.
20. Quoted in Vasil, 1984, pp. 134-35.
21. Quoted in ibid., p. 136.
22. Ahmed Ali, *Plural Societies*, Vol. 8, No. 1 (Spring 1977), pp. 57-69.

23. Ahmed Ali, 1982, p. 150.
24. *Report of the Royal Commission*, 1975, p. 10.
25. Ibid., p. 9.
26. Ibid., p. 7.
27. Ibid., p. 9.
28. Ibid., p. 11.
29. *Report of the Royal Commission*, 1975, p. 13.
30. Ibid.
31. Ibid., p. 11
32. Ibid.
33. Ibid., pp. 14-15.
34. *Fiji Times*, 22 May 1976, Editorial, p. 6.
35. Ibid.
36. Ibid.
37. See 'Ratu Mara Speaks on Government of National Unity', *Fiji Times*, 2 September 1980, pp. 8-9.
38. Ibid., p. 9.
39. Ibid., p. 8.
40. Ibid., p. 9.
41. See Ralph Premdas, *Pacific Perspective*, Vol. 10, No. 2, 1981.
42. Jai Ram Reddy, 1980, p. 3.
43. Ibid., p. 5.
44. Quoted in Premdas, 1981, p. 18.
45. Ibid., pp. 1-21.
46. Ibid., p. 17.

CHAPTER FOUR

THE 1977 ELECTIONS AND THE CONSTITUTIONAL CRISIS

We have lost the general elections and the National Federation Party have won. It is not only their right, it is their duty to form a government. I thank all who have supported me throughout these ten exciting and rewarding years.

Prime Minister Ratu Mara: resignation statement, 1977.

On 4 April 1977 about 20,000 Fijians voted for the radical FNP. For the first time in the country's political history the Alliance Party had been defeated. This defeat paved the way for the NFP to form Fiji's next government with the first Prime Minister of Indian origin: Siddiq Moidean Koya. But this event did not take place. Instead, Fiji entered into an epoch of political instability and confusion.

On 7 April 1977, 'the day that fooled Fiji', Koya went to the Government House at 4.30 p.m. to be a sworn in as the new Prime Minister. But the Governor-General, Ratu George Cakobau, told him that he had appointed Ratu Mara as Prime Minister and had asked his Alliance Party to form a caretaker government. A period of bitter racial and constitutional wrangling followed. If the Governor-General's action had stunned the nation, the defeat of Alliance was equally astonishing. The Nationalists had been waiting on the sidelines as both the Alliance and NFP prepared to embark upon the electoral campaign, a campaign in which several issues were on trial: the staying power of the Alliance, the strength of the Nationalists, the readiness of the NFP as a government-in-waiting, and, above all, the viability of parliamentary democracy.

The members of the House of Representatives had, on 10 February 1977, ended their last session before its dissolution for the 19 March to 2 April general elections with the claim that they had given Fiji a model government. The closest the House of Representatives had come to a constitutional impasse was when, following a vote of no confidence, the former Speaker, R.D. Patel, in 1975, refused to accept that his constitutional obligation was to resign as Speaker.

These March/April general elections clearly emerged as the most crucial. Indisputably, they were to be a three-cornered fight between the Alliance, the NFP and the FNP. Most political pundits thought the Alliance would remain in office, although the possibility of a coalition or minority government was widely anticipated. Elections in Fiji have always stirred up racial issues and the emergence of the FNP gave fresh impetus to the hatred for the Indians on the part of some Fijians. The Nationalists reiterated their persistent demands for constitutional changes, with Butadroka fervently hoping for an NFP victory so that it would reveal to the Fijians that the country was not exclusively theirs.

> That is the day Ratu Mara and his Alliance Fijians must look for. It is the very thing I want to prove to the Fijian people; that this Parliament does not belong to us. The Fijians take it for granted that a Fijian will always be Prime Minister, that a Fijian will always be Governor-General and the ministers for Fijian Affairs and Lands will always be Fijians. I tell them no. It is not in the Constitution. I wish for the day the Federation will come to power, because it is the very time it will dramatically point out to Fijians that the government is not ours.[1]

As election fever gained momentum Butadroka and his campaign members visited most rural Fijian areas and explicitly spelled out their message 'Fiji for the Fijians', and went on to lampoon the Alliance's performance, particularly its alleged failure to protect Fijian interests. While asserting that the FNP would form the next Opposition, Butadroka maintained that this would force the Alliance to seek a coalition with the NFP. He was convinced the 'FNP flag would fly in Parliament'.

The Alliance found itself in a dilemma: whether to focus its campaign exclusively on the Fijians or on the population as a whole. The party chose, however, to campaign in force across the country where the FNP threatened to make deep inroads into its support. The offensive, by several prominent Alliance ministers, was led by Ratu Mara who barnstormed across the country claiming that a vote for the FNP would turn Fiji into another Uganda.

Describing Fiji as a 'three-legged table', he went on to state that 'if Mr Butadroka's party evicts one section, the Indians, then next comes the General Electors and finally the Fijians will be left in Fiji, which will create a situation like the one Uganda is facing today.'[2] He also asserted that the FNP's main motives were to discredit the Alliance and to work for its downfall, and to create confusion and despondency.

In the past Ratu Mara had indicated his early retirement from politics. But now sensing the anxiety among some voters regarding who would replace him, he reassured the nation of his availability because:

> I found that [when] I mentioned my retirement then there were voices completely contrary to the principles of the Alliance that have ... formed a party. And as long as that party promotes its course and as long as it remains, I will remain in politics. I refer to the Butadroka party, which wants to send the Indians out of Fiji.[3]

This failed to appease the Nationalists or to allay the fears of the Indians. Many thought that it was simply an example of election showmanship. While campaigning on the platform of 'peace, progress and prosperity', the Alliance, to some extent, did specifically concentrate on Butadroka. It chose Tomasi Vakatora, a former Secretary for Communications, Works and Tourism, who was from the same province in which Butadroka had launched the FNP nearly three years ago, to fight him for the Rewa-Serua-Namosi Fijian communal seat.

The Alliance probably calculated that personal rivalry in the NFP between Koya, Ramrakha and Mrs Irene Jai Narayan, which for several months had made the quest for party unity frustratingly elusive, was sufficient to eliminate the Indian-dominated party from the political map. But if the Alliance found comfort in thus dismissing the NFP, it was equally aware of the political perils that lurked in its own backyard: the bitter Indian Alliance dispute over the rejection of Sir Vijay Singh as candidate for the safe Tailevu seat, coupled with the withdrawal from the Alliance by M.T. Khan (an Indian Cabinet minister who had been unsuccessfully prosecuted for corruption), could cost them a lot of Indian votes.

On the whole, the Alliance remained defiant and buoyant, with Ratu Mara apparently not too concerned at the prospect of ruling Fiji with a majority of one. He remarked that Malta's Dom Mintoff was one of the strongest prime ministers in the Commonwealth because he had spent so long in power battling with a majority of one. The Alliance also dismissed the electoral threat posed by a young but influential Fijian chief, Ratu Osea Gavidi, who decided to run for Parliament as an independent against the official Alliance candidate in his own Nadroga/Navosa constituency in the western belt of the country.

The NFP, meanwhile, entered the election battle as a collection of disparate groups, busily protecting its own vested interests and beliefs. It did, however, seem to be in tacit connivance with the FNP in an electoral arrangement to defeat the Alliance. The NFP had fielded 35 candidates only; with none for the Fijian or General Elector communal seats, and two for the National seats. Some of its Fijian candidates had secretly nominated FNP candidates in certain crucial or marginal seats. Despite the fundamental differences in personality of Koya, Ramrakha and Mrs Narayan and their acrimonious conflicts of the previous year[4] they formed an odd but strategic coalition.

The NFP's problem during the general election was to win Indian hearts, minds and votes. Equally pressing was the threat from disgruntled NFP politicians: notably R.D. Patel, who was standing against Koya as an Independent candidate for the Lautoka Indian communal seat; and Vijaya Parmanandam, another independent, who was contesting the Suva Rural Indian communal seat after failing to be nominated for the same seat on an NFP ticket.

In 1977 Patel, who had resigned as Speaker of the House and from the NFP in 1975, dedicated himself solely to eliminating the embattled Koya as NFP leader. Division within the NFP's grassroot members also widened with Hindus, Muslims and Gujeratis communally splitting along religious, linguistic and provincial lines. For example the contest between Koya (a Muslim) and Patel (a Gujerati) 'was no longer just an election battle between NFP and an Independent. It had become a Muslim versus Gujerati affair.'[5]

Religion is an important factor in Fiji politics and political parties have often made use of it as an election issue. But many Indian candidates realized soon that the use of religion was highly inflammatory; the political stakes were high on all sides. They needed the combined votes of all the factious groups, votes on whose backs they had ridden to power in the past. To avoid political suicide, therefore, the rival NFP factions once again entered into an electoral pact; religion became a secondary issue. The NFP's election strategies therefore concentrated basically on the economy, unemployment, inflation, education and land issues. In retrospect, and wracked by deep dissent in its Indian ranks, the party set out deliberately to instil fear in the minds of the Indian community by focusing on the Alliance's shortcomings is so far as the Indian population's interest were concerned.

The issue that probably more than any other was responsible for arousing and antagonizing Indian feeling against the Alliance was the implementation of preferential treatment in education. In 1977 the Indians had been told that Government policy was for half of the university scholarships to be reserved for Fijians and that all qualified and deserving Fijian students should receive them. As a direct result, admission to university courses required a minimum of 216 marks in the New Zealand University Entrance Examination for Fijians, while Indian and other students needed a minimum of 261 marks. Among other considerations, this policy was based on the principle of equalizing educational opportunities among various ethnic communities in Fiji. During the campaign, however, the NFP interpreted it as blatant discrimination and the perpetration of a double standard. Koya added: 'It is bound to produce recriminations, frustrations, bitterness, the destruction of the image and the reputation of the university and indeed the Government of the day in the eyes of the world.'[6] He reminded the Indians, inter alia, about discrimination not only in education but also in the military forces.

The Indians needed no persuasion. To them the NFP was still the 'voice of the voiceless', especially on the subject of education. In 1975, the Minister of Education had decreed that Government would not contribute funds for free and partly-free places in schools to non-Fijians from the third term of the school year. To Indians this smacked of racialism, prompting even the Alliance's own man, Sir Vijay, to state: 'the decision is deplorable because of its distressingly repellent odour of crude racialism'.[7]

The decree was finally rescinded on the grounds that the Minister had erred, but Koya's statement on the issue, demanding that the government 'remove this blatant piece of racial injustice' and 'the people of Fiji, irrespective of race or party affiliations, to rise in protest against this untenable decision'[8], was still fresh in the minds of the Indian electorate. The Alliance thought that the decree might sink into obscurity: 'for Indians the action spelled additional danger, because it affected education which had been the means of their progress and success' and 'to deny them educational opportunities was to sever one of their arteries'.[9]

The NFP, which had set out to recapture Indian votes, had succeeded in arousing the feelings of the beleaguered Indian majority, many of whom saw Alliance policies as hostile and hypocritical. The future of the Indians became the main topic of political conversation; and despite their religious and political differences, Indian leaders addressed the same question: how to protect the interests of their community in a land where political equality and equality of opportunity had become the key election issues?

At the height of the campaign, the racially oriented programme launched by the FNP against the Indian community, and the Alliance's difficulties, brought racial politics to the surface once more. The dialectic of history now seemed bound to drive the Indians and the Fijians along a path of no return.

In the March/April elections political discussion was largely dominated by the politics of coalition. Fiji had never experienced a coalition government, but many concluded that the 1977 general elections might see the country experiment with coalition politics. A senior member of the NFP stated that his party would seek a coalition with the Alliance if the NFP won the election by a slender majority. He believed that the split in Fijian votes would enable the NFP to win four national seats and have an overall strength of 27 or 28 in the House of Representatives. But Ratu Mara's election campaign speeches explicitly ruled out a coalition government and remained confident of increasing his party's majority in the House.

The FNP pressured for 'Fiji for the Fijians'; 'it's time for a change' charged the NFP; and 'share and care with us', the Alliance proclaimed pragmatically. In all, 132 candidates were contesting for the 52 seats in the House of Representatives. The Alliance fielded 52 candidates, the NFP 35 and the FNP 17. The FNP had put up nine candidates for the 12 Fijian communal seats and eight for Fijian national roll seats. When the nomination ended on 3 March, five candidates, all Alliance, including Ratu Mara, were returned unopposed. The question was: however; would the voters return the Alliance to power?

The answer came on 4 April 1977. After two weeks of polling and two days of counting, it emerged that the voters had dramatically ended the Alliance Party's monopoly of power. The party had lost nine seats: seven to NFP, one to FNP leader Butadroka and one to the independent Ratu Osea. Its Fijian support slid from nearly 83% in 1972 to about 64%; while its Indian support was slashed from 24% in 1972 to 16%.[10] The FNP obtained about 20,189 or 25% of the 80,369 Fijian communal votes cast. The Alliance, however, had retained the three General Elector communal seats. But with 16 per cent Indian votes, 67 per cent of Fijian votes and nearly 100 per cent of General Elector votes the Alliance had failed to retain a majority. The final election results were: NFP 26; Alliance 24; FNP one; Independent one.

For many Fijians the results signified the beginning of 'Indian rule'; for Indians a dream come true finally to inherit the political kindgom. Two factors contributed substantially to NFP's victory. Firstly, the fear of about 20,000 Fijian voters—shamelessly fuelled by the FNP during the campaign—that the Indians would 'strip' the Fijians of their birthright. Secondly the NFP's exploitation of the fear of further hardship under an Alliance government, and its play on the Indians' sense of duty to stand together against FNP racialism.

But with a razor-edge majority of 26 seats the NFP could not confidently govern the country alone. The party realized that it had no clear majority, and questions began to be raised. A leading member of the NFP, Reddy, in his local radio broadcast, said he believed that an NFP government, if formed, would not be viable at this time; there was more to forming a government than having ministers. Reddy then questioned the loyalty of the Civil Service, the Royal Fiji Military Forces and Police under an NFP government. He also pointed out the Great Council of Chiefs' control of the Senate on Fijian matters. Finally, he raised the question of leadership: 'Does the NFP have a person of the stature that he can truly claim to be a leader of the people of Fiji?' Reddy's opinion, later to be manipulated by the Alliance, was that there was no person of Ratu Mara's stature: 'Now with the greatest respect I do not believe that we have anyone at the present time.'[11] On 4 April, the panorama of political events began to unfold shortly after Ratu Mara, in a radio broadcast, announced that he was resigning and inviting the NFP to form a government.

The NFP, however, still favoured a coalition government. They invited Ratu Osea to add to their parliamentary numbers, but he refused. Ten years later, in February 1987, Ratu Osea disclosed that he was approached by Tora to join the NFP; he refused because, 'I was afraid of my Indian friends'.[12] Butadroka had already brushed aside any coalition deal with the NFP, but revelled in the Alliance defeat: 'We were able to prove to the Fijian race that the Constitution does not guarantee that the Fijians will remain forever as leaders of this country. The emergence of one of our candidates in Parliament has cost the Alliance its defeat and it proves the Alliance will not always be in power.'[13] The NFP feared that if it appointed one of its 26 successful candidates as Speaker, it would be left without a working majority in the House of Representatives. Since the Speaker has a casting vote, the NFP was bound to be defeated on every issue if the Alliance and the two independents, Ratu Osea and Butadroka, combined against it.

After Ratu Mara's resignation on 15 April, and unsuccessful attempts by the NFP to set up a coalition, Ramrakha and Mrs Narayan, in Koya's absence, informed the Governor-General that the NFP would proceed to form a government.

When they met to elect their Leader and Cabinet it soon emerged that the members were split down the middle over whether a Fijian member, Captain Atunaisa Maitoga, should be elected as Leader to reassure Fijian opinion, or whether Koya should be re-elected. On the first ballot each candidate received the same number of votes; in the second, Koya was re-elected by 14 votes to 12 with Captain Maitoga as Deputy Leader. Reflecting on the leadership ballot Koya claimed, nearly 10 years later in 1987, that 'It is our people (Indians) who went against me. First they put up a Fijian against me. Then they told me if not the Fijians would indulge in violence.'[14]

As we have seen, however, Koya was not to become the Prime Minister of Fiji. Instead, when on 7 April 1977 he arrived at Government House to keep his 4.30 pm appointment with the Governor-General he was told that Ratu Mara had already been sworn in as Prime Minister for a second term. He later reported to the NFP parliamentarians that the Governor-General had given two reasons for this: one was 'security' and the other that in his (the Governor-General's) judgement Ratu Mara commanded majority support in the country.[15]

Thereafter followed much recrimination and bad faith. In his defence Koya claimed he was deliberately and callously misled by Governor-General Ratu George Cakobau. But a month later Mrs Narayan, while dismissing a suggestion that the NFP was 'dilly-dallying' when asked to form a government, claimed there was no leadership crisis because Koya had always remained leader of the party: 'What Mr Koya lacked was decision-making', she said, 'Why didn't he act like a leader?'[16] Ramrakha has since provided an insight into the events leading to Koya's appointment and his missed opportunity to become Prime Minister. On 9 March 1987 he wrote:

> In 1977 I said to him: 'Let's work out the leadership by consensus.' His reply: 'My back is to the wall.' He called for leadership elections. When I said what if there is a tie, can we take the name out of the hat? 'No,' he said, 'it is not lottery.'
>
> Result: The whole world knew there was a tie; the whole world knew that in the second round someone changed his mind, and voted Sid leader. Was it Captain Atu? Did his military discipline take over, and tell him not to lead a hung party? We will never know. . . .
>
> When I told Sid to hurry to Government House and take charge he said, 'No, I must select my ministers.' . . .
>
> When I told him Whitlam had held so many portfolios and selected his ministers at leisure, he did not see the point. Result: The Governor-General lost confidence in Sid and appointed Ratu Sir Kamisese.[17]

Ramrakha argued that Koya had no realistic plan of his own. He then asked: 'Did Sid want the Prime ministership? Did he not upon being elected leader say he did not know how long his Government would last, whether it would be one month or one year, he did not know? Did he not come back from Government House and say he would advise all and sundry to quit Fiji? We are all living witness to those events and we have fought each other over the facts too long.' Ramrakha said it was Ratu Osea who held the key.

> If he had come in with us, we would have made a go for it. Even if Sakiasi Butadroka had told us he would not object to an NFP government that would have been a comfort. These two men were the real heroes, the real winners of that battle in 1977. It was they who defeated the Alliance, not us.[18]

Meanwhile, the people were bound to harbour their doubts and misgivings on the statements from the different political actors in the wake of the 1977 crisis. In reappointing Ratu Mara as Prime Minister to head an Alliance minority government on 7 April, the Governor-General justified his action in an official statement. Replying, Ratu Mara, believing in 'loyalty and respect to ultimate authority, presented his acceptance of the office as being the act of a subordinate chief with a duty of obedience':

> I obeyed the command of His Excellency the Governor-General, the highest authority in the land and my paramount chief. I obeyed him in the same manner that thousands of Fijians obeyed their chiefs when they were called to arms—without question and with the will to sacrifice and serve.[19]

He contended that he 'was not being invited to join in power sharing' but 'was being begged to bail out the Opposition from a position which they did not feel capable of sustaining.'[20] Unhappily, Ratu Mara 'raked up an old wound by an oblique reference to the refusal by many Indians to join the war effort when the free world was threatened by the Nazis and the Japanese imperial forces.'[21] Ratu Mara's explanation for his rejection of coalition proposals, in part undoubtedly dictated by the fear of advancing Butadroka's political cause, had elements of plausibility. 'We feel', he had said, 'that once we form a coalition with an Indian dominated party Butadroka will have to form branches all over Fiji because Fijians will be flocking to his side.'[22]

Finally, Ratu Mara told of his reaction to his summons to Government House on 7 April: '[It] really came out of the blue. . . . I took it as a command from the authority administering this country, and I am quite happy and pleased to carry it out.'[23]

In restrospect, the NFP's opinion was that the decisions of both the Governor-General and Ratu Mara had left a lingering discordant note for the future of democracy and of the country's domestic harmony. The politically bruised and battered Koya claimed that the Governor-General's decision to appoint Ratu Mara to head an Alliance minority government had 'eroded and devalued democracy', and he accused the Alliance of creating an 'alarming' situation. 'The country ought to know that Ratu Sir

Kamisese himself declared on more than one occasion that it was not only the right of the NFP to form a government but it was its duty to do so',[24] Koya said. The important point in all this is that both Ratu Mara and Koya, who earlier had hailed Fiji as a model for democracy, were now ascribing different meanings and interpretations to the democratic process that was open to the Governor-General in the current political crisis.

The conflict reached its climax when Koya deliberately whipped up Indian sympathy by charging that Ratu Mara's and the Alliance's acceptance to form a minority government was because they did not want an Indian Prime Minister in Fiji. He said their decision was an 'insult to the Indian community and its self-respect'.[25] And that a group of Fijians in the Alliance were determined to dominate permanently the political life of the country. Although Ramrakha categorically disassociated himself from these allegations saying they were 'extreme' and lacked wisdom, Koya had succeeded in driving a wedge between the traditional NFP supporters and the Doubting Thomases in the NFP hierarchy.

Furthermore, Ramrakha who, on 7 April, had stated that 'We have a written constitution and it is a pity that the constitutional processes were not allowed to take their due course',[26] on this occasion asserted that although the Governor-General's decision fully complied with the Constitution it was not 'politically defensible'. On 4 September 1978, Ramrakha wrote:

> I have thought and rethought this situation over, and I think the correct assessment of the situation was that the National Federation Party was afraid to come to power—these are very strong words but what other interpretation can be given? Why did we attempt again and again to persuade the Alliance to come into a coalition with us when Ratu Mara clearly rejected the idea? An NFP government would have come into power without enjoying any of the centres of powers, like the heart of the business world, the Native Land Trust Board, Fijian Affairs Board and indeed any significant voice within the Fijian community.[27]

It can be argued, however, that Ramrakha's soundness of judgement, political foresight, and subtle and shrewd understanding of the current temper does not correspond wholly with the political climate of the time. During the four days of political drama, the opinion of many members of the Great Council of Chiefs was that the NFP's emergence to power would not have undermined the traditional relationship between the Council and the government. One of the three Council members, Senator Ratu Livai Volavola, said that as long as the government stuck to the Constitution there would be no problems. What if an Indian becomes Minister for Fijian Affairs (the holder of this office is also Chairman of the Council)? Ratu Volavola replied that the Council would function and carry on its duties as in the past, irrespective of who was the Chairman. The former Assistant Minister for Communications, Works and Tourism, Uraia Koroi, also said he did not see any problem if this situation occurred, pointing out that a European had once held the chairmanship of the Council.

The possibility of disorder among the Fijian population is also debatable. Although they were 'shocked to learn of the election results there was no widespread uprising in the countryside'. On 4 April 1977, shortly before the final results were announced, Ratu Mara, in an interview in Suva with a senior political journalist, Robert Keith-Reid, had addressed this issue:

Keith-Reid: Do you consider that there is any possibility of a Fijian backlash should they find themselves suddenly with an NFP government in power?

Ratu Mara: We in the Alliance have been preaching peace and progress and we would be out of character now to go out and fan up the emotions of the people, because if we do that we have no right to aspire to come back into power.

Keith-Reid: Do you think there could be backlash from the Fijian people, out of the blue, as there was in 1968?

Ratu Mara: I don't think so, because there was 24 per cent of the Fijian vote which was already against us. This is probably what they want.[28]

Another, and perhaps more fundamental issue, involved the checks and balances inscribed in the Constitution, a Constitution which many saw as the epitome of true democracy. As we saw in the previous chapter the Alliance had maintained before the Royal Commission that the electoral system was the most appropriate one for Fiji's political problems and political process. In an interview with Keith-Reid after the Alliance's defeat, Ratu Mara reaffirmed his belief in the Constitution:

Keith-Reid: Having experienced this amazing election, would you adovcate changes in the present Constitution or would you say that the results have borne out the Alliance's contention that it is a perfectly fair Constitution?

Ratu Mara: If I had to change part of the Constitution, it is the stringent way that it is being carried out—for instance, we cannot get people into the Public Service Commission unless they have left Government for three years. . . . I would have to relax those bits of it. I have yet to find a Constitution in the world, and I have studied quite a number of them, which would improve on this one we have.[29]

Yet, on numerous occasions Ratu Mara, whether consciously or unconsciously, had displayed his willingness to sacrifice his seemingly unflinching belief in constitutionalism, particularly whenever the Alliance's control over the country's political affairs had come under threat.

Meanwhile, and before examining the constitutional role of the

Governor-General during the 1977 crisis, it is pertinent to recall Ratu Mara's response to Koya's allegation that he had been robbed of the prime ministership because he was an Indian. In his nationwide address Ratu Mara reprimanded Koya for fomenting racial discord:

> I and my party have been accused of racialism at its worst and that whatever happens an Indian Prime Minister should never be installed. To accuse me in this way who have been Prime Minister of this country for ten years, and devoted myself to multi-racialism and tried to lead the whole country along this road is not only as I have said a provocative and damaging racial statement. It is a deep personal insult and a gross lie. I hope on mature reflection and for the sake of the future harmony of this country he will publicly retract his statement.[30]

But Koya refused to retract. He reiterated his earlier claim. 'That is my conclusion, my prerogative. I am used to being threatened', he stated, adding: 'I ask the people of Fiji and posterity to judge.'[31] Butadroka also joined Koya in accusing Ratu Mara of 'sinful and shameful' conduct in accepting the Governor-General's call to form a minority government.

In other developments, Tora, an NFP vice-president and then president of the Fiji Council of Trade Unions (FTUC), flew to Australia on 10 April 1977 to seek Australian trade union support to ban trade with Fiji in protest against the Alliance minority government. Toro who, the NFP claimed, was 'out on a frolic of his own', went to seek advice from the then Prime Minister Gough Whitlam, and two other friends, Dr Jim Cairns, the ex-Deputy Labour leader whom Whitlam had sacked in 1975 for misleading the House on the 'Loans Affair', and Pat Clancy, the Communist trade union leader. According to newspaper reports Tora had also hoped to have an audience with the right-wing president of the Australian Council of Trade Unions (ACTU) and subsequent Prime Minister of Australia, Bob Hawke. Tora's one-man mission to Australia reportedly drew a blank.

Meanwhile, in an extraordinary statement the defeated but 'dissident' Koya supporter, Parmanandam, in a public meeting hinted that Koya had been disowned by two of his colleagues and erstwhile rivals, Mrs Narayan and Ramrakha, and the Governor-General had, therefore, not appointed him the Prime Minister. Parmanandam alleged that on the Thursday afternoon when NFP parliamentarians were discussing the formation of a new government, Mrs Narayan and Ramrakha had left the meeting and were driven to Government House by another NFP MP, Anirudh Kuver. Both Mrs Narayan and Ramrakha vigorously denied the allegations as 'sheer lies and mere fabrication'.

The denials did little to quash rumours that the two had engineered Koya's downfall, especially Ramrakha whose part in the political crisis had pushed him into the frontline of publicity. In the end, an astonishing series of provocations compelled Government House to issue a terse denial stating that no member of the Opposition had communicated with the Governor-General, and that the rumour was unfounded. At the behest of his constituents, Ramrakha took an oath in Parliament on the holy Hindu book, the *Ramayan*, that he had not been to the Governor-General as alleged. Mrs Narayan did likewise.

But why did the Governor-General change his mind that afternoon when his earlier message to the NFP had been so explicit? Who advised him? Was his action correct?

According to Professor David Murray, significant issues about the powers of the head of state in more recent versions of Westminster model constitutions were raised by the Governor-General's action. The Fiji crisis was the second involving a Queen's representative in the South Pacific; two years earlier, on 11 November 1975, in 'the most dramatic day in Australian political history, the Governor-General had dismissed Whitlam as Prime Minister of Australia'.[32] To some extent this event was not dissimilar to the Fijian crisis in 1977. Not surprisingly then even Koya sought for parallels: 'This may be a legal and constitutional question for someone else to decide, but I would equate this position to a minority government installed in Australia by the Governor-General, Sir John Kerr!'[33]

But Koya seemed to overlook the fact that in Australia Sir John dissolved Parliament to resolve the constitutional deadlock created by the Senate's refusal to approve the budget passed by the House of Representatives. Although Whitlam's labour government had a majority in the House of Representatives, the Opposition had one-vote majority in the 60-member Senate.[34]

Who advised the Governor-General of Fiji? There is a widespread belief that it was the then Chief Justice of Fiji, Sir Clifford Grant. Also, the NFP was of the opinion that Sir Clifford had himself drafted the Governor-General's official statement. In Ramrakha's words, 'an interesting parallel to be found in this is that Sir Garfield Barwick, Chief Justice of Australia, also gave advice to Sir John Kerr, the Governor-General of Australia in a somewhat similar crisis.'[35] On Sir Clifford's role Ramrakha wrote:

> Everyone was using the back entrance to Government House in Suva that day. We had tried to use the front entrance to be turned away by the guard. But that day, Sir Clifford had gone there by the front entrance. No one saw him. Everyone was concentrating on the back entrance. Sid Koya later said that when he entered the Governor-General's room, he thought he saw Sir Clifford leaving the room. It was Sir Clifford who gave last minute advice on which Ratu Sir George acted. I know that Sid Koya and his colleagues now know this to be the truth. Yet they wasted all those months trying to lay the blame elsewhere. . . . But then, politics in Fiji is one long stab in the back.[36]

Was the Governor-General right? In the opinion of Dr Mohammed Shamsud-Dean Sahu Khan, a local Fiji-born constitutional lawyer, 'unless and until at least three members of the National Federation Party had stated categorically that they would not only support Mr Koya but also that they would go ahead and support Ratu Sir Kamisese Mara, the Governor-General could have had no constitutional basis for deciding that Ratu Sir Kamisese Mara, and not Koya, commanded the majority support of the House.'[37]

He based his opinion on the assumption that Butadroka and Ratu Osea did not support the Alliance government: 'Even if both had supported the Alliance government, it would still need one National Federation Party member to give Ratu Sir Kamisese Mara the majority support.'[38] He also added that factors such as national security of the question of how an NFP government would have been received by the people were not within the Governor-General's jurisdiction to consider: 'He cannot form a judgement from rumours or from what he reads in the newspapers.' The term, 'In his own deliberate judgement', Dr Sahu Khan said meant that the Governor-General 'is not obliged to take advice from anyone.'[39] Koya's alternative, he said, was the possibility of seeking a Supreme Court ruling on the Governor-General's action in appointing Ratu Mara.

Although Koya was publicly urged to seek such ruling, he declined due to strong political and social factors. There was also 'the likelihood of the Supreme Court adopting a subjective interpretation of the discretion conferred on the Governor-General's exercise of judgement'. The NFP was also apprehensive of the role of the Chief Justice, Sir Clifford, and many doubted a fair hearing.

When Parliament met on 26 April 1977, a Speaker was elected from the Alliance, thus leaving the effective numbers in the parties as: Alliance 23; NFP 26; FNP one; Independent one. The House of Representatives then went into a four-week recess. Immediately before the House reconvened the 26 members of the NFP signed a letter to the Governor-General requesting him to invite Koya to form the government. But political events took an entirely different course.

When the House reconvened on 28 May the Alliance introduced a motion of confidence in the minority government of the day. To this the NFP moved an amendment in the following terms:

> This House expresses its considered view that the will of the people of Fiji as expressed through the secret ballot should be respected in order to maintain parliamentary system of government in Fiji and therefore requests the Governor-General not to dissolve Parliament should an advice in that behalf be tendered but to invite the Leader of the minority party in the House, namely, the Leader of the Opposition, to form the government.[40]

The NFP's amendment was carried by 26 votes to 23 with Ratu Osea abstaining and Butadroka remaining absent. On the following day, however, Ratu Mara advised the Governor-General to dissolve the

House, which he did. The House was dissolved in the middle of a debate on a motion to lower the voting age from 21 to 18 years. Shortly afterwards new elections were called, scheduled for 17-24 September 1977.

The role of the Governor-General in the appointment of Ratu Mara and the dissolution of Parliament has been thoroughly analysed elsewhere, notably by David Murray, who wrote:

> The constitutional crisis in Fiji has among other things focused attention on the standing of the section under which the Governor-General acted in appointing Mara as Prime Minister. It is unclear whether, in stating that 'the Governor-General ... shall appoint as Prime Minister the member ... best able to command the support of the majority', the intention of the Constitution was to set out an unenforceable description of hoped for conduct, a practice whose enforcement intendedly derives from political processes fashioned by the Constitution, or a legal provision with a judicially enforceable sanction. Whatever was intended the crisis has thrown some light on the significance of the section without wholly clarifying it.[41]

According to Professor Murray what the crisis did show was that the majority in the House had not, within the life of Parliament, the means of enforcing what it regarded as intended practice. Regarded the other way, the Governor-Genral 'was able to select as Prime Minister who he wished to have'.[42] Murray also noted that what the crisis did not resolve was whether the courts had any part to play in reviewing how the Governor-General exercised his deliberate judgement in this matter, and if the courts did have such a part, whether they would regard the wide interpretation placed on his power by the Governor-General as legitimate. On the Governor-General's role in the 1977 crisis, Professor Murray concludes:

> There is just a possibility, therefore, that the Governor-General acted in a way that went beyond what the words of the Constitution provided in order to safeguard government under the Constitution. If so, this might be taken to justify a greater degree of residual discretion that the Constitution conferred so that the Governor-General could play a part in handling certain sorts of political crises.[43]

The dissolution of Parliament, whereby the Governor-General justified his action with the statement that 'the Constitution provides that the Governor-General may dissolve Parliament at any time, but so doing, he shall act in accordance with the advice of the Prime Minister', inevitably tore the parties apart. In the September 1977 elections the NFP was beleaguered by factionalism splitting the supporters into rival political groups. The conflict revolved around the three old rivals: Narayan-Ramrakha-Koya. The two groups also fiercely fought for the custody of the NFP's traditional mango tree symbol, only to be told by the Supreme Court to choose a new symbol.

The Narayan-Ramrakha group chose the hibiscus flower and became known as the 'Flower' or 'Hibiscus' faction; the Koya group chose the dove and became known as the 'Dove' or 'Bird' faction. Briefly, the September election, in which the two factions fielded parallel candidates, became a Hindu-Muslim contest. As Ralph Premdas remarked later, it would be no exaggeration to report that the Hindu-Muslim theme dominated the factional struggle. The evidence clearly indicates that large numbers of Indians, who had no desire to be embroiled in the religious implications of the NFP internal strife, simply did not vote.'[44]

Since both Ramrakha and Mrs Narayan were Hindus, 'in the minds of some NFP supporters the Hibiscus faction was the Hindu group, while the Koya-led Dove faction was the Muslim group.'[45] The Hibiscus faction charged that Koya, as leader of the NFP, had sold out Indian rights at the London Constitutional Conference; he should have accepted the ALTO Act; he lacked the will to lead the country; was a divisive leader; could not get along with Ratu Mara; was a part-time leader; and that he promoted racial disharmony in the country.

In turn the Dove faction accused the Hibiscus group of deliberately using anti-Muslim campaign tactics against them; that it was purely a Gujerati party; and that it was power hungry.[46] The campaign revealed that far from reflecting a genuine desire to challenge the Alliance, the Indian candidates shamelessly displayed a clear and outspoken commitment to destroy each other at the polls.

The Hibiscus faction's sole objective was to politically crush Koya at all costs. It chose Reddy, who was tipped to become the next NFP leader, to fight Koya for the Lautoka Indian communal seat. Reddy's opinion of Koya and the climate of the contest between the two factions can best be illustrated by the following statement by Reddy:

- 'I am not frightened of Koya. I can face one thousand Koyas.'
- 'This general election will throw the Leader of Opposition, Mr Siddiq Koya, in such a place that he will never be able to come back to the political arena again. The man changes tune according to the crowd. How can they rely on him?'
- 'Mr Koya had been taken for a cheap ride by Ratu Mara during the constitutional conference. People who got fooled by others should leave the field and get out.'[47]

Others also joined in the personal attack on Koya. Mrs Narayan charged that he 'should be defeated in such a way that his political career will be buried so deep that even his ghost cannot come out'.[48] The Hibiscus group's campaign, seen by some as open collaboration with the Alliance, gained added political punch when Ratu Mara confirmed publicly that 'I'd rather step down than work with Koya again'.[49] Responding, Koya accused Reddy and Narayan of having sown seeds of discord in the Indian community, and alleged that they had deliberately set out to destroy his faction by setting Hindus against Muslims.

The Alliance greatly benefited from this protracted struggle between the two factions. Its chances at the polls were further enhanced with the imprisonment of Butadroka (gaoled for six months under the Public Order (Amendment) Act of 1976 for inciting racial antagonism) who was fighting for his seat from behind the prison bars. Consequently, the Alliance was this time free to conduct a 'nationalistic' campaign among the Fijians aimed at rallying them behind the party. Some of its candidates privately equated Fijian survival with dominance. The alternative to dominance, the Fijians were told, was domination by an Indian-dominated NFP government.

The election results were, therefore, a foregone conclusion. The Alliance Party won 36 seats in the House of Representatives, compared to only 24 in March. The NFP's strength was slashed from 26 to 15 seats, of which 12 went to the Hibiscus faction and only three to the Dove faction. Ratu Osea retained his seat. A total of approximately 196,000 votes were cast, out of which the Alliance obtained about 47%, the combined NFP vote 45% and the FNP only 9.2%. Interestingly, a good deal of the change in Indian votes was within the factional groups.

There were however two surprising results in this election: Koya was defeated by Reddy in the Lautoka Indian communal seat and Butadroka lost his seat, the FNP's only one in Parliament. Three other notable NFP veterans in addition to Koya—Chirag Ali Shah, M.T. Khan and Tora—were also defeated. While Fijians celebrated Alliance's victory, for the Indians it was an occasion of political mourning.

In the aftermath, there were skirmishes regarding Reddy's leadership between Ramrakha and Mrs Narayan. But to the Indians Reddy was seen as the sole unifying force in the face of impending adversity. They branded Ramrakha as a 'traitor' and condemned and ostracized those members of their own ethnic group who publicly expressed opposition to Reddy. Ramrakha later resigned from politics and migrated to Australia. Tora, along with about 500 of his supporters, crossed over to the Alliance, and became an Alliance vice-president and one of its most vocal anti-Indian members.

Some Indians abandoned the Alliance and later joined the NFP. On 19 January 1979, James Shankar Singh resigned as Minister for Communications and Works but remained as president of the Indian Alliance until his defection to the NFP in 1982. His nephew, Sir Vijay, also resigned from the Senate and the Alliance after a group of Cabinet ministers, led by the then Deputy Prime Minister Ratu Penaia, were responsible for his removal from the post of Attorney-General following his appearance as a defence witness in a criminal case involving the Government and the Flour Mills of Fiji; in 1982 he joined the NFP.

During this period many Indian politicians realized that politics cannot be the toy of the elite, nor can it be divorced from the harsh realities of Indians' plight in Fiji. Some Indian MPs no longer had faith even in the democratic process. The role of the Governor-General had confused the political climate further, even to outsiders. As David Murray noted: 'even if the actions of the Governor-General have produced conventions about his power which could be justified in the particular context of Fiji, the way this was achieved did not enhance the credibility of the Fiji Constitution.'[50]

Apart from the constitutional arguments whatever forces compelled Ratu Mara to reject coalition in April 1977 it was a right decision. In the light of the NFP's history shortly before and after the two elections, this coalition between two unequal parties at this period of time could have turned out to be like the relationship between the tiger and the young lady of Riga. Because despite political horse-trading the Indian community would still have been the losers. The plight of the Indians at this point can perhaps be best conveyed in David Murray's words:

> The Fiji citizens of Indian origin have been a disadvantaged community. At the time when Fiji became independent, this community accepted the position that the working of the Westminster model Constitution, combined with their majority position in the population, would mean that over time the extent of the discrimination against them would be moderated. The years 1977 and 1978 have brought out the weakness of their situation. Fijian citizens of Indian origin are extensively discriminated against, and the constitutional crisis of 1977 showed how little faith could be placed in the Constitution.[51]

In 1979 the parliamentary groups of the two NFP factions decided to reunite and act as one party in Parliament; they also agreed to merge totally into the former NFP under its old mango tree symbol. The Dove faction withdrew its candidate for the Labasa-Bua by-election leaving the Hibiscus faction candidate to contest the seat for the NFP. In order to facilitate a smooth merger Mrs Narayan resigned as NFP president.

In October 1980, when the NFP met for the party's 16th annual convention in the western township of Ba, unity seemed to have been achieved. In his address Reddy re-emphasized the need to preserve unity and integrity. He told the members to look ahead; to read their future in the 'Indian's eyes', and that, 'We must let our history rest in peace.' Reddy had set the political stage for the next contest—the 1982 general election.

Notes

1. *Fiji Times*, 31 March 1977.
2. *Fiji Sun*, 14 March 1977, p. 1.
3. Ibid.
4. See *Fiji Times*, 'Unity of Farce? NFP's two factions meet to heal wound', 11 January 1977, p. 7.
5. Ahmed Ali, 1980, p. 209.
6. *Fiji Times*, 18 March 1977.

7. Ali, 1980, p. 172.
8. *Fiji Times*, 18 March 1977
9. Ali, 1980, p. 173.
10. For more discussion see Ahmed Ali, *Journal of Pacific History*, Vol. 12, 1977, pp. 189-201.
11. Jai Ram Reddy in a Radio Fiji interview, 5 April 1977, See *Fiji Times*, 11 April 1977, p. 2.
12. *Fiji Sun*, 24 February 1987, p. 1.
13. *Fiji Times*, 11 April 1977, p. 2.
14. *Fiji Sun*, 24 February 1987.
15. Clause 73 (2) of the Fiji Constitution states: 'The Governor-General, acting in his own judgement, shall appoint as Prime Minister the member of the House of Representatives who appears to him best able to command the support of the majority of members of the House.'
16. *Fiji Times*, 23 May 1977, p. 7.
17. *Fiji Sun*, 9 March 1987, p. 7.
18. Ibid.
19. Quoted in David Murray, 'Fiji 1977: The Governor-General's part in a constitutional crisis', June 1986 (mimeo).
20. *Fiji Times*, 11 April 1977, p. 2.
21. Ibid., Editorial, p. 6.
22. Quoted in John Nation, 1978, p. 143.
23. *Fiji Times*, 11 April 1977, p. 2.
24. Ibid., 9 April 1977, p. 1.
25. Ibid., 11 April 1977, p. 1.
26. Ibid. (Election Special), 7 April 1977, p. 3.
27. *Fiji Sun*, 4 September 1978, p. 6.
28. *Fiji Times*, 5 April 1977, p. 3.
29. Ibid.
30. Ibid., 11 April 1977.
31. Ibid.
32. See David Butler, 1977, pp. 313-36.
33. *Fiji Times*, 9 April 1977, p. 3.
34. See Butler, 1977, and Sir John Kerr, 1979.
35. K.C. Ramrakha, 'One long stab in back, that's Fiji politics' (mimeo).
36. Ibid.
37. *Fiji Times*, 11 May 1977, p. 7.
38. Ibid.
39. Ibid.
40. Ibid., 1 June 1977.
41. Murray, 'Fiji 1977', op. cit.
42. Ibid.
43. Ibid.
44. Ralph Premdas, *Journal of Pacific History*, Vol. 14, 1979, pp. 194-207.
45. Ibid.
46. Ibid.
47. Compiled from *Fiji Times*, 15 August 1977 and 23 September 1977.
48. *Fiji Sun*, 12 September 1977.
49. Quoted in Premdas, 1979.
50. Murray, op. cit.
51. David Murray, 1980.

CHAPTER FIVE

THE 1982 GENERAL ELECTION

The Fiji election will be particularly interesting as the Indian dominated National Federation Party has a good chance of gaining a
majority. Unlike 1977 when this happened and the NFP failed to
form a government, the assumption is that should the NFP win this
time, the leadership would form a government ... which would be
the first non-Fijian government since independence.

William Boddie, Jnr., former United States Ambassador to Fiji.

The collapse of hopes for a government of national unity raised immediate speculations of a snap general election. Seasoned political observers
felt that Ratu Mara might call an early election because: (1) a majority of
the people favoured the idea of a government of national unity; (2) Fijian
support for the Alliance was at its all-time high; (3) the born-again NFP
might be caught on the wrong foot.

As the commentators dabbled in forecasts, however, both the major
political parties had begun to lay plans and develop campaign strategies
and tactics for the next general election. The Alliance Party took the lead
with setting up polling station committees of members and supporters of
the party.

At the national level, the Alliance set up an Election Planning Committee towards the end of November 1980. The committee, comprising
representatives from each of the constituent bodies, and established after
it became clear that the NFP had rejected the government of national
unity offer, was to be responsible for the overall direction of the campaign. A publicity sub-committee was also set up to deal with issues
arising during the election. A veteran newspaperman, Len Usher
(knighted after the general election), was appointed as its chairman.[1]

The NFP and the FNP also entered the campaign race with their own set
of assumptions and expectations, streamlining their respective party pri-
orities and strategies to court non-supporters. The Nationalists, as in the
past, continued to pronounce on land and other issues to attract floating
Fijian votes. In December, Ratu Mara reiterated the need for an early
campaign if the Alliance was to muster enough Indian support to win the
election.

Other election-related activites continued throughout December. But
much to the chagrin of political soothsayers, when 1980 finally came to
an end, so did the widespread speculations about a snap general election,
because Ratu Mara did not announce one. Instead, in an atmosphere
highly charged by economic pressure and fears of political backlash, Ratu
Mara's New Year's Day message to the people asked them to nurture

national consciousness based on tolerance, understanding and national participation. The NFP leader Jai Ram Reddy's message, however, furiously condemned the government's economic policies. He told the nation to become frugal to improve the quality of life, adding that if Fiji wanted growth she could no longer go on living on borrowed money. Inflation and unemployment were singled out as the two most pressing issues that required immediate attention in 1981.

These contrasting and forceful messages were largely election warm-up speeches indicating that inflation, unemployment, leadership, participation. The NFP leader Jai Ram Reddy's message, however, fu-campaigns—issues that were also in the minds of the electorate, according to a private survey carried out on behalf of the Alliance by a team of foreigners.[2]

For the incumbent party, the perceived issues were secondary as far as the Alliance's fortunes at the general election were concerned. One of the most serious problems it faced was the containment of traditional Fijian votes following the birth of a new Fijian political party: the Western United Front (WUF). This party was born in the wake of confrontation between a group of Fijian landowners in the west of the main island of Viti Levu and the Fiji Pine Commission (FPC) over proposals on how best to utilize the country's pine forests. WUF, which was to be led by the independent parliamentarian Ratu Osea Gavidi, was also seen as 'a party formed by Fijians jealous of the dominant role that powerful traditional leaders including Ratu Mara, hailing from eastern Fiji, have long tended to view as being their natural right'.[3] In the words of a Fijian lecturer in sociology, Simione Durutalo:

> The western Fijian peasantry remains potentially one of the most combative and class-conscious sections of Fiji's peasantry because of their double exploitation and history of class struggle through the years culminating in the confrontation with the eastern-based and neo-colonial Fijian state (and its transnational allies) in the dispute over the benefits to be derived from Fiji's resources and its exploitation.[4]

In 1985 the FPC sought proposals on how best to make use of the pine forests. Two companies, British Petroleum (BP) and the America-based United Marketing Corporation (UMC), were among those who responded. A group of pine landowners, led by Ratu Osea, contended with the FPC that the processing of the country's pine forests should be awarded to UMC but the Commission favoured BP on the grounds that UMC had no previous experience in forestry or national resources and that its proposals were unsatisfactory.

This provoked a boycott of meetings, and protests from the landowners. Ratu Osea and his group vigorously maintained support for UMC, claiming that BP's proposals were neither in the interest of the industry nor the landowners. The saga took a bizarre twist when the Alliance government revealed that UMC's president, American businessman Paul

Sandblom, had twice been convicted for fraud in the United States. The Fiji government therefore declared Sandblom a prohibited immigrant and subsequently used the connection to discredit Ratu Osea at the polls.[5]

Meanwhile, WUF's entry into the election contest and Ratu Osea's public disclosure of his party's willingness to join with another party—but not the Alliance—in a coalition further changed the political landscape of the country.

Realizing the need for a well organized campaign the Alliance sought a suitably qualified person to direct its election campaign as well as run the party office. In September 1981 the Alliance found such a person in Isimeli Bose, an employee of the Australian-owned multinational company, Burns Philp (SS) Ltd., in Fiji, Ratu Mara personally approached the company and they agreed to grant Bose,their shipping operations manager, leave without pay to enable him to work for the Alliance until the 1982 general election. Bose, whose salary the Alliance claimed had been met by the party, subsequently took up his appointment with the party as campaign director.

Like the pine saga, his appointment had all the hallmarks of becoming a political issue. Professionalism was also introduced into the campaign. The Alliance sent Bose to Australia and Papua New Guinea to study the campaign tactics of the then Prime Minister Malcolm Fraser's Liberal Party and Prime Minister Michael Somare's Pangu Party respectively. While in Australia Bose was told about the role of field officers and arrangements were made for him to learn details of the Liberal Party's election tactics and strategies from two officers of the party, one of whom had, between 1977 and 1980, been head of the research department of the Liberal Party's secretariat.

September also saw the visit to Fiji by the late Indian Prime Minister, Mrs Indira Gandhi. On 23 September, two days before Mrs Gandhi's arrival, the Alliance government ended months of speculation by announcing the next general election dates. Polling was to take place from 10 July to 17 July 1982, with nomination day proposed in June and the House of Representatives to be dissolved in May.

In October, two more events, one at home and one abroad, dominated the nation's attention. Ratu Mara attended the Commonwealth Heads of Government Meeting (CHOGM) in Melbourne, Australia, and Fiji hosted the 27th Commonwealth Parliamentary Conference for Small Countries. While in Australia, Ratu Mara addressed a group of Australian businessmen and economists on Fiji's economy at a meeting organized by the Committee for Economic Development of Australia (CEDA). He was also successful in selecting an Australian Broadcasting Commission (ABC) journalist, Clive Randolph Speed, as a media communications consultant to the Fiji Government for a period of 12 months. Speed's appointment which became a controversial election issue, and will be discussed in subsequent chapters, was made 'in line with a 1979 CHOGM committee recommendation in Lusaka, Zambia, for assistance to developing countries in communication work'.[6]

The Australian government provided an accountable cash grant of $A50,000 and on 2 December 1981 Speed began a one-year contract as a Fiji civil servant, to be paid under Australian aid. The terms of reference for Speed were apolitical. He later disclosed, however, that Ratu Mara had discussed the future of the Fiji Department of Information with him 'as an effective unit in relaying government decisions and activities and as a facility to transmit the views of the people to the government.'[7] But the Opposition claimed, as later events revealed, that Speed had breached his terms of reference and that the Alliance had misused the Australian aid money, for electoral advantages.

In November Ratu Mara made a controversial statement on the oft-repeated importance of Fijian leadership in national affairs and its direct impact on the Fijian community. In his presidential address to the Fijian Association on 11 November, two days before the party's annual delegates' conference, he said the Fijians could lose the things they cherished if the existing Fijian leadership was removed. He also tried to deflect bitter criticisms levelled against the Great Council of Chiefs—the sheet anchor of the Fijian way of life.

The speech was interpreted in different contexts in different quarters. Some claimed it was 'politics of fear' directed toward potential FNP and WUF voters, others thought that Ratu Mara was making a statement of fact, one that would in due course be challenged. The first to respond was Ratu Osea who described Ratu Mara's statement as racial emotionalism. He said the question of race should never arise in the struggle for leadership and stressed that leaders should instil in the minds of the people of Fiji the true meaning of democracy. He claimed that Ratu Mara was desperately clutching at the nation's leadership which was fast slipping from the Alliance Party's hands.

In December, the rift between the Indian Alliance president and former Cabinet minister, James Shankar Singh, and Ratu Mara was widening, disgruntled party stalwarts likely to miss out on election tickets were planning to cross the floor, and political heavyweights were working behind the scene to hold the party together as one strong and effective unit ready to lead the nation for another five years.

The NFP, like the Alliance, was beset with problems. Apart from raising funds for the election, the immediate problem was the distribution of seats among the 1977 Dove and Hibiscus factions who were to fight the 1982 election as one united NFP. Some lobbyists publicly demanded the allocation of a safe seat for the former Opposition leader Koya, who for the past five years had been waiting on the political sidelines. Others complained about gestures from would-be Alliance drop-outs for a safe political anchorage with the NFP.

Meanwhile another covert deal was being hatched to dislodge the Alliance. On 11 January 1982 after extensive talks between the NFP, led by Reddy, and WUF members led by Ratu Osea and NFP defector Isi-keli Nadalo, the two parties entered into what was to be called the NFP/WUF Coalition. In Reddy's summing up of the terms and agreements of the Coalition each party was to maintain its independent identity and objectives in a partnership of equals.[8]

While some praised the NFP for shaking off its pro-India image, others saw the deal as a marraige of convenience. The Alliance accused Ratu Osea of using the Coalition for political survival and Reddy of using it as leverage for a political foothold to win the election; further, that the pact probably concealed sinister motives.

If the New Year promised a bright future for the Coalition, for the Alliance the political horizon looked dark. The long-running personal rivalry between Ratu Mara and Singh became open confrontation when Singh failed to be re-endorsed as Ratu Mara's running mate for the safe Lau-Cakaudrove Rotuma Indian national seat; Ratu Mara was the Fijian member for this constituency and paramount chief of Lau. The seat was instead awarded to a university lecturer and political adviser to the Alliance, Dr Ahmed Ali.

Lacking majority support Singh had no choice but to resign from the party. This he did on 10 May 1982. In a statement he acknowledged that in many ways Ratu Mara was an outstanding leader who had done so much for Fiji, but claimed that, like many politicians, 'perhaps gradually love for power and position have overtaken his better attributes and sadly coloured his overall vision. . . .'[9] Replying, Ratu Mara, said the resignation would be no loss to the party.

Singh, who later joined the NFP, publicly castigated the Alliance leadership and its policies toward the Indian community. His fiery speeches, outbursts and defection strongly influenced some Indian members of the Alliance who, contrary to that party's expectations, left the party and followed Singh. Some even withdrew their nominations claiming that they were being treated as third-class members.

While the Alliance was struggling with the Indian Alliance defectors, it received another blow from a high-ranking western Fijian chief, the Tui Nadi and Alliance parliamentarian, Ratu Napolioni Dawai. He resigned from the party after refusing to support a government motion seeking $453,868 to build a meeting house and to restore Fijian historical sites and monuments on the chiefly island of Bau—the home of the Paramount Chief of Fiji, the former Governor-General, Ratu Sir George Cakobau.

Ratu Napolioni and Ratu Osea, both western chiefs, opposed the motion claiming that the money should be spent on other important projects for the benefit of western Fijians, who, Ratu Napolioni claimed, had been given a raw deal. His stand on the issue again demonstrated the rift that had been silently brewing between the eastern and western chiefs over the needs of the Fijians in general. Ratu Napolioni subsequently joined the WUF in order to again contest his old seat in the general election.

Meanwhile, the NFP was welcoming Alliance defectors and the Alliance was welcoming a handful of NFP personalities, notably disgruntled Muslims, and an Indian lawyer, Surendra Prasad. Three former members of the NFP formed a new party, the National Labour and Farmers Party and in an attempt to broaden their voter base initiated contacts and held discussions with the Alliance, including Ratu Mara. But the new party quickly faded into oblivion and the trio returned to the NFP fold. Apart from the Muslims, other minority groups also flexed their political muscles, threatening to split their votes and give race politics a dangerous, explosive ascendancy.

The Alliance Party's acting general secretary, Adi Losalini Dovi, was blamed for poor management and later Dovi resigned. Floor-crossings have always been a bane in Fiji politics during election time, and between January and May 1982 when the nominations closed, the political scene was all too familiar. As parties began to announce their slate of candidates, political infighting led to a spate of defections; antagonisms intensified. Some politicians defected out of personal disillusionment, others in disgust and a few out of political opportunism. After changing their affiliations they savagely attacked their erstwhile leaders and blatantly denounced their old parties' policies.

The House of Representatives met for the last time on 30 April 1982 and Parliament was dissolved on 15 May in preparation for the July general election.

The electoral roll showed that the Indian voters were in a majority with 142,529 compared to 141,846 Fijians and 7,966 General Electors. The Indian voters' majority over Fijians was 683 but the Fijian and General Elector voters combined totalled 149,812 compared to only 142,529 Indians.

When nominations closed on 21 May 1982, the Alliance and the Coalition had filed nominations for all 52 seats in the House of Representatives. The FNP had 28 candidates, and there were nine Independents. After the lapse of the objection and withdrawal period, the final line-up was: Alliance 51 candidates; FNP 27; the Coalition 51; and Independents seven, a total of 136 candidates. As part of the deal, WUF contested six Fijian communal seats and two Fijian national seats; NFP six Fijian communal seats, eight Fijian national seats and all Indian and General Elector seats, while the FNP contested 10 Fijian communal seats, 10 Fijian national, three General Elector communal and four national seats. The NFP candidate for the Savusavu Macuata East Indian communal seat, Subramani Basawaiya, was declared unopposed when the Alliance candidate and ex-NFP member and Bua farmer, Shiu Prasad, withdrew his nomination. Seven candidates, including two Indepndents had withdrawn their nominations—three each from the northern and western and one from the central division.

Most of the incidents faced challengers, including Ratu Mara and Reddy. Two candidates, a cargo truck owner and a farmer, were contesting against Ratu Mara, and Reddy faced challenge from Surendra Prasad, the NFP defector and national president of the orthodox Hir Ju religious group, the Arya Samaj, who was fighting the election on an Alliance ticket. Another NFP defector and former Suva city councillor, Raojibhai Patel (a Gujerati), stood against the Deputy Opposition Leader Mrs Narayan. The candidates included farmers, lawyers, doctors, businessmen and government ministers. The final election line-up promised a stormy political confrontation.

The release of the party manifestos set them on a collision course. In pursuance of their policies, restraint and caution took a hasty retreat. Both the Alliance and the NFP/WUF Coalition manifestos espoused a commitment to put the country on a more stable political and economic footing. The Alliance encapsulated its past, present and future policies in only eight pages, while the Coalition presented itself in an 82-page manifesto, mostly polemic and highly critical of the Government's economic policies, as an alternative government to the people.

The Alliance manifesto was largely a continuation and reaffirmation of its previous policies with slight changes to meet the demands of the day. For the criticism and critique of the NFP manifesto, comments were sought from other bodies, including foreigners. The Alliance called on voters to 'keep Fiji in good hands' by voting for the Alliance Party in the July general election.[10]

The NFP/WUF campaigning on the 1972 Australian Labour Party (ALP) slogan, 'it's time for a change', chose to offer a new approach, but nothing controversial or sensitive, to solve the country's problems. While the Alliance stressed multiracialism, the political catchword in many plural societies, the Coalition made the economy one of the key issues. It sought a mandate from the people to form the next government on the strength of its progressive policies and programmes and of its candidates' competence and capabilities.

The Coalition manifesto claimed that the government itself needed reform: Fiji's Constitution provides for parliamentary democracy; Parliament, not the Cabinet, is supreme. The last decade, it charged, was littered with instances of Alliance ministers' increasing arrogance towards Parliament. They had set themselves up as the supreme authority, and shown a propensity to make far-reaching decisions without prior parliamentary discussion and approval. What was required, the Coalition claimed, was a government with a sense of urgency, determination and dynamism. The NFP/WUF Coalition promised to provide such a government.

On the sensitive land issue, the Coalition emphatically stressed that it had no desire to interfere with the ownership rights of Fijians, but recognized that better utilization of land resources provided the key to future economic progress.[11] On the international front the Coalition promised to maintain an active policy of non-alignment, and to establish and strengthen Fiji's relationship with 'all nations without prejudice to their political ideologies'—stating, however, that it would not invite Russia to open an embassy in Fiji. It also promised to keep the Pacific region free of big power rivalries, and in co-operation with other countries in the region, to oppose all forms of nuclear testing or nuclear waste disposal in the Pacific.

While the Alliance and the NFP/WUF Coalition attempted to discredit each other's policies, the FNP offered itself as the only true champion of Fijian rights. In a seven-point platform it reiterated its earlier demands based on the theme 'Fiji for the Fijians'.

Following the release of the manifestos, the parties ruthlessly condemned and criticized each other's policies. The Alliance claimed that the Coalition's manifesto was merely a rehash of the government's Development Plan Eight (DP8)—'full of sound . . . signifying nothing'. One Alliance candidate, Dr Ali, summed up the Alliance's position *vis-a-vis* the Coalition, claiming that Reddy was offering a dream 'which will quickly dissolve into a nightmare. The inexperience of the NFP is laid bare by its proposals for bankruptcy with a manifesto for misery, a preamble for chaos in a society which for 20 years under the Alliance has known genuine economic growth, social justice and political stability.'[12]

Analysing other aspects of the Coalition manifesto, Dr Ali raised the spectre of 'reds under the beds' and suggested that the Coalition's policy on international matters implied, firstly, that the Russians would be allowed to open an embassy in Fiji; secondly, the present location of some of our embassies would be changed; in other words, 'our traditional ties and economic interests would undergo drastic change' in NFP/WUF hands.

The Coalition confined its attack to the field of unemployment, the shortage of drugs in the local hospitals and the treatment of prisoners. Both the Alliance and the Coalition consistently and persistently provided a litany of statistics, made speeches in defence and ran long series of articles in the newspapers to support their manifestoes. Meanwhile the traditional tone of degeneracy, mudslinging and character assassinations became the order of the day and was to continue with increasing recklessness until polling day.

Table 5.1

Extract from Alliance Party 1982 Election Briefing Document

Issue

Strength:
   Reddy
   Made for unity. He is policy oriented. He is seen to be safe. Seen by some not to be personally ambitious but to care for Fiji.

Osea (Ratu)
Special appeal to pine growers. Coalition with Reddy.

Butadroka
Appeal to Fijians.

Weaknesses:
Reddy
Gavidi connection. Conflict with Koya which divides the party. Conflict with Narayan which divides the party. Lacks strength, resolve wishy-washy. Anti-foreign and borrowing and investment therefore growth and standard of living for Fiji. Conflict in Hindu/Muslim. Cannot take tough decision or control his ministers. No answers to key economic problems. Can't lead united government.

Gavidi
Objective simply destructive. He is a crook. Associated with crooks. Policies frighten some groups. Disloyal—tried to work with Nationalists. Mad policies to be published. Reddy link. Dawai's speech to the Nationalists with NFP.

Butadroka
Anti-Indian. Benefited from Government loan $107,000. No strategy or policy.

Since voting in the past elections had always been on racial lines, it was hardly surprising that in his 1982 election personalities and ethnicity would be more crucial factors than party manifestos. As political commentators gave the NFP its best chance of winning the government since the disastrous split in 1977, it became abundantly clear that the Alliance would exploit the leadership issue to its maximum advantage. Its weapon lay in some of the Coalition candidates who had been principal actors in the March/April election debacle. Table 5.1, an extract from the Alliance candidates' briefing documents, reveal its preparedness to face the leadership issue.[13]

The row over leadership qualities began when Reddy, addressing a political rally, challenged Ratu Mara to state the extent of his political experience before he began ruling as Prime Minister of Fiji. The Alliance whose trump card, as always, was Ratu Mara said it was unfortunate that Reddy, who did not have a long and varied political career of Ratu Mara's standing both locally and internationally, chose to call into question its party leader's capabilities. Coalition candidates, including Reddy, were subsequently labelled stupid, lunatic, thief, crook. As Ratu Osea possessed the charisma that Reddy lacked he became a special focus of Alliance attention, being described as 'a smooth young chief with boyish features, dazzling smile and a way with words but there are so many questions hanging over him that one is forced to believe the worst'.[14] Apart from questioning his involvement with Sandblom, the Alliance also raised questions about Ratu Osea's alleged links with secessionist rebels in the neighbouring Vanuatu, a former Anglo-French condominium.[15]

As mentioned earlier, Reddy's aspiration was the unification of the NFP, and his emergence as party leader had signalled a commitment to changing the party's image. But to the Alliance the NFP was still leaderless and fragmented by ideological and religious divisions which would again rip it asunder. The Alliance repeatedly highlighted the Koya/Reddy battle of 1977, with Ratu Mara claiming that Reddy had gone out of his way to prevent Koya from becoming Prime Minister. He was immediately shouted down and Koya and Reddy accused Ratu Mara of trying to create disunity between Hindus and Muslims in order to rule for the next five years. The pettiness and character assassination took another ugly turn when Reddy, with uncharacteristic rashness, told a political meeting in the northern township of Labasa that Ratu Mara would even open a toilet to shake a few more Indian hands to get their votes. The Alliance branded him 'racist' and claimed that this remark had insulted the Fijian people.

In the course of the campaign both sides agreed that the level of debate had sunk to an all-time low but blamed each other for provoking it. The Alliance also accused the WUF of 'playing a dangerous tribal game and capitalising on the ancient rivalries which led to strife in the Fiji of old', [16] and charged that it was strictly a regional and racial organization with membership restricted to one race—created in the west with the objective of giving priority to the interests of the people in the west. Pointing out the disruptive effects of tribalism elsewhere the Alliance warned that the WUF's committed policies could lead to the growth of rivalries based on clan allegiances. This debate raised the issue of the role of chiefs in Fiji's national politics. Fijian chiefs have and still do play a vital role in ensuring Fijian unity, but their political role has been the subject of contention on many occasions, particularly during election time. Some Fijian chiefs see their participation in national politics as a natural extension of their leadership roles in the Fijian society, while others maintain that it should not be taken for granted that a Fijian chief should lead Fiji.

These conflicting views found their way into the campaign: some Alliance candidates warned that a change to a government dominated by Indians would mean trouble for Fiji; Fijians were persuaded that they could lose some components of their traditional heritage if the Alliance Party failed to remain in power. Even Ratu Mara warned that peril lurked where customs were trampled, implying that traditional Fijian rule was above politics. But Butadroka demanded that Fijian chiefs should get out of politics if they regarded criticisms levelled at them on the political battlefield as offensive. In another incident a group of villagers, led by a 'touchy' chief, demolished a temporary building where Reddy was holding a political meeting.

Perhaps the most controversial Fijian reaction was one chief's banning of Coalition candidates' holding public meetings at villages in the outer Yasawa islands. He later claimed that all political parties opposing the Alliance had been similarly banned. The Coalition claimed the ban was in breach of the Constitution which provided for freedom of expression, freedom of assembly and association, and protection of freedom of movement, a claim which was later upheld by the Royal Commission of Inquiry into the 1982 general election.

The FNP apparently lacked a base in the country, except in Rewa, the home of its leader Butadroka; his policies were also constantly discredited by the other political parties. Fijian voters were called upon to reject the FNP outright at the polls. On Butadroka's claims that the Alliance had failed to help the Fijians, Ratu Mara said even government agencies had advanced loans of $107,000 to a Rewa farming venture involving the FNP leader. The FNP seemed to offer little that was palatable to the Fijian voters. It had remained silent on the future of the Indians in Fiji, but had placed emphasis on the economic emancipation of the Fijians.

The parties also exchanged political barbs over the government of national unity and the coalition offers, the allocation of government scholarships, religion and politics, the plight of the squatters and the concept of multiracialism. The Coalition challenged the Alliance's portrayal of itself as the only truly multiracial party. Reddy thought that the Alliance did not practise what it preached. The racially disparate composition of the Alliance Cabinet was one of many examples which belied the Alliance's claim to multiracialism.

In his campaign message Reddy therefore pledged a 'genuine multiracial Cabinet' and not 'a Cabinet with only one Indian minister who is too sick'.[17] He promised Fiji a government based on the Singapore concept in which the president, prime minister and the ministers are selected from various races. In reply Ratu Mara deliberately distorted Reddy's references to the Singapore concept, charging that this would make Fiji a republic, abolish the post of Governor-General and sever Fiji's links with the Crown. In response the Coalition stated categorically that if it came to power the Governor-General would be invited to hold his office as long as he liked. The flattering comments of the Malaysian Prime Minister, Dato Seri Dr Mahathir Bin Mohammed, who visited Fiji at the height of the campaign, found their way into the Alliance campaign. Dr Mahathir had stated that the forthcoming election bore eloquent testimony to the democratic and stable record of peaceful political development in Fiji.

What was supposed to be a 'clean campaign' characterized by promises of providing one kind of amenity or another broke all rules of the political game. The personalization and vituperations disrupted the calm of a 'budding democracy' and revealed all the political depravity and often ugly competitiveness characteristic of a plural society in which restraint imposed by traditional values was ignored. Two accusations in particular were to change the character of the campaign permanently: the spectre of poll rigging; and foreign interference in Fiji politics.

Mrs Narayan claimed that Ratu Mara might 'rig the election' and went on to allege that the former Australian journalist, Speed, was 'churning out election propaganda for the Alliance'. Reddy claimed at a meeting that four expatriates had prepared a master plan for the Alliance on how to win the 1982 election. The Alliance effectively denied the claim but Reddy's allegation suddenly changed the complexion of the campaign, creating consternation in Australia, New Zealand, United States, Canada, India and the Soviet Union.

The allegations gained wider international attention when the Australian Broadcasting Commission (ABC-TV) current affairs programme, 'Four Corners', exposed the foreign team claiming that it was headed by the Australian businessman and Speed's friend, Alan Carroll, an international economic and business consultant. While placing emphasis on the alleged domination of Australian big business interests in Fiji's 1982 general election, the programme disclosed that the team had prepared a 'How to Win an Election' kit—which subsequently came to be known as the Carroll Report—for the Alliance Party. 'Four Corners' further alleged that the Carroll Report had recommended the exploitation of racial and ethnic tension between the different communities; bribery; character assassination and other offensive and undemocratic dirty tricks. Meantime, and amid hysteria in the Alliance camp, the NFP/WUF Coalition managed to obtain a copy of the 'Four Corners' programme from Australia. It was now poised to exploit the programme to its maximum advantage, hoping to crush the Alliance at the polls.

The Coalition also tried hard to raise the political temperature by portraying the Carroll episode as Fiji's Watergate, and in their bid to reach the populace at large, they released more than 300 video tapes of 'Four Corners' which were screened with increasing regularity.

The message was loud and clear—the Alliance must be punished at the polls for indulging in a Nixon-type campaign. The party was virtually under siege. Claiming that he literally wept when he saw 'Four Corners', Ratu Osea called on Ratu Mara to resign. But an opinion poll showed that despite their different political affiliations, most people still preferred Ratu Mara to continue as Prime Minister, and in Suva his Alliance Party commanded most support among the voting population. The Alliance, however, was not prepared for a political gamble. But how could the Coalition be swiftly silenced?

The answer lay in the opening words of the 'Four Corners' programme that Fiji's present leaders were descendants of the Fijian chiefs who 'clubbed and ate their way to power'. Branding the quote as 'racist', the Alliance hit back through various newspaper advertisements, claiming that by introducing the programme into Fiji the Coalition supported 'this foreign racism', and, furthermore, 'a vote for NFP-WUF is a vote for racism'. In reply the Coalition denied that the programme was racist. In an attempt to appease the Fijian voters, statements from two Fijian chiefs, Ratu Osea and Ratu Napolioni, were effectively used, urging the electorate not to be fooled. The programme's 'cannibal' quote was now in the forefront of the campaign and dominated it until polling day.

Even Butadroka condemned the programme as anti-Christian, anti-Pacific and anti-Fijian. According to Ratu Mara the allegations contained in the programme were 'a deliberate fraud perpetrated against the people of Fiji to confuse the voters' mind'.[18] He had earlier condemned the 'Four Corners' team's visit to Fiji 'as an act of political sabotage against a sovereign nation'. Consequently, and because of its impact on the election results, especially among the Fijians, the issue was taken up with them. The Coalition had, through introducing the programme into Fiji, trampled on Fijian customs and traditions, the Alliance claimed.

The Coalition, as it turned out, had played into the hands of the Alliance. In a political rally speech that electrified Fijian voters Ratu Mara, while denigrating the Coalition for insulting him and his Fijian people, stated that the Coalition's actions 'cannot be forgiven and will not be forgotten'. Ratu Mara later told an Australian audience after the election:

> The producers showed, in the programme, that they cared nothing for the welfare of Fiji or the sensitivities of our people, nor did they know or understand Fiji. So they introduced a comment which was an insult to me, as a democratic leader, and through me an insult to the chiefly ·ancestors of the Fijian people.[19]

He further said that the Fijian reaction was 'swift, indignant and decisive' and 'Fijian voters turned out in record numbers to support the Alliance, and this was an important element in our success'. Meanwhile, on 17 July, the eve of the polling day, voters, and especially the Fijians, were treated to another dramatic statement from Ratu Mara. He told a reporter that he would resign if he got fewer than 30 seats in the House of Representatives, thus putting his credibility on the line.

His political act probably reaped a dividend by spurring more Fijian people into the polling booth on Saturday. As he put it: 'On Saturday morning we had 600 Fijian votes to look for in Suva and by the time the polls closed we had 580 who turned up to vote.'[20] About 86% of the voters turned out on the polling day, a clear reflection of the feelings whipped up by the stormy campaign. The elections were conducted without any ugly incidents; candidates of the same race faced each other in so many constituencies and only a handful were too bigoted to vote for any but their own race.

The interim peace during polling seemed an act of affirmation in the country's democratic process. The Fiji election, in the words of a long-time friend of Ratu Mara, Singapore's Prime Minister Lee Kuan Yew, was 'better than elections in other countries which feature bloodshed, gunfire and riots'.[21] The election results, however, were followed by allegations and counter-allegations of fraud, coercion, bribery, and that the election was not 'free and fair'.

The outcome of the final results on Sunday, 19 July, after a week's polling, contained many surprises and saw the Coalition within hair's breadth of wrenching power from the Alliance. Although the voters returned the Alliance to power, they cut its strength from 36 seats to 28; the NFP won 22 seats, an increase of seven; and WUF won two seats. All 12 Fijian and three General Elector communal seats went to the Alliance, all 12 Indian communal seats went to the NFP, and the 25 cross-voting seats were shared fairly equally. The two WUF candidates squeezed through only because of the large pro-Indian vote in the two cross-voting constituencies.

As in the past, 81.9% of the Fijians rallied behind the Alliance, and 75.6% of the Indians behind the NFP. There were many casualties: both Ratu Osea and Ratu Napolioni, the two key figures of WUF, lost their seats, as did the firebrand Nationalist leader Butadroka. All his candidates failed, many losing their deposits. The Fijian voters had predictably punished Ratu Osea and Ratu Napolioni at the polls. As for the Nationalists, they appeared to be a spent force.

Total votes cast were 1,003,448 (86.8% of a possible total of 1,155,969),[22] distributed as: Alliance (519,909) 51.8%; NFP/WUF (4,42,800) 44.1%; FNP (27,399) 2.7%; Independents (3,093) 0.3%. Tables 5.2a and 5.2b provide a provisional breakdown of the voting.

Table 5.2a

Breakdown of Voting in 1982 Election

Party	Indian communal seat	Seats	Fijian communal seat	Seats	General Elector seat	Seats
Alliance	29,382	0	101,533	12	5,937	3
NFP	93,194	12	–	–	570	0
Independents	616	0	1,010	0	–	–
Nationalists	–	–	9,385	0	108	0
NFP/WUF	–	–	11,943	0	–	–

Table 5.2b

Party	Indian national seat	Seats	Fijian national seat	Seats	General national seat	Seats
Alliance	129,727	5	126,215	5	127,115	3
NFP	113,314	5	–	–	112,548	2
Independents	1,924	0	353	0	–	–
Nationalists	–	–	9,949	0	7,957	0
NFP/WUF	–	–	111,688	5	–	–

Total seats 52; Alliance, 28; NFP/WUF 24; FNP 0; Independents 0.

The voting pattern was once again on racial lines, but more Indians (23.8%) voted for the Alliance than did Fijians for the NFP (9.6%). (See Table 5.2a.) The Nationalists, who polled 25% of the votes in the March-April 1977 elections, this time secured only 7.5%. Interestingly, while the Alliance now had a smaller majority in the House of Representatives, it actually polled a larger percentage of votes than it had in the September 1977 elections, having improved its position by 8.6 per cent, capturing about 52 per cent of the total votes cast.

In 1977 it formed a government after receiving only 44 per cent of the votes but won 36 seats because of the split in the NFP. Although the Coalition made a dent in the Alliance hold on General seats by picking up two National General constituencies, the Alliance remained unscathed in the General communal areas.

The GEA president, Ted Beddoes, later claimed that the General Elector support for the Alliance was because the Coalition believed that minority groups 'are over-represented in Parliament'. The results also showed that the General Electors did not support the 'insults' levelled at Fijians through the 'Four Corners' progamme. But given the past history of their voting pattern, their choice came as no surprise.

The Indian support for the Alliance seemed to have come from the minority Muslim and Gujerati voters. During the campaign the Alliance had tried to exploit the religious differences among the Indians by making special appeals to the Muslims. It was discreetly supported by a faction of the Fiji Muslim League, formed in 1926 to protect and promote Muslim interests, and whose president was an Alliance senator. Ratu Mara personally courted the Muslims, through speeches in their mosques, opening Muslim-run schools, promising better times ahead under an Alliance government and expressing his readiness to work with his one-time arch political rival Koya. The Gujeratis, particularly the big businessmen, flocked to the Alliance in order to protect their financial interests in the country.

The election results, however, marked the beginning of the chain of contentious events to follow. They had torn apart the two principal races, the Fijians and the Indians. When the election results were announced, some defeated candidates refused to accept them. An NFP candidate, Mumtaz Ali, objected to the final count which gave victory to his Alliance opponent and government minister, Mohammed Ramzan, in the tensely and closely fought Suva Indian national seat. He subsequently filed a writ in the Suva Supreme Court claiming that the method of delivering , checking and counting of votes was not in accordance with the electoral regulations, and claimed corrupt practices; he was followed by Ratu Osea, Ratu Napolioni and Joape Rokosoi, Lord Mayor of Suva, and an Alliance defector. These actions put the electoral process in question. Argument also broke out regarding postal ballots. A handful of arrests around the country of people accused of voting offences further compounded the conflict. The Alliance was again the centre of political controversy when

three women, pleading guilty to illegal voting and voting when not registered, claimed they had become prey to a 'mystery man' who advised
them to go to the Alliance Party voting booth at the Fiji Institute of
Technology polling station.[23]

Recriminations against the Alliance continued. The defeated Nationalist leader Butadroka attributed the loss of Fijian support for his party
to the 'racial utterances' by the leaders of the two major parties. He said
the last-minute Alliance tactic to virtually 'dictate' to the people whom to
vote for by offering them transport, and literally 'leading them to the
polling booth' was responsible. While proclaiming that 'I will be still
around in the next five years',[24] he said 'all indications were that we were
going to win some strategic seats including the one I contested but the
results swung completely to the opposite'.[25]

Other members of his party made more sensational claims. According
to them, beer, whisky and barbecues lavished by the Alliance campaign
team seduced many Fijians away from the FNP. The FNP's new general
secretary summed up their case:

> We were not able to use the expensive strategy used by the Alliance
> Party. They were actually buying the voters. That is why there was a
> lot of Fijian block voting. Even though we had established more than
> 100 branches throughout the country, the final week of entertainment
> made the difference. The voters had no choice really. In one report
> received from Kadavu, a police officer even told voters to tick the
> wheel [the Alliance's voting symbol] or they would regret it. Some
> voters were threatened that national development would not reach them
> if they voted for another party other than the Alliance. Some were
> told that the boxes would be opened and authorities would be able to
> tell who betrayed the Alliance Party.[26]

In short the allegation of vote rigging gained widespread currency.
The 1982 general elections can be characterized as a direct replay of the
1968 by-elections; for the Fijians once again felt that the Indians were
determined to wrest political power from them: Fijian unity alone would
ensure their political dominance in the country.

If the events of 1977 general election were unhappy for the Indian
community, events in the aftermath of 1982 were even more so. Some
Fijians saw them as 'angels in disguise' while one likened them to dogs
'who would not wag their tails when loved'. The scene was now set for the
next phase of post-election confrontation. While the Indians claimed that
the Australians and the Americans tried to keep them out of power, Ratu
Mara in an interview with the Australian magazine, the *Bulletin*, made
one of the most serious and sensational charges against the NFP, claiming that the party received as much as $A1million from Soviet Union
sources to help destroy him in the election campaign. He also claimed
that the Indian Embassy in Fiji and in Australia had been used to further
Soviet interests in the South Pacific, and alleged that India's High Com-

missioner to Fiji, Mrs Soonu Kochar, had actively involved herself in party politics, and spent much of her time trying to heal the split in the NFP.

Ratu Mara also suggested that Mrs Kochar's husband, Hari, had acted as the 'middle-man' in the rouble deal. 'He's a former Indian Foreign Affairs officer, who had links with the Russians. Our reports show he was very active in assisting the NFP right up to the elections and met some of the leading members of the NFP in Sydney in this period.[27] Meanwhile, if the 'Four Corners' programme had incited the Fijians, the *Bulletin* interview had equally aroused Indian indignation. Their leaders were seen as taking Fiji down the road of communism. The allegations made by a paramount chief of one community against the leaders of another community at last plunged the country's racial parties into turbulence.

As in 1968, the country was heading more closely towards the rocks. The 1982 general elections doused the flame of multiracialism in a sea of racial antagonism. As Ratu Mara put it: 'It will be a long time before we achieve a non-racial Fiji.'[28] The internationalization of Fiji politics ignited the dormant racial volcano, started by the outflow of 'political lava' from the 'Four Corners' programme.

Notes

1. Compiled from Ratu Mara's prepared statement to the Royal Commission of Inquiry into the 1982 Fiji General Elections, 8 April 1983; a copy of the published statement is in author's possession.
2. The survey prepared by the Carroll team was entitled 'Strategic Issues Facing The Fijian Government', November 1981.
3. See *Far Eastern Economic Review* (Hong Kong), 'Indians Galore, but can they be chiefs?', 6 November 1981, p. 80.
4. Quoted by R.T. Robertson, in *The Journal of Pacific Studies*, Vol. 12, 1986, p. 48.
5. For more discussion see Parliament of Fiji, *Report of the Royal Commission of Inquiry into the 1982 General Elections,* Parliamentary Paper No. 74 of 1983, pp. 93-96 (subsequently referred to as *The White Report* because the Commission was headed by a retired New Zealand Supreme Court Judge, Sir John White).
6. Disclosed by Ratu Mara to the Royal Commission, op. cit., Ref. 1.
7. Statement of Clive Randolph Speed to the Royal Commission, 1983 (mimeo).
8. *The Coalition Bulletin*, No. 1, February 1982.
9. *Fiji Sun*, 11 May 1982, p. 1.
10. *The Alliance Manifesto* (mimeo).
11. *The NFP-WUF Manifesto.* For an exposé, see also *Fiji Sun*, 5 June 1982, pp. 17-24.
12. Ahmed Ali, 'A Critique of the NFP/WUF Manifesto', in author's possession.
13. Obtained from an Alliance candidate who prefers to remain anonymous.
14. *Fiji Sun*, 5 July 1982, p. 2.
15. Ibid., p. 7.
16. Ibid., p. 2.
17. Ibid., 31 May 1982, p. 1.

18. Ratu Mara's statement to the Royal Commission, 8 April 1983.
19. He was the guest speaker at the Royal Prince Alfred Hospital Centenary Dinner, Sydney, Australia, 30 July 1983. A copy of Ratu Mara's speech is in author's possession.
20. *Fiji Sun*, 21 July 1982, p. 3.
21. Ibid., 15 October 1982.
22. Tabulated from *Fiji Sun*, 19 July 1982, p. 28.
23. For more details see Victor Lal, *Fiji Sun*, 8 October 1982, p.1.
24. Ibid., 19 July 1982.
25. Ibid.
26. Ibid., 24 July 1982.
27. *The Bulletin Magazine* (Australia), 10 August 1982.
28. *Fiji Sun*, 21 July 1982, p. 3.

CHAPTER SIX

THE CARROLL AFFAIR

> It quickly appeared obvious to Dr Race and me that there were
> some striking similarities to the Malaysian political environment of
> the 1960s and we structured a scenario type analysis to demonstr-
> ate outcomes should the Alliance Party approach the 1982 elec-
> tions under differing assumptions.
>
> *Alan Carroll*, (Australian business consultant, 1982).

Some days after Reddy's allegation, in June 1982, that there was a
'treacherous master plan' produced by four expatriates to enable the Alliance Party to defeat the NFP/WUF Coalition at the polls, he named
four 'experts' who had produced it and detailed various strategies he
claimed it contained.

This document later came to be known as the Carroll Report and the
team who wrote it as the Carroll team. Alan Carroll, Geoff Allen, Rosemarie Gillespie (Australians) and Dr Jeffrey Race (American) were the
four 'experts' in question. Reddy also alleged that Speed's appointment
as media consultant to the Fiji government was part of the Carroll plan.
These allegations subsequently led to claims and counter-claims over the
existence and contents of the Carroll Report. The *Fiji Sun* chronicled the
claims and counter-claims relating to this report, and these are summarized below.[1]

June 22: Reddy alleges Speed is working for the Alliance government
under Australian aid funding. Ratu Mara replies that Speed works for
the Ministry of Information, assisting the department on policy matters.

June 23: Reddy alleges there is a 'master plan' produced by four expatriates for the Alliance government.

June 25: Reddy names four people alleged to be the 'experts' who produced the report. He says 'the contents have to be seen to be believed',
and claims that Speed was hired by Carroll, one of the four experts, at
the request of Ratu Mara.

June 28: Ratu Mara admits experts were employed but that expert advisers are needed; it was normal practice in any democracy. He reminds
the electorate that in September 1979 the NFP invited Australian Labour
Party secretary, David Combe, to address its convention and to advise
the party on political matters . . . 'we had to follow suit'.

He claims the four advisers conducted a sample survey concentrating
on economic, not political, issues; that issues emerging from it included
attitudes towards statutory bodies; unemployment; education; the economy, including the private sector; and the level of support for the gov-

ernment within the Indian and Fijian communities. Adding that Reddy's claims that government had received advice from foreign experts were 'stupid' and an attempt to 'bamboozle the electorate'; and that the Alliance does its own planning.

June 29: Reddy asks who paid for the four foreign experts; claims Carroll found Speed, not Ratu Mara and Dr Lasaqa; that Speed was hired to help the Alliance; calls for the report to be made public.

July 1: Ratu Mara denies the Alliance government paid for a political survey, saying the report is confidential. He neither denied its existence or that it could have suggested exploiting ethnic or religious differences to assist the government. He challenges Reddy to release the report.

July 2: Reddy replies that as the report is for the Alliance, they should release it.

July 3: The ABC's 'Four Corners' programme reveals the Carroll team's involvement, placing emphasis on domination of Australian big business interests in Fiji's election. Ratu Mara charges the ABC TV film crew with 'political sabotage'. The Coalition release video tapes of the programme, dubbing it Fiji's Watergate.

But who commissioned the Carroll Report? How did it all begin? In November 1980, a prominent Indian Gujerati businessman and member of the Alliance Management Board, Mahendra Motibhai Patel (M.M. Patel), needed someone to advise his firm, Motibhai and Company, on the future planning of their company. Discussions with Adam Dickson, a partner of the Fiji branch of the multinational firm, Coopers and Lybrand, auditors and advisers of Motibhai since 1961, led to further talks with Dickson's counterpart in Sydney, Australia, John Goddard, who subsequently recommended Carroll of Business International (BI) as the best choice for the project. BI is a world-wide advisory organization describing itself as a global research and advisory corporation 'serving corporations doing business across borders and those who support and govern them including bankers, attorneys, accountants, consultants, colleges and universities and government officials.'[2]

In December 1980 Carroll visited Fiji at Mr Patel's invitation and, following negotiations, tentatively agreed to provide an economic and business survey for Motibhai, at a cost of $20,000. It was also agreed that the survey would not be conducted under the auspices of BI because the company 'would charge twice as much for it'. On 17 December 1980, Carroll also gave a talk to various executives of Motibhai and Company at Motibhai's Administration Office about 'economics and how politics in America has affected the politics of many countries in the world'. He also raised questions relating to Fiji government policies.[3]

Carroll's high-powered presentation impressed Mahendra Patel who, thinking that Ratu Mara 'could derive some benefit', introduced the two men to each other. Carroll's suggestion to Ratu Mara that it would be useful for the Alliance Party to have a professionally conducted opinion poll in Fiji was accepted.[4] It was further agreed that Patel should arrange for Carroll to return to Fiji in March 1981 to explain to Ratu Mara in greater detail his views on the world economy and its likely impact on Pacific nations. The public opinion poll suggestion was carried further when, shortly afterwards, Ratu Mara, on his way to London for a Privy Council meeting, again met Carroll, in Sydney. It has since been claimed that the Alliance Party was not at all involved in that agreement between Carroll and Ratu Mara.

The two men also agreed, according to the Alliance, that the proposed survey would be grafted onto the Motibhai economic review at 'no extra cost', which Ratu Mara felt was a personal gift to him from a staunch Alliance supporter. Given the close political and business links between Ratu Mara and M.M. Patel, however, this explanation would be unacceptable to the country's political observers. Three years later the NFP/WUF Coalition's lawyer at the Royal Commission, Bhupendra Patel, was to question M.M. Patel's motive in introducing Carroll to Ratu Mara. His view was that:

> M.M. Patel was and still is a very close personal friend of the PM of Fiji. And that friendship has assisted MMP and his family to amass a large fortune in a relatively short span of time, in fact Motibhais have built a little empire. Being the astute businessman he is, MMP's foresight told him that his empire could be in danger if the PM lost power in the 1982 elections.[5]

Whatever the underlying motive, the Carroll/M.M. Patel/Ratu Mara meeting of 17 December 1980 led to the recruitment of Allen, Gillespie and Race. As Carroll's telexed statement to the Royal Commission of Inquiry into the 1982 general elections, admitted:

> A professional report was provided by me to Mahendra Patel, chairman of Motibhai and Co. at his request in April 1982. The report took a detailed look at the political economy of Fiji, but in the context of the business strategy options for Mr Patel's company.
>
> Given the company's structure and base of operations being centralised in Fiji, it was obviously important to explore a risk assessment profile of the political/economic environment of that country. I then enlisted the aid of Dr Jeffrey Race as an Asian expert and political consultant based in Thailand to assist with that assessment.[6]

The enlistment of Race, an expert on Malaysian politics, and head of the Asian Strategics Company, added a new dimension to the survey of Fiji's political scene. It quickly became clear both to Race and Carroll that there were some striking similarities to the Malaysian political environment of the 1960s and they devised an analytical structure to enable them to demonstrate alternative possibilities should the Alliance Party approach the 1982 elections under differing assumptions.

According to Gillespie, following the recruitment of Race, Carroll telephoned her at her Melbourne office in late April/May 1981 to say that he and Race were 'developing a political strategy for Fiji', and would she be willing to undertake the research component; she agreed to do this.

After their preliminary surveys and assessments, and with the overall view of the 1981 political climate as, according to Gillespie, Race perceived it:

> The ruling party is like the ruling party in Malaysia [it is] falling apart at the elite level [there is] squabbling in the Cabinet. At the mass level [the Alliance Party] is losing popular support.[7]
>
> Everyone says the PM is becoming very isolated. Nobody there dares tell him he is becoming very isolated from everybody including his own cabinet . . . things are falling apart . . . if nothing is done, the Alliance Party will be out on its ass.[8]
>
> [Under these circumstances] the outsider performs a crucial role.

On 17 September, the 'outsiders'—Carroll, Race and Allen—who had 'run three Liberal Party campaigns in Australia' met Ratu Mara and a few selected senior Alliance members and informed them of the results of the economic survey and the public opinion polls. There was also a draft report with a segment by Carrol entitled 'Outlook and Outlook and Implications', and a set of three scenarios by Race. What transpired at this meeting has since been disputed with varied and controversial interpretations put upon it.

The scenarios[9] that dominated the election campaign , reproduced below, provide a guide to events described in the subsequent chapters:

SCENARIO ONE—"ALLIANCE WINS"

Aspect	Risk	Strategy
Fijian support intact. Biggest problem and first priority is consolidating Fijian support.	Dictation by leader won't work. Must use carrots.	1. Widen range of contacts and advice in elites of PM's own camp— * Press * cabinet * opinion leaders * business.
* point made by both friends and opponents of PM. * feudal allegiances crumbling		*Means* * organised 'stroke' * kitchen cabinet 2. New carrots for support— * honours. * stroke * other payoffs.

		3. Recognise that NFP despite pretence is businessmen's party and push economic growth (see economic section).
PM shows decisive leadership.	Split in Alliance ('Autocracy')	Stroking/appointments Good start already made 8/81.
Boundary redistribution slightly favours NFP.	'Throw of the dice' but probably more than slightly favours NFP.	Must be handled right. *Must* handle carefully. Carefully analyse likely constituency-by-constituency campaign strategy.
Poor economic conditions in 1982 increasing urban unemployment.	NFP pushes 'issue' (class) politics.	(See 'Image')
Election policies * economic policies. * sugar. * television. * housing. * fiscal stance. * medical. * education.	Timing is crucial. NFP has but irresponsible; Alliance needs Possible cost/benefit Seen as pro-Fijian Too conservative	Think out ahead, have in readiness. Release in studied succession to further support image of movement
Image * Get credit for pro-Fijian stance currently without jeopardizing expansion of Indian support.	Reddy will hit here Difficult. 'Fine line' Need professional expertise.	1. Firness 2. Expanded effort/ 'zip' 3. More for all locals by cutback for foreign share (but no one hurt since pie will grow due to # 2).
* Renewed direction— vigour versus perception of present stagnation.	Need firm support from top Danger of split in Alliance.	All above refer Malaysian precedents/success. 3. New stocks— * 'Toc-cutter to plan and implement might be useful.
Gain 1 Fijian communal seat	In fact shaky, need major effort—difficult (see above)	
Marginal deterioration of Federation unity	Marginal at best	

* Muslim leakage to
  Allaince
* Koya/Reddy battle
  smoulders
  Improve quality of
  Alliance candidates.

Expand Indian Support while Spliting NFP Base

(secondary priority but
still essential)

1. Gain Muslim sup-   Can't be blatant.
   port.
   Many observers say it
   can be done and will
   affect marginal seats.

* appointments
* oral commitment to
  Muslim represent-
  ation in Alliance
  government (not
  change constitution)
* improve business.

2. Make it respectable   Must handle very
   for Indians to sup-   carefully or will
   port Alliance and   undercut Fijian
   build on that.   Strategy (this election

1. Malaysian method—
* articulated program-
  (NEP)
* hard-charging ethic
  parties as coalition
  constituents (segment
  marked).
* pitch—'responsible
  leaders' vs. ranting
  madmen.
2. Get more/better
   Indian candidates
   (Incentive needed).

Miscellaneous and Organizational Aspects
'Got to get organized'

too slack now
inadequate professiona-
lism

De-emphasize international
aspects and concentrate for
next 12 months on getting
domestic problems settled.

After Election:
1. Total re-think of strategy for next five years.
2. Possible restructure of voting system—preference voting, single electorates.

Image/Communications Aspects

Nature of campaign two levels:
1. Emotional
   Most observers agree will be mostly emotional
   not rational.
   Get ready for it—hit back quickly or hit first.
   Segment the markets (Malaysian method)

NEP Strategy:
* build Fijian support
* 'fear in the pubs'.
* get in coalition
* wait for chance to take over.

Some issues:
racial component of
* civil service
* diplomatic service
* military service
* policy
* statutory bodies

The Pitch:
* responsible
* have a program
* fresh blood/new ideas
* equity/fairness
2. Rational
Programs:
* well-thought-out
* have answer for everything.

Timing:
Don't fire all your guns at once.

Professionalism (refer to Organizational Section)

Events:
He becomes increasingly autocratic and isolated after 8 years in office. (Foe example in 1965 he kicks Singapore out of Federation without even consulting the Cabinet; he insists on autocratic selection of candidates for office.)
Increasing intercommunal tensions.
In the May 1969 election, the Alliance achieves an unsatisfactory win, gets scared. (Opposition: DAP = Chinese party and PAS—Malay Islamic party).

Outcome:
Riots a few days after the election.
A 'coup' against the Tunku by his own party (organized by Dr Mahathir, now PM and Musa Hitam, now DPM). Tunku resigns.
The Alliance brings the PAS into coalition from position of strength.

Lessons:
Increase sensitivity in *time* to potential divisions. Timely shifts of direction to keep opposition off balance. Stroking.
Do the necessary before elections, not after.
Organized restructuring/*a program* both political and economic = NEP and coalition strategy in Malaysia.
Successor anointed early.

Fijian variant:
Alliance looks to lose election or win marginally, so the Cabinet preempts by having coup against PM *before* election.

SCENARIO TWO—'Malaysian Replay'
(Marginal win, leader compromised and out)

Receives less attention because it is less appealing but it certainly is possible if timely corrective action is not adopted. It is so named because there is an uncanny likeness between certain features of the current political situation in Fiji and that which occurred in Malaysia in the late 1960s and 1970s.

In the Malaysian case, the 'Father of his country'—Tunku Abdul Rahman, leader at the time of Independence and prince from a relatively unimportant state on the periphery of the country—came under increasing attack from elements of his own party after an uncovincing 'win' in the 1969 election, which threatened a coalition or even loss of the government in Selangor, the state where is located the Federal capital. Though the Tunku survived the election, and even succeeded in purging two of his critics, Dr Mahathir and Musa Hitam, he was ultimately removed himself as head of the party and PM. Mahathir and Musa made a comeback, indeed are PM and DPM respectively this day. They went into a coalition with certain of the opposition parties (though from a position of great strength, unlike the Fiji situation) and then developed the programs (the NEP) which consolidated their hold on the government. In their view, however, the 1969 threatening electoral loss never would have occurred had the proper policies been adopted in time. That may be the most important lesson for Fiji.

Background:
1957 Independence.
Malaysia's first prime minister is Tunku Abdul Rahman, prince from Kedah. (Not the key political state.) He is 'the father of the country'. He heads multi-ethnic coalition of elites (Malay 51%; Chinese 35%; Indian 11%).

SCENARIO THREE
(Alliance Loses)
Fijian Support and Constituencies Fragment over Next 12 Months
Public:

FNP and WUF take voter support away from Alliance in its natural constituency.
Apparent sense of drift and confusion cause voter apathy.
Elite:
Other Alliance politicians moving around issues;

(e.g., Singh ex AG)
(e.g., process selection).
Redistribution scares them.

Federation Unity Going into Election
Koya sits out election waiting to strike; accommodation with Reddy.

Strategy:
   Fijian support by getting chiefs on ticket.
   Electoral cooperation with splinter Fijian parties.
   Hit on emotional issues
      education quotas
      stagnation/lack of direction
   Pocket book issues
      sugar
      copra
      unemployment
      housing
      land

Alliance Candidates do not Improve in Public Perception.

Candidate Selection Process Further Fragments Unity of Alliance Base.

Boundary Redistribution Further Favours NFP/NO Response from Alliance.

The designer of the scenarios, especially with regard to parallels with Malaysia, was clearly Race, who was well-versed in the Malaysian political scene as his following analysis of Malaysia's political structure at a 1979 Business International seminar in Melbourne reveals:

   (a) The ruling party of Malaysia is a coalition of the elite segments of the three ethnic communities: Chinese, Malays, and Indians.
   (b) Those in Malaysia without political power include: non-elite Malays, non-elite Chinese, and non-elite Indians.
   (c) The three ethnic communities are not integrated, and there is significant tension between them. The Chinese are powerful in business, the Malays are powerful in politics. The Malays are given preferential access to education opportunities and credit facilities.[10]

By substituting 'Fijian' for 'Malay' and 'Indian' for 'Chinese', significant parallels between the political situation in Malaysia and that in Fiji may be observed. It was these similarities that Race saw fit to expand upon and apply, with variations, in Fiji.

The 17 September meeting set in motion the second stage of the project. The public opinion exercise of the teams' survey was thought to have produced some useful results and that it should be repeated in

March or April 1982, when the Alliance campaign was to be advanced, in order to see if voters' attitudes on the issues covered had changed. Gillespie's services were again accepted and the Alliance agreed to pay for this second survey. The results were to assist the team, particularly Allen, to develop a framework for an analysis of the political strategy to be presented to senior members of the Alliance at a subsequent meeting on 24 April 1982.

While this meeting was still impending, however, another controversial event occurred. In November 1981 M.M. Patel received a copy of a report entitled 'Strategic Issues Facing the Fijian Government'. He did not send this to Ratu Mara believing that he already had one; Speed also received a copy of the report from Carroll. Another copy, and an undated covering letter, which referred to meetings and advice previously given to the Alliance, were addressed to Ratu Mara with Section One specifically noting it as 'Report of Consultants to the Prime Minister of Fiji on the Economic and Political Outlook and Options for Strategy and Political Organization'. Ratu Mara has denied ever receiving either the report or the letter.

The report, with slight variations, included the papers supplied to the participants at the 17 September 1981 meeting but with significant updating. Amongst the recommendations were explicit strategies to bribe the FNP leader, Butadroka, and by manipulating the criminal justice system, to prevent the WUF leader, Ratu Osea, from contesting the election. In Butadroka's opinion it was a 'Mafia-type operation', and he stated that 'if anyone is thinking of trying to buy us off, he better forget it, we are priceless'. Butadroka subsequently called on Ratu Mara to seek clarification.

In the meantime, Ratu Mara publicly claimed that this copy of the report did not include the 'Private and Confidential' page recommending strategies on how to cripple political opposition in order to retain political control of the country. This page read as follows:

(Private and Confidential)

SCENARIO THREE—EXPANSION

STRATEGIES

Public:
   FNP—either buy off or take him out of running.
   Gavidi—since he is going to jail anyway, best to pile all effort on and accelerate prosecutions so he cannot run.
   Two other parties forming—got to make an accommodation.
   Nationalist and other party challenge in general—accept the challenge—'We hear what you are saying, we have well-thought-out, responsible programme. Our opponents are madmen.'

Elite:
> Ratu David and allies—got to have accommodations with Alliance.
> Voluntary or involuntary drop-outs from Cabinet—either let them
> leave happy (appointments) or make sure they understand they will
> be sorry if they challenge the Alliance. (Get something on them.)

General Notes:
> Need and enforcer (PM's surrogate).
> Combine divide and rule with stroking.
> Need both means of disciplining people now in and incentives to
> attract more good candidates.
> Mechanisms of planning.
> Rest is obvious.

Ten months later, what had begun as a business survey turned into a
political nightmare for Ratu Mara. He had either to admit or deny the
NFP charges that the Alliance was implementing the Carroll Report; he
completely denied them. He maintained that until Reddy's allegations he
did not even read the 17 September draft report.

> At the meeting most of us did no more than look casually, if at all, at
> the scenarios and they were certainly not discussed at the meeting. It
> was 10 months later, when Mr Jai Ram Reddy commented in public
> about this report, before I examined these papers again.[11]

Regarding the second survey, he said:

> I have earlier stated that it had been felt that another opinion poll
> similar to [that] undertaken in 1981 should be conducted sometime
> closer to the time of the 1982 general elections.
> This second opinion survey was later conducted and was completed
> in early April 1982. Messrs Carroll and Allen came to Suva to pres-
> ent the results at a meeting on April 24th, 1982.[12]

The Coalition, however, viewed this with scepticism. In their opinion the
purpose of the Carroll team was to develop a political strategy to enable
the Alliance Party to win the 1982 general election. The 24 April meeting, they maintained, including the draft and the final report, were part of
that strategy. Later they alleged that 'perhaps Mahendra Patel was only
an innocent victim used in getting access to the Prime Minister by organizations such as the CIA and Business International.'[13] The economic
and business survey for M.M. Patel was also interpreted as 'a hastily contrived smokescreen designed to cover up the real nature of the Fiji project'.[14]

The Alliance stand was that 'the election campaign waged . . . was the
planning the party itself had put into campaign' and 'the Carroll surveys
and accompanying report . . . played no part in the Alliance election
campaign'.[15]

But what was the truth? Who signed the undated letter? What were its contents? What was discussed at the 24 April meeting? Was Speed part of the Carroll team? How did the Coaliation and the ABC get hold of the Carroll Report?

These are some of the vital questions that must be fully addressed before judgement can be passed on the Carroll Report which still casts its shadow on Fiji's political landscape.

Notes

1. *Fiji Sun,* 5 July 1982, p. 2.
2. Disclosed by the Australian market researcher, Rosemarie Gillespie, to the Royal Commission of Inquiry. The Carroll team's background is contained in BI's promotional literature; copy in author's possession.
3. See transcript of tape recording to Carroll's talk, quoted in Vijay Maharaj's submission (Counsel of Gilespie) to the Royal Commission, 19 August 1983 (mimeo).
4. See Ratu Mara's prepared statement to the Royal Commission, 8 April 1983, p. 7.
5. Cited in Parliament of Fiji, *Report of the Royal Commission of Inquiry into the 1982 General Elections(The White Report),* Parliamentary Page No. 74 of 1983, pp. 42-43. Sir John White regarded the suggested inference 'as greatly overstating the effect of the evidence'. In his opinion there was no evidence to justify the comment in the second sentence.
6. Carroll's telexed statement of 17 June 1983, cited in *The White Report,* November 1983.
7. Quoted in Vijay Maharaj's submission, op. cit.
8. Ibid.
9. Copy in author's possession.
10. Quoted in Vijay Maharaj's submission, op. cit.
11. Ratu Mara's statement, op. cit., p. 11.
12. Ibid., p. 13.
13. *The White Report,* pp. 40-41.
14. Ibid., p. 41.
15. Ibid., p. 74.

CHAPTER SEVEN

FIJI'S WATERGATE

What is unusual about Fiji is that it is our Third World. We helped
make it what it is.... This is one of the faces of politics in Fiji.
There is another face. It is imported. It is white. It is Australian.
And it is out to win by whatever means are necessary.
The Australian Broadcasting Commission TV 'Four Corners', July 1982

The covering letter attached to the copy of the November Carroll Report
is still a mystery. It was a photostat copy with neither heading nor date,
and purportedly written by Carroll to 'Ratu Sir Kamisese Mara, Prime
Minister of Fiji'. Ratu Mara denied receiving it; Carroll initially claimed
it was a forgery. The Royal Commission of Inquiry into the 1982
General Election treated it with suspicion, and evidence tendered at the
inquiry suggested that Mrs Carroll might have signed the letter on her
husband's behalf.

Despite its aura of mystery, however, the letter's contents were specific:
mentioning the September 1981 meeting; the implementation of recommendations in the report; and foreseeing future dealings with the Alliance Party. The contents of the letter also provided the required catalyst
to set the political parties on a confrontation course. It was also to provide the ABC 'Four Corners' team and the *National Times* of Australia
with a solid base from which to investigate the possible 'meddling' of
certain Australian interests in Fiji's internal political affairs. To understand and evaluate the later turn of events, the letter must be quoted in
full:[1]

Ratu Sir Kamisese Mara, Prime Minister of Fiji.

Dear Prime Minister,

I attach a report on strategic issues facing the Fijian Government and Alliance Party a draft of which was discussed in depth with you between September 16-20th, 1981.

Attached also are results of a genral political survey conducted in six electorates selected on the basis of perceived political sensitivity, between June/
July 1981. A selection of parliamentary results of this survey and their implications were also discussed with you and close colleagues at these meetings. Apart from recommendations embodied in the attached report, your
consultants, Dr Jeffrey Race, Mr Geoff Allen and I made a number of recommendations during the course of these discussions. These included:

1. The need to upgrade the party organisation by the appointment of a
new General Secretary and to re-examine the functions of the Party Secre-

tariat and its relations with the Government and Alliance Party.

2. The need to make the conduct of election campaign more professional.

3. The advantage of a visit to Australia and Papua New Guinea by an executive of the party who would have responsibility for the implementation, if accepted, of recommendations 1 and 2.

4. The need for improved grassroots relations between the Prime Minister's office and the media, including increased direct contact between reporters and the Prime Minister. Apart from policy and attitudinal considerations the appointment of a media liaison consultant to the Prime Minister, as is a common minimum facility in most countries, was recommended.

5. The further regular polling be conducted to assess and identify marginal electorates for positive discrimination in electioneering effort and to assess and evaluate approaches to key election issues prior to the forthcoming election. The sensitivity of polling results was identified and the need for confidentiality stressed.

6. A committee of senior party supporters, led by a dynamic and respected chairman, who would be most likely found in the business community, be set up quickly to conduct a major fund-raising campaign. These funds would be necessary to finance new professionalism in the development of the party and the conduct of the election camaign.

Following these recommendations I am happy to note the appointment of Mr Ismail [sic] Bose to the party until the next election. We were pleased to arrange contacts and details of a short study program by Mr Bose with the Australian Liberal Party, and The Pangu Party of Papua New Guinea in early October 1981. We note that Mr Bose was able to research in some considerable depth the role of political polling by parties in Australia.

Following these recommendations we were pleased also at your request to search for and recommend a journalist of exceptional talent to work in media relations with the Government. Mr Clive Speed, Executive Producer, Current Affairs, for the Australian Broadcasting Commission who is strongly recommended to you is one of Australia's most mature and experienced working journalist with a breadth of background that includes particularly the production of radio news, current affairs and documentary programs. This background together with his personal qualities makes him particularly well suited to the task that would be required of him in Fiji.

We stand ready to provide further assistance as required and believe a review of developments and further assessment of requirements by us would be of importance early in 1982—most appropriately during April. Ms Rosemarie Gilliespie who conducted the attached survey would be of further assistance in the conduct and analysis of polling should that be desired—preferably in March.

We are happy to have been of assistance, have valued very much your courtesy and consideration, and look forward to further close association.

Yours sincerely,
Alan M. Carroll
Signed

It may be relevant at this point to recall certain events already outlined which accord with the contents of the letter, such as:

(1) The need to upgrade the party organisations by appointing a new

general secretary, etc. (In early January 1982, the acting general secretary Adi Losalini Dovi was blamed for poor performance, resulting in her resignation. Ratu Mara's response was that the Alliance headquarters needed 'a washing and brushing up'.)

(2) The need to make the conduct of the election campaign more professional. (Bose was appointed as Alliance's campaign director on 21 September 1981.)

(3) The advantage of a visit to Australia and Papua New Guinea etc. (Bose did indeed go to Australia and Papua New Guinea.)

(4) The appointment of a media liaison consultant to the PM. (We have outlined in detail the appointment of Speed as media consultant and Ratu Mara's evidence stating that Carroll had suggested Speed to him on 17 September 1981.)

(5) Further regular polling to be conducted to assess and identify marginal electorates. (Approval was undoubtedly given for Gillespie to conduct a second survey.)

(6) A committee of senior party supporters led by a chairman from the business community be set up to conduct a major fund-raising campaign. (M.M. Patel was indeed appointed chairman of an ad hoc subcommittee of the Indian Alliance to undertake fund-raising.)[2]

Did the Alliance deliberately implement the recommendations? Or did the recommendations merely coincide with the party's strategy?

The most plausible explanation put forward by the Alliance was that there 'may have been coincidences, or the recommendations may have been in line with known Alliance policy in action'. But what is the truth? Even the Royal Commissioner failed to provide a convincing answer:

> While the implementation of the recommendations in the report (mentioned especially in the letter) is a very important matter of inquiry, the fact that they are referred to in a document with such an unsatisfactory history must, in my view, reduce the value of that circumstantial evidence.[3]

The Royal Commissioner, Sir John White, went on to note that 'the letter may be self-serving in giving the Carroll team credit for having been responsible for some actions taken by the Alliance and that it is unsupported by other evidence of weight to corroborate what is stated in it.'[4] The Alliance, as has been shown, strongly disputed that either Speed or Bose was appointed to their respective posts as a result of the Carroll Report.

Whatever the truth, the involvement of the Carroll team in the 1982 election preparations was later to prove a disaster for the Alliance; similarly even the scheduled 24 April meeting when electoral strategies for the Alliance were discussed in detail.

The contents and purpose of this meeting are revealed in Gillespie's notes while participating as a member of the Carroll team. The participants included Ratu Mara, Dr Lasaqa Len Usher, Speed, Bose, Carroll, Allen and Gillespie. Apart from Dr Lasaqa and Speed, who attended as observers on Ratu Mara's direction, the other Alliance members belonged to the party's publicity sub-committee. Allen was a 'Johnny-come-lately' but given his experience with the Papua New Guinea political environment, he attended the meeting as a personal favour to Carroll.

Several crucial issues were discussed: Gillespie's second survey; ways to tackle the question of inflation during the campaign; the Alliance's chances of winning three Indian communal seats; and the popularity of the political leaders. The eventful meetings could be summarized as follows: Carroll introduced the meeting saying 'the bottom line of today is to choose the issues and what to do about them', put the session in perspective, talked on strategy; Gillespie gave summary of issues and Allen talked on implications, poll results, personalities, unemployment, housing, Opposition strength/vulnerability, food prices, etc. Emphasis was also placed on strategy and timing.[5] Examination of the content of the meeting reveals one controversial issue which later became part of Carroll saga: the proposed involvement of the former Australian Prime Minister and later co-chairman of the Commonwealth Eminent Persons Group (EPG) to south Africa, Malcolm Fraser.

Although it cannot be ascertained if the Carroll team managed to involve Fraser, it is public knowledge that, in May 1982, Fraser invited Ratu Mara to Canberra for a private visit as his guest during the annual Federal Council Meeting of the Australian Liberal Party, which at that time, led by Fraser, had the majority in the House of Representatives.

The relationship between the two leaders was further strengthened when Ratu Mara, speaking at a dinner in Canberra, declared that Fraser was 'the best friend I have in the Commonwealth'. Fraser, in his 15 May speech, thanked Ratu Mara for visiting Australia and praised him for providing Fiji with stability, a sense of direction and economic management for over 30 years. Fraser said he had first met Ratu Mara about seven years ago at a meeting where some bi-lateral problems between Australia and Fiji had emerged. It was agreed at this meeting that if necessary Ratu Mara should pick up a phone and speak to Fraser.

Meanwhile, if Fraser's praise of Ratu Mara at the height of the campaign was a soothing balm in some quarters, his statement in the same speech that 'Australians who fell for the slogan, "it is time for a change", got the lesson of a lifetime', was a bitter political pill for Fiji's Opposition to swallow.

The Coalition, which was campaiging on the 'time for a change' slogan, quickly interpreted this as a call for voters to reject them at the polls. They also read into the statement 'political interference' in Fiji's internal affairs by Fraser who was reported as saying:

If it is some encouragement, and I am not sure that any encouragement is needed, Australians once fell for the slogan, 'It is time for a change', but they paid such an awfully high price for it in the years afterward that it should be a lesson to anyone who has been promised that it is time for a change. They just have to look at Australia's example and anyone would run right in the other direction.[6]

In a highly polarized society like Fiji, such a statement was certain to provide a strong reaction, particularly during election time. The wrath of the Coalition was manifested in a cable sent to Fraser by the president of the NFP Youth Movement, urging him to stay out of Fiji politics. Another cable, sent to Fraser's political opponent, the then Federal Leader of Opposition, Bill Hayden, asked him to seek clarification of the alleged interference, and to oppose any such interference, if it was found to exist, in the political affairs of an independent democratic country such as Fiji.

It is difficult to estimate what influence Fraser's statement had or could have had on Fiji voters but it remained a burning political issue as more 'Australian involvement' began slowly to emerge as the campaign advanced.

Meanwhile, the Coalition's prompt reaction was only the beginning of troubled times ahead for the Alliance, which had by now rejected Carroll's offer for Gillespie to return to Fiji to conduct the third survey as planned. They also failed to realize that the exercise was to be exposed by a member of the Carroll team—Gillespie did just that. She decided to cut loose the tight-rope on which the Carroll team was balanced. Her outlet was through the Australian media, specifically the ABC and the *National Times.* Her motive can be found in her statement to the Royal Commission.

> I did so because I felt that the operation conducted by the Australian contingent [Dr Race, Alan Carroll, Geoffrey Allen and Clive Speed] was nothing short of a rape of democracy. Since I also had been involved in the project, I felt I had a duty to let the people of Fiji know what was being done to their country. I also felt that the people of Australia had a right to know about the misuse of Australian aid funds to pay for Clive Speed's salary while he was stationed in Fiji.[7]

Her view was that the Carroll team was engaged in a manipulation exercise; the Alliance was merely 'ham in the sandwich'. The team used the Fiji project as a front to further the interests of its Business International clients. She also considered that Carroll and Race were exerting pressure on Ratu Mara to carry out their recommendations if he wished to remain as Fiji's Prime Minister, citing as evidence two specific events: Race's recommendations about the Malaysian Replay and Carroll's 'aggressive' questioning of Ratu Mara when he spoke at a meeting of CEDA in September 1981.

She said that Carroll told Ratu Mara that compared to most developing countries, Fiji had a very low level of overseas borrowing, and questioned (1) whether Fiji's borrowing capacity could be 'more aggressively used for development? and (2) did he (Ratu Mara) think more risks could be taken?

Gillespie had clearly become disgusted with the contents of the Carroll Report and other circumstances surrounding the Fiji operation and had therefore decided to act swiftly before the voters went to the polls. Since her motive would later be questioned, it is pertinent to briefly recall Ratu Mara's initial reaction following the screening of the 'Four Corners' programme. In his election speech of 8 July, he claimed 'revenge' as her motive, and that he 'decided to discontinue the opinion poll supervised by a Rosemarie Gillespie; she became hostile, stole papers from Mr Carroll's office and became the centrepiece of 'Four Corners' project on Fiji.' Gillespie firmly rejected these allegations, claiming that she was told only in June 1982 that her services were not required for the third survey; she had decided to expose the Fiji operations in May.

Following this decision her contacts led to her meeting the ABC television personality, Peter Manning, in May; he immediately saw merit in making a programme on the Fiji election. Meantime, Gillespie also contacted Australian journalist, Marian Wilkinson, of the *National Times*. Subsequently, the *National Times* and the ABC decided jointly to research and report on the whole Carroll saga.

In June, Manning and his television crew visited Fiji, interviewing and filming many leading political personalities including Gillespie, Ratu Mara, Reddy and Sir Vijay. During this visit Manning also briefly showed Reddy parts of the Carroll Report and the undated letter purportedly written to Ratu Mara, which later became the basis of the Coalition's claim that the Alliance had a 'treacherous master plan'.

The *National Times*, however, faced a hostile reaction. Answers sought to questions from those involved in the Carroll affair went unanswered from the Alliance camp, including Ratu Mara. Reddy as Opposition leader, however, when contacted by telephone did answer questions put to him by Marion Wilkinson. According to her: Carroll would not accept her calls; Allen refused to discuss the matter and would only make one brief and incomplete statement and Speed would not answer several pertinent questions related to whether or not he had participated in election work in Fiji.

The most bizarre reaction came from Race, who in June, following a telephone call from Wilkinson to his headquarters in Thailand, allegedly telexed the Editor of the *National Times*, Brian Toohey, threatening a libel suit. The telex read as follows:[8]

Urgent
Attn. Editor . . . not for publication.

Sir: In connection with your Miss Marion Wilkinson, kindly be advised that mentioning in print the name of a private citizen of the USA without his consent (which I do not grant you) exposes you to grave legal liabilities in several jurisdictions under relevant laws of invasion of privacy and libel. Please accept this message in its intended friendly spirit to avoid unnecessary expense and aggravation all around.

Sincerely, Jeffrey Race.

In another separate development, an unsigned letter understood to have 'originated from Mrs Adriane Carroll' and containing threats of dire consequences was also sent to Gillespie. In an atmosphere of intrigue and suspicion, the 'Four Corners' programme, nevertheless, finally went to the air on 3 July in Australia, mainly directed toward the Australian audience: 'Today, the Fiji general election enters its final week in an atmosphere of controversy. The cause is the programme you are about to see which reports the disclosure of a Melbourne Market Researcher.'[9]

The programme focused on the November Carroll Report, the accompanying undated letter purportedly addressed to Ratu Mara, the role of Speed, the Carroll team, the alleged misuse of Australian aid fund, and so on. The *National Times* article (4-10 July) by Wilkinson, under the headline 'Australian involvement sparks Fiji election row', contained similar allegations. Stressing Australian involvement, she wrote: 'The spectre of Australia as the overbearing brother in the South Pacific has emerged as an explosive issue in the Fijian elections.'[10]

Indeed, the disclosures had triggered a time bomb that proved fatal not only to the Alliance but also to the Coalition. The transcript of the 'Four Corners' television programme must be set out in full to capture the whole Carroll saga and to assist in understanding and analysing its after effects in the weeks ahead.[11]

Jims Downs: The Kava Ceremony precedes any matter of importance. So before they talk politics they drink kava ... a ritual which predates by centuries the forms and words of party politicking. This is one of the faces of politics in Fiji. There is another face. It is imported. It is white. It is Australian. And it is out to win by whatever means are necessary. Today the Fiji general election enters its final week in an atmosphere of controversy. The cause is the program you are about to see which reports the disclosures of a Melbourne Market Researcher. Documents in her possession, some of which we will be showing tonight and which will be published in detail in this weekend's *National Times*, reveal that a trio of foreign consultants, two of them Australian citizens, have been secretly engaged to help the Prime Minister of Fiji win the election. Some of the tactics they have proposed are highly questionable. Further controversy surrounds the role of a former ABC executive who is now a key man in the Fiji Government Ministry of Information. Already there is resentment enough in Fiji about the role of imports from Australia in the national economy. The fact that we are also exporting our style of politics is seen there as an outrage. Britain bequeathed the Westminster system of government to Fiji and it has worked for the 12 years since Independence in spite of the lingering remains of an old Feudal System: Government by the descendants of the Great Chiefs who clubbed and ate their way to power in these islands centuries ago. The democratic chief of

Fiji for the past 12 years is such a descendant. A Ratu, a Chief, and a Knight too, Sir Kamisese Mara.

Mara: What Mr. Reddy is saying is that the Opposition will make Fiji a Republic.

Downs: Under the old ways anyone who challenged such a chief would do so at his peril. But democracy leaves him open to challenge and the election which begins on July 10 will see Prime Miniser Mara fighting for his political life.

Is this what they mean by time for a change?

Fiji's problems are not much different from those of other Third World countries. There's poverty though a benevolent nature guards against famine. There is serious and rising unemployment. People are leaving the villages and coming to towns. That means there is a housing problem. What is unusual about Fiji is that it is our Third World. We helped make it what it is. When a Fijian talks of a multinational company he's probably talking of an Australian company. It was Australia's CSR which historically controlled sugar and through sugar much of Fiji. The sugar industry is Fijian-owned now but sugar markets have fallen. Copra is down too and together that means serious recession for Fiji. The Australian-owned trading companies have redirected their efforts into importing, distributing and selling and their influence has become a major political issue.

Gavidi: This is lemon. This is the mandarin, the orange and the lemon season right now. You go to that market. You go to the Nadi, Sigatoka, Nausori or Suva market, you'll find thousands, thousands of mandarins and oranges being sold out there. Ladies from inland trying to sell these oranges and yet you get it from Australia! Ratu Mara is buying the citrus from Australia! You trying to sell it to New Zealand, sell it in Fiji first. Stop that from Australia!

Downs: Business can be frightened by such Opposition rhetoric. Not that the Government, particularly Prime Minister Mara, was necessarily all that much a friend. But he was a known quantity.

Mara: Investment confidence in Fijian land leaseholds has been vastly enhanced.

Downs: But Prime Minister Mara was seen by some of his business supporters as getting out of touch. He was too autocratic. Too chiefly. And reluctant to interest himself in political organising. So they decided to get outside help to improve both his public appeal and his party organisation.

The originator of the plan to reshape the Prime Minister's image seems to have been one of his foremost supporters Mahendra Motibhai Patel known as Mac Patel. He is the biggest of Fiji's Indian businessmen and a real power in the country. At a conference in Melbourne, Patel met Alan Carroll, the Director of client services in Australia for Business International Corporation. B.I. is a world-wide business advisory organisation. Its headquarters are in New York, and its offices are spread across North and South America, Europe, Asia and Australia. The list of Business Internationals clients reads like a multinational roll of honour—banks, oil companies, manufacturers, food companies. It specialises in providing these clients with political and economic intelligence. Patel decided that Alan Carroll was the man he needed. In the middle of 1981 Carroll went to Fiji. Carroll has been visiting Fiji intermittently ever since. When we caught up with him outside a Nadi Hotel two weeks ago he refused to be interviewed but he did insist that his work in Fiji had nothing to do with Business International. We're not suggesting that it had. What is certain is that through his work for B.I., Alan Carroll has widespread connections throughout the political and business world. Some of Business International's clients are companies with significant investments in Fiji. Take for instance Bowater Scott, the paper company, which wrote to Alan Carroll in September last year. At the time they had a 29 per cent share in a packaging company in Fiji called Kiwi United South Pacific. The letter asked Carroll: 'Do we go in harder or pull out now with capital profits? And of course how will the latter be viewed by the Fijian government?' In view of these connections and of the Fijian sensitivity about multinational, and especially Australian, business influence, it is perhaps not surprising that Carroll's political work in Fiji was kept very secret. Indeed, when we asked Mr Mac Patel why he had asked Carroll to come Patel denied any political motive at all.

Patel: We called him here to look at the business prospect generally. I think he is doing some work for business companies overseas who want to set up companies here or invest in Fiji and primarily that was his role. Nothing beyond that.

Downs: You said 'we called him here.': Who are the 'we'?

Patel: First of all, Motibhai Company. As I've said Motibhai Company has called him here and I think he is just being used by other people as he's made himself known.

Downs: So, there was no political purpose in your calling him, inviting him to Fiji?

Patel: Not really, no.

Downs: The truth is very different. As these documents show Carroll was invited to Fiji to give advice to help the Alliance Party win the election. On that first visit he was accompanied by another man, also with connections to Business International, a man so retiring it's impossible to find a photograph of him. His name is Dr Jeffrey Race and he's based in Bangkok. Paul Lockyer has been seeking to speak with Dr Race.

Lockyer: Jeffrey Race has his centre of operations here, a Thai-style bungalow on the outskirts of Bangkok. He is said to be very security conscious and has installed a sophisticated alarm system connected to the local Police Station. Through his company, Asian Strategy, he offers advice to clients on economic, political and military trends in the region. He is highly sought after and apparently charges accordingly for his time. After completing an impressive academic course at Harvard University, Jeffrey Race went to the Vietnam war. During those war years, according to reliable sources, he spent at least part of his time working for American Military Intelligence. According to one source, Jeffrey Race is well plugged into the American State and Defence Department and has done occasional consultancy work for Washington, although it is unclear what that work has entailed. Mr Race travels widely in South East Asia and keeps a low profile when he is at home. He declined a Four Corners request for an interview.

Downs: Back in Australia from their first Fiji visit Mr Carroll and Jeffrey Race recruited a third man, Mr Jeffrey Allen, the Director of the Australian Industries Development Association. Like the other two, a man with very top business connections and he's got close links to the Liberal Party. The three decided they needed to know more about Fiji. Alan Carroll recruited a Melbourne Market Researcher, Rosemarie Gillespie, to do an on-the-spot political survey. What were you told was the purpose of the Fiji job?

Gillespie: To help the ruling party win the next election.

Downs: From the start, Rosemarie Gillespie found herself in an atmosphere of secrecy and intrigue.

Gillespie: Jeff Race was the first one to brief me on what I was to do and the first thing he did was tell me what I should know about what he called 'the sensitivities' of the project. He gave me explicit instructions that I was not to mention either his name or Alan Carroll's name. I was to pretend that I had nothing to do with either of those two men. I was to explain my presence in Fiji and my role in Fiji if I was asked that I was a professional consultant to the Alliance Party.

Downs: Once in Fiji Rosemarie Gillespie checked her cover story with Mahendra Patel.

Gillespie: Mahendra Patel said straightaway that that wasn't possible. He said, 'You had better go incognito.' I said, 'What do you mean.' He said, "Well, it hasn't been approved by the Alliance Party.' And then I said, What do I go as?' And he said, in his characteristic voice, 'You'd better talk about that to the PM.' So then we went to the next part of it, where he was to tell me who I was supposed to see and also set up appointments for me with different people in Suva. So I got him to write them down for me.

Downs: Do you recall your instructions to Rosemarie Gillespie of what you expected from her?

Patel: No, I was not directly involved with that lady.

Downs: You were not directly involved?

Patel: No, no.

Downs: Did you meet her?

Patel: Yes, I met her a couple of times.

Downs: And you didn't instruct her where to go and who to see?

Patel: No.

Downs: Sir, would you examine this piece of paper and tell me if in fact it is your writing.

Patel: Yes, it is my writing.

Downs: It was indeed his writing. This is the list he wrote of four men who knew what was afoot: Adam Dickson of the multinational accounting firm, Coopers and Lybrand; Charles Walker, the Minister of Finance; Dr Lasaqa, the Secretary to the Cabinet, and the Prime Minister himself. Which of those four gave you the detailed instructions, that you obviously had to have?

Gillespie: Well, I discussed the whole matter in the Prime Minister's office. Dr Lasaqa, the Prime Minister and myself were there and since the project had not been approved by the Alliance Party we had to work out a suitable cover for my work.

Downs: A cover to keep it secret from the rest of the Alliance Party or from the electorate or from whom?

Gillespie: From everybody.

Downs: So, into the villages of six decisive island electorates went big-city Market Researcher Rosemarie Gillespie with her set of questions devised in Melbourne. She was provided with some local university students to help her, students selected for their political trustworthiness or their lack of political involvement. Dr Race had demanded those conditions.

Gillespie: My research was supposed to tell them what they had to do by way of political strategy. Do you drop the candidate, do you use patronage?

Downs: On the basis of Rosemarie Gillespie's survey, a draft report was prepared by Messrs Carroll, Race and Allen. It was in effect a 'how to win' for the Alliance Party. It's a fascinating document. Not surprisingly perhaps, it urges on the Fijian government policies that favour private enterprise and foreign investment. Among its recommendations are these: 'a stronger commitment to mobilising the energies of the private sector; the establishment of a business council to work directly with the Prime Minister to help establish a more pro-business image for the Alliance Party' and much more in like vein. The report tries to impose upon a Third World country the values and techniques of a foreign school of political manipulation. 'Conduct an image-building campaign emphasising some such themes as rebirth, renewal, a new sense of movement and the like. Conduct detailed constituency-by-constituency desk analyses to identify marginal seats and conduct field polls to determine the decisive issues.' Implicit in it is the end of politicking Fiji-style in which the candidate reached his voters by whatever means were available, taking with him along the rivers, beyond the reach of power lines, his own loud-speaker powered by the battery from his car. What the Alliance Party needed, the consultant said, was upgraded organisation and professional campaigning. The party found its professional in this man, Isimeli Bose, Operations Manager in Suva for the Australian-owned company,

Interviewer: Is Burns Philp still paying your salary?

Interviewer: Is Burns Philp still paying your salary?

Bose: Burns Philps' part of its contribution is to loan me to the Alliance Party and cover part of my salary.

Downs: Yet, curiously enough, Burns Philp has emphatically denied to us that the company is contributing to Mr Bose's salary. In October last year, Mr Bose visited Australia to see how the Liberal Party did things. That contact was arranged by Messrs Carroll and Allen.

Bose: Really this role is just advisory . . . because I was new in the game. He just advised me on things like newspaper tactics, what sort of an issue you can look at, analyses of the issues, these are the things. Generally talk about what I can do and then apply them in my own situation.

Downs: Even Isimeli Bose, the Campaign Manager, apparently was excluded from the inner circle which knew about the Consultants' Report to the Prime Minister. So he remained unaware of the more unscrupulous tactics which the report recommended. In a section of the report marked 'Private and Confidential' the consultants suggests how to deal with political opponents if the Alliance Party appears to be losing. 'FNP, either buy off or take him out of the running': 'Gavidi, since he's going to jail anyway let's pile all effort on and accelerate prosecution so he can't run.' And this is how to deal with potential deserters from the Cabinet—'Either let them leave happy—appointments or make sure they understand that they will be sorry if they challenge the Alliance. Get something on them.' And there are many more, obscure and intriguing. It says here 'Dictation by the leader won't work, must use carrots, new carrots for supporters, honours, stroke, another pay-off.' Stroke and stroking are words that often appear. Stroke used to be a Nixon word and when he used it as President he meant 'contrived flattery' and here the need for new ways of discipline—the stick as opposed to the carrot—and need toe-cutter to plan and implement it.

Butadroka: The Nationalists began in 1974. There was only one member in Parliament at that time . . .

Downs: The tactics of professional politics, while par for the course in Australia, are regarded here with deep suspicion. And there is in Fiji the Third World fear of multinational business domination.

Q: Do you see the prospect here of rather large-scale conflict of interests?

Reddy: Well, I think there already is that conflict of intersts. The Prime Minister of this country, it is generally believed, has tilted so heavily in favour of big business that he has forgotten the ordinary people. And this I think is a confirmation of that belief. Here is the Prime Minister who was quite willing to engage these consultants, be advised and guided by them and at the same time claims to further the interests of the ordinary people of this country. Now, I just don't see how he's going to do both. I think he has compromised his position on this.

Q: Prime Minister, is it all contradictory to you from your history and your determined nationalism that you should employ foreign nationals, especially foreign business cousultants to advise you on political matters.

Mara: Well, there are streams of civil servants from Fiji that go out to international organisations practically every week to learn. After all, we are developing towards a western standard of living and it would not be surprising if the political standards also approximate to the western standard of politics.

Q: But, as I understand it, Sir, the advisers who came here were not civil servants.

Mara: Quite frankly, you seem to know more about these people than I do. All I knew, they were consultants who were willing to help our organiser and we sent him there and further than that I know little.

Downs: But, could the Prime Minister have forgotten this letter addressed to him personally and signed by Alan Carroll? It accompanied the final version of the consultants' report dated November 1981, and it reads in part 'I attach a report on strategic issues facing the Fijian Government and Alliance Party, a draft of which was discussed in depth with you between September 16—20, 1981. Apart from recommendations embodied in the attached report your consultants, Dr Jeffrey Race, Mr Jeff Allen and I made a number of recommendations during the course of these discussions.' One of those extra recommendations was especially significant. 'The appointment of a Media Liaison Consultant to the Prime Minister as is a common minimum facility in most countries is recommended.' Within a few weeks of the despatch of that letter observers in Fiji began to notice a new sophistication in the handling of the Prime Minister's press relations.

Sir Vijay Singh: Well, it's very noticeable to me because I have worked with the Prime Minister since party politics began and I see a very noticeable difference between this election and previous elections in the way the news media is being utilised. The professionalism behind statements. I doubt very much whether it's his local advisers because they've been round here for all these decades that party politics has been here but there is this very new angle to the use of the media.

Downs: But if local advisers weren't responsible for the new sophistication, who was? That letter from Alan Carroll to the Prime Minister provides the answer. 'We were pleased also at your request to search for and recommend a journalist of exceptional talent to work in media relations with the Government. Mr Clive Speed, Executive Producer of Current Affairs for the

Australian Broadcasting Commission, is strongly recommended.' Clive Speed and Alan Carroll are friends of long standing. Carroll's recommendation was accepted by Mara. At the end of last year Mr Speed resigned from the ABC and in January began work in Fiji.

Q: Might I ask who advised you that Mr Speed was the man for the job?

Mara: I, myself, made enquiries.

Q: Did you seek advice from anyone as to who would be available and who might be best in this job?

Mara: I had my Permanent Secretary to do the enquiries, the detailed enquiries. I said an Australian seems to be the man available. You go and find out when we were in Melbourne who are the ones to be available. It is our decision: it is our responsibility. Nobody else advised me. I am rather finicky about people telling me what to do. And if you think that anyone tell me what to do about Mr Clive Speed, then you are barking up the wrong tree.

Downs: Mr Speed was appointed to a post called Government Media Consultant. It's a non-political job. Its non-involvement in party politics demanded as a condition of its funding. For the whole cost of Mr Speed's services for one year—$50,000—is being paid by the Australian Government as part of Australia's aid to Fiji. But, according to Rosemarie Gillespie, Mr Speed's role since he arrived in Fiji has been hardly non-partisan.

Gillespie: Clive Speed was supposed to pick up the campaign if Bose wasn't able to handle it. They were in fact working in tandem but Clive Speed's role was more obscure because officially his appointment was not supposed to be political. But, in fact, he was fulfilling the role that a press agent for the Party would normally fill.

Down: Two weeks ago the presence and purpose of Mr Speed became an election issue.

Mrs Narayan: Well, Mr Clive Speed has come here under Australian aid and when he first came we were told that he was going to be attached to the Ministry of Information but one of his responsibilities would be training a local to do the work that he's supposed to be doing now. But in fact ever since he has come he has not been with the Ministry of Information but he has been attached to the Prime Minister's Office where he has been acting as the Public Relations Officer for the Prime Minister and apart from that he has actually been involved in writing out, churning out propaganda material for this election, helping the Alliance Party.

Q: Did you see Mr Clive speed as a public servant or as a worker for a political party, the Alliance Party?

Gillespie: I didn't see him as a worker for the Alliance Party. I saw him as working closely with Alan Carroll and being Alan Carroll's man in Suva.

Q: To your knowledge was there any on-going contact between Mr Clive Speed in Suva and Mr Alan Carroll in Melbourne?

A: Yes, Clive Speed would write back little cryptic messages which would summarise the political situation as it was at that particular date of reporting. He would send these back roughly every two weeks to Alan.

Downs: This is one of those messages. It's headed "Situation Report" and signed by Clive Speed. It was sent to Alan Carroll on 28 February this year. Not only is it clearly partisan, but it does convey the impression that Speed was, in Rosemarie Gillespie's phrase, Alan Carroll's man in Suva. The general feelings within the Alliance are that things are going to be tough. There are some who openly give the NFP a good chance of winning the election. I am still optimistic. One, NFP power struggle has yet to surface. Two, Alliance is more likely to mount an effective campaign. And, three, Ratu Mara is still the best thing the Party has going for it and the country.'

Q: Has Mr Speed had any part at all in shoring up the Alliance Party?

Mara: No, I don't think so. He is more or less a help in our public relations office, which has been pretty poor for I don't know how many years.

Q: Is it part of Mr Speed's role to report politically to Mr Alan Carroll?

Mara: If he does I do not know. I don't think so.

Q: Would it seem to you odd if he were to do so?

Mara I would find it very odd if Mr Speed reports back to Mr Carroll as you say. Mr Speed is a civil servant in Fiji.

Q: Paid by the Government of Australia?

Mara: Paid by the Government of Fiji.

By the Government of Fiji?

Mara: By the Government of Fiji through the supplementation of aid, of technical aid from Australia. We have many other people from Australia, from New Zealand, through technical aid. I do not wish to carry on any further, if you don't mind.

Downs: At that point the Prime Minister terminated the interview.

Reddy: Surely the Australian taxpayer doesn't want to see his money spent here to further the political interests of the Party in power, but rather to see that money spent for the welfare of the people of this country.

McDonald: I've seen no evidence of Clive Speed being politically involved. He's certainly working at the Ministry of Information which I suppose, is a sensitive area.

Downs: Mr Colin McDonald is Australia's High Commissioner in Fiji. What does he say to the suggestion that Mr Speed is reporting politically to an Australian Business Consultant?

McDonald: I doubt that very much but I certainly have no knowledge of it.

Q: If he were so doing, would you call that an impropriety?

McDonald: Oh definitely.

Downs: So, to sum up. An Australian journalist paid for by Australian Aid has exceeded the bounds of his appointed duties in Fiji. On top of that he's been reporting back to another Australian, Alan Carroll. Carroll is a Melbourne Business Consultant, many of whose clients have investments in Fiji. Carroll arranged for the Government Party's Campaign Manager who is on leave of absence from an Australian company to be coached by the Australian Liberal Party. Carroll recruited an Australian political lobbyist and an American specialist in economic intelligence and together they wrote a secret report for Prime Minister Mara intended to help him win the election. Some of the tactics they recommended were anything but respectable. Australia's influence throughout the Pacific has up to now mostly been regarded as benign but that reputation is fragile and operations like the Fiji Project will do nothing to enhance it. Three months ago in early April there was a crucial meeting in the Cabinet Room in Suva. Present were the Prime Minister, some of his closest Fijian advisers and four foreigners—Alan Carroll, Jeffrey Allen, Clive Speed and Rosemarie Gillespie.

Gillespie: One of the major issues that came up was unemployment and various strategies were suggested by Alan Carroll and Jeff Allen how to defuse the unemployment issue and several suggestions were put forward and one of them involved sending young people back for further training. And Ratu Mara quite rightly pointed out that what's the good of sending them back when there's no jobs for them when they come out at the other end because all you'll get is more highly trained people who can't get jobs and Alan Carroll said that "Well, it'll reduce the number of unemployed on the books, makes you look like you are doing something. It buys you time. And Jeff Allen chimed in, "Well, if we don't win we're stuffed!"

Downs: And, after all, winning is what it's all about. The voting in Fiji begins next Saturday, July 10.

Meanwhile, sensing that Reddy did not have the full report, Alliance, in a paid advertisement, challenged Reddy to release the whole Carroll Report to the public. Since it raised the question of credibility, the Coalition finally decided that one of its most senior members and former Alliance Attorney-General, Sir Vijay Singh, should go to Australia to arrange for the video tapes of the 'Four Corners' programme to be brought back to Fiji.

In Sydney, Sir Vijay, after contacting Manning and Wilkinson, traced Gilliespie, who not only agreed to meet him but was also willing to give him all the documents in her possession. Sir Vijay then paid $400 for her air travel from Melbourne to Sydney to hand over to him the documents and information, which he later brought back to Fiji.

Among the documents were confidential government papers including a file relating to the Suva City Council, known as the Red File C45/16/1. Gillespie later claimed that Ratu Mara's Cabinet Secretary, Dr Isireli Lasaqa, had given it to her for the purpose of providing material discreditable to an NFP candidate and former Suva Lord Mayor, Joape Rokosoi, who had failed to win an Alliance ticket. Dr Lasaqa later claimed that Gillespie had stolen the Red File from his office, a charge which she strongly denied. According to Gillespie, Dr Lasaqa gave her the Red File in a 'Jiffy' bag to conceal it from other people in his office suite. In his election broadcast on 9 July 1982 Ratu Mara said that Dr Lasaqa had assured him that he did not give Gillespie the file, adding, 'I believe it.'

But, nevertheless, it seemed clear that Lasaqa did give her the file. According to the Royal Commissioner White there was no dispute that he had shown Gillespie the file. White, who described the substance of Lasaqa's evidence as 'unreliable' and in one instance 'wrong', had earlier stated that 'Dr Lasaqa's evidence was not only important because of the weight which it should be given because it was important that there be a clear finding on Miss Gillespie's credibility'.[12] As a result he concluded that 'having regard to the manner in which he gave her access to other files with confidential material, it would not be remarkable that Dr Lasaqa would let her take the file away';[13] he, therefore, preferred Gillespie's evidence. On whether Gillespie took the file with the object of finding something in it to assist her as a part of her assignment as a member of the Carroll team, White further noted that 'is the only reasonable inference'.[14]

In the face of mounting rebuffs, the Alliance ran into further trouble; contact with Gillespie led to the disclosure that M.M. Patel had brought Gillespie to Fiji for the second survey in 1982 on 'contra tickets' provided by the Australian airline Qantas to the Fiji Visitors Bureau, of which he was the chairman. Although M.M. Patel claimed his company had paid back the full sum involved, the NFP claimed before the Royal Commission that 'the Alliance Party used financial channels of a statutory body for their support and benefit in preparing strategy to fight the general election'.[15] There was also suggestion of corruption. White, however, ruled that although the method of obtaining the ticket was wrong, he did not consider the evidence established that M.M. Patel did not intend to make the refund (which in fact was made). There was also no need for further action.

Earlier, armed with the above information and a copy of the 'Four Corners' video tape, Sir Vijay was back in Fiji on 4 July 1982 and addressed a political meeting the same day. Some prominent members of the NFP who saw a private screening of the 'Four Corners' tape were of the opinion that it should be released; and accordingly the tape was released for public viewing, inevitably gaining the proportions of a Fiji Watergate.

As already noted, the programme sparked intense political confrontation unparalleled in Fiji's political history; a host of questions had to be answered by all sides, including the Australians. The Carroll team's role came under searching scrutiny even in their own media, as the following editorial in *The Australian* (5 July 1982), headlined 'Australians meddling in Fijian power game',[16] demonstrates:

> Australia obviously has an interest in elections that take place in neighbouring countries. . . . It also goes without saying that Australia would prefer that parties whose policies might ultimately lead them closer to Moscow not be elected.
>
> But this interest does not give Australia any right to interfere in democratic elections in another country, and if it has any role at all to play in the Fijian elections, that role should be limited to ensuring that democratic principles are observed.
>
> It is, therefore, very disquieting to learn from the ABC 'Four Corners' television program, that the Foreign Minister, Mr Street, approved the use of $50,000 of foreign aid for the appointment of Mr Clive Speed, an experienced broadcaster, to act as media consultant to the Fijian Prime Minister, Ratu Sir Kamisese Mara, during the run-up to the election.
>
> Had Federal Parliament not been in one of its long recesses this week the Opposition spokesman on foreign affairs, Mr Lionel Bowen, might well have subjected Mr Street to some embarrassing questioning, especially as it is probable most Australians believe the purpose of our overseas aid is to help the poor countries of the Third World,

not provide ruling princes with public relations men. That does not mean Mr Street can evade the issue, for the public has a right to know exactly to what use taxpayers' money is put.

... There is also the curious role of Melbourne business consultant, Mr Alan Carroll, and Mr Geoffrey Allen, director of the Australian Development Association. Together with a US consultant they filed a report to the Fijian Prime Minister on tactics for the coming elections, including 'accelerating' prosecution against one Opposition leader so that he could not run, and shedding old candidates of the ruling Alliance Party by using 'carrots such as honours, stroking and other pay-offs'. There was also the suggestion that there should be voluntary or involuntary drop-outs from the Cabinet—'either let them leave happy (appointments) or make sure they understand they will be sorry if they challenge the Alliance (get something on them)'.

Mr Carroll says his work with commercial and political contacts in Fiji is an innocent commercial exercise. Certainly there is no suggestion that he is doing anything illegal. But those companies numbered among his clients might well question whether the publicity attracted by activities such as those disclosed in the past few days are in their best interests.

And Sir Kamisese Mara should try to win elections without outside help.

On the Fijian front the reaction had ranged from scepticism to indignation. How far the Australians would go to wash their hands in public was as yet unclear.

Notes

1. Copy in author's possession, obtained from the Australian market researcher, Rosemarie Gillespie, November 1983.
2. See NFP counsel Bhupendra Patel's submission, quoted in Parliament, Fiji, *Report of the Royal Commission of Inquiry into the 1982 General Elections*, Parliamentary Paper No. 74 of 1983, pp. 53-55 (*The White Report*).
3. *The White Report*, p. 50.
4. Ibid.
5. For full details see Gillespie's prepared statement to the Royal Commission, June 1983; a copy of the notes of the meeting in author's possession.
6. Malcolm Fraser quoted in the *Fiji Sun*, 2 June 1982.
7. See Gillespie's statement to the Royal Commission, Ref. 5.
8. Quoted in Vijay Maharaj's submission (Council for Gillespie) to the Royal Commission on Issue 1, Group 1, 19 August (mimeo), p.35.
9. Quoted in *The White Report*, p. 145.
10. The *National Times* (Australia), 4-10 July 1982.
11. Quoted in *The White Report*, pp. 145-57.
12. Ibid. For further details see pp. 179-85.
13. Ibid., p. 185.
14. Ibid.
15. Ibid., p. 222.
16. *The Australian*, 5 July 1982.

CHAPTER EIGHT

THE AUSTRALIAN CONNECTION

While various claims and counter-claims were inevitably made in the heat of the election campaign, assurances had now been received on three separate occasions from the Fiji government that the consultant's activities had been within the guidelines set down at the time of his appointment.

The then Australian Minister of Foreign Affairs, Tony Street, on Clive Speed's role.

The previous occasion when the Australians found themselves in a peculiar and embarrassing predicament was during the 'Loans Affair' scandal that hit the Gough Whitlam government in 1975. This was in connection with the activities of the then Deputy Labour Leader, Dr Jim Cairns' stepson and electoral secretary Philip Carins, who, while still on Australian government payroll, held several discussions with Fiji government officials about private investment opportunities in Fiji. As an Australian journalist, Paul Kelly, in his book *The Dismissal* records:

In April the Fiji high commission in Canberra was notified that two Arab representatives, Mr S. Nassar and General M. Galal, wanted to have discussions with government officials about investment opportunities in Fiji. The high commission was told the Arabs would be accompanied by Philip Cairns on an official visit as private secretary to the deputy prime minister. On 7-8 May talks were held in Suva between Galal, Mr Ian Richardson and Philip Cairns and a number of Fiji government ministers and officials. Mr Nassar never arrived. Both Galal and Richardson were directors of an import-export company, Rawia International (Australia) Pvt. Ltd., incorporated in Melbourne a short time later on 20 May 1975. In the talks Cairns stated he was acting in his official capacity and the Fiji ministers and nine officials were involved in the two-day talks. The discussions were exploratory, covering oil and sugar refineries, fishing and timber industries and access for Middle East airlines to Fiji. During the talks Galal said he and his associates could arrange for investments in Fiji once they assessed the needs of that country. He said it would be possible to arrange for investors in the Middle East, who would examine the question of setting up an oil refinery once they had further details from the Fiji government.

Philip Cairns made a number of visits to Fiji in this period. According to the Fiji government his second visit was on 19 June when he indicated he was acting in an unofficial capacity and held further ministerial talks on behalf of Rawia International. In these talks Cairns advised that interests in Australia wanted to breed prime beef cattle in Fiji. Subsequently the Carins' visit became the centre of a major political controversy in Fiji after it was reported that Jim Cairns had been dismissed and a series of allegations made about Philip Cairns' activities.[1]

In view of the gravity of the matter Ratu Mara subsequently wrote to then Prime Minister Whitlam, who 'sent back a brief but devastating reply to the effect that Philip Cairns was in no way a representative of the Australian government, that his visit had no official status and that his activities were an embarrassment to the Australian government.'[2]

According to Kelly, the Australian government was alarmed by the auditor-general's report indicating that telephone calls, accommodation and travelling allowance during Cairns' visit were costs on the government. At the same time the auditor-general uncovered a payment that had been made to a woman in Fiji who had lived near Philip Cairns in Melbourne. In 1982 the Australians found themselves in a similar situation, except that it was Malcolm Fraser's Liberal Party which had to provide the answers regarding Speed's role and persistent claims of Australian 'involvement' in Fiji's domestic politics.

The first time Speed's name surfaced was at a political rally in June 1982 when Mrs Irene Narayan claimed that Fraser had sent Speed to Fiji to help the Alliance Party win the general election. Accusing Speed of 'churning out election propaganda' for the Alliance, she further accused him of being Fraser's PRO. She was subsequently proved wrong. In Gillespie's opinion Speed was Carroll's man planted in Suva as a political watchdog to monitor and report back political developments in the critical six months before the voters went to the polls.

Speed's appointment and terms of reference were briefly outlined in Chapter 5. What follows is an attempt to trace the root of the controversy, the claims and counter-claims, the Australian reaction, the link with Carroll and the Royal Commission of Inquiry's findings on the issue.

The political temperature was already running high when Mrs Narayan suddenly focused the voters' attention on Speed's alleged activities, thus tilting the scale of political debate. Since Ratu Mara had been personally involved in Speed's recruitment, he promptly replied detailing the circumstances surrounding Speed's appointment. Charges that Australian aid money had been misused were also firmly crushed. The Alliance also later denied that Speed was appointed in accordance with recommendations in the Carroll Report. Whatever the truth, the fact was that Carroll and Speed had known each other for a long time. As Speed himself explained: 'I had known Alan Carroll as a contributor to programmes I produced and as a friend.'[3] Ultimately it was this friendship which shaped and dictated Speed's conduct toward Carroll, conduct for which he had to pay dearly: being subjected to public scrutiny, a political tool for Coalition exploitation, and cause for ABC 'Four Corners' intervention. The gravity of his involvement could be ascertained from the following questions. The Royal Commission specifically enquired whether he:[4] (a) Was appointed on Carroll's recommendations? (b) Was appointed to, and did, in fact, assist in the Alliance's election campaign? and (c) Had his salary paid (directly or indirectly) by the Australian Government?

After taking up his new appointment as media consultant in December 1981, Speed contacted Carroll on 13 January 1982 by a letter which, though personal in tone, provided an assessment of the political climate. Despite the personal tone, the letter's content was to be the source of troubles for him. This letter also provided the Coalition with an effective political weapon to exploit to its maximum advantage.

In February Speed sent Carroll another letter entitled 'Situation Report—15-2-82'. This letter included a detailed report of the political controversies of the day, especially the Ratu Mara-James Shankar Singh rift, the former US Ambassador Boddie Junior's prediction of an NFP victory, and Ratu Mara's proposed visit to address the Liberal Party's annual Federal Council meeting.

Superficially the two letters suggest a partisan attitude on the writer's part. According to Speed, however, they were simply to impress Carroll: 'The letters were written in a cryptic style to someone who places a great deal of value on his personal time. The heading "Situation Report" was somewhat tongue-in-cheek as the information contained in the letters could have been gleaned from the local press. They were intended to impress Alan Carroll with my local knowledge.'[5]

But the Coalition thought otherwise. In NFP's opinion, as Sir Vijay later put it, 'Clive Speed's appointment as media consultant was an essential, in fact, a critical and crucial component of the Carroll Report, and of Carroll's efforts on behalf of the Alliance Party in Fiji. The Alliance executive politicians went ahead and put on the government payroll a person who was primarily intended to churn out party political propaganda and improve the image of the Alliance Party.'[6] The submission of Gillespie's counsel, Vijay Maharaj, however, portrayed a different scenario. Relying, apart from Speed's other activities, on a telex received by Speed while in Fiji with instructions such as 'Talk to Mac' and 'Demand clarification' etc., Maharaj submitted that:

> Clive Speed was never formally part of the Alliance Party organisation, but he was uniquely placed to play a significant role in assisting the Alliance Party in its campaign material and in media relations of the Prime Minister and other Ministers of the Alliance Party Government.[7]

The Alliance's defence is noteworthy: they firmly maintained that 'there was no evidence before the Commission that Speed's work was to organize in or conduct any of its constituent bodies during the election campaign'.[8] Even during the campaign, they steadfastly supported Speed, and in response to sustained Opposition onslaught on him, they attempted to quell the political uproar by an announcement in the press.

One of the most damaging charges made against Speed was Gillespie's: she accused him of 'fixing' the 1980 Australian election. She told the Royal Commission that in 1980 the Labour Party was found to be vulnerable on the 'Capital Gains' question. Speed, while working for the ABC in Sydney, sent Jim Bonner to 'set up' Bill Hayden, the then ALP leader, over the issue. She said:

> Bill Hayden, tired from long days of campaigning, was caught unprepared and spoke vaguely about a 'wealth tax'. This was subsequently reported in such a way as to make it appear that a Labour Government would impose a 'wealth tax' on small homeowners. This provided the basis for a long hard running Liberal Party fear campaign which swung the election for Malcolm Fraser.[9]

She further claimed that Bonner was later to become Press Secretary to Fraser. 'The timing of the operation was such that it did not give the Labour Party time to clarify the ALP position.' Speed, in a signed affidavit, has since refuted most of Gillespie's allegations. He also claimed that he had never been a member of a political party or worked for a political party. 'Mr Jim Bonner's appointment to Mr Fraser's staff is not relevant as other reporters on my staff accepted similar positions with Labour ministers', he said.[10] But despite the claims and counter-claims, it was in Australia that Speed's role caused political rumblings.

The seriousness of the issue was expressed in the submission of John Rabone, the counsel assisting the Royal Commission:

> The gravity of this issue lies in the concern of the public that party political work not be done at the taxpayers' expense. That, in this case, it was the Australian taxpayers and not the taxpayers of Fiji doesn't affect that basic issue but rather that circumstance adds another aspect for concern, namely whether foreign aid had been misapplied.[11]

Meanwhile, the Royal Commission considered that:

> The history of the matter underlines a point made by the High Commissioner for Australia answering questions on the 'Four Corners' programme when he said Mr Speed's position in the Ministry of Information was 'a sensitive area'. That the matter has not passed unnoticed is clear from the evidence. Various press reports were referred to and there was an Australian press editorial suggesting that guidelines should be better defined 'to prevent aid ever becoming an issue in domestic politics.' I agree and recommend accordingly.[12]

In considering the evidence the Royal Commissioner, Sir John White, found that Speed 'was happy to be of assistance to Carroll', as was clear from facts such as his possession of a copy of the report that Carroll had given him in confidence, and his reports to Carroll which confirm that. Ratu Mara, White said, had made it quite clear during the 'Four Corners' programme that he thought it would be 'very odd' if Speed had such communications with Carroll because Speed was 'a civil servant'. On the other hand Ratu Mara said in evidence that he had 'given directions for Dr Lasaqa and Speed to attend the meeting on 24 April as observers'.[13]

Pointing to his reference to the accepted modification of the 'non political' rule for press secretaries, to take account of the practical realities as far as that aspect of the matter was concerned, Sir John found evidence that 'Mr Speed broke the rules by direct assistance to the Carroll team, but that it was not a kind which amounted to an infringement of the stated principles' to be satisfactory.[14] In sum, while considering the allegations that Speed had acted for the Alliance, he found that 'of his own volition, or at the behest of Carroll, Speed had assisted members of the Carroll team in a minor role'.[15]

Like Speed, Carroll had also been strongly criticized in Fiji. The Coalition embarked on a sustained campaign to highlight Carroll's other alleged activities in Australia. Relying on press cuttings, Reddy claimed that Carroll had interfered in Victorian state politics, and had been known to have made several reports similar to that received by the Alliance and had spoken to the US Chamber of Commerce in 'secret'. Sir Vijay went further; he told the Commission that, according to Gillespie, Carroll was also involved in the move to depose Bill Hayden as leader of the ALP. It was the same move that made Bob Hawke leader of the Labour Party, and Prime Minister of Australia.

Was Carroll 'involved' in these events? Although there is no concrete evidence, several writings and documents contain similar claims. For example, The Committee for Labour Integrity and Progress, in a document marked '*Top Secret—The Ultra File*', purportedly an inside report on co-ordinated action by big corporations and the extremist right to manipulate and influence the Labour movement, carried the following report on Victorian politics. Headed *Influencing a Labour Government*, it noted:

> BI (Business International) sold this report, 'A Victorian Labour Government 1982-85: An Analysis of the Strategic Implications for Business', to corporations at $2,500 a copy, rather expensive for 114 pages plus appendices. It was written by Dr Jeffrey Race, an American Researcher for BI who worked 'on contract' for the CIA and claims special expertise on Southeast Asia.
>
> Dr Race's report is more scholarly than Carroll's racy jargon, but it comes up with the same advice. Labour will win Victoria (they needn't have paid $2,000 for the tip, the dogs were barking it) and the corporations will have to accept this. The report details the balance of forces in the Victorian ALP, its politices, leader and candidates, then explains how a Labour government can be 'influenced'.[16]

Sir Vijay's claim that 'Carroll tried to topple Hayden' seems to be an overstatement, perhaps made on the strength of first available details during the days of intense political struggle when various claims and counter-claims were made in the heat of the moment. Evidence reveals that Carroll likes to style himself as someone 'very much in the know', a trait vital to a business consultant dealing with international business cartels. He did just that during the Hawke-Hayden leadership struggle in order to impress his business clients.[17] Carroll made an inspired, though not entirely accurate, forecast of Hawke's rise to power, as John Hurst's *Hawke PM* revealed.[18]

Meanwhile, the sharpest attack on Carroll came from Joan Coxsedge, a prominent member of the Socialist Left faction in the Victorian ALP. Coxsedge, a member of the Victorian Parliament, while delivering the Evatt Memorial Lecture at the University of Adelaide, claimed that Hawke's challenge for the leadership of the Federal Parliamentary Labour Party was supported and manipulated by Carroll and the CIA. On Carroll's alleged role in the leadership struggle, she said:

> One of the key Australian activists in the campaign is Alan Carroll, who is as boastful as he is influential. Over the years, Carroll spilled the beans to his corporate mates at various meetings of the upper echelons of the industrial establishment. Who is this Alan Carroll? Son of an American, with one of his degrees from Georgetown University, Carroll is probably best known for his boring and jargon-ridden economic commentaries on ABC current affairs programme. He is a lot less well known for his involvement in more important activities. . . .[19]

She went on to 'read some extracts from an actual transcript of a tape of Alan Carroll made at Business International's Asia-Pacific forecasting round-table at Noah's Hotel in Melbourne on 13 April 1981, more than 5 months ago', noting that 'Carroll has some interesting things to say, not only about Bob Hawke, but about other key figures in the Labour Party, about the economy and Australia generally.'[20]

After outlining Carroll's role, she went on: 'it would appear as if the accuracy and specific nature of Carroll's predictions years ahead of their happening can therefore hardly be either clairvoyance or coincidence';[21] this was not the first time, she said, that 'Carroll has functioned as an unofficial king-maker'. She claimed he undoubtedly played a major part in the downfall of the ex-Premier of Victoria, Rupert Hamer, 'who was considered to take too moderate a line for certain vested interests'.[22] Coxsedge than touched on the Fiji imbroglio:

> As well as analysis of the strategic implications for business of a Labour Government 1982-1985, compiled by Carroll and a Dr Jeffrey Race, a former US military intelligence officer who runs a company called 'Asian Strategies' out of Bangkok and is a graduate of Harvard, bears a not unexpected resemblance to a similar document pre-

pared for the Fijian Government by the same two gentlemen, entitled, would you believe it, 'Strategic Issues Facing the Fijian Government' which sparked off an election row in Fiji and was exposed on the ABC 'Four Corners' programme.[23]

Her allegations did not go unnoticed. Excerpts of her speech were later reprinted in Fiji, with one press report screaming 'Carroll did same back home'. In another development, Button, by now the Federal Opposition on communication, called for a freeze on the use of Carroll's services by the ABC radio programme 'AM' and 'PM' until the alleged misuse of aid funds had been investigated. The ALP also called on the Federal Parliamentary Committee to investigate the claims.

Caught in the crossfire, both in Fiji and Australia, Carroll, suggesting forgery, signed a statutory declaration saying he had never written, signed or seen the letter used in the 'Four Corners' programme. He also, through his solicitors, notified the Victorian police that certain letters and other materials (particularly concerning Fiji elections) were missing from his files; Gillespie was singled out as the prime suspect. Carroll's solicitors sent a letter to Gillespie, which she later described as 'a fishing expedition', inquiring about the missing documents and her involvement in the 'Four Corners' programme.

This intervention by Carroll provided the Alliance with a 'political card' to play with to temporarily keep the Carroll saga at bay. Through press statements, they informed the electorate of Carroll's denial, adding that the letter used in the 'Four Corners' programme was an attempt to damage Ratu Mara's credibility. But the ABC believed that Ratu Mara had received the final report. Its executive producer, Jonathan Holmes, said in Sydney, 'the report was completed by a team of four overseas consultants about November last year and we believe the final report reached the Prime Minister'.[24] The letter, he said, 'was signed by him [Carroll] and we believed that it was his letter'. He discounted the theory of forgery and conspiracy involving the ABC.

The Royal Commission, therefore, ruled that 'as far as the ABC was concerned the "Four Corners" programme was directed against Australians, for home consumption, and was not deliberately directed against any political party in Fiji'.[25] The Alliance had also sought a ruling on the allegation that 'the "Four Corners" programme contained . . . deliberate insults on Fijian chiefs, and . . . a grossly offensive reference to the Prime Minister's ancestors, and that this aroused strong feelings of resentment among Fijian voters'.[26]

John Rabone (counsel assisting the Royal Commission) had pointed out that there was evidence that 'a history of cannibalism is deliberately fostered and projected to visitors' in Fiji. The relevance of that, he submitted, was that persons coming to Fiji acquired the impression that once 'cannibalism was rife' and 'the clubbing and eating of one's rivals were aspects of the gaining by chiefs of territorial advantage'.[27]

Accordingly, Rabone submitted that the programme's opening words should be taken as having little effect on any Australian television viewer with a popular impression of Fiji, and further, that it would not be regarded by TV producers, who held that popular image, as likely to give offence. Nevertheless, White found that the cannibal comment would be taken by any attentive viewer as 'intended to be disparaging in describing the system of government and the Prime Minister',[28] and that resentment in Fiji would be natural. Consequently he cleared the NFP of collaborating over the cannibal quote.

During the campaign Gillespie was also accused of collaborating with the ABC and the NFP. Ratu Mara had claimed in his election speech that Gillespie had 'stolen' certain letters and also had 'forged a document', but he was simply making a calculated guess, as his statement under cross-examination at the Royal Commission reveals:

> *Q:* More, still referring to your Kinoya speech, in the same paragraph, you said 'she became hostile and stole papers'. What evidence did you have, Prime Minister, to say that she stole the papers?
> *A:* That was just a calculated guess. I just didn't think that Mr Carroll would have done something to incriminate himself.

On the allegation of forgery:

> *Q:* Do you have any evidence to support the forgery aspect of your allegation?
> *A:* I thought that was forged because I did not receive any letter.[29]

While the verbal war was raging over the letter's authenticity during the election campaign, Carroll claimed that Wilkinson or the *National Times* paid Gillespie $12,000 for the documents relating to the Fiji elections. Ratu Mara, in a nationwide radio broadcast in the Fijian language, alleged that Gillespie had received $12,000 from the NFP with a promise of a further $6,000. But he was unable to substantiate this claim, even after making inquiries in Australia. Cross-examined before the Royal Commission upon whether he had 'any evidence of the NFP giving $12,000 to Miss Gillespie' he could only reply, 'I heard about it but I don't think I can say that I have evidence.'[30]

In her statement to the Royal Commission, Wilkinson described Carroll's claim that she or the *National Times* paid $12,000 as completely false. She also discounted the conspiracy theory. 'On the issue of whether I or the *National Times* was involved in some sort of "conspiracy"—according to some of the more fantastic reports with the Russian KGB—this is a nonsense and in my opinion clearly designed to shift attention away from the facts of the matter.'[31]

The uncomfortable situation in which political leaders found themselves led to their acting either to accord with the perceived mood of the electorate, or, perhaps more often, oppose the fractious mood of their rivals. For example, Ratu Mara, in an after-dinner speech at the Royal

Prince Alfred Hospital in Sydney, on 30 July 1982, deliberately mis-stated certain facts concerning the Carroll saga and the 'Four Corners' programme, as the record of Rabone's cross-examination shows:

> *Rabone:* It might be taken from that speech, Sir, that the reason why you then rejected what was tendered to you in September was because you found the outsiders' advice both foreign and repugnant to your philosophy and principles.
>
> *Ratu Mara:* It was a way of trying to diffuse, undermine or counteract this line taken by the 'Four Corners' that undesirable election tactics suggested had been used. There may be better way of doing it, sticking to the truth, but I thought that's not strong enough.
>
> *R:* I see, so you thought, to strongly reject your 'Four Corners' challenge it was justified to depart from the truth to give sufficient impetus.
>
> *RM:* They were not telling the truth. So, you might as well get to the same ground and beat them there, Sir.
>
> *R:* Very well. So, if I use these words without offence, did you in your Sydney speech make a deliberately incorrect statement for that purpose?
>
> *RM:* I have perhaps liked poetic licence.[32]

Against this background it was hardly surprising that Ratu Mara accused the NFP leadership of making a 'million dollar deal' with the Russians, and subsequently diving for political cover under the umbrella of Crown privilege, as is revealed in the next chapter.

Notes

1. Paul Kelly, 1983, p. 220.
2. Ibid., p. 221.
3. Quoted in Parliament of Fiji, *Report of the Royal Commission of Inquiry into the 1982 General Elections*, Parliamentary Paper No. 74, of 1983 (*The White Report*).
4. Ibid., p. 39.
5. The affidavit of Clive Speed quoted in *The White Report*, p. 5.
6. Quoted in *The White Report*, p. 117.
7. Ibid.
8. Ibid., p. 122.
9. See Gillespie's prepared statement to the Royal Commission, June 1983.
10. Affidavit quoted in *The White Report*, Ref. 7.
11. A copy of John Rabone's submission in author's possession.
12. *The White Report*, p. 142.
13. Ibid., p. 141.
14. Ibid.
15. Ibid.
16. Obtained from Gillespie; copy in author's possession.
17. For an excellent account of the Hawke-Hayden battle, see John Hurst, 1983; and Anne Summers, 1983.
18. Hurst. 1983, pp. 266-67.

124   *The Australian Connection*

19. Joan Coxsedge, 'What Price Socialism?' (Evatt Memorial Lecture, 21 July 1982). Transcript in author's possession, pp. 8-9.
20. Ibid., p. 9.
21. Ibid., p. 13.
22. Ibid.
23. Ibid., pp. 13-14.
24. Quoted in *The White Report*, p. 166.
25. Ibid., p. 178.
26. Ibid., p. 144.
27. Ibid., p. 169.
28. Ibid.
29. Quoted in Vijay Maharaj's submission (counsel for Gillespie) to the Royal Commission, 19 August 1983 (mimeo).
30. Ibid.
31. Marion Wilkinson's statement to the Royal Commission, quoted in *The White Report*.
32. Quoted in *The White Report*, pp. 174-75.

CHAPTER NINE

THE INDO-SOVIET CONNECTION

Russia wants me out because it has been my influence that has successfully blocked Russian incursions into the Pacific Islands. With me gone, they think they can pick off the island states separately and gain a permanent foothold in the South Pacific.

Ratu Mara, August 1983.

We categorically refute any allegations that India has been or could indeed be a tool for furtherance of Soviet objectives in the area. We find it difficult to believe that the Prime Minister Ratu Mara could have said what he is reported to have said.

The Indian Ministry of Foreign Affairs, New Delhi, India, 1983.

Fear of the 'Red Peril' haunts most Pacific island leaders, as it does Australia, New Zealand, the People's Republic of China, Japan, and the United States, who want the region free of Soviet influence. Why has the South Pacific, hitherto a neglected area in the geopolitical calculation of the superpowers, become an area of special interest? What can be said about the region's place in Soviet foreign policy? Where does Fiji fit in, both ideologically and politically in the theatre of big-power rivalry in the South Pacific? What effect has this interest had on Fiji's domestic politics?

These questions need to be addressed in order to assess the allegations and refutations about the alleged Soviet interference; the role of the Indian Commissioner to Fiji, Mrs Soonu Kochar, and of her husband, Hari Kochar; and, given India's close relationship with the Soviet Union, the role of the Indian High Commissions both in Fiji and in Australia in allegedly furthering Soviet interests in the region.

In recent years the superpowers' gunboat diplomacy and political upheavals in the small states have enhanced the region's strategic value. The growing awareness in the 1970s of the Pacific region's marine resources (especially tuna), sea floor mineral deposits, and the sea lanes for new patterns of trade and military manoeuvres has contributed greatly to its geopolitical importance. As Richard Herr wrote: 'It abuts Indonesia, Japan and the Philippines in Asia; lies athwart the Pacific approaches to Antarctica, Australia and New Zealand; is the route for Asian access to South America; and it dominates the sea lanes from Australasia to North America.'[1]

Post-independence developments, such as the establishment of the South Pacific Forum, the emergence of New Zealand's Lange government in July 1984 which culminated in the drafting of a South Pacific

Nuclear Free Weapon Zone Treaty; tuna fishing agreements between some island states and the Soviet Union; France's repeated nuclear testings at Mururoa Atoll; and the left-neutralist Vanuatu's diplomatic ties with Cuba and Libya have, however, to some extent, upset traditional Western hegemony in the region.

The underlying struggle in the South Pacific is the USSR's effort to gain some influence in the region and US determination to preserve it as an 'American lake'. So far the Americans have been successful in spreading their influence through a barrage of propaganda about the Soviet threat to the Pacific and, especially, the South Pacific; its allies have been equally active in perpetuating the myth of a Soviet threat. The official stand of the US has been that its presence in the region is to defend the interests of the islands' peoples.

The Soviet Union has never been a colonial power in the South Pacific. The US, on the other hand, sees its role as custodian of the Pacific islanders, in the same way that US policy in Central America is rationalized as necessary to contain the spread of communism.

In some Pacific island states a Soviet takeover of the South Pacific has become accepted as truth, even though there is not a single Soviet base anywhere in the South Pacific. The USSR firmly rejects suggestions that they are out to obtain bases for themselves, contending that they can operate in the South Pacific without base facilities. Their ships are supplied by their own support vessels.

Yet Soviet overtures, however sincere, continue to inspire paroxysms of hysteria in US admirals, Pentagon spokesmen, ambassadors and anti-Soviet propagandists. On the political front, apart from Ratu Mara, the traditionally right-wing Malcolm Fraser, as Prime Minister of Australia, was a leading crusader against any Soviet presence in the region. As Prime Minister he spoke out strongly against the Soviet invasion of Afghanistan, and at many South Pacific regional meetings won support when he spoke of the dangers posed by the Soviets. He views have been vigorously championed by the National Civic Council (NCC) in Australia, the anti-communist organization formed in the 1950s, and the International Democratic Union (IDU) which he had been active in setting up as a counter to the Socialist International. But what does Soviet policy toward the Pacific island nations including Fiji really mean? In a speech to the UN General Assembly on 26 September 1978, former Soviet Minister of Foreign Affairs Andrei Gromyko said:

> Oceania is very far from us, but we wish to maintain normal and where possible friendly relations with the countries of that area as well. Here too we regard with sympathy the aspirations of the people to gain independence and to free themselves from foreign tutelage, in both the literal and figurative term of the word.[2]

In general, the statement has been interpreted as the Soviet Union's readiness 'to develop its basis of equality, mutual advantage, respect for sovereignty and territorial integrity, and non-interference in the internal affairs of each other'.[3] In July 1986, in his speech at the port of Vladivostok on the Sea of Japan, the base of the Russian Pacific fleet, the Soviet leader Mikhail Gorbachev asserted the Soviet Union's claim to be a Pacific power with legitimate reasons to be involved in the affairs of the region.[4] The USSR has also identified four characteristics of the southern Pacific region in the following terms:

1. The region has strategic importance which has been left virtually untapped.
2. Soviet presence in the region will provide the USSR with a close link to South-East Asia—the fastest growing economic zone in the world.
3. There is a substantial power vacuum in the region and while the US did have influence, it has progressively worn out its welcome.
4. The Pacific islands have just emerged from colonial administrations, are anxious to assert their independence and have a sceptical view of patronising Western governments.[5]

The US, however, continues to display a 'holier than Soviet attitude' in the region, repeatedly warning of the impending Soviet 'invasion'. What is the truth? In 1984 the Bureau of Intelligence and Research of the US State Department commissioned two Pacific island experts, Richard Herr and Robert Kiste, to provide an answer. Their findings strangely failed to support Washington's official line about Soviet policies in the region, but they found that the rigid policies of the US and France are, in fact, mainly responsible for instability in the region. While agreeing that efforts should be made to deny the USSR access to the region, their report entitled 'The Potential for Soviet Penetration of the South Pacific: An Assessment', made these specific statements based on their investigations:

1. The region is 'almost extraordinarily devoid' of any communist parties or Marxian political groups.
2. Except for some extreme right-wing claims, mainly by French colons (settlers), 'even allegations of front parties for communists intervention are all but non-existent'.
3. While the South Pacific ranks as one of the most vulnerable regions of the world (by usual objective criteria), 'it has perhaps the least Soviet influence of any area of the globe'.
4. There is no evidence to show that trade unions in the region are controlled by outside influences.
5. Factors which aided Soviet penetration of other parts of the world are 'largely absent' in the region. They include wide social discontent, weak democratic institutions, deep ideological cleavages and a 'paucity of exploitable circumstances'.
6. Russia has a 'spectacular lack of involvement' in the region, with no embassies at all and virtually no trade or other links.

7. Russia's official stance of atheism and explicit opposition to Christianity make it 'somewhat of an anathema' to usually devoutly Christian Pacific islanders.[6]

Against this background, Ratu Mara's allegations and the variety of motives advanced for the Soviet Union's involvement in the 1982 general elections may now be examined. Firstly, Fiji regularly plays on the West's fears about communist involvement in the South Pacific; the Soviets are seen as spies. Such rhetoric often strikes a responsive chord at home and abroad. It was not surprising, therefore, to be told by Ratu Mara that the Russians were meddling in Fiji's internal affairs.

In his view, the Soviets finally found in the general elections the right opportunity to achieve their long-term objectives in the region. They allegedly entered into a secret deal with the NFP/WUF Coalition through a letter, later known as the 'Koya Letter'. The letter, purportedly bearing the signature of the former NFP leader Koya, committed the Coalition to full political co-operation with the Soviet Union. Among other concessions was included the possibility of an embassy and research facilities in Fiji but without any interference in the military standing of the Fiji government.

Koya however dismissed the document as forgery and in evidence before the Royal Commission of Inquiry subsequently suggested that it was manufactured in preparation for the military overthrow of the new NFP government if the Alliance had lost the election; he further claimed that the CIA was prepared to help in the planned coup. This issue will be dealt with in the next chapter. As for the source of Ratu Mara's allegations about the Soviet interference, a leading South Pacific magazine, *Islands Business* (IB), traced it to the Australian Security and Intelligence Organization (ASIO).

The first signs of the Soviet saga surfaced during the election campaign when Dr Ali, as already noted, suggested that the Coalition Manifesto implied that the NFP would invite the Soviets to Fiji. In the course of electioneering other supposed links with the USSR emerged. Rumours were rife that the Coalition was involved in a dubious deal with a 'foreign power'. Shortly after the election results became public, Ratu Mara provided the dramatic finale by exposing alleged NFP/Soviet/Indian links. As already stated, he claimed that the USSR funnelled $1 million into the Coalition's election coffers in order to oust him from power. He further charged that Hari Kochar had acted as an intermediary to facilitate part of the money transfer. While elaborating that the NFP had not perhaps realized where the money was coming from, he asserted he would be naming more names 'at the right time'.

Large sums of money, he claimed, had been channelled to the NFP via Canada and Australia. Some of the money originating in the Soviet Union had come through Middle East sources and other cash came from sources in India. A Mr Naidu, of Naidu Enterprises in Los Angeles, USA, was allegedly one of the 'Mr Fixits', and Kochar, Ratu Mara alleged, was another. He was said to have passed $55,000 to a member of the NFP in a Sydney hotel room. Ratu Mara also claimed that the Fijian Coalition candidates were given $10,000 each to stand against Alliance candidates.

His claims had profound and diverse effects. In the Opposition camp the mood was one of anger and the allegations were completely denied. In Mrs Narayan's view Ratu Mara was trying to portray them as pro-Soviet so that countries such as the United States, Australia and New Zealand would get together and help him. Reddy, while emphatically denying that his party received 'one red cent', questioned Ratu Mara's motives in making the allegations to a foreign journalist. He considered the allegations to be a ploy to divert the people's attention from the Carroll saga, and also to refurbish Ratu Mara's image: 'The Prime Minister needed to refurbish his image particularly before the Australian people, and what better tactics than to raise the bogey of Russian help to the NFP in order to obscure the seriousness of foreign involvement in Fiji's general election.'[7]

While prepared to open their accounts for inspection to prove that the party had received no financial or technical advice from outside Fiji, Reddy said it was 'common knowledge throughout the country that it was not the NFP-Western United Front Coalition but the Alliance that was treating people so generously to vote for the wheel [the Alliance symbol]'.[8] He also recalled his earlier campaign pledge that an NFP/WUF government would not allow a Soviet embassy in Fiji. As far as India was concerned, he said: "It is ironical that the Prime Minister should also unjustly attack the Indian Government whose Prime Minister, Mrs Indira Gandhi, Ratu Mara appeared to be so warmly welcoming to Fiji only eight months ago and whose praise of Ratu Mara was so generously used by the Alliance in the campaign to stay in power."[9]

The Alliance, however, rejected Reddy's denial as 'wrong and evasive', and expressed the opinion that in view of the lavish expenditure by some WUF and NFP candidates during the election campaign, Reddy would find it difficult to persuade the people of Fiji to accept the statement that the entire campaign expenses of his party were raised locally and came from the proceeds of two lotteries and small contributions from local supporters. His offer to open NFP books for inspection, the Alliance considered to be 'a meaningless gesture'. They also dismissed Reddy's claim regarding India, asserting that Ratu Mara did not, as Reddy had alleged, 'attack the Indian Government'. His criticism was 'directed at Mrs Kochar and her husband about whom he made formal representations to the Indian Government'.[10] When these representations eventually reached Mrs Gandhi, Mrs Kochar was transferred.

Did the NFP receive Soviet money? Who signed the 'Koya Letter'? Was it of any intrinsic value? Did the Alliance have proof to support its claim about Soviet interference? What had the Royal Commission to say on the issue?

One of the major issues the NFP insisted before the Royal Commission was the Soviet link. Their counsel submitted that the history of the matter showed that the allegations of a 'Russian connection' was viewed very seriously indeed, not only by the NFP and its supporters but by every citizen of his country who is understandably apprehensive of any invasion of a different ideology in these islands. He further submitted that 'the stigma which has been so easily imposed on a party, its leader and its supporters, ought to be inquired into and decided, once and for all'.[11]

The onus to prove the claims lay with the Alliance. From the start it seemed that they were dithering. Frantic behind-the-scene negotiations reveal that they were prepared to take refuge under the umbrella of Crown privilege. Earlier, there were suggestions that both the parties wanted to cut short the inquiry, with the Alliance offering to withdraw all its complaints against the NFP, except with regard to the matter of Soviet support, if the NFP did likewise. The NFP leadership, however, in particular Reddy, insisted that the inquiry into the 'Russian connection' must proceed; whatever evidence was available must be placed before the Royal Commission.

Ratu Mara, however, embarked upon another plan. Late in the afternoon of 17 May 1983, on the advice of Falvey, a former attorney-general and senior Alliance counsel for the inquiry, he despatched Alliance Party Management Board member, Usher, to the local newspapers and Radio Fiji to deliver two pieces of paper. One was a photostat headed Sydney, March 1982, 'Secret In Confidence'. Bearing a signature purporting to be Koya's, it appeared to commit the NFP to allowing the USSR to open an embassy and scientific bases in Fiji contingent upon an NFP election victory and formation of government. The second announced that Ratu Mara had decided to respond to 'widely-expressed concern about the length and cost' of the inquiry. Attempts to limit it had been fruitless. It was apparent that the major issue concerning the public was the allegation regarding the USSR, including the financial arrangements, Ratu Mara's statement ran. It added that 'the money is of relatively minor importance when weighed alongside the arrangement which is indicated in the document which he has directed to be distributed to the media today.'[12]

The grammer, spelling and appearance of the photostat partially destroyed the credibility of Ratu Mara's claims. But the gauntler had been thrown down and Koya could neither evade nor ignore the claims, which by now had attracted widespread public interest. 'This document is a false document', he claimed. 'Where is the original? If this is a genuine document those responsible should say so on oath in judicial proceedings. I invite them to do so.'[13] Taking issue with Ratu Mara, he said, 'as a decent and responsible citizen of this country if he believes and has proof that Russians have provided money to me and that I have received it on behalf of the NFP, he should come forward and testify.'[14] According to Koya, the release of the paper was a ploy to goad him into suing those responsible: 'The object is to sufficiently agitate the victim of this false allegation, that is me, to issue a writ in court of law thus forcing the commission of inquiry to say that the matter is subjudice.'[15]

Koya indicated, however, that only after the Royal Commission of Inquiry was completed would he take legal action against the 'perpetrators' of the document, including the press for their part in reproducing it. His action would give an opportunity for all concerned to prove the allegations, including Alliance propagandist Usher who delivered copies of the document to the press in the name of the Prime Minister. Rumours of the document's existence had been spread by one of the Alliance's lawyers at the Commission, G.P. Lala. Koya said: 'I have never, never in my life signed such a document. It is utterly false for anyone to say that the leaders or any of the members at any time received any money from the USSR or any other foreign power.'[16] Subsequently, the NFP, including Koya, authorized all the banks in Fiji, and abroad, to release to the Royal Commission accounts of any money they had in order to prove their innocence.

According to the so-called Koya Letter, the NFP, at a meeting in Sydney made the following alleged deals:[17]

(*Note:* The spelling is as that in the document given to the media.)

SECRET
IN CONFIDENCE

I, S.M. Koya of Suva, Fiji herein make the solemn confirmation for self my colegue Mr. Jairam Reddy and our party in Suva Fiji that we are being helped in good will in the interest of our Nation of Fiji, by the USSR Govt. to contest and put up our party candidates on all seats in the forth-coming FIJI General Elections.

In consideration, I am authorised to confirm that in acknowledgement and appreciation of the assistance and help thus received, and in the event that our Party is able to form the Government, our Govt, shall be:

a. co-operative and maintain friendly political and economic relations with USSR,

b. at all times willing, agreeable and receptable to permit USSR to organise their scientific experiment base in/or round FIJI Islands, park experimental ocean floats, without causing disturbance to Military standing of Fiji Govt. and the Island, within International rules of ethics, at their own cost,

c. through due approval in Fiji Parliament/Senate approve establishment of USSR Embassy for South Pacific, at a suitable station/s in Fiji.

It is agreed that all such co-operation and political tie-up shall be only in keeping with the laws and rules of the land.

And upon default on our part, the USSR representative can encash the Bank Guarantee, separately given by me; expose this agreement against us any where they choose to, to seek enforcement of the terms. In case of adverse results the agreement shall be null and void after July '82.

Sydney, March 1982.

[Signed: S.M. Koya]

When the inquiry resumed on the morning of the publication of the 'Koya Letter', the NFP asked Royal Commissioner White to set aside all other issues before him in order that the alleged Soviet connection could be probed immediately. The Royal Commissioner, however, ruled that because he had not been formally informed of Ratu Mara's evidence the Commission must ignore it until he had been. On 23 May he announced an adjournment of the Commission's inquiries until 14 June.

During this adjournment the Alliance took another step. On 10 June 1983, Falvey wrote to the Commission indicating that the Alliance would call no evidence on the Russian issue when the Commission resumed. Although the Prime Minister was satisfied as to the origins of the documents to which he had referred he could not disclose their origins to the Inquiry for reasons of security. It now became apparent from the letter that Crown privilege was likely to be sought.

The issue had obviously attracted wide publicity. The USSR which had previously denied any involvement reiterated their denial in a letter to the Royal Commission:[18]

EMBASSY OF THE UNION OF SOVIET SOCIALIST REPUBLICS
78 CANBERRA AVENUE, GRIFFITH, A.C.T. 2603
TELEPHONE 95 9033

Mr. J.D. Rabone,
Counsel Assisting the
Royal Commission of
Inquiry into the 1982
General Election,
Suva, Fiji

March 9, 1983

Dear Sir,

Regarding the issue you raised in your letter of february 23, 1983, I would like for your information to state the following.

Our position in respect to the speculations on the alleged 'Soviet interference' into the parliamentary elections in Fiji was put forward in the Embassy statement of the Fiji High Commissioner in Australia on August 12, 1982.

In no uncertain terms I wish to reiterate that, proceeding from the basic principles of its foreign policy, the Soviet Union has never interfered and has no intentions to interfere into internal affairs of Fiji, as well as of any other state. This is our firm policy.

Allegations about 'the Soviet involvement' in the Fijian election, which seem to have been inspired from outside, have nothing to do with reality.

We hope that good relations between the USSR and Fiji will be maintained and developed and that the obstacles, with the emergence of which the Soviet Union has nothing to do, will be eliminated.

Yours faithfully,
[Signed]
E. Rogov,
Minister-Counsellor of the USSR Embassy,
Australia.

Meanwhile, Vijaya Parmanandam, who earlier had rebelled against the NFP and accepted the office of Deputy Speaker of the House of Representatives, alleged that Reddy did 'woo' the Russians. It was at the Socialist International's Asia-Pacific Organisation conference in Sydney, Australia, which was attended by many Labour party representatives from around the world, including 'many communists'. Reddy, Parmanandam claimed, made bids for communist help for the 1982 elections.

When, on 14 June, the Royal Commission resumed, Koya seemed to command centre-stage. Meanwhile the Alliance had decided upon the course they should follow. Later, on 7 July, Falvey confirmed that the Alliance did not intend to call evidence in respect of the third group of issues and gave notice that he would submit that the Commission was thus precluded from considering those issues further. This was opposed by the NFP counsel who submitted that they were entitled to proceed and call evidence. The following day, Falvey said that the election to offer no evidence in the proceedings did not mean that the inquiry into the matters which had led to the allegations in the third group of issues would not continue. Further, it was claimed that there was relevant evidence which was subject to a claim of Crown privilege. He also added that should the Commission permit the NFP to call evidence, the counsel representing the Alliance would not apply to cross-examine any witness so called.

Following legal arguments, Dr Sahu Khan filed a certificate on behalf of the Crown by the Prime Minister, the Ministers of Home Affairs and Foreign Affairs and the Cabinet. He made it quite clear, on behalf of the Crown, that he was giving notice that if any matter 'pertaining to Crown privilege' arose in the evidence of any witnesses who might be called regarding the allegations Crown privilege would be raised; this would include any case where any minister or civil servant appeared on the subpoena. This statement made it clear that a claim of Crown privilege was not relied upon, or not stated as, in the view of the Crown, terminating any further consideration of the allegations. The Commission upheld Crown privilege but also ruled that the NFP could put its case forward. On the issue of Crown privilege, White said:

> In my view the present case illustrates the fact that there are some documents and information which can be specified and described and there are some which for sufficient reasons cannot because of their nature. Those reasons are given in the certificate and were explained further in argument, namely that slight additional detail would be liable to provide information leading to disclosure.[19]

Judge White also ruled that 'the NFP should be permitted to place on record sworn testimony in support of its positive assertions that there was no involvement of the kind alleged'. The ruling thus enabled the NFP to prove its case. Most NFP members who subsequently testified before the Royal Commission categorically denied the allegations. Alliance members were taken to task in explaining their views about the 'Koya Letter'. The NFP also summoned the general manager of the Central Monetary Authority (CMA), Savenaca Siwatibau, who told the Royal Commission that no money had been remitted to the NFP from overseas sources.

It was, however, the evidence and cross-examination of witnesses by Koya that kept the nation on tenterhooks. While calling on the Royal Commission for a 'categorical statement of complete exoneration of the alleged part I played', he claimed that his signature on the photostat document was a forgery, lifted from the visitors' book kept in New York by the Fiji mission to the UN. Claiming to be a firm adherent of the democratic system of government, Koya said he regarded the Soviet Union as a foreign country outside the Commonwealth. He also protested that the content of the document portrayed him as being on the 'verge of committing illegal parlance' with foreign superpowers; adding that although such parlance might not be described as treason, it could be seen as sedition. He also maintained that the transposition of his signature was possible and to prove his point, he transferred the signature of Ratu Mara and some other Alliance members on to the same document. 'Whoever had concocted the letter hadn't even made a good job of it.'

In his statement to the Royal Commission, Alliance Party Management Board member Usher had claimed that the visitors' book was given to him two or three days before his testimony, although he knew it had been in Fiji for five weeks. Usher said Ratu Mara had seen the book while en route to London during the Commission's brief adjournment in May. He said the book was brought to Fiji at the suggestion of Ratu Mara.

At the inquiry, Koya accused Usher of transposing the signature. Vowing to destroy Usher's credibility, he put to him that he was 'a past master' at interposing photographs and signatures. Koya was referring to a newspaper advertisement in which Usher had interposed a picture of

Koya, sitting beside Sir Vijay, unsmiling, during the election campaign. Usher, while admitting having doctored the picture, claimed he was portraying the truth about dissensions in the NFP, but he denied fixing Koya's signature to the 'Koya Letter'.

Apart from accusations and denials, nothing could be extracted from Usher. At one stage a question raised by the NFP counsel involved Crown privilege. Such became the feature of the inquiry, and as Rabone pointed out, White had also been frustrated in some aspects of the hearing. Frustration was also rife in the Alliance camp as political and national pressure was growing over the authenticity or otherwise of the 'Koya Letter'. As far back as 29 March 1983, the Alliance was trying to get hold of the 'original' letter; Falvey had even sent a telex to the Soviet Embassy in Sydney to 'supply the original of the contractual document from their own file or from those at their New Delhi embassy'.[20] There was no response from the Embassy. In August it seemed that the Alliance had finally crumbled. One of their counsels, G.P. Lala, who during the election had defected from the NFP to the Alliance, made the following statement to the Royal Commission:

> The Alliance Party, in consultation with its leader, assures this Royal Commission that it has been unable to obtain or provide evidence or offer to this Royal Commission to prove that Mr S.M. Koya had signed the documents concerning Russian involvement in Fiji with the National Federation Party.[21]

At this, the NFP counsel said his party was ready to close its case immediately. White said that after an adjournment of a few days he would be ready to hear closing addresses, since no more evidence was to be offered on matters before him.

On the last day of the hearing, however, the NFP discovered that a new situation had been created. The Alliance counsel, Falvey, dismissed the idea that the Alliance had abandoned its case. 'Nothing could be further from the truth and I categorically deny the implication', he said. While recalling his June letter he added that 'the Alliance maintains that the Koya letter is authentic, that the original was in fact signed by Koya and that money was paid to or for the benefit of the National Federation Party in exchange for the promise made to the USSR in that letter.'[22]

It now seemed that the battle lines would be redrawn. The clarification did nothing to help the Alliance; instead it spurred Koya to angrily demand the recall of Ratu Mara to the witness box to 'clear the air'. But this request was refused. White ruled that it had already been agreed that there was no further need to question Ratu Mara. The NFP's fury was later expressed in the submission of its counsel, Bhupendra Patel, who claimed such allegations should not have been made 'with the ease and carelessness' that they had been. He claimed that the proper inference to draw from the evidence was that Ratu Mara's allegations were false and without foundation. He also contended that the impact of such allegations was even greater for a multiracial society such as Fiji's than it would be for larger, more sophisticated countries, saying:

> It is especially so, My Lord, when the allegations have the appearance of racial connotations, when they are made by a paramount chief of one community against the leaders of another community; when references are made to a friendly but foreign country with ethnic similarities to the community which the leaders accused represent.
>
> Such allegations, My Lord, must create misunderstanding amongst the various communities living in this country, and at least arouse suspicion towards one half of its people in the minds of the governments and people of the South Pacific.[23]

Koya also addressed the Royal Commission. He objected at the outset to what he described as Falvey's 'subjective views'. Secondly, he submitted that the Alliance was bound by what had been 'verbally declared' that they had no evidence to prove that he signed the so-called letter. He also submitted that Ratu Mara's statements on which the allegations in group three were based 'were wild and irresponsible'. Amongst other things he also pointed out that the letter was 'easy to concoct'.

The counsel assiting the Royal Commission, Rabone, said the issue was 'both sensational and of inevitable concern to both the international community and to the people of Fiji'. All that was available was a photostat document which, said Rabone, was of 'no intrinsic value' and 'quite unsafe' to accept as evidence. It was open to the Commission to find as a fact that Koya had not signed the letter. Accordingly, White ruled that Koya's evidence was 'uncontradicted' and there was no evidence to show that he signed what had been described as the Koya Letter. The NFP was also cleared of receiving any funds from the Soviet Union. White also found that there was no evidence that Usher had fabricated the letter.

The ruling was just the beginning for Koya who had threatened to take legal action against those responsible for releasing the letter. In 1986 it seemed he was vindicated when Falvey and Usher in an out-of-court settlement paid him undisclosed damages and in a statement before a Supreme Court Judge formally apologized:

> Sir John Falvey and Sir Leonard Usher have apologised and expressed regret to Mr S.M. Koya for their contribution to the publication of allegedly defamatory material in the 'Russian Letter' which was released to the media on the instructions of the Prime Minister in May 1983.
>
> They accept without reservation a categorical denial by Mr Koya that he ever signed the document or had any part in, or any knowledge of, any such document.
>
> They agree that Mr Koya is a loyal citizen of Fiji.

A Supreme Court action by Mr Koya against Sir John and Sir Leonard arising from the publication of the document had been settled.[24]

The settlement, however, failed to arrest the progress of anti-Soviet propaganda in the region. As already pointed out, Libyan involvement in the Pacific is almost certainly independent of the Soviet *démarche*. In 1987, five years after the 'Russian episode', one Australian journalist, James Crown, claimed that the Libyans were also actively involved in influencing the outcome of the 1982 Fiji general elections. In the January 1987 edition of the Australian magazine, *Penthouse*, he claimed that the Libyan leader, Muammar Qaddafi, had 'planned to deliver the American-dominated South Pacific—a vast net of small, generally impoverished island nations—into the hands of the Russians, a gift to ingratiate himself with the Kremlin'.[25]

Crown claimed in his article that Australian security service (ASIO) contacts in Singapore put him in touch with one of the two Libyan agents (named only as 'Farhart') about the Fiji operation. According to Crown, 'Farhart', reportedly a 39-year-old Libyan former soldier who, in 1971, attended an intelligence course at the Patrice Lumumba Friend-ship University in Moscow, told him that his partner was executed on Qaddafi's orders for his failure to influence the outcome of the 1982 Fiji general elections. Fiji 'went bad' because Libya was trying to buy the same people as the Soviet Union in those elections. According to Crown's article, 'Farhart' confessed that:

> What happened was that the Russians were involved. They were fun-nelling money through Indian interests. Ours was going direct. I made three vists to Fiji on a yacht hired for the purpose. On each visit I carried in $10,000. That was mostly American dollars. We spread the money around. NFP got some, but so did members of the Alliance, the party in power, and the Western United Front (WUF).
>
> You see, the difference between what we were after and what the Russians were after was the Russians wanted to destroy Ratu Mara. Moscow thought they could advance their plans if he was out of the way. All we wanted was an invitation for Libya to become a friend of Fiji at least as a first step.
>
> When the Russians were publicly cited by Ratu Mara, the people we'd cited got scared and did nothing for us. Then the Russians found out about us and got mad.[26]

Crown's article went on to claim that the Russians ordered the Libyans to stop their Fiji operation after the Soviet 'connection' was exposed by Ratu Mara. Meanwhile, although the article received cautious response in Fiji, it did reopen a controversial issue which the Royal Commission seemed to have permanently closed.

Similarly, the Royal Commission had also cleared the Kochars of 'meddling' in the internal affairs of Fiji, but this issue needs further examination. As already noted, the Alliance had announced the date of the election two days before Mrs Gandhi arrived in Fiji. It was clear from the outset that Mrs Gandhi's visit, at the invitation of Ratu Mara during his visit to India in 1971, would have strong political connotations.

Mrs Gandhi was the first Indian Prime Minister to visit Fiji. To the Fiji Indians, linked to India through historical, cultural, emotional and religious ties, Mrs Gandhi's presence and messages during the tour gave them a sense of security and respite at a time when the fate of their brethren overseas in East Africa and other former British colonies hung in the balance. Mrs Gandhi's father, Jawaharlal Nehru, was remembered by many Fiji Indians for his participation, during his early political days, in the agitation against the system of indentured labour in Fiji. Some of them probably recalled Nehru's vision of free India and its impact on overseas indentured Indians, especially his presidential address to the Lahore Congress on 29 December 1929, in which he said: 'This is not from any want of fellow-feeling with our brethren in East Africa or South Africa or Fiji or elsewhere who are bravely struggling against great odds. But their fate will be decided in the plains of India and the struggle we are launching into is as much for them as for ourselves.'[27]

Similarly, Mrs Gandhi, while calling on the Fiji Indians to pledge their loyalty to their new found home in the South Pacific, said, 'India wants to see the Indians, wherever they have settled, adopt the country as their own and continue with their traditions, culture and religion'.[28] She also praised Fiji's multiracial image including the contribution of Fiji's Indians toward its success. The most moving event for the Indians was when she officially opened the Girmit Centenary Centre in the western township of Lautoka built to commemorate the 100th anniversary of the arrival of the first Indians in Fiji under the indenture labour system.

In his welcome speech, Ratu Mara had praised the Indians saying that 'today as citizens of Fiji, they comprise a valued component of our multiracial society, contributinig to its progress and benefiting from its prosperity'. He said that the vast majority of Fiji Indians regarded the islands 'as their home and, like the other members of our multiracial community, are proud citizens of independent Fiji'.[29] And, at a state banquet he told Mrs Gandhi that 'like good wine, the friendly close ties between Fiji and India had matured and improved with the passing years'.

Although the Indian High Commission is one of the oldest embassies in Fiji, dating back to 1946, it was not until the end of 1986 that the Alliance government appointed a non-residential High Commissioner to India. Even the choice, in the person of James Maraj, a Trinidad-born but naturalized Fiji citizen and Permanent Secretary for Foreign Affairs, failed to please the Fiji Indians, provoking charges of racial discrimination.

In line with the fundamental principles of its foreign policy, India has, in a modest way, tried to help South Pacific countries through economic assistance under the Indian Technical and Economic Co-operation

(ITEC) programme. The role of the Indian High Commission in Fiji is to promote Indo-Fijian bilateral relations in all fields. The supposedly good relations between Fiji and India were, however, becoming sour due to the activities of the Kochars, whose alleged involvement in NFP politics Ratu Mara considered to amount to interference in Fiji's internal affairs.

Indian High Commissioners' role in former British colonies with a large Indian population has always been controversial, with any statement expressing concern about the welfare of the Indians construed as interference. In late 1948, the Colonial Governor had warned the Indian High Commissioner to Fiji against such interference:

> We continue to hope that his presence in our midst will promote a genuine spirit of co-operation, and that nothing will be said or done by the Commissioner or his associates which will have the effect, directly or indirectly, of diverting the Indian population of Fiji from that undivided loyalty towards the Colony of their adoption which forms the only possible basis for their future happiness and prosperity.[30]

In Ratu Mara's opinion Mrs Kochar's statements held all the ingredients of interference. He had registered his displeasure with the Indian Ministry of Foreign Affairs during Mrs Gandhi's tour, resulting in Mrs Kochar's early transfer to the Netherlands. Ratu Mara had complained about her to Dr P.C. Alexander, later to become India's Ambassador to Great Britain. It will be useful here to recall the text of Mrs Kochar's speech, as published by the *Fiji Sun* on 16 April 1982.

She had told a meeting organized by a group of Suva politicians that circumstances and lack of time had prevented her from visiting other parts of Fiji, particularly the western division, where the bulk of the Indians reside. She said India and Fiji were bound together by ties of kinship and heritage which Mrs Gandhi so 'tenderly described as a mother and a married daughter who lives far away'. At the same time, she added, if the daughter is unhappy or ill-treated, it pains the mother and even a mother's patience is not inexhaustible. This implied that India was bound to speak out on behalf of the Fiji Indians if it was felt that their survival in Fiji was under threat. She then spoke specifically on the role of the Fiji Indians. The interests of the indigenous peoples were everywhere subordinated to the needs of the white invaders, she said, but this was not the case in Fiji, and Mrs Kochar did not hesitate to point out:

> The Indian contribution to Fiji is no less a feat of pioneering endeavour than that of European settlers in Australia, New Zealand or USA, but with one notable difference. The Indians did not decimate the indigenous people. Instead in many ways they became shock absorbers in the harsh reality of a colonial era.[31]

She went on to express her candid views on three most crucial issues:

the fear of insecurity among the Indians, land issue, and the spectre of racial violence, and warned that to tell the Indians to get out of Fiji was a recipe for disaster. On a personal note, she reminded the Fiji Indians of their true status in Fiji: 'To those Indians who themselves want to migrate, to seek greener pastures, I have always said that they are chasing mirages. This is the piece of earth on which you were born, shaped, made aware; whose flowers you have learned to love and whose paths to roam. You belong here.'[32]

In another forthright outburst, she called upon the government to open up more land to the Indians, recognize the potential for the outbreak of racial violence, and exhorted the bickering Indian leaders to close ranks and fight for improved conditions for the Indian community in Fiji. These demands gained widespread acceptance in the Indian community but not by Ratu Mara. It also seemed to frustrate the Alliance's divide and rule electoral tactics. As far as the Indian government was concerned, the statement did not violate the rules of non-interference. It stated that it was the Indian government's duty and responsibility to protect the rights and interests of all Indian citizens living abroad and to take appropriate action in this regard whenever called upon to do so.[33]

Past experiences abroad have made many Fiji Indians wary of the influence of the Indian High Commission in Fiji in times of crisis. The following analogy with Guyana, as Ramrakha saw it, suffices to explain this caution:

> The Government of India has never been able to help any resident group of Indians abroad, and if some trouble occurs in Fiji, it will be no exception.
>
> The Indians in Guyana were stunned when the Indian High Commissioner failed to take action, or condemn the open shooting of Indians during the civil disturbances in that country.
>
> And the Indians remain a repressed majority in that country, cheated of their democratic rights by an openly rigged ballot system, a racially lopsided police and army. . . . What did the Indians do when the crisis there arose? The High Commissioner for the Government of India continued to extend his courtesies to Mr Forbes Burnham—and one of the stories was that they continued to drink their Royal Salute together.[34]

In general, Ratu Mara's claims about the activity of the Kochars brought strong denials and protests from the Indian Ministry of Foreign Affairs in New Delhi. In a hard-hitting response, it described the allegations as 'deplorable' and 'mischievous'. The statement also categorically refuted the allegation that India had been or could indeed be, a tool for furtherance of Soviet objectives in the South Pacific, adding: 'We find it difficult to believe that the Prime Minister, Ratu Sir Kamisese Mara, could have said what he is reported to have said. This can only have the effect of a deliberate attempt to spoil the relations between the two countries.'[35]

In summary, these diplomatic exchanges inevitably frayed the relationship between the two countries; the aftermath events hardened it. Furthermore, if the Indian High Commission was secretly aiding the Russians in Fiji, often called the 'Little India of the Pacific', the Americans on the other hand saw their own intervention as a necessary safeguard against such foreign 'communist' influences.-

Notes

1. See Richard Herr, in Ron Crocombe and Ahmed Ali (ed.), 1983, pp. 290-308.
2. Quoted in D.D. Tumarkin, in Crocombe and Ali, 1983, p. 145.
3. Ibid., p. 146.
4. Text of speech by Mikhail Gorbachev, 28 July 1986 (Moscow: Novosti Press Agency, 1986).
5. *Fiji Times*, 3 October 1986. For further discussion see Ernest Kux in *Pacific Community*, April 1970, and A.W. Grazebrowk in *Pacific Defense Reporter*, *September 1980, pp. 15-24.*
6. *Islands Business* (Fiji), February 1986.
7. *Fiji Sun*, 5 August 1982, p. 3.
8. Ibid.
9. Ibid.
10. Ibid., 6 August 1982, p. 3.
11. Quoted in Bhupendra Patel's submission (counsel for NFP) to the Royal Commission of Inquiry, 22 August 1983 (mimeo).
12. *Fiji Sun*, 18 May 1983, p. 1.
13. *Fiji Times*, 18 May 1983, p. 1.
14. Ibid.
15. Ibid.
16. Ibid.
17. Ibid.
18. A copy of the letter in author's possession
19. *The White Report*, p. 197.
20. Quoted in ibid., pp. 206-7.
21. Ibid., p. 212.
22. Ibid., p. 215.
23. Ibid., p. 208.
24. *Fiji Times*, 6 June 1986, p. 3.
25. Quoted in ibid., 20 February 1987.
26. Ibid.
27. Dorothy Norman (ed.), 1965, p. 209.
28. *Fiji Sun*, 28 September 1981, p. 1.
29. Ibid.
30. Quoted in Ahmed Ali, 1974, p. 29.
31. *Fiji Sun*, 16 April 1982, p. 1.
32. Ibid.
33. Personal communication with the Indian Ministry of External Affairs, New Delhi, 11 February 1986.
34. *Fiji Sun*, 2 October 1982, p. 6.
35. Ibid., 13 August 1982.

CHAPTER TEN

THE AUSTRALIAN/AMERICAN CONNECTION

We discussed the Fiji operation and, in putting our ideas together, it appeared to us that the nature of the Fiji operation was such that the CIA may have had a hand in it somewhere.

Rosemarie Gillespie, Australian market researcher.

The Fijian nation he so ably represents is a model of democracy and freedom, a tremendous example for all the countries of the developing world, and we, again, have found ourselves standing shoulder to shoulder in our condemnation of the brutal invasion of Afghanistan and the deliberate shooting down of a civilian Korean airliner. Americans also deeply appreciate your support of our efforts to rescue our students and restore democracy to the people of Grenada.

US President Ronald Reagan to Ratu Mara at the White House, 1984.

The Americans have maintained a significant presence in Fiji since the middle of the 19th century. In fact, it was the unscrupulous activities of the United States commercial agent, John Brown Williams, and others, which partly influenced the Fijian chiefs, particularly Ratu Cakobau, to surrender their sovereignty to Great Britain in 1874.[1] The Deed of Cession specifically stressed the US factor:

And being heavily indebted to the President and Government of the United States of America, the liquidation of which indebtedness is pressingly urged, with menaces of severe measures against our person and sovereignty. We do hereby transfer and convey unto Victoria, by the grace of God, Queen of Great Britain and Ireland, Her heirs and successors for ever, the full sovereignty and domain in and over our aforesaid islands and territories.[2]

The rest is history. Britain turned down the offer and Cakobau then offered the country to the US, but the US government, preoccupied with the Civil War, ignored the offer. Sixteen years later, however, Fiji became a British colony. This also opened a new chapter in the relationship between Fiji and the US, which has since stood the test of time.

The relationship was given real meaning during the outbreak of the Second World War when the South Pacific became a major theatre of war. Both the Americans and the Fijians found themselves fighting side by side against Japanese imperialism. US troops had used Fiji as a transit base in the South Pacific, an important contribution which still lingers in the minds of the Americans. As Ronald Reagan recalled nearly 40 years later when he met Ratu Mara at the White House in 1984:

> Mr Prime Minister, when you return to your country, I hope you will convey to your citizens the deep respect and admiration of the American people. Fijians are our brothers and sisters in the family of nations. We share values that are at the heart of our societies, the most important of which is our abiding love of human liberty. That was underscored to many Americans who fought alongside Fijians in the Second World War, during the Solomon Island campaign, a turning point in the Pacific theater. We stood together then in the cause of human freedom.[3]

The defeat of the Japanese also saw the Pacific island states gradually taking shelter under the wings of the American eagle. The ANZUS Treaty, signed between Australia, US, and New Zealand, in Presidio, San Francisco, on 1 September 1951, afforded the island states further comfort because most of them saw it as the cornerstone of security in the Pacific region.

In the previous chapter we noted the geopolitical importance of the South Pacific's geographical location and the myths and realities of the Soviet threat in the region. Conversely, what are US interests, objectives, and policy in the South Pacific? Where does Fiji fit in? Were the CIA and ASIO secretly conspiring with the Fijian armed forces to overthrow an NFP government if it was elected to power in 1982? Could there be a Grenada in the South Pacific?

To respond to these questions and to understand the developments and ensuing claims and counter-claims during the 1982 general elections, it is necessary to turn briefly to US policies within the region. Reagan has described the Pacific as the 'ocean where the future of the world lies'. The US considers itself as part of the Pacific, and its policy, as one US Ambassador to Fiji, Carl Edward Dillery, put it, 'is not toward the Pacific but is a policy of a country which is part of the Pacific basin'.

This perception of the region, therefore, makes the South Pacific—no longer a colonial backwater—more important for the US Administrations to keep within its sphere of influence. 'Our relationship with the Pacific island region', according to Reagan, 'is a partnership'. He noted that other common interests held were 'a strong belief in freedom and democracy, respect for human rights, and faith in the power of the free market'.[4] The overall US policy has been aptly summed up by a Pacific island expert, and Senior Foreign Service Officer in the Office of Australia and New Zealand Affairs in the State Department, John Dorrance.[5]

Overall, it may be argued that the US South Pacific policies have been driven by two conflicting approaches: (1) to view the region in terms of the strategic US competition with the Soviet Union; and (2) to deal with the region on its own terms.

In the final analysis, it is quite clear that the 1947 Truman Doctrine enunciating the 'containment of communism' overrides all other US policies and interests in the South Pacific. An Indiana Republican and chairman of the US Senate Foreign Relations Committee, Richard G. Lugar, while urging the South Pacific states to develop stronger ties with the US and Australia, asserted, 'intelligence gathering comes right along with the fishermen', an apparent reference that innocuous fishing agreements were the thin end of a Soviet wedge, aimed at providing opportunities for spying and subversion in the South Pacific.[6]

Today, and in view of the increasing chaos in the South Pacific, Fiji has indisputably become 'the jewel in the American crown in the region. Soon after Fiji became independent on 1 November 1971, the US established an Embassy in Suva with Rober W. Skiff as Chargé d'Affaires ad interim. In 1978, as Fiji became a key Melanesian regional power, the US appointed John Condon as its first resident ambassador.

In many countries US ambassadors have been accused of conspiring with or freely encouraging the US clandestine organizations, especially the CIA, to destabilize 'hostile' governments. Although it is not contended here that the American ambassadors to Fiji were involved in such activities, the issue has to be taken further in the light of the NFP charges of CIA complicity during the 1982 elections. There is also Speed's letter to Carroll in which he notes that the former Ambassador Boddie 'can't be given a diplomatic rap over the knuckles' for predicting an NFP win in the general elections.

As far as the South Pacific is concerned, many US experts agree that 'personal relationships with and between political leaders affect governmental attitudes and decisions'. Therefore, US ambassadors to the islands should 'be selected with particular attention to their ability to relate to proud but usually extremely informal leaders. Patience, informality, straightforwardness, a sense of humour, and mastery of soft-sell techniques are essential embassadorial traits.'[7]

In November 1980, the US political scene underwent a major transformation when Ronald Reagan was elected the 40th president. This gave him the opportunity to reshape the defence and foreign policies, more in accord with his own ideology and conviction that communism should be consigned 'to the ash-heap of history', denouncing Soviet communism as 'the focus of evil in the modern world'.

US ambassadors were also changed. Reagan personally nominated advertising personality and New York State Senator, representing the Rochester area, Fred J. Eckert, as the next Ambassador to Fiji. He arrived in Fiji on 22 February 1982, and very soon made a great impact on Ratu Mara. His diplomatic manoeuvres also resulted in Fiji gradually becoming one of the most pro-US island states in the South Pacific.

Ratu Mara was given an 'open' invitation from Fiji's US ambassador, and the US government, to visit high-ranking officials and hold discussions whenever he was in the US. This was revealed when Ratu Mara made a 'confidential' visit to Hawaii in September 1982 where he met Admiral

Robert Long, then Commander of the US Pacific Command (CINPAC). On his return Ratu Mara categorically denied press reports that he was seeking US military assistance. In a subsequent press release his office disclosed: 'What is most significant really is that the Prime Minister, while in Hawaii to relax following a long political campaign, took the time to pursue discussions on US-Fiji relations.'[8] This visit, as events will show, was merely a smokescreen. Soon after, Fijian soldiers began training in the United States.

In recent years behind-the-scene diplomatic arm-twisting has achieved its objectives. At the end of 1984 Ratu Mara became the first Pacific island leader, since the post-colonial independence process began in the region in 1967, to be given a royal reception at the White House; he had gone to Washington with high hopes and returned home fully satisfied. Ratu Mara also deeply impressed Reagan who praised him for turning Fiji into 'a model of democracy and freedom, a tremendous example for all the countries of the developing world'.[9]

Reagan also found Ratu Mara a valuable ally in times of crisis, as he put it:

> He is a man to look up to in many ways. Oxford-educated and deeply religious, a man of conviction and wisdom, he has provided exemplary leadership for his people in the crucial stages of democracy. His support of free enterprise and a market economy has enabled his people to enjoy stable economic progress. He has kept Fiji on a steady course and has always defended the principles on which his country was founded, principles that we Americans share.[10]

In conclusion, Reagan reiterated that the region must be kept free of Soviet influence. The White House meeting between Ratu Mara and Reagan, both ardent opponents of communism, also saw Fiji become the first South Pacific nation to have a bilateral agreement with the US. Ratu Mara later told the Fiji Parliament that he had been promised favourable deals for sugar, landing rights for Fiji's national airline, Air Pacific, and a fisheries agreement. The US Defense Department also agreed to give $300,000 for the standardization of rifles for the Fijian military, without specifying the real motive for this magnanimity. The US's attitude to Fiji was actuated, firstly, in order to defend its own security interests in the region, and, secondly, to reward Fiji for re-opening its ports to all US naval vessels; and also to check the spread of communism.

Before examining the charges made against the US and Australian intelligence services, and that the infamous 'Koya Letter' was manufactured to pave the way for the Fijian army and the CIA to overthrow an NFP government had it won the elections, it is important to briefly consider the US-Fiji military axis.

The military connection between the two countries has been assiduously cultivated through officer-to-officer contacts and military aid. In addition the US has two programmes: (1) the Pacific Armies Management

Seminars (PAMS), organized by the Western Command of the US Army from Fort Shafter in Hawaii; and (2) the Pentagon's International Military Education and Training Programme (IMET), operative since 1983. The US spends thousands of dollars a year putting selected Fijian officers through major US military staff colleges and courses. The PAMS programme is reportedly directed at young majors and colonels 'because they'll be in their services for a long period of time'.

In recent years the US has also totally re-equipped the Fijian army. The elite American Green Berets frequently train the Fijian peace-keepers bound for Middle East duties—particularly the US-sponsored multi-lateral force in the Sinai—in the use of sophisticated US weapons. Furthermore, the pride of Fiji's navy is her possession of three 44 metre ex-US Navy Bluebird class minesweepers which were sold to her at a nominal cost. The vessels proudly reflect the 'Americanism' in them as they try to keep an eye on 370,000 square miles of Fijian ocean.

Fiji's participation in the US-sponsored Middle East peace process, however, evokes the strongest criticism. While the Alliance government maintained that the Middle East commitment provided a chance to boost employment, the NFP always asserted that the participation exceeded the country's capacity. It also affected Fiji's relations with the Arab world; in 1982, for example, Fiji was the only Third World country to vote against a resolution to condemn Israel's annexation of the Golan Heights.

More radical NFP members have publicly condemned the racially lop-sided composition of the Fijian troops in the Middle East, some claiming that the soldiers were 'satellite troops of the US', trained to effectively quell any wide-scale Indian rebellion in the foreseeable future. In its election manifesto the Coalition had criticized the Alliance government for committing Fijian troops to the Middle East without prior parliamentary discussion and approval.

The first wave of fear at the role of the Fijian military in the 1982 elections erupted when, at the height of the election campaign, a new commander was appointed to lead the Royal Fiji Military Forces (RFMF). He was Ratu Epeli Nailatikau, a distinguished career diplomat and professional soldier, who, prior to his new appointment on 22 June 1982, had commanded Fiji troops in Lebanon, and had received an OBE. He was later appointed the Chief of Staff of the RFMF, with the rank of Colonel, replacing a New Zealander, Brigadier Ian Thorpe.

There was nothing irregular about the appointment, but it evoked genuine fears because Ratu Epeli was Ratu Mara's son-in-law. Although Ratu Epeli later dismissed Koya's charges as 'hogwash' and clarified his relationship from a military standpoint, saying 'that's got nothing to do with the price of fish',[11] arguments over the role of the military in domestic politics continued.

It will be recalled that during the 1977 political crisis the military made no move to intervene. Reflecting on the events of 1977, it can be argued that the subsequent appointment of an Alliance minority government, under the leadership of Ratu Mara, discouraged military intervention. In 1983 Gillespie told the Royal Commission that she was told that a 'leading' army officer, now widely thought to be Sitiveni Rabuka who mounted the 1987 military coup, asked Ratu Mara if he wanted to bring in the army at the time of the 1977 general election. 'I understand the Prime Minister had refused', Gillespie said.[12] During the same period, Mrs Narayan had also commented that:

> In other countries experience had shown that when one race controlled the army and security forces and then found its position threatened by the ballot box, it made use of the forces. I do not mean to suggest that this would have happened here. We have much more faith in the leaders of Fiji. Identity of interest between them and the armed forces leaders was a guarantee that the latter would not move without the approval of the former.[13]

In 1982, however, she claimed at a political meeting that Ratu Mara was out to grab power by wit or grit. She also called on him to give an assurance that the ballot boxes would not be tampered with during the election. Furthermore, Mrs Narayan considered that Ratu Mara, in a moment of weakness, might decide to rig the election, referring to events in Guyana, as she put it: 'During the election in Guyana the opposition party was set to win the election but Sir Forbes got the army to deal with the ballot boxes and he was returned with a great majority.'[14]

In short she suggested that the Fijian army might also do the same; she was immediately criticized. The President of the Fiji Public Service Association (FPSA), Dr Timoci Bavadra, who himself was overthrown as Prime Minister by Rabuka in 1987, said that in making such a suggestion it must have been clear to Mrs Narayan that she was questioning the integrity of the civil servants, who were charged with the responsibility of supervising the elections. He also added that the FPSA had justifiable reason to be proud of their members' record, particularly their integrity and of the clear demonstration of their independence (despite expressed doubts to the contrary) following the May 1977 elections.

Regarding the 1980 Guyanese elections, the international observer team's report, while concluding that the election had been 'rigged massively and flagrantly', said of the Guyanese military:

> The military presence in some areas was intimidating. The boxes were collected by military personnel who prevented accredited officials of the opposition, sometimes by force or threat of force, from accompanying or following the boxes. Military personnel refused accredited representatives of opposition parties access to the count at gunpoint in some areas.[15]

No similar incidents were apparent during the elections in Fiji, but allegations against the Fijian military continued. One Coalition candidate, Mumtaz Ali, claimed that more than 700 soldiers serving abroad on peace-keeping missions had been bloc registered in one area only—Na-droga/Navosa—the home of WUF leader Ratu Osea. Claiming that he had evidence to prove this, Ali expressed his fear of possible vote rigging; the Supervisor of Elections, however, denied any bloc registration. Yet, fear of the military had become widespread in the Coalition camp. In another, and perhaps the most serious outburst, one Coalition candidate, Arthur Jennings, alleged that the Fiji troops serving in Lebanon and Sinai were being trained to take on military rule of the country. The RFMF maintained silence but the Minister of Home Affairs described the allegation 'as an insult to the loyalty and devotion of men who have volunteered for service, even at the risk of sacrificing their lives, in the cause of international peace', adding that it was also an insult to those who trained and commanded the Fiji troops for such service, and turning Jennings' outburst to political advantage, an emotionally charged plea, told the voters: 'I hope that all Western General National constituency, especially Fijian voters, will remember on the polling day that [Jennings] is the man who has so wantonly and disgracefully insulted the soldiers of Fiji, of whom they have always been, and always will be, greatly proud.'[16]

Against this background, charges against the CIA and two Australian agencies, ASIS and ASIO, will be examined.

We have already noted that although the Fiji project for the Alliance was not carried out under the auspices of Business International, the thrust of the allegation against the party was that it was in collusion with big business and, as Gillespie had claimed, the Fiji operation was a front to further the business interests of BI's clients. The CIA was specifically implicated in the 1982 Fiji general elections because of the alleged links of Race and BI with CIA.

The genesis of this kind of thinking was brought to attention by the 'Four Corners' programme and it became known to the NFP. Later the local press focused its attention on Race. An editorial in the *Fiji Sun* wanted to know:

> ... why the report was prepared by the shadowy Bangkok-based Dr Jeff Race, while Mr Alan Carroll is claimed to be the front man in the operation.
>
> Is Dr Race a front for the ... CIA? More unusual things have happened in Third World operations of this type. He has all the classic qualifications—Harvard education, Vietnam Military Intelligence experience, 'a close link with the US Defense Department', and is now engaged in Asian Strategies Studies from a well protected base in Bangkok.
>
> Why, for instance, did the pay Ms Rosemarie Gillespie in US dollars with a personal cheque drawn on a bank in Boston, Massachusetts?

Surely Fiji or Australian dollars from Motibhai and Co. or the Alliance would have been quite acceptable.[17]

These questions remain unanswered. Very little is known about Race, who refused to co-operate with the ABC, the *National Times* and the Royal Commission.

In his book, *War Comes to Long An—Revolutionary Conflict in a Vietnamese Province*, Race notes that, in 1967, when he was serving in the Army as an adviser to a Vietnamese district chief in Phouc Tuy province, 'It was clear from my experience that my fellow officers and I frequently had to make decisions affecting people's lives with an insufficient understanding both of actual conditions and of the nature of the conflict itself of which we were a part.' And that, 'this widespread failure of understanding permitted a belief at higher levels of government in possibilities that did not actually exist, in turn leading to increased intervention and to the high costs which the failure of that intervention has subsequently entailed'.[18]

Despite this admission it could be suggested that, in view of his 'repugnant recommendations' in the Carroll Report, Race had failed to learn the lessons of Vietnam. He was, as Judge White ruled, the architect of the scenarios suggesting sinister tactics. Judge White also found that it was impossible to pronounce judgement on a person who had refused the opportunity to be heard, as Race had done. After the Royal Commission's report was published, Race, in a personal communication to me, in December 1985, had this to say about his role in the Fiji project:

I did indeed do some work on Fiji, for a businessman who was close to the ruling party at the time (perhaps still—I haven't followed events there). I didn't know much about Fiji, having spent only two weeks there in my whole life; the reason I was asked to go was because I know a lot about Malaysia and there are many similarities since the British set them up the same way for the same reasons.[19]

But he denied having any knowledge of what the various governments' intelligence agencies were doing in Fiji, adding that he was sure they must be doing something (especially the US, USSR, People's Republic of China and Australia) or they would hardly be earning their keep. Yet, during and after the elections, he remained the principal suspect. Gillespie insisted at the Royal Commission that Race's behaviour in his dealings with her was always consistent with that of an intelligence man—a 'spy'—Carroll, she alleged, was another. One of the interests he was serving on the Fiji project was the CIA. She added, 'I am not saying that I know this for sure but there are suggestions, indications that this may well be the case.'

It was not the first time she had voiced this suspicion. On 2 July 1982 while discussing the Fiji operation with Sir Vijay in Sydney, both had concluded that the CIA may have had a hand in it somewhere. Gillespie had based her conclusion on an alleged earlier link between the CIA and BI, and the remarkable similarity between BI's research and the CIA's espionage and evaluation work and the multinational corporate interests both serve. Gillespie then gave evidence of the earlier links.

In December 1977 the *New York Times*, in three lengthy articles on the Agency's use of the US media, exposed BI's alleged clandestine collaboration with the CIA.[20] Regarding BI, after three months' investigation of the CIA's manipulation of the media, following a story by Carl Bernstein (of Watergate fame), the article published on 27 December drew the following conclusions:

> Among the lesser-known organisations were the College Press Service, Business International, the McLendon Broadcasting Organisation, Film Daily and a defunct underground newspaper published in Washington, *The Quicksilver Times*.
>
> Another who acknowledged a connection was Elliot Haynes, with his father a co-founder of Business International, a widely respected business information service. He said that his father, Eldridge Haynes, had provided cover for four CIA employees in various countries between 1955 and 1960.

While testifying before the Royal Commission, Gillespie alleged that in an interview with the Washington correspondent of BI she was told that its links with the CIA continued after 1977. The correspondent said that he came to know of this after an interview between the editor of the BI publication, Ken Gott, and a senior vice-president of BI, William Pearson. Gott resigned in 1978 after the disclosure of the European cover.

In 1975 Gott had selected Carroll to head BI's Australian operation. In January 1978, the Australian newspaper, *Melbourne Age,* reported that Gott, an Australian who had held senior positions with BI for seven to eight years, setting up its Hong Kong office, and then editing its main journal for corporations in New York, had resigned saying that he had never been involved with the CIA. He 'did not know that Business International had any such involvement', and added that, 'I am not out to taunt the already tattered CIA. While there is a KGB, America needs a CIA.' He believed the CIA needed cover, Gott said, adding, 'I'm not concerned if they get cover from salesmen, accountants, lion-tamers or morticians. But I must be concerned if they operate, or pretend to operate as journalists.'[21] In support of her conspiracy theory Gillespie also claimed that, in another context, BI had wanted information for a pharmaceutical company on the number of blood banks in Australia but she refused to co-operate because:

> My suspicion was that it was some intelligence agency wanting to have background information on Australia about the military and medical nature, that this might have been the CIA, it could also be the defence

intelligence agency or whatever it is called. There are a number of intelligence bodies, it could have been any one of a number.[22]

The CIA links had apparently come home to roost. The US embassy in Fiji declined to comment. Ambassador Eckert said it was 'standard United States policy not to comment on such accusations, even when they are as preposterous as those of Gillespie'.[23]

In 1982, and immediately preceding the election, the NFP continued to highlight the 'Australian connection'. Two other events need to be added. In 1980 the NFP had been unhappy about the appointment of an Australian, Sir Arthur Tange, under Australian aid assistance to review the organization, esablishment and operations of the Fiji Public Service Commission (FPSC). Tange was highly regarded in Australia as an able and experienced public servant and had been Secretary for External Affairs for 11 years, Ambassador to Washington for one year and High Commissioner in India for five years. He retired in 1979 after serving as Secretary for defence for almost 10 years. His review of the FPSC was completed on 18 August 1980.

The NFP was not protesting about Tange's qualifications to carry out the review but his rumoured role in the fall of the Whitlam government in 1975, and the alleged long arm of the CIA in the whole affair.[24]

Another event, involving an Australian diplomat, shook the NFP's confidence in the Fraser government. Gordon Upton, Australian High Commissioner to Fiji from 1976 to 1979, then in October 1980 High Commissioner to India, sent a secret report to Fraser suggesting that the Indian Army could oust a faltering Mrs Gandhi. This document, leaked to Canberra political journalist Laurie Oakes, headed 'India—Indira Gandhi's Faltering Leadership', said that Mrs Gandhi had 'failed to solve or even offer effective solutions to India's major domestic problems'.[25] Upton accused the *Melbourne Age*, which had quoted excerpts from the report in Oakes column, of misrepresentation and of publishing only selected parts of his report. But this failed to convince the NFP's pro-India and anti-Fraser factions who became extremely cautious and suspicious in their dealings with Australian diplomats in Fiji.

The subsequent allegations that Australian aid money had been misused; that three Australian consultants were helping the Alliance; and that Fraser was interfering in Fiji's internal politics, as well as the charges made after the election, further strained the relationship between NFP politicians and Australia.

In his evidence to the Royal Commission, Sir Vijay claimed that the Australian Ministry of External Affairs had been hostile towards journalist Wilkinson, who was gathering information on Speed's appointment to the Fiji government. He also alleged that ASIS, and an official in the Australian High Commission in Suva, might have been involved in Speed's appointment. Relying on information supplied to him by Wilkinson, Sir Vijay said the Australian official was definitely an ASIS man. Sir Vijay also claimed that Race had access to a military/navy officers' club in Melbourne, one largely restricted to senior military or navy officers. But it was Koya's evidence that hinted at the final conspiracy theory.

While cross-examining Usher, Koya had put to him that the groundwork for a military coup had been worked out by the Alliance in the event of the NFP winning the election. Usher described the allegation as 'complete nonsense' and 'utterly untrue'. The cross-examination, however, collapsed after Usher's lawyer claimed that Koya was exceeding his role in the inquiry. Koya had put to Usher that the 'Koya Letter' had been in the possession of the Alliance during the campaign period, and if the NFP had won the election the Alliance would have disclosed its contents to pave the way for a Fijian army coup to overthrow the new government; the coup was to have been aided by the CIA.

The US Ambassador Eckert, who had declined to comment on Gillespie's evidence, in an indignant statement bitterly criticized Koya, saying that such an accusation was 'irresponsible, reckless and foolish', and that 'to accuse my country, which is a great friend of this country, of such thing is an intolerable insult'. Eckert added that he wished he did not have to criticize remarks made by a Member of Parliament, that he would not make public statements about Fiji's domestic politics, take sides or show favouritism, 'but I cannot sit silently by and let anyone— even a Member of Parliament—make false and malicious accusation against the United States'.[26]

Koya did not have the opportunity to prove his claim before the Royal Commission, but two top NFP officials have since pieced together the following reasons why they considered that a military coup would have taken place:

1. The very close and personal relationship between the US and the Fiji governments.

2. The Coalition manifesto was critical of Fiji's nuclear policies and of committing Fijian troops to the American-sponsored peace proposals in the Middle East—two issues which directly affected American interests.

3. The Coalition had also promised to maintain, establish and strengthen Fiji's relationship with 'all nations without prejudice to their political ideologies'. This was interpreted by the Alliance that the USSR would be allowed to open an embassy in Fiji.

4. The public condemnation of the Fraser government had signalled warnings to Canberra as to the kind of relationship an NFP government would have with its counterpart in Australia.

5. The highly critical and inflammatory remarks by some Coalition members against the Fiji military must have caused some irritation and discomfort to the Fijian soldiers.

6. Finally, the contents of the 'Koya Letter' went against the very grain

of what Fiji, US, and Australian governments had been struggling to achieve—to keep the USSR out of the South Pacific.

In its findings, the Royal Commission concluded that the evidence submitted by the NFP did not support the inference that the CIA or BI was involved in the Fiji project. Nor was there any evidence to support the allegations regarding the connection between the CIA and the Fijian military put by Koya in his cross-examination of Usher.

The allegations and counter-allegations raised another question: Could Fiji become Grenada? When, in October 1983, the US invaded Grenada one Fiji journalist asked: 'Grenada: could it ever happen in the South Pacific?'[27] Political observers and intelligence officers also began to suggest that the South Pacific could become another Latin America, Caribbean or Middle East if the US continued to restrain the spread of communism in the region. The Grenada episode had also seen the establishment within Britain's, Australia's and New Zealand's armed forces of units designed to respond within hours to any call from South Pacific regional governments for help against political 'hijacking'.

Whether the US would have acquiesced in the overthrow of the government if the predominantly Indian NFP had won the 1982 general elections is, of course, a matter of conjecture. The US interventions, in Guatemala (1954); British Guiana (Guyana) (1962-64); the Dominican Republic (1965); Chile (1973); and Grenada (1983) were all mounted in order to stamp out the 'communist threat'. As already noted, the 'Koya Letter' apparently committed the NFP to allowing the USSR to open an embassy and scientific bases in Fiji if it won the election and formed a government; also, Ratu Mara alleged that the NFP received $1 million from the USSR to oust him from power. K.L. Holsti, in outlining the contemporary conditions that encourage intervention, argues that 'the greater the ethnic, religious, economic, or ideological conflicts within a society, the greater the probability that an external government will intervene to serve its own interests'.[28]

In 1982, the US, Australia and Fiji all saw the USSR as a threat to democracy and security in the region. Without subscribing to the conspiracy theory, certain factors do at least indicate that this viewpoint should be seriously considered. The contents of the 'Koya Letter', if we are to believe Ratu Mara's assertion of its authenticity, posed a serious threat to the pro-US government of Fiji and the US's most powerful ally in the region—Australia.

Would the US and Australia have maintained a neutral position and allowed the NFP government to 'go communist'? The NFP's failure to win the election means that we shall never know, but was the election then free and fair?

Notes

1. See R.A. Derrick, 1950, Vol. 1, pp. 95-135.
2. Quoted in Sir Alan Burns, 1963, pp. 76-77.
3. Text of speech by Ronald Reagan, 27 November 1984 (Suva: US Embassy, 1985).
4. Caroline Yacoe, in *Pacific Magazine*, May/June 1984.
5. John Dorrance, June 1980, pp 33-34.
6. The Soviets, however, refute the claim. As the Third Secretary at the Soviet Embassy in Canberra, Vladimir Valkov, put it: 'We fish for tuna in the Atlantic and also in the Indian Ocean, but the South Pacific is the richest region for tuna. That's why we want to fish here also. We are here to fish. It is a straight commercial proposition.' (*Pacific Islands Monthly*, August 1986, p. 20).
7. Dorrance, June 1980.
8. *Fiji Sun*, 9 November 1982, p. 1.
9. Speech of Ronald Reagan, 27 November 1984.
10. Ibid.
11. Interview with Ratu Epeli Nailatikau, 30 April 1985.
12. *Fiji Times*, 22 June 1983, p. 10.
13. Quoted in R.S. Milne, 1981, p. 117.
14. *Fiji Sun*, 8 July 1982, p. 12.
15. Source: The Report of the International Team of Observers at the Elections in Guyana, December 1980.
16. *Fiji Sun*, 7 June 1982.
17. Ibid., 8 July 1982.
18. Jeffrey Race, 1972, Preface.
19. Personal communication with Jeffrey Race, 14 December 1985.
20. *New York Times*, 25, 26, 27 December 1977.
21. *Melbourne Age*, 19 January 1978.
22. Quoted in Parliament of Fiji, *Report of the Royal Commission of Inquiry into the 1982 General Elections*, Parliamentary Paper No. 74 of 1983 (*The White Report*) p. 66.
23. *Fiji Sun*, 25 June 1987, p. 7.
24. See Paul Kelly, 1983, pp. 31-32.
25. *Fiji Sun*, 8 November 1980.
26. Ibid., 23 July 1983.
27. *Islands Business* (Fiji), December 1983.
28. K.L. Holsti, pp. 275 and 292.

CHAPTER ELEVEN

RACIAL POLITICS IN TURBULENCE

Blood will flow whether you like it or not. I can still start it. Any race which does not bear along with Fijians can pack and go home.

A Fijian senator, 1982

The NFP should be careful with what they say, bearing in mind that Fiji's not exempted from what is happening in other countries such as Lebanon, Uganda, South Africa.

Do Indians want another South Africa, with its policy of segregation here?

Letters to the Editor, from Fijians, *Fiji Sun*, 1982

The whole Indian community in Fiji was savagely criticized for the actions of some of its political leaders, who were branded as disloyal and power hungry. Some Fijian leaders considered that Indians' attitude, behaviour and political loyalty had reached a nadir; radical Fijians publicly encouraged racial confrontation. Furthermore, the Great Council of Chiefs evolved its own strategy for maintaining future political control. In short, it was time for realistic political stock-taking. The Indians reacted with disbelief; there was a sense of injured pride, in that having contributed so much to Fiji's development they were still seen as transient visitors whose aspirations could never be incorporated into the political system. The well-orchestrated condemnations also signified that the Alliance had regained its lost paradise of power. The FNP had lost its appeal, but the resurgence of new Fijian nationalism created a historic phase in Fiji's political development that could be described as the era of the 'politics of survival'.

Shortly after the 1982 election results became official, some Indian leaders claimed that their political supporters, especially Indian voters, were being intimidated for failing to support the Alliance. These claims gained credence when one prominent Alliance supporter, trade unionist Navitalai Raqona, called for Indians to be evicted from native land in the western township of Ba because they had failed to vote for the Alliance Party. Party supporters claimed that the Indian tenants had deceived them by going through the Alliance's voting booths but voting for the Coalition candidates.

The Alliance's apparent reluctance to dissociate itself from Raqona's call inevitably prompted a reaction from the Opposition. The newly elected NFP's Indian national member for the area, Sir Vijay Singh, characterized it as politics of intimidation. The stoning of an Indian home in a nearby Ba area was also interpreted as another example of political bullying. Sir Vijay called upon all right-thinking people of all political parties to make it clear that intimidation and lawlessness had no place in Fiji. For the Alliance, however, one government minister, Militoni Leweniqila, claimed that Indian voters were frightened into believing their future in Fiji would be jeopardized unless they united and elected an Indian prime minister. He said the perpetrators of such actions were doing to Indians what the FNP leader Butadroka was doing to the Fijians. He also disclosed that many Fijians were disillusioned and saw their sacrifice for a multiracial existence wasted, a statement which dramatically exemplified the problem of communalism in Fiji. He warned that there were signs that there could be problems in the next decade unless people were careful and considerate. 'I think it has been fully appreciated by the majority of the people in this country that once goodwill and trust is shaken and shattered it would indeed be very difficult to restore', the said. Leweniqila also reiterated the observations of the newly appointed Minister of State without Portfolio and former NFP parliamentarian, Apisai Tora, that peace should not be taken for granted. He said further that the Fijian voters in his constituency had indicated to him that they would 'retreat, regroup and consider' the position, particularly their attitude toward other races because of events in the 1982 election; he also reminded other races of the ability of the Fijian landowners to deny them the 'small amenities' which they had enjoyed in the past.[1]

Ratu Mara told an Australian audience after his election victory that although the NFP/WUF Coalition campaigned publicly on the slogan, 'it is time for a change', in private, canvassing such change was translated into 'this is your chance to have an Indian prime minister'. Ratu Mara also charged that the Coalition had misled the Indian voters when they asked why he had walked away from the ABC 'Four Corners' interview. He alleged that Coalition members told a group of illiterate Indian farmers that he had refused to answer questions about maintaining Indian rights in Fiji.[2]

It has already been noted in Chapter 3 that Ratu Mara's offer of a government of national unity was partly influenced by Zimbabwe's Prime Minister Robert Mugabe's statesmanlike solution in his country. But the ensuing Fijian reaction toward the Indians had all the features of Mugabe's reaction to the role of Zimbabwe's white voters in the 1985 general elections: 'We showed them love, they showed us hatred; we forgave them, they thought we were stupid; we regarded them as friends, but they were wicked witches.'[3] Some Fijians thought along similar lines; as we have seen, trade unionist Gavoka had likened Indians to dogs. But on the floors of the Senate and Parliament some leading Fijian senators and parliamentarians warned that interracial tension in the country was reaching danger point. Their speeches epitomized the bitter racial tension that had become the dominant feature of life throughout Fiji. The Indians and their leaders were the main topic of debate; they had to be reminded of their rightful place in society.

The 'Four Corners' cannibal quote was again called into service in this upsurge of racialism. The NFP convert of old, Tora, warned that racial tension and political instability would be the order of the day unless the NFP changed its provocative political stance, and that it should realize the foolishness of the path it had pursued in recent months and apologize to the Fijian people. Tora reiterated that tradition, culture, ancestral beliefs and systems that had served Fiji so well should be above politicking.

Tempers flared when Tora claimed that the action of the NFP in the bitterly fought campaign was a show of arrogance (*viavialevu*) and insults heaped on the Fijian chiefs could only be made by people belonging to the lowest caste (*kaisi bokola botoboto*). An NFP parliamentarian, Jai Raj Singh, protested against the Fijian terms used by Tora, but the Alliance Speaker Tomasi Vakatora (who earlier had defeated the FNP leader Butadroka in his Rewa constituency) overruled the objection saying the words had been used in the Fijian Parliament.

Tora's passionate outburst, however, came as no surprise to many political observers who had closely followed his political career. Five years before he had been the most anti-traditionalist Fijian in the NFP camp. Reflecting on the 1977 constitutional crisis, he had told a political gathering in September of the same year that the former Governor-General, Ratu George Cakobau, had set a dangerous precedent by reappointing Ratu Mara as Prime Minister. Within 10 years, he said, people would be convinced the action was wrong, and would question the validity of having a governor-general instead of simply a prime minister.

He had also told another political rally in September 1977 that the Fijian chiefs were out to 'threaten' Indians by indirectly telling people not to vote for the then Leader of the NFP, Koya. 'Do not subjugate the future of Fiji in the hands of the power-hungry Ratu Sir Kamisese Mara. And whatever provocation people are under we do not want any violence in this election', Tora added. In 1977 too he branded his electoral opponent, Raqona, as one of Fiji's most irresponsible trade unionists. Tora had also hit out at the chiefly system in Fiji and said many Fijians were getting 'fed up' with the 'archaic' system, and that Fijian chiefs were using their chiefly status to gain and keep power.[4]

But in 1982 Tora was speakinig a different political language. He was directing his criticisms against his old colleagues and foes, especially the NFP Flower faction. It may be recalled that Tora lost his seat on an NFP Dove ticket in the September 1977 elections, and since then had continued to grind a political axe against Reddy who had defeated Koya—the shortlived leader of the Dove faction of the NFP. The disastrous failure of the Dove faction had largely forced Tora to make peace with his arch rivals in the Alliance camp, an action seen by many as political opportunism. Therefore in 1982 it was perhaps hardly surprising to witness Tora demanding an unqualified apology from the NFP for insulting his former political opponents in the Alliance, and especially the Fijian chiefs whom he had once considered to be the bane of Fiji politics.

The NFP, regarding Tora as someone notable for making strong statements, remained united, with the exception of Vijaya Parmanandam, who earlier had rebelled against the party and, as we have noted, had accepted the Deputy Speakership of the House of Representatives. He then accepted all the accusations levelled at the NFP by Ratu Mara and his Alliance colleagues.

But the most vicious attack on the Indian leaders was made in the Senate where one Fijian senator, Inoke Tabua, who in 1976 had suggested that the Fiji Indians should be deported to relieve the 'population pressure', stoutly defended Ratu Mara, his paramount chief. He warned: 'I want to make it clear in this House that whoever hates my chief, I hate him too. I do not want to make enemies but to a 'kai Lau' like me, if someone is against my chief he is also against me and my family right to the grave.'[5] He also claimed that he was assured by the Fijians in rural areas that they were ready 'to fight for the leadership of our country'.

Tabua refused to isolate politics from chieftaincy. Understandably, as Ratu Mara himself had told the Royal Commission that his evidence should be considered and treated in the light of his three main roles in Fiji.

> On the one hand I live, think and act as an ordinary citizen of this state and also as a chief in the Fijian traditional social system. I am also a politician and leader of the Alliance Party, which is closely interested in these proceedings. And, lastly, I am Prime Minister of this state and leader of its government.[6]

It was these three roles that dominated the sentiments and minds of Fijians when it came to passing judgement on the actions of Indian leaders during the general election. They invoked their traditional ties with their chiefs to condemn the Indian leaders.

Another Fijian senator, Ratu Tevita Vakalalabure, while calling on the Indian High Commission in Fiji to 'pack and go' (over the rouble connection), warned that unless Indians united with Fijians and if what happened in the 1982 general elections was repeated at the next, probably 1987, election, 'Blood will flow, whether you like it or not. I can still start it. It touched me, and also touched my culture, tradition and my people. We have carried this burden for too long.'[7]

The Ra Provincial Council and the Great Council of Chiefs, through two resolutions, tried to reassure the Fijian people of their determination that Fijians should, and always would, rule Fiji.

The first tentative step was taken during a meeting of the Ra Provincial Council which resolved that the offices of governor-general and prime minister must be reserved for Fijians and that this should be the subject of constitutional changes, a demand voiced by the FNP. The Council also proposed that the composition of the House of Representative should be two-thirds Fijians and one-third all other races. The Council also re-solved that the two resolutions be forwarded for inclusion on the agenda of the Great Council of Chiefs meeting scheduled for November 1982. Council members were of the opinion that the issues should be discussed at the Bau meeting, when the chiefs from the various traditional Fijian confederacies discussed issues of Fijian interests.

Both resolutions were condemned by the WUF and the NFP. The WUF expressed surprise that some Fijians still felt so strongly about the last general election and dismissed as totally unfounded the allegations that the Fijians and their traditional systems had thereby been insulted. WUF also considered that there was nothing derogatory in the 'Four Corners' programme. While linking the programme with the Alliance's involvement with the Carroll team, WUF's general-secretary said, 'Cannibalism was part of life in Fiji in the early days and we Fijians are descendants of cannibals. What is wrong with that? Only powerful chiefs in those days enjoyed on *bokolas*. I cannot find why some Fijians are annoyed about the Four Corners programme.'[8]

The country's press also entered the debate. Commenting on the resolutions, a *Fiji Sun* editorial called for its rejection as well as a firm statement from the Alliance government, and put the issue in a historical perspective:

> During the election campaign we noted that Mr Sakeasi Butadroka's campaign was rather a sad attempt to turn back the clock of history. Now the Ra Provincial Council is echoing similar views, but with extending differences. Inherent in Mr Butadroka's theme is the conviction that the indigenous Fijian people must retain control over not only their destiny but also that of the other fellow travellers who inhabit these islands, whether born here as citizens or not. This is an understandable view but one that must be rejected in the interests of the future as it belongs in the past.
>
> This underlying fear of loss of control comes through again in the resolution of the Ra Council, but it is based on wrong assumptions. This is evidenced by the Government's commitment to the democratic process and the Prime Minister's view that Fiji is being steered along the path of Western-style government.
>
> The sticking point is the question of the place and role of the chiefly system, now and in the future. It is not possible for the two systems to operate in tandem successfully at national level. At the same time it would be hard to accept that any responsible politician would advocate anything less than the total preservation of the Fijian culture, but equally the culture of the Indian part of the population needs nurturing and the impact on Fiji from the various other races is a matter of importance. The time is right for some firm statements from the Government on its feelings on these matters to allay unnecessary fears.[9]

The FNP hailed the resolutions as falling in line with their own demands for exclusive political rights for the Fijians. A letter to the *Fiji Sun* from a Fijian writer, saying, 'We Fijians also want changes in the country, as we are fed up with a lot of talk which insults us due to derogatory remarks uttered by non-Fijians', and that, 'laws made by men can also be changed by men. We only recognise the law made by God which no one can change',[10] expressed the general feelings of Fijians on the issue.

The Great Council of Chiefs moved to endorse the two resolutions thus presenting itself in the eyes of the Indian community as the political champion and promoter of Fijian nationalism, as preached by the FNP. The proposed sanction of Fijian political domination by further constitutional changes served only to increase hostility between Indians and Fijians.

The resolutions were finally passed despite a lukewarm reception from Ratu Mara and the then Deputy Prime Minister, Ratu Penaia, who pointed out that to change the Fiji Constitution required the consent of a two-thirds majority in both Houses.

The role of Ratu Mara, who abstained from voting, did nothing to allay Indian fears. As an NFP/WUF Coalition statement later charged: 'It should be apparent even to a political novice that the whole exercise was carefully stage-managed to intimidate non-Fijians, especially Indians and the Fijian supporters of the NFP-WUF Coalition.'[11] The Coalition also expressed surprise that Ratu Mara had abstained from voting rather than opposing the two resolutions.

It was during the debate on the resolution that trade unionist Gavoka had linkened Indians to dogs; and Mrs. Narayan, branding the Bau resolution as racist, went on to state:

> To liken Indians to dogs . . . is a grave and unwarranted provocation to the entire Indian community. It is now obvious that those indulging in the abuse of Indians are not reacting to any so-called insults . . . [but] because the NFP/WUF Coalition dared to challenge for power in the last general election and came within a whisker of wresting it from the Alliance.

Mrs Narayan further observed:

> It is indeed curious that the controversial motion came up while the Prime Minister claims that the worst insults he received were from Fijians themselves, why the focus of attack and resolution adopted by the Great Council of Chiefs have been designed to rob of the few rights they (Indians) have left to live in the country of their birth.[12]

Clearly, the statement continued, racial policies espoused by the FNP leader, the commoner Butadroka, had found greater favour with the chiefs than had the so-called multiracial policies of the paramount chiefs leading the Alliance Party. In sum, the resolutions only enhanced the prospect of a race war, prompting the *Fiji Sun* to beg to the chiefs, 'Let us not march backwards', and write in its editorial:

The Great Council of Chiefs has passed an incredible resolution calling for a constitutional change which, if it occurred, would change Fiji
overnight from a democracy to an autocracy, or even a dictatorship. It
is a horrendous thought. . . . For many years Fiji has been held up to
the world as a multi-racial society which works—where two races with
widely disparate religions, culture and ethnic backgrounds have lived
and worked harmoniously for a hundred years. Now, with a stroke of
a pen, a group of our most respected elders and statesmen are prepared to throw all that away and march backwards into the 19th
Century and beyond.[13]

The same editorial also called on the elected politicians to set their
minds to governing in the interests of all citizens, regardless of race, religion, and colour, and asked the Great Council of Chiefs to regather and
concentrate its accumulated wisdom on the traditional guidance of the
Fijian people.

Meanwhile, some tried to steer a middle course in the face of imminent racial strife. Kolinio Qiqiwaqa, a backbencher, called for revision of
the Constitution to ensure long-term peace and stability, claiming that it
may have outlived its usefulness. In his view it was leading to a racially
divided and segmented society and thus to dictatorship and instability,
and, therefore, was a real threat to peace. Regarding comments that Britain would never have allowed a constitution biased towards Fijians,
Qiqiwaqa said that in fact Britain was only too glad to grant independence at the stage because it was allegedly aware that Fijian nationalism
would emerge at some stage. The Fiji Constitution, in his opinion, was a
recipe for a caretaker government and a continuation of the colonial
government. A government minister said that the Indian population's
presence in Fiji was no fault of their own, and reminded the radicals of
the horrors of Amin's regime.

The dabate, on the whole, did more than demoralize the Indians, it
shattered assumptions about the role and character of the chiefs, a group
of revered elders whom Robert Norton views as 'boundary keepers'[14] or
mediators in relations with other ethnic groups in Fiji. But their racial
pronouncements in 1982 revealed their desire to preserve and promote
the traditional dynasty.

Thus the future of race relations and parliamentary democracy depended on the findings of the Royal Commission of Inquiry into the
1982 general elections. The Commission, which sat for 76 days, opened
for a preliminary hearing on 14 December 1982. The general issue before the Royal Commission was, according to the NFP counsel Bhupendra Patel, 'the preservation of democracy in its true sense and the integrity of Parliament'. As the principal political actors were put to the test,
however, two questions stood out: Was the election free and fair? Who
was telling the truth? As already noted Ratu Mara's concern when announcing the Royal Commission was 'the circumstances under which

certain Australian journalists tried to influence the results of the elections in Fiji'. The NFP leader Reddy said that his reason for pressing for a judicial inquiry 'was the need to gauge the depth of foreign influence, to check if such influence was calculated to undermine the electoral process'.

The Commission's terms of reference were to *inquire* into the truth of and the circumstances surrounding the various allegations and complaints relating to and made during or after the period of campaigning for the 1982 Fiji elections, *and to determine* the nature and extent of any infringement of any principles:

1. . . . of fundamental freedoms and protection safeguarded and guaranteed under the Constitution of Fiji;
2. . . . which underlie the foundation of freedom, justice and peace and the inherent dignity and equality of all races in Fiji;
3. . . . which safeguard the existence and maintenance of the democratic process in Fiji with particular reference to the integrity of the elections, committed by any person or body within or outside Fiji.

Efforts were also made to obtain overseas witnesses; to this end, Rabone (counsel assisting the Commission) approached: the Chairman of the Board of Governors of the ABC; John Fairfax and Sons, publishers of *The National Times*; Clive Speed; Rosemarie Gillespie; Alan Carroll; Geoffrey   Allen; the Ambassador of the Union of Soviet Socialist Republics (Canberra); Mr and Mrs Soonu Kochar; Joan Coxsedge; Dr Jeffrey Race. The Kochars, Race, Allen and the USSR embassy in Canberra declined to attend; Speed, Carroll, and Wilkinson of the *National Times*, sent signed affidavits through their solicitors stating their roles in the Carroll saga; the ABC indicated that Mannings, Downs and others would not be available.

The only positive and enthusiastic response came from Gillespie, who agreed to testify before the Royal Commission provided she was granted immunity from prosecution; a legal counsel was made available to represent her at the inquiry. On 20 July 1983 she took to the witness box as the only foreign witness and for the next seven days kept everyone on tenterhooks by her history of the involvement of the Carroll team and herself in the political affairs of Fiji. The office of the Director of Public Prosecutions in Fiji also granted immunity for anything she may have done while previously in Fiji. The broad issues before the Royal Commission were as follows:

Group 1:
1. Whether the Alliance commissioned the Carroll Report.
2. Whether some or all of the recommendations contained in the Carroll Report were implemented deliberately or otherwise by the Alliance Party.
3. Whether Clive Speed was appointed on Carroll's recommenda-

tion; and was appointed to, and did in fact assist in the Alliance's election campaign; and had his salary paid (directly or indirectly) by the Australian government.

Group 2:

4. Whether the ABC people involved in producing the 'Four Corners' television programme (and the persons involved in writing the *National Times* article) collaborated with the National Federation Party both in the content of, and the time of release of, that programme.

5. Whether Miss Rosemarie Gillespie at first assisted the Alliance (through Carroll and also directly), but later took documents also from Carroll and obtained the 'Red File' and supplied them to ABC television, the *National Times*, and the National Federation Party.

Group 3:

6. Whether the NFP (or the NFP/WUF Coalition) received 'as much as $A1,000,000' from the Soviet Union to assist it during its election campaign.

7. Whether Mr Hari Kochar, husband of the former Indian High Commissioner to Fiji, was an intermediary between the NFP and the Soviet Union.

8. Whether whilst Mrs Kochar was in Fiji as High Commissioner for India, she actively supported the NFP.

Miscellaneous allegations

'That the Alliance Party used financial channels of a statutory body for their support and benefit in preparing strategy to fight the general elections.'

'That NFP/WUF candidates were refused permission to go and hold public meetings at villages in the Yasawas.'

There was no disagreement between the parties that the bitter political confrontation which arose during the 1982 election campaign and its aftermath was a matter of serious concern to the people of Fiji. The dispute between the parties was as to the cause and its implications. The general statements of both the NFP counsel, Patel, and the Alliance counsel, Ramanlal Kapadia, as Judge White pointed out, revealed the broad clash on the issues before the Royal Commission.

In his general submissions on all the issues before the Royal Commission, Patel alleged that it was a matter of serious concern that the peace and harmony so critical to the development and prosperity of the country, depending on a fair balance between the conflicting political, social and economic aspirations and interests of the various groups, had been deliberately upset by the introduction of concepts and tactics calculated to heighten interracial doubts and suspicions. Further, that it was a matter of serious concern that tactics were introduced to set groups against groups by playing on religious or cultural prejudices, so that fear and prejudice were accepted as legitimate tools in the pursuit of votes. In a broader context:

> What is at issue is a way of life: expressed in the faith that it is the right of the people to choose their government. Elections to be meaningful have to be honest and fair. A just election connotes not only a choice for the voter between parties and candidates but also a right to make a free choice without any fear or prejudice. A fair election also connotes the right of all competing parties and persons to participate as equals according to the one and the same rules of the game.[15]

Similarly, the Alliance, through Kapadia, contended that it was unthinkable that the party would introduce strategies and tactics directly in conflict with the principles of multiracial harmony and the Constitution itself. In his primary submission Kapadia reiterated the Alliance defence that the party had implemented none of the recommendations in the Carroll Report; that at no stage did the Alliance gain its inspiration from the Carroll recommendations in deciding its policy for the general elections; and that neither the Carroll Report nor any member of the Carroll team had any connection with the devising of the Alliance's election policy.

As Judge White pointed out, the Royal Commission had a situation where each political party claimed that its view of the facts was correct, confronted one another on that basis and set out to justify their actions accordingly. The task for the Commission was to judge whether or not there were infringements of the principles the Commission was called to consider. As we have seen, in his findings, released of 22 November 1983, Sir John White surprisingly absolved all participants of any deliberate malpractices. He also found that no infringement of the stated principles, with particular reference to the integrity of elections in Fiji, by any person or body, within or outside, had been established. Gillespie's disclosures were not intended to, and did not, infringe the principles of democracy or the integrity of elections in Fiji. Judge White further noted that Race and other members of the Carroll team had played no part in the publications of their confidential report, but, he stressed, there was no doubt that there 'has been a strong and very natural reaction against Dr Race as the author of the wholly repugnant recommendations and proposed strategies', although Race did no more than contribute to a confidential report; he also found that it was not established that the strategies were either adopted or implemented. Overall, in his view,

> A valuable outcome of the universal abhorrence shown for such proposals, and the examination of the policies of the political parties, and the statements of the political leaders in Fiji in evidence, will be recognised as a sign of the integrity and the political maturity and stability of this country.[16]

Patel was more specific. In his submission he invited Judge White to recommend to the Governor-General that a code of conduct for candidates and political parties, with appropriate penalties, including automatic disqualifications, be enacted for use in future general and by-elections. Judge White did not make such recommendations but concluded his report on an optimistic note. While endorsing the necessity of the inquiry he said there was no reason why confidence should not be restored.

Reactions to the Commission's Report varied. Reddy said he was 'reasonably satisfied' since the NFP was cleared over its alleged links with the USSR. The Alliance reserved its opinion on the grounds that the report had just been tabled in Parliament. The only voice of dissent was Gillespie's, who described the report as a whitewash, claiming that it was as if the whole Carroll affair had been put through the laundry so that everybody came out looking clean, with the exception of Cabinet Secretary Dr Lasaqa, 'who appears to have been made the scapegoat in the whole affair'. She said that understandably Judge White wished to handle the issues with kid gloves in view of the political implications of firm findings, citing White's finding with regard to the role of the former media consultant to the Alliance government, Speed. She argued that if Speed assisted the Carroll team and the Alliance had commissioned the team, it would follow that Speed was helping the Alliance. 'So, the judge, like a matador, danced around the issues rather than grappled with thorny issues', she said.

The mood of the electorate and the country's future could be best illustrated by press comments: 'Inquiry report does not end debate', said the *Fiji Sun* and while the inquiry still left many contentious issues unanswered, hoped that people would 'let bygones be bygones';[17] and calling for positive stock-taking, the *Fiji Times* headline said, 'Now let's look ahead'.[18]

Political fighting continued both inside and outside Parliament. Both Ratu Mara and Reddy, instead of defusing racial polarization, accelerated its progress. The war of words during and after the election campaign drove them deeper into two extreme camps. The aftermath dashed any hopes of reconciliation and finally forced Reddy from the centre of the country's political stage. The first signs of a widening rift between the two leaders emerged following the appointment of Vakatora as the Speaker of the House of Representatives. The NFP immediately claimed that Ratu Mara had not consulted Reddy as the established parliamentary convention had required of him.

Vakatora had accepted a position that carries both great dignity and high authority. An event on 15 December 1983 provided him with the opportunity to live up to that tradition when Reddy refused to stand when objecting to a ruling made by Vakatora against his one-time adversary, Koya. An angry clash between the two followed and Vakatora called the Sergeant-at-Arms to eject Reddy from the House for the day. On 15 April 1984, however, Reddy announced his resignation both as party leader and as a Member of Parliament, and told the NFP to elect a new leader by 15 May, the date on which despite pleas, both from the Party and its supporters, he officially relinquished both positions.

Reddy's departure almost tore the NFP apart, as the two diehard rivals, Mrs Narayan and Koya, duelled for party leadership. Although Koya emerged victorious, the crown of NFP leadership, which had lost most of its glitter by now, never again sat comfortably on his head; in fact, as we shall see in the next chapter, he lost it for all time. The Alliance, and especially the chiefs in the party, tried to maintain the facade of parliamentary democracy minus its democratic contents. As the Great Council of Chiefs struggled to make the Indians politically impotent through 'conditional democracy', there was polarization along racial as well as class lines.

In 1985 the country saw the birth of yet another political party—the Fiji Labour Party—led by a group of trade unionists promising to establish a new political order. By the end of 1986 the nation had become both economically and politically bankrupt under the Alliance government, forcing Ratu Mara to call an early election in April 1987. The road ahead seemed arduous—both frustrated urban Fijians, reeling from the impact of a blanket wage freeze, and Indians were determined to make the Alliance's political journey to power difficult.

In the 17-year history of its rule the Alliance leaders finally realized that the political kingdom was no longer a bed of roses but a crown of thorns. In the past they had employed every domestic tactic to cling to power. Perhaps, as a last bid for power, in the name of ethnicity, the law of force might be invoked by the Fijian dominated military, supported by the chiefs, to overturn democracy.

Notes

1. *Fiji Sun*, 26 August 1982, p. 6.
2. A text of Ratu Mara's speech to the Royal Prince Alfred Hospital Centenary Dinner, Sydney, Australia, 30 July 1983.
3. *Concord Weekly*, 11 July 1985.
4. *Fiji Times*, 12 September 1977.
5. *Fiji Sun*, 16 September 1982.
6. Ratu Mara's prepared statement to the Royal Commission of Inquiry into the 1982 General Elections (mimeo).
7. *Fiji Sun*, 16 September 1982.
8. Ibid., 23 August, 1982, p. 3.
9. Ibid., p. 2.
10. Ibid., 14 July 1982, p. 2.
11. Ibid., 6 November 1982, p. 1.
12. Ibid.
13. Ibid.
14. See Robert Norton in *Journal of Commonwealth and Comparative Politics*, November 1981, pp. 309-28.

15. Bhupendra Patel's submission (counsel of NFP) to the Royal Commission of Inquiry, 22 August 1983 (mimeo).
16. *The White Report*, p. 187.
17. *Fiji Sun*, 23 November 1983, p. 6.
18. *Fiji Times*, 23 November 1983, p. 6.

CHAPTER TWELVE

THE RISE AND FALL OF THE FIJI LABOUR PARTY

The Fijians have always viewed the Alliance as being the Fijian party. That base is being eroded. For the first time Fijians are being offered a list of credible Fijians standing against the Alliance. These Fijians can match the Alliance on its own front. They have comparable experience and know-how. For the first time there are Fijians who are willing to sacrifice their jobs and positions. Fijians will no longer elect people merely because they are chiefs.

> *Dr Tupeni Baba*, National Federation Party/Fiji Labour Party Coalition spokesman, January 1987.

In historical perspective, the formation of the FLP and the statements of its leaders saw the rebirth of the 'agitational politics' whose origins can be traced to militancy among the Indian labourers on the sugar plantations. The most notable were the strikes and riots of 1920, which the Australian historian K.L. Gillion recorded as 'of great importance in the history of Fiji: they threw the reality of the colonial system into sharp focus, and they had an important influence on later European, Fijian and Indian attitudes in Fiji, and on opinion in India.'[1] The strikes, in Ahmed Ali's words, 'heralded a new facet of Indians: their assertiveness and willingness to enter into confrontation with other groups in their effort to obtain what they considered equality of treatment in a land to which they had come as immigrants but where they were fast anchoring permanent roots'.[2] Their descendants have since continued the struggle and, with one notable exception, the strikes these days have assumed a multiracial rather than a racist dimension.

As was noted in the previous chapter, the FLP came into being after the Alliance government unilaterally imposed the wage freeze in November 1984.[3] The Alliance's main economic argument was that the country would save $36 million that otherwise would have been paid out in wage increases. The government's share of the savings could be made available for job-creating projects, helping the poor and the unemployed. During this period Fiji's economically active population was estimated to be 230,000, of which approximately 79,000 or 34.5 per cent were estimated to be in paid wage and salaried employment, and 132,000 or 57.4 per cent occupied in other forms of employment. The remaining 18,600 or 8.10 per cent were classified as unemployed.[4]

The trade unions in Fiji, which are the best organized in the South Pacific and for many years had been apolitical, condemned the government for not consulting them through the Tripartite Forum, set up to deal with such issues by discussion among the government, the trade unions and the employees. The machinery for further confrontation was now set in motion. The Fiji Trade Union Congress (FTUC), the largest organized workers' body, to which 37 unions, with a total membership of approximately 40,000 workers, are affiliated, began to explore the formation of a political party. Its national secretary, James Raman, a trade unionist of long standing and formerly a pro-Alliance man, said there was 'a real threat' that political power would be used in 'a brutal and unmitigated manner' to suppress the trade unions in Fiji. In a paper entitled 'Fiji Trade Unions and Party Politics' Raman said that, to avoid being 'victims of the arrogant use of political power', the movement must play an active role in political and community issues. The struggle of workers could not be divided from the political struggle in the community, and workers were fighting for the same goals as the community.

Comparisons were also made with the role of trade unions in the national politics of Britain, Australia and New Zealand. A Fijian lecturer in sociology at the USP in Fiji, Simione Durutalo, who later became a vice-president of the FLP and contested the elections as a Labour candidate, in his analysis on 'Social and Political Options for the Labour Movement in Fiji' blamed the British for introducing communal politics into Fiji and creating a situation of occupational specialization along communal lines. Durutalo, in terms of class struggle, condemned the Alliance and the NFP for perpetuating those divisions. He accused the NFP of outliving its usefulness, as far as labour was concerned, because it had never questioned the relevance of the existing social relations of production despite widespread poverty, unemployment and increased hardship among the people. He said this was to be expected in the light of the composition of Fiji's Parliament, whose members were either from the traditional chiefly landowning class, or were capitalists, settler descendants (local Europeans) and former opportunist union leaders. Durutalo also pointed out that given the absence of fundamental differences between the two major parties, it was not surprising that members could easily change party loyalty: the case of Apisai Tora and Vijaya Parmanandam were instructive.

He further maintained that the political nature of the crisis confronting the people of Fiji could not be discussed without a closer look at the state structure built up during the colonial period. He noted that in the phase of decolonization, power was transferred through virtually unchanged government institutions to largely hand-picked heirs, the new ruling group in Fiji. For example, laws were changed from Ordinances to Acts but their contents remained the same. The colonial parliament changed its name from Legislative Council to House of Representatives (with an appendix, the Senate) but its whole racial foundation and electoral system remained the same, as did the education and public health system, the Council of Chiefs, and the army and bureaucracy.

Durutalo recalled the remarks of Professor Ron Crocombe that many Fijians failed to realize that what they believe to be their ancient heritage is in fact a colonial legacy. He claimed that the British used the economic disparity between the Indo-Fijians and the Fijians to increase the Fijian ruling class dependence for protection on the colonial government. The creation of the 1944 Fijian Administration, the NLTB and the constitutional guarantees on Fijian matters were cited as examples.

It has been claimed elsewhere that the ruling Fijian class had greatly benefited from colonial education, as the Council of Chiefs demanded that Fijian commoners should not receive education in the English language. The result was that very few Fijians, mostly of chiefly rank, entered the civil service as junior members of the 'bureaucratic bourgeoisie'.[5]

Durutalo charged that the British manipulated local regional and ethnic differences to emphasize divisive rather than unifying national interests. Such divisions were then deposited in the independence constitution to assail the cohesion and survival of the new Fijian state from its inception. Ethnic differences, he maintained, and the use of the new Fijian chiefs, were the main instruments used by the colonialists to defuse and neutralize the 1959 Oil and Allied Workers' strike. In summary, Durutalo, himself a commoner, indirectly appealed to the underprivileged Fijians and Indians to unite and undermine the established political order. In his opinion this could be achieved 'if Fijian society produces the political will that is required to overcome the present impasse, and the labour movement, with the trade unions at the centre, is the only force which now has the potential to produce that political will to take us out of the present inertia'.

From this analysis emerge two inherently contradictory tendencies of exclusivism and accommodation among the conservative, nationalist and moderate Fijians. While the traditionalists were advocating the retention of the old established order, Durutalo was calling upon the disgruntled Fijians, especially the Fijian workers, to respond to the demands of practical politics, rather than surrender to the forces of conservatism.

In March 1985, the 7,300 strong Fiji Public Service Association (FPSA)—the main public service trade union—had changed its constitution by 2,914 votes to 326 so that it could be 'free to associate itself with any organization in pursuit of workers' rights'. Against this overall background the FLP was finally launched on 6 July 1985: the party's aim to establish itself as a political force, influencing the balance of power in the event that a coalition government was formed following the election of 1987; and eventually to replace the long established but shaky NFP as the main opposition to bring the Alliance government down in the future elections. Led by the former president of the FPSA, Dr Timoci Bavadra, the FLP promised to revolutionize Fiji politics. In 1981 Bavadra, a medical doctor and son of a village carpenter, had spoken strongly against the formation of a Labour Party because, as he explained later, 'I was Alliance at the beginning'.

In 1985 his political affiliation had changed, dictated partly by the economic crisis and the Alliance's failure to bring the different races together. While promising to promote 'the principles of democratic socialism', he stated that his party would seek to cut across the traditional, racially-arranged, voting system in a country where 'race is a fact of life'.

Others besides Bavadra at the heart of the 1987 breakthrough by the FLP—and its downfall—were: Mahendra Chaudhry (Indian), FPSA general secretary, FTUC assistant secretary, secretary of the National Farmers' Union (a cane growers' association), appointed Minister of Finance and Economic Planning in the new Bavadra Government in 1987; Krishna Datt (Indian), president of the Fiji Teachers' Union, general secretary of the FLP, former principal of Suva Grammer School, appointed Minister of Foreign Affairs and Civil Aviation in the Bavadra Government in 1987 Joeli Kalou (Fijian), Fijian Teachers' Association (FTA) general secretary, a vice-president of the FLP, appointed Minister for Labour and Immigration in the Bavadra Government in 1987; Dr Tupeni Baba (Fijian), a former registrar of the USP, a vice-president of the FTA, cheif NFP/Labour Coalition spokesman, appointed Minister of Education, Youth and Sport in 1987.

In January 1985 the FTUC seemed likely to close the country down with a general strike in protest against the wage freeze. Ratu Mara threatened to declare a state of emergency and call out the army and the police to run the country. Although the government won the standoff, this challenge by the FTUC provided a foretaste of its capacity to inflict substantial damage to the Alliance's hold on the country. Ratu Mara subsequently charged that the FPSA was 'politicising the Civil Service'. On 4 June 1986, in another dramatic action, interpreted by the FLP as purely political, the Alliance government withdrew recognition of the FTUC as the sole representative body of the trade unions and organized labour, on the grounds that it had aligned itself politically with the FLP.

Many Alliance politicians branded the FLP as 'leftist', claiming that they had abundant evidence to prove that it was a 'communist' front set up to disrupt the political and racial equilibrium. As in the 1982 general elections, the Alliance thus tried to whip up the spectre of a Soviet 'invasion' of Fiji through the FLP, should it win power. In making these allegations, the Alliance also hoped, as in 1982, to win the sympathy of its allies overseas, notably the Australian and New Zealand Labour governments. The FLP's constitution had drawn on its British, New Zealand and Australian counterparts. Bavadra had also earlier indicated that he planned to visit Canberra to discuss possible technical help in getting his party established from the Australian Labour Party.

The first signs of 'communist links' were raised by the Alliance in the Senate. Its acting party secretary and nominee in the Senate, Jone Banuve, while on 28 March 1985 speaking on a motion about the state of industrial unrest in Fiji, claimed to have evidence that Libya, Cuba, and the USSR were trying to destabilize the South Pacific. While expressing concern over the confrontations between New Zealand and the United States on a nuclear-free zone, and claiming that the dispute would open the Pacific Basin for other countries to come in, Banuve accused Libya of fomenting disturbances among the Kanak separatists in New Caledonia. He then claimed that according to evidence available to him 'some of our militant unionists [have] very close ties with people from these three militant countries'.[6] Banuve did not name the so-called militants but they were widely believed to be Chaudhry and Raman, the two most active unionists from Fiji in the Pacific Trade Union Forum (PDUF), a regional grouping of left/liberal trade unions. In May 1985 Raman had chaired the Forum's meeting in Auckland, New Zealand, at which Chaudhry also attended.

In August 1986 the right-wing Australian magazine *Bulletin* accused the PDUF of being anti-American and controlled by far-left unionists, saying that most of the unionists were affiliated with or sympathetic to the Soviet-backed WFTU. It was at the expense of the non-communist International Federation of Free Trade Unions (ICFTU). *Bulletin* also claimed that the Forum's anti-American approach did not accord with the espoused foreign policy of the Australian Prime Minister Bob Hawke's government.

Chaudhry, in reply to the article, said he disagreed, stating 'It depends on what position one takes. If you are conservative you might look at issues differently. As far as the congress (FTUC) is concerned we take an independent view. We are no puppets of any superpowers.' He asserted that the Forum was pro-Pacific but stressed that it wished to be dominated neither by the US nor the USSR.[7]

During the Forum meeting in Auckland the unionists had criticized the United States for trying to infiltrate their ranks in a bid to sabotage their growing anti-nuclear stance. In his address, Jim Knox, the President of the New Zealand Federation of Labour, told the Forum that the unionists were well aware of US attempts to infiltrate their ranks. 'No matter how much money the Americans pump into the Pacific that won't reduce support for anti-nuclear policies', he said. Knox said ICFTU's most recent meeting had ended with an indication of disquiet about anti-American moves by the unions in the Pacific.

The Forum had expressed concern following reports from Sydney that a Reagan administration backed organization, the National Endowment for Democracy (NED) and the US Agency for International Development (USAID) had spent $1 million funding conservative political activities in the South Pacific. In 1982 William Paupe, who had served in Vietnam from 1966 to 1975, and was later accused by Bavadra of funding anti-government demonstrations, came to Fiji as director of USAID's South Pacific Regional Office.

In 1984 the Asia-America Free Labor Institute (AAFLI), stepchild of the CIA and closely linked to USAID and NED, was set up in Suva to counter anti-American protests in the region. AAFLI's executive director, Morris Paladino, has been described by the former CIA officer Philip Agee as 'the principal CIA agent for control of the International American Regional Labor Organisation (ORBIT)'. ORBIT is the Latin American regional body of the ICFTU, and from 1961 to 1964, Paladino worked out of ORBIT's Mexico City office. It has been claimed elsewhere that Paladino, working closely with the Labor Committee for Pacific Affairs (LCPA), whose major objective is to undermine PDUF, moved into Fiji to counter the PDUF's growing anti-nuclear protests. Interestingly, AAFLI's move into Fiji coincided with ICFTU's decision to establish a branch of its Asian Regional Organization (ARO) in Fiji.

AAFLI, however, characteristically denied the allegations. In 1985 Vincent Suazo, its South Pacific regional director, who had worked with Paladino in Mexico, said the allegations were mere smears. He also discounted the theory that AAFLI was set up, at the invitation of the Alliance government, to stage a 'coup' against the unions in Fiji. But Paladino, in an unpublished interview with *National Times* journalist Marian Wilkinson, is reported to have said that 'the office in Suva was set up to counter the spread of the WFTU and the nuclear-freeze campaign'. Not surprisingly, therefore, when a resolution declaring the Pacific a nuclear-free zone was defeated at the PDUF's meeting in Auckland, critics blamed the CIA for masterminding the defeat. According to an article in the *Sydney Morning Herald* (based on papers secured under the US Freedom of Information Act) it was AAFLI's $1 million spending in the region that directly led to the resolution's defeat.

Yet the concerted campaign against the Soviets, Libyans and Cubans continued, with Australia and New Zealand leading the battle, with Pentagon and US State Department officials heightening the cold war fever against Soviet and Libyan activities in the region. Some influential US soldiers and diplomats, including US Secretary of State George Shultz, visited Fiji. While rapping New Zealand's knuckles over her anti-nuclear policy Shultz, during a brief stopover in 1986, praised Ratu Mara and his Alliance government for their decision to welcome US warships, and also warned of the dangers of Libyan intrusion into the South Pacific. The unspoken message to the anti-nuclear unionists, including the FLP front, the Fiji Anti-Nuclear Group (FANG) which opposes the presence, transit, dumping, testing and support of nuclear devices in the Pacific, was to abandon their allegedly Soviet-inspired plot.

These unqualified charges, however, failed to deter the FLP, whose leaders said the electors would be the final judge. The party's fortunes soared when it captured control of the Suva City Council, which in turn promised to declare Suva a nuclear-free city. In another bid the FLP's Chaudhry narrowly lost a by-election for a seat made vacant by the resignation of Sir Vijay Singh from the NFP and Parliament.

Defections of the many disgruntled supporters from the conflict-ridden NFP further strengthened the FLP's vision of its role in the country's national politics. The party, which had promised not to accept any NFP defectors, however, changed its stance by accepting Dr Satendra Nandan as its first Member of Parliament. Nandan had resigned from the NFP to demonstrate his displeasure over Koya's 'imperial style' of politics but remained in Parliament as an Independent MP; he was subsequently joined by three other NFP MPs.

Meanwhile, the NFP continued to be wracked by internal dissension. Its Youth Wing launched scathing attacks on Koya's leadership, and fielded a rival candidate during the by-election for the seat made vacant following Reddy's resignation from Parliament. The NFP, under Koya, continued to diminish in strength, morale and effectiveness. His re-shuffles of the shadow Cabinet, in which he unceremoniously dumped the deputy opposition leader, Mrs Narayan, one of the most consistently vocal critics of the Alliance for several years, and the only woman in Parliament, angered many party stalwarts. Mrs Narayan was replaced by a Fijian, Koresi Matatolu, as Koya's deputy. In May 1986 a group of NFP parliamentarians forced Koya, who had guided the party inter-mittently for over a quarter of a century, finally to relinquish the leadership to a moderate Indian lawyer Harish Sharma. 'It is time for a change', Koya said.

There were changes also in the Alliance camp. It even accepted some well-known former FNP politicians to prevent the rising tide of intellec-tual Fijian hardliners in the FLP. One notable example was Taniela Vei-tata, a trade unionist whom the Alliance deliberately selected to split the workers' vote. Veitata, known as 'Big Dan' to his friends, was general sec-retary of the Dockworkers' and Seamen's Union. In the 1970s he led the dockworkers in a number of strikes, that resulted in the jailing of several of them, including Veitata. In 1972 he formed the Liberal Party and un-successfully fought for a seat in Parliament. In 1977, he stood as a can-didate for the FNP but was again unsuccessful. The Alliance, however, retained Isimel Bose who featured prominently in the Carroll saga, as the party's 1987 election campaign director.

One of the greatest political shocks in pre-election horse trading was the defection, and the Alliance's acceptance into its fold of Mrs Nara-yan. Born in Lucknow, India, in 1932 and living in Fiji since 1955, Mrs Narayan said she was convinced that the Alliance would remain in power for years to come because 'it is the party that has stood the test of time'.

By the end of 1986, the Alliance leadership, unable to handle the threatening political situation, began to whip up Fijians' emotions on the theme that if Fijians were not united, power and land would slip out of their hands. Tradition was mixed with politics. For example, Ratu Mara, in his September 1986 address to a mini-convention of the Fijian Asso-ciation, called upon the Fijians to remain united in order to retain the nation's leadership. He told the meeting that despite being outnumbered by Indians, Fijians had political leadership; if they became divided this leadership would slip away from them.

He was immediately criticized for raising the race issue. Bavadra, as leader of the FLP, lodged a formal complaint to the Director of Public Prosecutions asking him to investigate whether Ratu Mara's remarks contravened the Public Order Act, under which the Nationalists' leader Butadroka was jailed for six months in 1977 for inciting racial hatred. The Alliance had greatly shifted to the right after the 1982 elections, and its overt racial statements encouraged many Indians to turn to the FLP with its multiracial philosophy.

The FLP, however, realized that in view of the external as well as internal pressures it needed to co-operate with the NFP rather than go it alone. But the NFP, troubled by the growing personal divisions within the more important branches of the party, had doubts about its own survival. Since both had singled out the Alliance as their principal opponent, the idea of a coalition began to gain foothold. In November the NFP/FLP Coalition was officially endorsed at a working committee meeting following secret talks. Reddy, who had previously negotiated the NFP-WUF Coalition in 1982, was once again instrumental in hammering out the deal. Bavadra was chosen as coalition leader, with the NFP leader Sharma as his deputy.

Faced with an unprecedented challenge from all quarters, Ratu Mara announced his decision to hold the April general elections; voters were to go to the polls six months before the election was due. Parliament was dissolved on 18 December in preparation for the most bitter and hotly contested election in which Bavadra, an indigenous Fijian, was leading a major opposition party against the traditional Alliance comprising ratus (chiefs) including Ratu Mara.

The electoral balance in Fiji became much more precarious and potentially interesting than at any time. Many political observers saw the NFP/FLP deal as a victory for coalition politics. But some diehard elements, spearheaded by an NFP parliamentarian, Shardha Nand, resolutely opposed the coalition. He warned Indians that if they were not careful they would suffer the same fate as Dr Cheddi Jagan and his Indian supporters in Guyana. The NFP dissidents were later joined by Koya, after the Coalition released the names of the prospective candidates. Both Koya and Nand's names were absent, along with the names of several veteran NFP politicians. The Labour leaders, who had an upper hand in the selection of candidates, allocated only three seats to former NFP parliamentarians before the House was dissolved, considering others as political liabilities. But the NFP was only a junior partner in the Coalition.

The NFP drop-outs consequently formed a breakaway group. Initially led by Koya, who declared that 'Indians were not for sale', and that 'civil servants should not indulge in politics', the group formed a coalition with Ratu Osea's WUF and threatened to field rival candidates. The NFP groups also filed a writ in the Suva Supreme Court for the custody of the NFP's electoral symbol, the tree. The Supervisor of Elections resolved the dispute by banning the symbol altogether. This was the second time that the tree symbol had been frozen, the first being in the 1977 September elections.

The NFP splinter group was issued the *diya* (earthen lamp), and the NFP/FLP Coalition candidates Labour's germinating coconut palm or *vara* symbol; the Alliance retained its wheel symbol. While waiting for the final nomination day—9 March—it clearly emerged that the races were split. The General Electors, who play a decisive if not divisive role, seemed to have shifted from the Alliance to the FLP. The Fijians, who form the Alliance's power base, were split. There was a relative shift on the part of urban Fijian voters to the FLP. The Nationalists also managed to regain some of their lost Fijian support in certain crucial marginal seats. The Indians spread their loyalties among four groups: the Coalition, NFP/WUF Coalition, Labour rebel groups and the Alliance.

When the nominations closed on 9 March, the Alliance and the NFP/FLP Coalition had filed nominations for all 52 seats in the House of Representatives. The splinter NFP/WUF group had 10 candidates, the FNP 6, and there was also 11 Independents, including a former Alliance parliamentarian, Hugh Thaggard, and Epeli Kacimaiwai, Fiji's High Commissioner to Australia, who had earlier resigned from his post only to learn later that the Alliance selection committee had turned down his application for candidacy. After the lapse of objection and withdrawal period the final line-up of candidates was 131.

Earlier, the Alliance had dropped 11 sitting parliamentarians from its line-up of 52 candidates; they included four Cabinet ministers, notably the Minister for Employment and Industrial Relations, Mohammed Ramzan, whose seat went to the newcomer and NFP defector, Mrs Narayan. The Alliance also brought in the former executive of the NLTB, the permanent secretary of the Fiji Public Service Commission, the chairman of the Fiji Electricity Authority (FEA), and a former Indian soldier and civil servant, Major Veer Vijay Singh. The surprise new inclusions were Veitata and Mahendra Sukhdeo, a former vice-president of the FLP.

An examination of the FLP/NFP candidates revealed that most of them were newcomers but with impressive academic or career records. The two big names in Indian politics—Koya and Reddy—did not appear in the final list of 131 candidates. Reddy declined to join the Labour Coalition platform and Koya had fallen out with the NFP splinter group. He later disclosed that he chose not to run for Parliament in order to preserve Indian unity. But it was the list of Fijian candidates that surprised the electorate. They included some of the leading names in trade unions and the academic world. One notable example was Dr Tupeni Baba, who resigned as head of the School of Humanities at the University of the South Pacific, to contest against the Deputy Fijian Prime Minister, Ratu David Toganivalu. Baba, who became the chief Coalition spokesman, explained the sudden shift in Fijian political thinking, especially among the intellectuals:

The Fijians have always viewed the Alliance as being the Fijian party. That base is being eroded. For the first time Fijians are being offered a list of credible Fijians standing against the Alliance. These Fijians can match the Alliance on its own front. They have comparable experience and know-how. For the first time there are Fijians who are willing to sacrifice their jobs and positions. Fijians will no longer elect people merely because they are chiefs. Now they are voting more intelligently. They will look at it in terms of what the people they supported before have done for themselves. The government has become very arrogant and alienated from the people. It is obvious from the people's point of view that political leaders are fairly well off. They are building houses, getting free land, linking up with big business. Corrupt practices have been alluded to, but very little account of this has been taken by the government.[8]

Meanwhile, the final electoral roll for the April general election showed 353,691 voters, 61,350 more than in the 1982 elections. There were 174,611 Indian voters, 169,398 Fijian voters, and 9,682 General Electors. The Indian voters' majority over Fijians had risen significantly from 683 in 1982 to 5,213 in 1987. Fijians and General Electors combined totalled 179,080, the Indians and General Electors combined totalled 184,293 voters.[9] There had also been significant changes in the marginal national seats, mainly in the Coalition's favour.

Four critical seats were identified: the Suva national Fijian seat, contested by Ratu David and Dr Baba; and the Suva national Indian seat, contested by Mrs Narayan and Navin Maharaj, a businessman and former Indian Alliance official who had also served as an Alliance mayor for the capital of Suva. Other critical seats were: the Suva eastern national Fijian/Indian seats, contested by the ex-chief executive of the NLTB, Ratu george Tu'uakitau Cokanauto (Alliance), and Coalition's Joeli Kalou, a former school teacher and trade unionist; and another contest was between Alliance's Major Veer Vijay Singh and Coalition's Fida Hussein, a respected leader of the Muslim community in that area.

The election became a straight two-way contest between the Alliance and the Coalition. When the campaign officially opened, the Alliance followed its previous style. While promising to maintain the status quo along with its 'share and care' slogan, it attacked the merger between the two parties and stated that Coalition members were from two opposed political philosophies, with the 'capitalism of the NFP married to the socialism of the FLP'.

As the campaign gained momentum, candidates of all parties found it expedient to make overtly racist appeals. The Nationalists, championing Fijian rights, reiterated their demands for constitutional changes; the NFP splinter group made use of the race issue to attract rural Indian voters, especially Indian cane farmers on whose backs they had ridden to power in the past.

But it was the Alliance candidates who shamelessly whipped up the racial issue, fanning fears that the Fijians could lose their land rights under an NFP/FLP Coalition government. While inciting communal antipathy, they claimed that a group of Fijians in the Coalition team, particularly USP intellectuals, were hatching a plot to undermine traditional Fijian leadership. Some leading Alliance candidates demonstrated the resurgence of Fijian nationalism in a bewildering variety of pronouncements. For example, Ratu David warned that the Fijian chiefs must remain a force for moderation, balance and fair play against such extremism. He said the chiefs were a 'bulwark' of security for all and custodians of Fijian identity, land and culture. Ratu David, himself a high chief, said to remove chiefs would 'pave way for instability'.[10]

As already pointed out, Ratu Mara also joined in the racially-oriented campaign. Declaring that 'I will not yield to the vaulting ambitions of a power-crazy gang of amateurs—none of whom has run anything—not even a bingo',[11] he charged that there was an FLP plot to destroy the chiefly system. Other Alliance campaigners ominously warned that 'without the Alliance in power, this country could turn into another Uganda where Indians were made to leave'.[12] The Alliance also maintained that a Labour government would dismiss the Fijian governor-general. Baba, speaking for the FLP, denied these charges. He accused Ratu Mara of attempting to reverse the tide of history in order to prevent the old Fijian order from dying, saying it was a desperate bid by Ratu Mara to cling to power, and added that political manipulation of people's emotions on the eve of a general election devalued democratic leadership. Also, that the baseless remarks were reminiscent of Ratu Mara's claim about the 'Koya Letter' in the 1982 election campaign.

Baba was supported by a former government backbencher and dropped Alliance candidate Kolonio Qiqiwaqa, who claimed that 'the traditional chiefly system has been cleverly manipulated to support a party [Alliance] that is neglecting the interests of the Fijian race; the ordinary *lewe ni vanua* [people of the land] are being fooled and so is the Fijian traditional establishment'.[13]

Earlier that year the Alliance government had announced that it was adopting the Cole Report which recommended that some aspects of the old Fijian Administration which were abolished in 1967 should be restored. The Report was prepared by researcher Rodney Cole and two others, the trio commissioned by the Pacific Islands Development Programme of the East-West Centre in Hawaii. The recommendations were designed 'to restore discipline in Fijian villages, where the breakdown of communal society meant that young Fijians no longer respected the authority of the elders and chiefs'. In 1982 Ratu Penaia, then Minister for Fijian Affairs and president of the Great Council of Chiefs, had expressed deep concern at the decline of chiefly influence and exhorted Fijians to preserve their traditional heritage under chiefly guidance. Inevitably, the Cole Report was endorsed by the annual meeting of the Great Council of Chiefs that took place on the island of Tavenui, the home of Ratu Penaia, who also opened the meeting.

The highlight of the meeting of the 76-member Great Council of Chiefs was its agreement to appoint Fijian magistrates to dry only Fijian offendrs charged with breaking Fijian customs. But a week after this meeting, a group of young men in Ratu Penaia's locality went on the rampage, smashing up the town as police, outnumbered, watched in vain. This action clearly signalled the young men's disapproval of the proposed system, particularly the chiefly power and Ratu Penaia, their paramount chief.

It was not surprising, therefore, that for the Alliance the FLP symbolized a Fijian commoners' challenge to the entrenched Fijian chiefly system. The NFP/FLP Coalition election strategies thus concentrated basically on economy, unemployment, inflation, education and land issues. It was committed to 'open and caring' government; it accused the Alliance of having become corrupt, wasteful and of doing little for the country's underprivileged and unemployed.

While accusing the Alliance of being a 'rich men's party', it said it would review the 12-year contract awarded to Australia's Channel Nine company to bring television to Fiji later in 1987. Earlier, and in an effort to win grassroot support, the FLP had publicly stated its intended policy to nationalize the country's Australian-owned gold mines and brewery. But to facilitate a smooth merger with the NFP—a party with a populist slogan but capitalist to the core—the FLP dropped many of its declared policies, including nationalization. Instead, in its manifesto the Coalition promised to set up a Native Lands and Resources Commission which, in full co-operation with the NLTB, would 'seek to maximise the use of land, sea, forests and mineral resources; provide and ensure greater security of tenture of all tenants; and secure fair returns and other national resources'.[14]

As explained in the previous chapters, land is a sacred issue. During election times it becomes an item of blackmail. It has always been an item of blackmail because, as Ramrakha correctly observed, 'the Indian is blackmailed because he does not have it' and 'the Fijian is blackmailed because the land is all the has—if he loses it, he will lose his culture, his traditions and indeed his identity'. In the 1987 election campaign the land issue therefore became political dynamite, its significance enhanced by the Alliance government's announcement that it was transforming about 4,800 hectares (12,000 acres) of Crown land into a native reserve, with a further 4,800 hectares to be transferred in the foreseeable future.

The FLP, on the other hand, asserted that reservation of this land would cause untold hardship to the Indian tenants, and questioned the need to reserve Crown land. The FLP viewed land as a national asset which should be made productive. Some party stalwarts expressed resentment at the economic role of the chiefs who received a major share, over four-fifths of revenue from renting communal Fijian land to Indians:

under a Labour government, they could lose this. The party also attacked the NLTB for inefficiency and promised to overhaul its operations. The position on land was well put by Bavadra when he outlined the FLP's manifesto:

> One of the key institutions that must be dealt with is the Native Land Trust Board. [It] must be democratised so that it comes to serve the interests of all Fijians and not just the privileged few and their business associates. In-addition, more efforts must be made to see to it that those whose land is being used get more for their money out of the NLTB. It is impossible at present to see how the level of administrative charges that are levied are justified on the basis of the few services performed. If the NLTB is to take the money that it does, then it must do more to those who it is supposed to be serving. It is also important that steps be taken to rationalise the benefits derived from land use in Fiji. The system must be rationalised so that all Fijians, not just a few, benefit more. In addition a great deal more must be done to enable the people of Fiji to increase the productivity of their land. More services and better infrastructure must be provided. This may be difficult, but ways must be found.[15]

The Alliance resorted to its old but depressingly familiar communal card, scaring Fijians that they could lose their land under a new government. Through press advertisements and political columns, dubbed by the local press as 'The Great Land Debate', it charged that the FLP was hell-bent on destroying the structure of the Fijian communal system by changing the land administration practices. Ratu Mara said the planned establishments of the Native Lands and Resources Commission could result in the Fijian landowners losing their land. He also charged that the FLP was trying to gain political mileage over the disclosure that some Crown land would be transferred to native reserve. Yet he himself, in a politically calculated move, announced that the Alliance government would soon set up an appeals tribunal to look after Fijian land disputes. Although the Great Council of Chiefs has eight out of 22 seats in the Senate, that is, more than one-third of the seats capable of blocking any constitutional changes without their consent on matters relating to land, Ratu Mara had skilfully frightened the Fijian voters. Thus Bavadra was forced to reply:

> The Alliance's so-called peace and stability rests on something insidious and treacherous—it rest on threat and fear. The tactics of the Alliance in the current election campaign mark a very sad chapter in the history of our country. There is absolutely nothing in the pronouncements of the Coalition—either written or in verbal form—which threatens land ownership in this country. And the advertisements in today's newspapers are [the] total and utter lies ... of desperate men clutching on to the last vestiges of power and privilege. The Coalition

respects and will defend the land rights of the *Taukei* as it also respects and defends all ownership of all our people.[16]

In addition, the Coalition listed crime and corruption, discrimination against women and secrecy in government as major targets of a Coalition government. It charged that big businessmen had laundered money to protect their interests. The FLP recalled the controversial release of a Suva businessman who had served only 37 days of a two-year jail term for fraud. The Coalition reminded the voters of the Auditor-General's report which detailed waste and mistakes in many government departments, including the Prime Minister Ratu Mara's own.

Externally, the Coalition promised to follow a strict non-aligned policy, ban US nuclear warships from Fijian ports, oppose nuclear weapons and waste dumping, refuse the Soviets permission to open an embassy in Fiji, and support the independence struggles in New Caledonia, French Polynesia and 'West Papua' (Irian Jaya).

The Coalition spokesman, Baba, told the voters that every time Fiji allowed nuclear-armed and powered ships into her ports it put the population in serious danger. He also asserted that the US refusal to sign the nuclear-free treaty (which included just about every condition the US wanted) revealed the insincerity of the Alliance's protestations that it supported a nuclear-free Pacific. Baba also criticized the Alliance for not adhering to its non-aligned policy and charged that since 1983 the Alliance Party had kept the country under the United States' defence umbrella.

In reply, some Alliance candidates falsely accused the Coalition of being a stooge of the Soviet Union. The former vice-president of the FLP, Sukhdeo, who before his defection to the Alliance had accused the government of being tied to the apron string of the US, on this occasion alleged that the Coalition did try to obtain Russian help. He named Krishna Datt, the general-secretary of the FLP and later the Foreign Minister in the Bavadra government, of being the contact between the two parties. Sukhdeo, like Dr Ali and others in the 1982 general elections, told a political rally: 'Let me admit it. There was an attempt made to get a contact with the Russians with the view to seeking help and aid for Fiji. An attempt was made to get some help for the Labour Party or the trade union movement.'[17]

He further alleged that he had accompanied Datt to East Berlin for a trade seminar and on their way back had visited Moscow. Sukhdeo, while claiming that the Eastern Bloc had paid their fares, thus warned the electorate: 'The FLP has two types of teeth. If you look at their manifesto they are going to follow a strict non-aligned policy. What is in the back of their mind when they say they will not allow the Russians here?'[18]

Meanwhile, others sought parallels elsewhere. A Coalition campaigner and senior USP lecturer, Dr William Sutherland, who later became Permanent Secretary to Prime Minister Bavadra, said South Africa had some relevance for the people of Fiji. 'Most of us have been victims of racism. I can't understand how ideas of racism are rationalised', he said. Sutherland accused the Alliance of trying to keep the Indians out of power by isolating them politically since 1972. But as far as the FLP was concerned, he noted that 'for the first time we have a representation of all major races. We have a group of educated informed Indians, Fijians and General Electors who have come together in this historical union of races.'[19]

In July 1986, the FLP's main arm, the FPSA, had also written to the Alliance government and to the South African Embassy in Australia condemning the detention of thousands of blacks and trade unionist leaders under the South African emergency laws. While expressing solidarity with the workers and people of South Africa and Namibia for the elimination of apartheid, and the release of the black nationalist leader Nelson Mandela, the FPSA asserted that it 'is in solidarity with thousands of brothers and sisters and even children who had sacrificed their lives in their fight for freedom, equality and social justice'.[20]

The Coalition seemed to have caught the people's imagination. Earlier it sought and had won the blessing of the paramount chief of Fiji and the former governor-general, Ratu Sir George Cakobau, to take its campaign to the Fijian villagers. The message to them was clear, as Bavadra had told one Fijian political gathering: 'There is a need to realise the difference between the traditional role and our democratic rights as citizens of this country.'[21]

He also called on the Alliance to stop employing abuse of Fijian tradition as a means of furthering its political ambitions. In a statement apparently directed at other Fijians caught in the traditional struggle, Bavadra made his position clear:

> I have great respect for both my great uncles the Tui Vuda and the Taukei Nakelo in so far as the traditional chiefly system is concerned. But I beg to differ from both of them as far as political belief and standing are concerned. . . . My loyalty to the Tui Vuda as chief of the Vanua is unshakable. But as far as my political affiliation is concerned I owe allegiance to my party. We belong to two different parties and we have different ideologies.[22]

In another surprising move the FLP, claiming that the Party stood ready to assist the common man and the underprivileged, disclosed that it was providing financial support in a legal battle between a group of Fijian villagers and the wife of Ratu Mara, Adi Lady Lala Mara, whom the group wanted dismissed as the sole governing director of Nakuruva-karua Ltd. The company manages the income received in rents from the owners of The Fijian, a resort hotel, and is supposed to distribute it to the owners of Yanuca Island where the resort is situated.

The owners of The Fijian, Fiji Resorts Ltd., pay basic rent of $20,000 a year to the company, plus two per cent of the resort's gross income above $1.8 million. The group insisted before the Supreme Court that they were unhappy with the way Adi Lala had been managing Nakuru-vakarua Ltd., and therefore wanted her dismissed.

The FLP also criticized the Alliance government's resource distribution policy, accusing Ratu Mara of diverting the country's wealth for the development of his island of Lau. The government sets aside $3.5 million each year to promote Fijian education; during the campaign, Ratu Isimeli Cokanasiga, the USP assistant registrar, asked why, in 1985 $169,278 worth of scholarships went to Lauans as against $19,278 for the people of Lomaiviti. Meanwhile, Bavadra also claimed that resources poured into Lakeba, Ratu Mara's home province in Lau, were derived from wealth produced elsewhere in the country, mainly the western division.

The anti-Lauan campaign demonstrated the historically deep hatred some Fijians hold against the Lauans who are descendants of Tongans. They settled in Fiji in the nineteenth century with their chief Ma'afu, a relative of the King of the neighbouring Polynesian island of Tonga. Ma'afu, who settled in Fiji in 1848, had gradually acquired authority over the eastern part of the Lau group and became a threat to the rule of King Cakobau in the central and western islands. He pioneered a modern system of government in Lau, but before the Cession, in which he played a leading part, came to terms with other chiefs. Intermarriages between Bauans, whose paramount chief now is the former governor-general, Ratu George Cakobau, and the Lauans brought them closer in the running of the country.

Furthermore, Ma'afu was the first Tui Lau, a title now held by Ratu Mara; and many radical Fijians assert that because of his family background, Ratu Mara does not have the right to champion Fijian rights and criticize the Indians' right to rule. It was not surprising, therefore, that Tora took pains to condemn the anti-Lauan campaign; he accused the FLP of dividing the Fijians in order to reduce their political influence in Fiji. The FLP, he said, was a political party whose main goal was to reduce the Fijian voice in their own land. Tora pointed out that the attack on the Lauans was part of that deliberate strategy. In particular, he stated: 'Now the development of Lau is criticised. Next it will be Lauans living outside Lau and their achievements that will be condemned. The ultimate goal will be to remove all Lauans back to Lau because these Lauans are obstacles to the ambitions of Dr Timoci Bavadra and the Labour Party.' Tora then charged that the FLP would take the Fijians back 200 years and leave them as divided, weak, and vulnerable to exploitation as they had been in 1798, not as they are in 1986. What the government has done for the western division, Tora said, was before the people to see.

The heated debate on the distribution of resources had reopened the long running battle between the eastern and western Fijians. While astutely defending the Alliance government, Tora seemed to have forgotten that Bavadra was merely repeating what he himself highlighted when he was part of the opposition. In 1963 Tora, who then unsuccessfully contested the western Fijian seat in the Legislative Council against his opponent Ratu Penaia Ganilau, an eastern chief, had charged that the easterners ignored the western people, telling his followers in the western township of Ba:

> You have been ruled by leaders from other areas who treated you with calculated contempt. Your division is the most important because from it comes the economic lifeblood of the colony. You deserve to be treated as first-class citizens. You must confess that deep inside you there was a longing to see the day when your kinsmen in western Fiji ... would rise to become leaders in their own domain and perhaps of the whole Group. The party offers your own kinsman who like you comes from the humble surroundings of a village, who knows what it is to be ignored by officials, to be discouraged by *Rokos* and chiefs and strait-jacketed by the system under which you and I live.[23]

A review of the campaign at this point shows that the different races, including the Fijians, had become increasingly polarized along racial, class, and regional lines. The nation, as Ratu Mara observed in his closing campaign speech, was at the crossroads of its history. While sensing that Fiji was perilously close to the abyss, Ratu Mara thus begged: 'If we take the wrong direction, we will finish up in blind alleys.... Remember where there be hatred, let us show love. Where there is injury, pardon. For we are one nation, one people, with one destiny regardless of race or creed.'[24] Whether real substance would follow the political rhetoric, however, remained to be seen.

Conversely, the NFP/FLP Coalition's campaign gained added punch when Reddy became the leading speaker at its hustings. He accused the Koya group of being in cahoots with the Alliance, and warned Indians of grave times ahead under an Alliance government. His timely intervention, much to the chagrin of the Alliance who claimed that, 'Jai Ram Reddy, the real boss, now pulls the strings and Bavadra dances', paid political dividends: on 12 April the voters ended the Alliance's monopoly of power.

The Alliance found that the Coalition had won the four identified key seats, the same four seats that had gone to the Alliance in 1982 and which had enabled them to win that general election. The final election results were: 28 for NFP/FLP Coalition; 24 Alliance; FNP nil; and NFP/WUF Coalition nil. The Alliance's votes had declined from 59 per cent of the total in 1982 to 49 per cent. The Coalition won the election with only 47 per cent of the popular vote, based on the first-past-the post voting system; all 12 Fijian and three General Elector communal seats went to the Alliance; all Indian communal seats went to the NFP/FLP Coalition; of the five cross-voting seats three went to the Alliance and two to the NFP/FLP Coalition. The voting pattern for the communal seats was once more on racial lines: some 10 per cent of Fijian voters favouring the Coalition and a further 20 to 40 per cent expressing support for neither of the two major parties.

If, however, the 1987 election figures are compared with those for 1982, the Indian communal support for the NFP/FLP Coalition was 82 per cent while the Alliance support remained at 15 per cent. The Fijian communal support for the Coalition was nine per cent while Alliance Fijian support *dropped* from 82 per cent to 78 per cent. Support for the old NFP dropped from one per cent to nil, FNP from eight per cent to five per cent, WUF from seven per cent to three per cent, and Independents increased their support from one per cent to four per cent.

The Indian communal support for the old NFP dropped from 83 per cent to one per cent. The General Elector support for the Coalition was 17 per cent while the Alliance support *dropped* from 89 per cent to 86 per cent. The voter turnout for the Fijian communal seats dropped to 70 per cent compared to 88 per cent in 1982, and for the Indian communal seats the voter turnout declined from 79 per cent in 1982 to 70 per cent in 1987. The overall voter turnout in 1987 was low: 71 per cent compared to the 85 per cent in 1982.[25]

There were many casualties: both Ratu Osea and Butadroka, the Fijian nationalist leader, failed in their bids to win seats. The rebel NFP splinter group was also rejected by the Indians who preferred to elect the Indians from the Coalition slate. The NFP's former deputy leader, Matatolu, who was moved from his national seat in favour of Bavadra, lost his bid to capture a Fijian communal seat for the NFP/FLP Coalition.

There were, however, two surprising highlights of this election: the former Fijian deputy prime minister, Ratu David Toganivalu was defeated in the Suva Fijian national seat by the flamboyant Fijian academic, Dr Baba; and Mrs Narayan failed by 659 votes to capture the Suva Indian national seat.

The political fate of the two parties lay in these four seats, described by the veteran NFP parliamentarian, Karam Ramrakha, as the 'Bermuda Triangle of Fiji's Politics'. Strong FNP support and 2,112 informal votes stopped Alliance men Ratu George and running partner Major Singh from winning in the Suva eastern national Fijian and Suva eastern Fijian seats. Both Baba and Maharaj managed to attract the vital middle-class vote, especially from the Fijians who were prepared to entertain shifting loyalties in the national seats where a candidate needed the votes of both Indians and Fijians. In the Suva national seat the Indians openly displayed their hostility to Mrs Narayan, thus ruining Ratu David's chances of retaining his seat. The counting clerks, while checking through the informal votes for this seat, found that one voter, instead of ticking, had written, 'Sorry Irene I can't vote for you this time. Maybe next time around. See ya.'[26]

The overall election results saw 31 new members in the House of

Representatives, and 21 former parliamentarians, of whom 16 were members of the Alliance. After independence, Bavadra became the second Fijian prime minister but for the first time the Indians dominated the government—the 28 strong NFP-FLP Coalition consisted of 19 Indians, seven Fijians and two others. In Ramrakha's words, 'a new marriage is taking place, a meeting of minds of the educated elite in Fiji, an elite which will bring in a new era to the country'.[27]

As for the change in the political landscape with the Alliance, comprising mostly chiefs, becoming the major opposition party with Ratu Mara as opposition leader, Ramrakha further added:

> And the Chiefs who have yielded so much power, and have made Fiji what it is today. Yes, they too have to recognise this change . . . a political adjustment has to be made. The genius of the Fijian people allowed them to cede this country and remain in charge of it. Their society has come down the centuries intact; their people still cling to their valued culture, tradition and customs.[28]

In his ministerial appointments Bavadra therefore tried to preserve these traditions. He slashed the Cabinet from 17 to 14, and appointed six Fijians, seven Indians and one General Elector in a bid to strike a racial balance in his team. Bavadra himself became the first Fijian from the western part of the country to lead the nation as prime minister, and appointed the NFP leader Sharma as his deputy — the first Indian to hold such a post.

Bavadra, however, gave the key ministries close to native Fijian interests to his Fijian Coalition members. While retaining for himself the sensitive portfolios of Fijian Affairs, Home Affairs and the Public Service Commission he appointed Fijian members to the ministries of education; labour and immigration; agriculture and forests; lands; energy and mineral resources; and rural development.

The most surprising appointment, however, was that of Jai Ram Reddy, the former NFP leader and a highly respected lawyer, who was named the new Attorney-General and Minister of Justice, replacing the Fijian, Qoroniasi Bale. On 13 April, the Bavadra government was sworn in by the Governor-General, Ratu Penaia, to lead the nation for the next five years. Although the election was fought along racial lines, the election results demonstrated that 'Democracy is alive and well in Fiji', to use the outgoing Prime Minister Ratu Mara's words.

Bavadra, on the other hand, praised Ratu Mara for accepting the change in government 'with grace and dignity', and added that 'the smooth and peaceful transition to the new government is something of which we can all be proud. For above all else it testifies to the depth and strength of democracy in our beloved country.' In his acceptance speech as Prime Minister, Bavadra further stated that his government would adopt a strictly non-aligned policy, but confirmed that Fiji would not al-

low a Soviet embassy in Fiji. His government would ban all nuclear warships from Fijian ports and reduce the number of diplomatic missions
overseas in order to cut costs. While promising to probe allegations of
corruption in high circles, Bavadra said his government had no intention
of changing the present Fijian administration system which controls Fijians at all levels. As a gesture of respect, Bavadra paid homage to
the Fijian chiefly establishment.

He was aware that not only was the election fought primarily over the
issue of race and power but that he had inherited the chairmanship of
the Great Council of Chiefs. As already pointed out, the Minister for Fijian Affairs, a post that Bavadra had retained for himself, is also the
chairman of the Great Council of Chiefs. During his first days of office
Bavadra visited the chiefly island of Bau where he was greeted 'effusively'
by the former Governor-General and the paramount chief of Fiji, Ratu
George Cakobau, who 18 months earlier had given his blessings to Bavadra's plan to take his party's message to the Fijian villages.

In April 1987 it seemed that a majority of Fijians had quietly accepted
the leadership change. That a Fijian remained Prime Minister calmed
Fijian anxieties regarding the country's future under an 'Indian-
dominated' Bavadra government. Ratu Mara's resignation statement
was also greeted quietly. He told the people:

> . . . we have come to the end of a long, hard campaign. You have given
> your decision. [It] must be accepted. While I am naturally disappoint-
> ed at the outcome, I am proud that we have been able to demonstrate
> that 'Democracy is alive and well in Fiji'. May I . . . thank all who
> gave their support to the Alliance Party. I know how hard many of
> you worked and the disappointment some of you must feel that the
> Alliance has not been returned to Government. It is important, how-
> ever, that you now put that disappointment behind you. The interests
> of Fiji . . . must always come first. There can be no room for rancour
> or bitterness and I would urge that you display goodwill to each other
> in the interest of our nation. We must now ensure a smooth transition
> to enable the new government to settle in quickly and get on with the
> important task of further developing our beloved country. I wish them
> well. . . . Fiji was recently described by Pope John Paul as a symbol of
> hope for the rest of the world. Long may we so remain. God bless Fiji.[29]

But almost as soon as Bavadra and his government were sworn in, a
Fijian nationalist movement called the *Taukei* (native Fijian), led by Tora
and a few prominent Alliance personalities, sprang up. Tora said the
group had been formed to mobilize the Fijian people and give them a
more unified voice on national affairs in their own country. He then announced a campaign of civil disobedience, and called for the Fiji Constitution to be changed in so far as to guarantee Fijian chiefly leadership in
government permanently. At meetings and demonstrations he charged
that the Bavadra government was a front for Indian interests and that

their immediate objective was to rob Fijians of ownership and control of their land. Tora declared:

> We shall recover the rights of Fijians sold out in London in 1970. We have no need for your system, your democracy. We shall never have such things imposed on our own paramountcy. They [Indians] have tried to blackmail us with economic power. It is becoming Fiji for Fijians now. We took in the Indians which Britain brought us, let them live in peace and harmony and let them make money from our generosity. There has been no single act of reciprocity. They won't learn our language, our customs, join our political parties. It is time for them to pack up and go.[30]

Such words suggest that he was a revolutionary Fijian hero, but Tora was simply a turncoat. Since he crossed to the Alliance camp before the 1982 general election he had acquired Ratu Mara's respect and confidence and had finally become a Cabinet minister. Thus his racist outbirsts were quite understandable, though contrary to his past political outlook. Born Apisai Vuniyayawa Tora, he had changed his name to Apisai Mohammed Tora after becoming a Muslim while serving with the Fijian forces in Malaya.

He had provided the prefix 'National' to the Federation Party to form the NFP in 1968. During this historic merger, he said that his decision had been influenced by the Indian leaders' statements on the special place for Fijians. In 1972 Tora had publicly apologized to the Indian electorate for having suggested, during the 1965 constitutional talks, that Indians should be repatriated from Fiji; he told a political rally in the same year that he had been wrong and no longer held such views. As recently as July 1986 he asserted that 'the Government policy is that Indian people are here to stay whether people like it or lump it. Without Indians Fiji would never have been what it is today, economic-wise and otherwise.'[31]

In addition to Tora's group, there was a group of Alliance ex-Cabinet ministers who could not accept the decline in status and financial reward imposed by their position as opposition backbenchers. Shortly after the Alliance's defeat, its most powerful arm, the Fijian Association, convened a meeting and passed a vote of no confidence in the NFP/FLP Coalition. Among those who attended this meeting which was chaired by the newly-elected Alliance MP and FNP convert of old, Taniela Veitata, were Ratu Mara's eldest son, Ratu Finau Mara who was a lawyer in the Crown Law Office; Qoriniasi Bale, the former Attorney-General; Filipe Bole, the former Minister for Education; and Jone Veisamasama, general secretary of the Alliance Party who, in 1983, was secretry to the Royal Commission of Inquiry into the 1982 general election. Veisamasama told the meeting that the Coalition government contained more Indians at the decision-making level.

The Fijian Association meeting, as had Tora's *Taukei* group, resolved that the Constitution should be changed to guarantee that Fijians always led Fiji, and agreed to organize protest marches through the capital, Suva, and other centres, and to submit a petition to the Governor-General against the Bavadra government. In complicity with the Great Council of Chiefs, this group subsequently set out to manipulate and mobilize the Fijians to destabilize the Coalition government.

The planned marches took place on 23 April in Suva and at Lautoka on 24 April and other centres in Fiji. The principal agitators brought in Fijian demonstrators from the rural and outlying areas, all reminiscent of the racially tense days of 1968. Some of the placards displayed by the Fijian crowds proclaimed:[32]

> We Fijians have no confidence in the Coalition
> Fiji my Fiji
> Change the Constitution immediately
> Out with foreign puppets
> Fiji belongs to the Fijians
> K.C. Ramrakha—the deserter, shut up
> Reddy gun, Bavadra bullet
> Fijians have given away so much for so long it hurts
> Bavadra stop selling lovely government to communist government
> Stop this Indian government
> Fiji now little India, say no
> We shall not be misled by a puppet
> We came to Fiji with nothing. Now we have cars, houses and the country? Bloodshed.

The public demonstrations were quickly followed by road blocks, attacks of Indian politicians' homes and fire-bombings of premises owned by Indian businessmen (including the law offices of Jai Ram Reddy and Harish Sharma). The outright racist appeals to Fijians prompted the Bavadra government to arrest and charge Tora with sedition and inciting racial tension. Another Fijian senator and chairman of the Young Alliance, Jona Qio, was also arrested and charged in connection with a fire-bombing incident.

The politically orchestrated campaign had finally plunged the new government into deep crisis, prompting Prime Minister Bavadra to hold a crisis security meeting with the Governor-General, Ratu Penaia, and the Commander of the Royal Fiji Military Forces, Brigadier Nailatikau. Later Ratu Penaia and his predecessor, Ratu George, both made radio broadcasts in which they appealed to Fijians to restrain their actions and give the new government an opportunity to prove itself. But their calls fell on deaf ears.

Moreover, the political uprisings were met by what the New Zealand Prime Minister David Lange subsequently described as 'thundering silence' by Ratu Mara.[33] At home, the President of the Suva Indian Alliance, Maan Singh, while asserting that the Indian Alliance had always been treated as a stepchild in the Alliance, strongly criticized Ratu Mara for his failure to make a public statement to calm the Fijians. Singh charged that Ratu Mara 'should have shown some respect for the Indians in the party and for the sake of democracy'.[34] But Ratu Mara left Fiji during the height of the crisis for a two-week visit to Hawaii before returning for the swearing-in of the new government. Nineteen of the 24 Alliance MPs boycotted the swearing-in ceremony determined to seriously embarrass and disrupt the Bavadra government, or, maybe, as the FNP leader Butadroka suggested: 'It appears to me that these ex-ministers are worried that Dr Bavadra will conduct an inquiry into their affairs and this is why they are reacting now. The way things are going it appears that they are doing this purely for monetary gains.'[35]

Some observers, including the Bavadra government, thought the destabilization campaign was inspired by external interests. Bavadra would himself subsequently accuse the CIA of instigating his government's downfall. Meanwhile, by 14 March 1987 a contingent of ex-Alliance Cabinet ministers and their supporters had reduced the effectiveness as well as the legitimacy of the Bavadra government, facilitating the process of military intervention in the politics of Fiji.

Notes

1. K.L. Gillion, 1977, p. 18.
2. Ahmed Ali, 1980, p. 67.
3. For further detail on the wage freeze, see Wadan Narsey, in *The Journal of Pacific Studies*, Vol. 11, 1985, p. 12.
4. *Labour News*, Vol. 2, Issue 2, 1985, Ministry of Employment and Industrial Relations, Suva, Fiji.
5. See Nii-k-Plange, *The Journal of Pacific Studies*, Vol. 11, 1985, p. 100.
6. *Hansard* (Fiji), 28 March 1985.
7. *Fiji Sun*, 15 August 1986, p. 1.
8. *Islands Business* (Fiji), January 1987.
9. *Fiji Times*, 13 March 1987.
10. Ibid., 4 March 1987.
11. *Fiji Sun*, 4 April 1987, p. 3.
12. Ibid., 28 March 1987, p. 1.
13. Ibid., 3 January 1987, p. 1.
14. *Sunday Sun* (Fiji), 22 February 1987, p. 1.
15. The NFP/FLP Coalition Manifesto.
16. *Fiji Sun*, 26 March, p. 1.
17. Ibid., p. 3.
18. Ibid., 3 April 1987, p. 14.
19. Ibid., 5 July 1986, p.1.
20. Ibid., 21 June 1986.
21. Ibid., 2 July 1986.
22. Ibid., 25 October 1986, p. 2.
23. Quoted in Robert Norton, 1977, p. 68.
24. *Fiji Times*, 4 April 1987, p. 3.

25. *Sunday Sun* (Fiji), 19 April 1987, p. 6.
26. *Fiji Sun*, 13 April 1987, p. 4.
27. Ibid., p. 5.
28. Ibid.
29. Ibid., p. 3.
30. Quoted in *The Times* (London), 21 July 1987, p. 8.
31. *Fiji Times*, 28 July 1986, p. 1.
32. *Fiji Sun*, 25 April 1987, p. 3.
33. *New Zealand Listener*, 6 June 1987, p. 17.
34. *Fiji Sun*, 24 April 1987, p. 2.
35. *Fiji Times*, 23 April 1987, p. 2.

CHAPTER THIRTEEN

'SOLDIERS IN PARADISE'

Sit down everybody, sit down. This is a takeover. We apologise for
any inconvenience caused. You are requested to stay cool, stay
down, sit down and listen to what we are going to tell you. Please
stay calm, ladies and gentlemen.
 Mr Prime Minister, please lead your team down to the right.
Policemen, keep the passage clear, stay down and remain calm. Mr
Prime Minister, Sir, will you lead your team now.

With these words, 38-year-old Fijian soldier, Lieutenant-Colonel Sitiveni
Ligamamada Rabuka, and a 'hit squad' of ten soldiers, led by one Captain X, launched the first military coup against a democratically elected
government in the South Pacific, ending the NFP/FLP Coalition's one
month and two days in office. In short, democracy died in Fiji on Thursday 14 May 1987.

The Fiji Indians awoke to mark the day on which exactly 108 years
ago the first Indian 'coolies' arrived in Fijian waters aboard the *Leonidas*.
The former Prime Minister Ratu Mara, who had celebrated his 67th
birthday the previous day, was still struggling to come to terms with his
new role as Leader of the Opposition. It was exactly three years since his
predecessor and arch-rival, Jai Ram Reddy, had resigned both as leader
of the NFP and as Member of Parliament.

In one way or another, therefore, May was of personal, political, and
historical significance. It was important, too, for Rabuka. Disenchanted
with the victory of the Coalition, he had started looking for a non-
military job. Two days before he seized power, he was interviewed for the
post of Commissioner of Police, then held by an Indian. 'I had had a
gutful. I wanted to leave the Army because I knew deep inside me that I
could not support a Coalition Government', [1] Rabuka now admits.

It has also been disclosed that the RFMF had booked airline tickets in
his name to arrive in Sydney, on 11 May, three days before the coup, but
Rabuka had not collected the ticket. Fiji's army had been invited to participate in a 'skill at arms' competition organized by the Australian Army
for the week 11-15 May in preparation for Australia's bi-centenary.
Various armies throughout the world were involved and Rabuka was to
have attended the events as observer. Rabuka and others, backed by a
racist faction of the influential Methodist Church of Fiji, however, had
already secretly planned to overthrow the Coalition government. Two of
them, the Reverend Tomasi Rakivi, a cousin of Rabuka's, and General
Secretary of the Fiji Council of Churches, and Ratu Inoke Kubuabola,
President of the Fiji Council of Churches and Secretary of the Bible

Society of the South Pacific, were to play a key role in the future course of events.

It was Kubuabola, a cousin of Ratu Penaia, who first termed the extreme Fijian nationalist organization as the *Taukei* Movement, and he was its direct link with Rabuka. While contradicting Rabuka's assertion that 'there was no complicity beyond the essential military personnel who were involved in the pre-coup organisation', Kubuabola told *Islands Business* (IB, May 1988), that for more than six hours on April 19 he and Rabuka, later joined by Jone Veisamasama, 'talked about different options'. It was on 19 April that the groundwork for the coup was laid and according to Kubuabola, 11 May was the day his co-conspirators decided to proceed with its execution. He also claims that when it was learnt that Parliament would not sit on Friday they had agreed to bring forward the coup to Thursday:

> By four [p.m. 19 April] we spent some time in prayer and options and we asked Rabuka to prepare his side of things, you know, the military option. And all the things we were doing were the lead up. We asked Rabuka to prepare that side and when the time, when we reach a stage when he must step in, he must be ready to step in. We changed it [the coup] to Thursday on Wednesday night in my office at the Bible Society with Rabuka.[2]

The other crucial intermediary between the *Taukei* Movement and the military, Rev. Rakivi, was to provide his house in suburban Suva as a centre for overall planning. Thus it was there that Rabuka met the other conspirators on Easter Monday, nine days after the defeat of the Alliance Party. In a book, *Rabuka; No Other Way*, by two journalists, Stan Ritova and Eddie Dean (a former press secretary to Malcolm Fraser), Rabuka claims that it was at Rakivi's home that he first learnt of the *Taukei* group's plan for massive 'demonstrations and the possibility of widespread arson and possibly murder'. According to Ritova and Dean Rabuka (his words in italics) went to,

> ... what he understood was an ordinary 'grog' party at the Rev. Rakivi's home, in suburban Suva. It was early evening, and he just walked in, as he normally would, throwing his 'sevusevu' [gift] of yaqona towards the bowl where the 'grog' was being mixed. *'I saw all these people sitting down, and realised it was some kind of a meeting. Some of the people greeted me, although I could not see everyone clearly because it was fairly dark in the lounge-room. Nobody asked me to leave.'* When his eyes adjusted to the darkness, he discovered the gathering was *'quite a formidable group'*. He says it included Ratu Finau Mara, the son of Ratu Sir Kamisese Mara; Ratu George Kadavulevu, son of the Paramount Chief of Fiji, Ratu George Cakobau; Ratu Inoke Kubuabola; Ratu Keni Viuyasawa, the brother of Brigadier Nailatikau; Mr Filipe Bole, formerly a Minister in the Mara govern-

ment; Ratu Jo Ritova, of Labasa; Ratu Jale Ratu; 'Big Dan' Veitata, and the host, Tomasi Rakivio. . . . Another leading light at this meeting was Apisai Tora.[3]

This handful of allegedly God-fearing men, some of chiefly rank, told their plans to Rabuka, exchanged opinions, and turned to God for help. To quote Ritova and Dean again:

> The link with God and Christianity surfaced here, too. At the end of the meeting, which was full of fire and brimstone talk about what to do with the Coalition and the 'flawed' Constitution, which had allowed the election of an Indian-dominated Government, they joined hands and prayed to God. Their prayer, in summary, was simple: 'Save us, and save our land. You saved the Israelites when their land was taken from them by foreigners. Dear God, please answer our prayer and do the same for us.'[4]

There were, apparently, other reasons which compelled the group to turn to God for help. One was the unfounded fear that the Indian-backed new government would unseat, or move sideways, senior Fijian public servants closely aligned with the Alliance government. The Indians, Rabuka thought, would 'move to get their own back on senior [Fijian] civil servants who were perceived as having given the Indians a hard time... An element of "pay back".' Another was the frontal attack on the 'chiefly system' and its rightful place in national politics; and the personal attacks on Ratu Mara, that Rabuka claims were too much for ordinary commoner Fijians to accept. He seems to have had Bavadra in mind, who had remarked during the campaign:

> . . . democracy provides [that] one person's vote is exactly the same as another's. A chief, be he ever so high in the traditional system, does not have five votes where his people have four. In previous elections, the Alliance fear tactic [included] asking people whether they wanted an Indian Prime Minister; now, with the historic uniting of all races under the umbrella of the coalition, the leader is a Fijian, so the question is whether a non-chief should be Prime Minister. One would thus imagine that if an equivalent chief from another province challenged Ratu Sir Kamisese, the Alliance question would be: 'Can we let a Prime Minister of Fiji come from any province but Lau?'[5]

The third reason was probably the fear that the Coalition government, comprising some of the best Indian legal brains in Fiji, would vigorously fulfil its promise to 'weed out' and bring to justice those suspected of corruption during the reign of the Alliance government. Nevertheless, Thursday 14 May 1987 was a typical May day in Fiji's capital, Suva, the citadel of parliamentary democracy in the South Pacific. Most parliamentarians had taken their seats in Parliament for the morning session, except for Ratu Mara who was at The Fijian in the country's finest resort in Sigatoka, 125 km west of Suva, chairing a conference of the Pacific Democratic Union (PDU), an association of conservative political parties, including Ratu Mara's Alliance Party.

As already explained, the PDU had been set up to promote and foster the conservative movement and democratic ideals in the South Pacific. The date of the Sigatoka conference had been agreed at a PDU meeting in Sydney in August 1986; funding was to be from the PDU budget, augmented by a grant from the National Republican Institute for International Affairs, an arm of the US Republican Party. Several international figures participated in the conference, including Malcolm Fraser. Fraser, however, had not been in Fiji on the day of the coup. As later events will show, this conference would suddenly assume a special character, in that it would provide the coup theorists with their supposedly vital links when analysing the coup's external dimension.

Meanwhile, Ratu Mara's absence did not deter his Alliance parliamentarians — some of whom were well aware of the imminent arrival of Rabuka and his troops — from carrying on their stately rituals. Rabuka, the third most senior army officer in Fiji's army, had for some time been planning the scenario for such an intervention; before the election he had already begun to train a group of 60 handpicked officers, some of whom were Middle East veterans; others had trained with the crack New Zealand Special Air Services unit.

A career soldier in the RFMF for 19 years, Rabuka was well qualified and had the backing, both internally and externally, to successfully stage a coup. He had trained in Australia and New Zealand, had served with the 6th Gurkha Rifles in Hong Kong, and commanded Fiji's UN peacekeeping contingent in the Middle East, an assignment for which, in 1981, he was awarded an OBE. The possibility of staging a coup had first occurred to Rabuka in 1977, when the NFP had won the elections but failed to form the government and it was while he was studying at India's Defence Staff College in the southern Indian state of Tamil Nadu, in 1979, that he expanded and finalized his plans.

On the day of the coup the army Commander, Brigadier Ratu Epeli Nailatikau, a high chief and Ratu Mara's son-in-law, was in Australia. The forces that Rabuka had at his disposal were preponderantly indigenous Fijians, including *Taukei* agitators and some Fijian members of the former Alliance Cabinet with whom he had all along been in collusion.

In Rabuka's coup document — Operation Order — three individuals: William Sutherland, Ratu Mosese Tuisawau and Tevita Fa were especially mentioned as principal targets. We already know that Sutherland took an active part in the formation of the Labour Party, becoming Permanent Secretary to Prime Minister Bavadra. In Rabuka's view, Sutherland had engineered the Coalition's strategy in the election, and had introduced unacceptable foreign terms, such as 'brothers' and 'sisters' and 'comrades', into the political debate. Such terms were, in Rabuka's opinion, 'socialist terms, deployed by somebody who'd had contact with Eastern bloc countries'.

Ratu Mosese Tuisawau was an even greater thorn in the traditional Fijian establishment's side. A high chief, half-brother of Ratu Mara's wife, and a Hull University (UK) economics graduate, Ratu Mosese was always a harsh critic of the Alliance government, especially its land policies. A former member of the NFP, and until his resignation as President of the FNP in October 1978, he constantly argued that the rights of native landowners were being denied because Fijian leaders were misguided by some past legal adivsers. In October 1986, Ratu Mosese alleged that in some cases the landowners received only $F3.75 while the Native Land Development Corporation (NLDC) got $95 and the Native Land Trust Board (NLTB) $1.25 from every $100 generated from the sub-division of native land. 'This is the kind of ridiculous situation which to my mind is criminal liability', he said. During the election campaign in April 1987 Ratu Mosese returned to the political arena, alleging that the Alliance Party was robbing Fijians of their land through the NLDC and the NLTB, both of which were under the influence of large business companies.

In June 1988 he was arrested and charged with conspiracy to 'instigate invasion and conspiracy to import arms and ammunition' following the discovery of a huge cache of arms in Sydney, Australia, reportedly destined for Indians in Fiji. The third individual, Tevita Fa, of Rotuman descent, was former government prosecutor and the Fijian Association's national treasurer, who crossed the floor and joined the FLP. He immediately projected himself as the champion of the oppressed, featuring prominently in trials involving both Ratu Mara and his wife. A month before the coup he had filed a writ in the Lautoka Supreme Court against Ratu Mara, the Native Lands Commission (NLC), the Attorney-General, Bale, and the NLTB, claiming that Ratu Mara, as Tui Lau, was not the rightful owner of 400 acres of land at Sawana village in Vanuabalavu, Lau, the home province of Ratu Mara.

The writ, filed on behalf of two descendants of Tongan conquerors, Alipate Fatafehi and Lupe Puleiwai Fatafehi (Ratu Mara's first cousins), further sought an injunction from the court to stop Ratu Mara from entering the land in dispute on the grounds that he had no right to ownership or occupation of it. In historical context the writ, filed at the height of polling, rekindled, privately, the debate about the place of Lauans in national Fijian politics. The writ claimed that the title, Tui Lau, was created by Enele Ma'afu, the Tongan chief, after he conquered and settled with his Tongan followers in Sawana in the Lau Group.

The late Ratu Sukuna had been the second Tui Lau after Ma'afu and the Tongan elders had conferred the title on Ratu Sukuna; this title was now borne by Ratu Mara. The writ pointed out that following a dispute over the land in 1939, Ratu Sukuna, as chairman of the NLC, ruled that the land belonged to the two plaintiffs' father. In 1966, however, following another dispute, the NLC dealt with the question of ownership and ruled that the land belonged to Ratu Mara.

In retrospect, it may be argued that in Rabuka's view Fa's actions were probably another example of 'mudslinging' against high chief Ratu Mara. Thus Fa had to be stopped.

By eight in the morning of Thursday 14 May people in Suva had settled down to their daily routine, except for the parliamentarians who were still heading towards the grey stone Government Buildings for the morning session of Parliament. So was Rabuka—a convoy of trucks carrying soldiers in full combat gear and armed with M16 assault rifles were also on their way from the RFMF barracks in Nabua, the army headquarters, some 15 km from Suva, and were to link up with Rabuka at the Government Buildings.

Rabuka reached Parliament House in time for the sitting and, first nodding to his uncle, Milton Leweniqila, an Alliance MP who was in the Speaker's Chair, took a seat in the visitors' gallery. As a visitor said later, 'a stranger walked into the House wearing a grey suit and a neck tie of green with maroon stripes and a sulu skirt'.

Two weeks before the coup Rabuka had discussed the effects of a coup with Leweniqila, who told him, 'if you are going to successfully execute a coup, you may have to take some lives for people to believe there is [one] because no one believes a coup is possible in Fiji ... [also] that a coup will be economically disastrous for the country'. Leweniqila further told Rabuka, 'You have to go to Government House first and remove His Excellency, then take over Radio Fiji.' Today Leweniqila claims for his part the discussion was never intended to be translated into practice, and he still feels guilty that he failed to order the sergeant-at-arms to stop Rabuka and his men.

That Thursday morning another MP, Veitata, was already on his feet, delivering an address on the conversion of the Fijian people to Christianity, especially the chiefs, in the late 19th century. By this time Rabuka's soldiers in battle fatigues, balaclavas and gas masks had assembled in the car park adjoining the offices of the Leader of the Opposition. Veitata, presumably aware of that morning's impending coup, continued with his speech: '... a life of peace and harmony has been the governing principle upon which the Fijian people have been living ... ever since the arrival of Christianity in Fiji, 150 years ago [that] peace is quite distinct from the philosophy of Mao Tse Tung, who said that political power comes from the barrel of a gun. In Fiji, there is no gun, but our chiefs are here. ...'[6] At this moment, as the Government Buildings clock chimed ten, Captain X and his team burst into Parliament. Four minutes later Rabuka and his 'hit squad' had brought an end to the parliamentary proceedings of their former rulers. They abducted Prime Minister Bavadra, his Ministers and backbenchers, and put them in waiting army trucks to be taken into custody.

Without a single bullet having been fired, a Pacific paradise became a military dictatorship. The coup was swift and bloodless, and the residents of Suva went on as usual, oblivious of the momentous events of the morning. Shortly afterwards a group of soldiers took control of the capital's telephone exchange, cutting off communications with the outside world, but withdrawing after a few hours. The Nadi international airport still remained open to any interventionist force, and the coup plotters made no apparent attempt to restrict people's movement in downtown Suva or in other major centres around the country. The first military coup in the South Pacific remained for more than 12 hours a low-key affair.

Not until 3.15 p.m. did Rabuka call a press conference of local and foreign journalists in Suva, to announce that he had taken control of the government, sacked his superiors, made the Governor-General redundant, reorganized the police force, suspended the Fiji Constitution and the judiciary, and had asked lawyers to draft a new constitution to restore political dominance to the Fijians in their own country. He also said that Christianity was to be the official religion of Fiji.

This belated and intrinsically racial announcement immediately attracted a crowd of Fijians who converged on the quadrangle of the Government Buildings to celebrate the military takeover. As rumours, confusion and fear swept the streets, the Indians began to leave the city. The state of siege was to continue for another eight months culminating in the army's second seizure of power; the direct intervention of Queen Elizabeth in the Fijian crisis; the Governor-General's resignation to become the first President of the new Republic of Fiji; the return of his former political colleague and traditional high chief, Ratu Mara, to the Premiership; the bid by a faction of the Rotuman community to secede; the discovery of a huge cache of arms in Sydney bound for Fiji; constant harassment of the Fiji Indian community; and the imposition of several draconian internal security decrees, in some ways similar to those operational in South Africa under the state of emergency (see Appendix for detailed chronology).

The Fijian Military

If a military coup had to occur at all in the South Pacific, then Fiji was the most likely place for it. Apart from being the most experienced armed force in the island states, it has always constituted a trump card in the hands of the chiefly oligarchy, available to maintain the status quo ante in the unlikely event of Fijian hegemony being challenged. In other words, the military, which in 1985 comprised 1,852 (92%) Fijians, 88 (4%) Indians and 88 (4%) from other communities, guaranteed the smooth functioning of parliamentary democracy as long as the chiefs remained in power.

In addition, the overlapping family connections between Ratu Mara and Brigadier Ratu Epeli Nailatikau, Ratu Penaia and his soldier son, who was with the Fijian peace-keeping contingent in Lebanon at the time of the 1987 coup, and the fact that Ratu Penaia is the high chief of Rabuka's tribe, inevitably raised several important questions especially among local political commentators. In its editorial on 15 May, the *Fiji Sun*, while inveighing against the coup, before being shut down by Rabuka, asked:

> What right has a third-ranking officer to attack the sacred institutions of Parliament? . . . to presume he knows how best this country shall be governed for the good of all? The answer is: None.
>
> But . . . was he encouraged by others to act? And if so, who were they? Did others stand by and lend silent approval to these unlawful actions?[7]

The Army Commander

The appointment of Brigadier Nailatikau as commander of the Fijian armed forces in June 1982 heightened speculation about a possible military intervention in Fijian politics. After the 1982 elections the army was increasingly viewed with extreme suspicion. At cocktail parties and in political circles the question frequently raised was: will Brigadier Nailatikau intervene to protect his father-in-law's political kingdom?

In their obsession with the Brigadier, the 'prophets of coup' overlooked the internal politics of the military, assuming that the commoner soldiers would respect their commander, a man of noble brith. This belief was mistaken because several officers were of the opinion that there were more deserving candidates. Among them was Rabuka who, reportedly, bitterly resented being passed over for the leadership of the armed forces. Thereafter, an uneasy alliance existed between the two men with Rabuka awaiting his revenge.[8]

In 1986, a top Cabinet document, leaked to the press by the Governor-General's official secretary, Josefa Vosanibola, revealed a serious rift between the army and the then Home Affairs Minister, Rabuka's uncle Militoni Leweniqila; this document was prepared by Leweniqila who was sacked after he tabled it in Cabinet. He had strongly urged that Rabuka be appointed army commander; he had also called for a review of Brigadier Nailatikau's appointment and argued that the army was disobeying Cabinet directives. Vosanibola was given a six-month jail sentence, suspended for two years, after he admitted leaking the document to the *Fiji Sun* in order, he said, to 'boost the morale of [Fijian] soldiers in Fiji, the Middle East, my chief [the Governor-General] and the people of Fiji'. The defeat of the Alliance Party in 1987 seems to have provided the excuse for Rabuka to fulfil his own military ambitions. Nevertheless, what did Brigadier Nailatikau know about the coup, and when did he know? We already know that he was in Perth (Australia) when the coup took place. The Royal Australian Air Force immediately flew him to Canberra for talks with Australian Prime Minister Bob Hawke and his Defence Minister Kim Beazley. While deploring the coup, Nailatikau strongly advised against any military intervention, pointing out that it was practically impossible, and could result in a considerable loss of life.

The first hint of a joint invasion came from New Zealand Prime Minister David Lange, who said his country would be ready to play a role along with Australia and other South Pacific countries 'in a peace-keeping function' and would respond to a 'cry for help' from the legitimate Fijian government. It was later reported that Australia had considered—and rejected—a request from Bavadra supporters in Fiji for Australia to provide at least logistic support to bring Fijian soldiers home from the Middle East, so that Brigadier Nailatikau could lead them back to Suva for a counter-coup; more than 50 per cent of these troops overseas had voted for the Coalition. Brigadier Nailatikau could see no circumstances in which military intervention was justified.

He disclosed, however, that he would fly home as soon as possible to resume control of the military. But on his return to Fiji he found that he had been placed on indefinite leave with full pay until his future was decided. One concession was that he was allowed to remain in the Commander's residence—which raised further speculation about his role. In an interview with the *Fiji Times* on 2 June 1987 he replied to his critics, categorically denying any foreknowledge of the coup. This interview left some key matters untouched. For example, did the Brigadier inquire if Rabuka had arrived in Australia? The coup took place on Thursday May 14 and, as already noted, Rabuka had been expected in Sydney on Monday 11 May. Brigadier Nailatikau's chief of staff, and acting commander at the time of the coup, Colonel Jim Sanday, who was also suspended by Rabuka, later expressed surprise that the Brigadier had left for Australia at a time when there were protests and demonstrations in the country. Moreover, Brigadier Nailatikau's eventual appointment as the new Ambassador of the Republic of Fiji to Great Britain leaves two questions unanswered: when did he know about the coup and what did he know? Brigadier Nailatikau maintains that he took it for granted that Rabuka was already in Sydney on 11 May, and stresses that as a traditional high chief he was obliged to accept the Ambassadorship to Great Britain.[9]

The Governor-General

The management of Fiji's protracted political crisis was thrust into the hands of the Governor-General, Ratu Sir Penaia Ganilau, the Queen's representative on the island. A former Minister for Fijian Affairs and Deputy Prime Minister in Ratu Mara's Alliance government, on 12 February 1983, Ratu Penaia had been officially sworn in by the Chief Justice, Sir Timoci Tuivaga, as Fiji's third Governor-General, the second high chief to hold such a position.

In his acceptance speech Ratu Penaia stressed that 'Fiji's link with the British Crown is a long and treasured one, and I feel deeply honoured to have been chosen to perpetuate that link into the future'.[10] He declared that he would practise political neutrality in discharging the heavy responsibility laid upon him. In turn Ratu Mara, welcoming Ratu Penaia to his new position, said the appointment was 'the culmination of a long and distinguished career that has been characterised by a commitment to the best interest of the country'; and that as soldier, administrator, Minister of the Crown and leader of men, Ratu Penaia had demonstrated 'in full measure to the people of Fiji tolerance, understanding, goodwill, cooperation, mutual respect, dedication and loyalty'. He reminded the nation: 'We live in difficult times and this is a time of rapid change. But there are enduring qualities that will remain steadfast throughout the age. We are confident that these qualities will be upheld from Government House in the future, as they have been in the past.'[11]

On 14 May 1987, however, in his capacity as the Governor-General Ratu Penaia suddenly found himself in an awkward position trying to reconcile three conflicting forces: loyalty to the Queen; protection of Fiji Indian interests; and his duty as a chief to safeguard the interests of his Fijian population.

Ratu Penaia's initial reaction to the coup was one of 'shock' and surprise, until Rabuka called upon him at Government House to explain his actions. The following exchange between Ratu Penaia and Rabuka shortly afterwards is worth recalling here as we examine the Governor-General's role in the whole crisis. According to Rabuka, as told to Dean and Ritova,[12] the conversation began in English:

Rabuka: Sir, I have just taken over the Government. I have detained all Dr Bavadra's team. They have been taken up to camp, where they will be detained until we find suitable accommodation for them.

Ratu Penaia: What have you done?

R: I have suspended the Constitution, or abrogated the Constitution, and that means, Sir, that your appointment as Governor-General now ceases to exist.

RP: You mean that I have no job?

R: (Now speaking in Fijian): Yes, Sir, but I would ask that you stay here with full pay and all your privileges and honours that go with your office, until we ask you to come back as President.

RP: Couldn't you have given them (the Coalition) time to carry out their policies?

R: Sir, it would be very dangerous to let them run the Government for a few more months.

RP: Have you thought about what you are going to do next? ... What about the Tui Nayau (Ratu Mara)?

Rabuka disclosed that his next steps were: the formation of a Council of Ministers comprising former Alliance ministers to run an interim government, prior to holding another election; and that he wanted Ratu Mara on the Council because he would be a 'trump card', a 'must' as Minister for Foreign Affairs. Ratu Penaia was sympathetic to Rabuka's essential aims, but, according to Rabuka, told him what he had done was unconstitional, and he (Ratu Penaia) would not go along with it.[13]

But in the light of the Governor-General's role later it remains possible that he endorsed Rabuka's overall aims if not the causes. That the Governor-General had initially accepted his dismissal is another example of apparent indifference to the coup. Had it not been for the intervention of the Chief Justice, Sir Timoci Tuivaga, events at that time might have taken a different turn. Sir Timoci has disclosed that he was in his chamber when his Chief Registrar notified him of the coup. He waited for a call from the Governor-General, which never came. Sir Timoci eventually telephoned the Governor-General, and said: Sir, there's a political crisis on our hands. What are we doing about it?

> I went to Government House to see him but he said he couldn't do very much because he had been advised that the Constitution had been abrogated and he was no longer the Governor-General. I don't know where that advice came from but it was plainly wrong. I expect whoever gave him that advice will lose his head over it. He said, 'Chief Justice, I'm sitting here not as Governor-General but as chief of the (northern province of) Cakaudrove'. I said, 'Sir, that is not so. You are the repository of power and authority now. You have temporarily lost your prime minister and your Cabinet and under the Constitution you now take over the executive authority.' Then he bucked up and said, 'Oh, is that so?' I said, 'Yes, sir', and he said, 'Will you put that in writing?' I said, 'Gladly.' I said, 'I'll do better than that. I'll go back to my office and get things moving for you.'[14]

Thus urged to give some semblance of legitimacy for the viceregal role a Governor-General was expected to play in such a crisis, Ratu Penaia was spurred into action. In a recorded radio message broadcast on a private Suva radio system FM 96, before it was seized by the military, Ratu Penaia expressed his deep shock and regret at the usurpation of power by the military. While deploring the coup he called on the mutineering troops to end their rebellion, declared a state of emergency, and said that he, personally, was taking charge of the government in the absence of his Cabinet. Unabashed, Rabuka announced shortly afterwards that he had appointed his own Council of Ministers, with prominent among them, Ratu Mara and many of his former Alliance ministers. The ex-Minister of Education, Dr Ahmed Ali, and a former Finance Minister, Peter Stinson, in fact, sat on either side of Rabuka when he gave his press conference declaring that he was firmly in control.

The Governor-General, to whom Rabuka had disclosed his post-coup plans, surprisingly, was allowed to remain in Government House, half a mile from Government Buildings in Suva and it was from there that he would persistently assert that he was the sole repository of legal authority in the islands, although he wavered as Rabuka, fully supported by the Great Council of Chiefs, moved gradually forward to fulfil the objectives of his coup. Moreover, Rabuka's apparent reluctance to act against the Governor-General, his own paramount chief, and the latter's 'secret' swearing in of Rabuka's Council of Ministers on 17 May, naturally began to raise doubts about Ratu Penaia's integrity. Although subsequently, on the advice of the Chief Justice, he refused to swear in Rabuka as head of government, it now became obvious that some sort of deal had been struck between them, as would be subsequently confirmed (as outlined in the Chronology), with the dissolution of Parliament, a total amnesty for the coup plotters, including Rabuka, and the setting-up of an eight-member sub-committee of the Council of Advisers to review the Constitution in order to see if it could be revised to guarantee Fijian political hegemony over the Indians before the next general election. This was necessary as a first step towards 'national reconciliation' and 'a path to democracy'.

But the plan to revise the Constitution, which smacked of racialism, was sure to be rejected by the Indian community, further thwarting the path of 'national reconciliation'. With the Indian members of the Coalition solidly against any changes in the Constitution, and Bavadra supporting them, a parting of ways became obvious. Thus the only hope for both the rival groups now was the Queen, the Chief of the Chiefs, and Queen of 'all the people of Fiji'.

The Queen

Her Majesty Queen Elizabeth II had been closely monitoring the crisis in Fiji, and had personally intervened to call upon Ratu Penaia to stand firm against Rabuka. In a speech during the crisis the Governor-General had proudly revealed that he had received a message from Buckingham Palace stating that the Queen 'wishes you to know how much she admires your stand, as her personal representative in Fiji and the guardian of the Constitution'. He also disclosed that when the time was opportune he would go to London to seek further advice from her regarding his present assertion of authority.

A month later, however, it was Bavadra who headed for London, to persuade the Queen that the coup was an illegal act and ripe for reversal. But for Bavadra it was a fruitless journey. He was granted an audience only with her private secretary, Sir William Heseltine. The Queen declined to see him after consultations with the Governor-General in whom she had reaffirmed her confidence in the restoration of parliamentary democracy.

The Governor-General had been successful with another 'royal coup' to secure his own future. In the end, however, the loser was not Bavadra but democracy, as he told an audience in London afterwards, 'the issue is the destruction of democracy in a Commonwealth country. We are all for democracy, aren't we? After all there are elections here next week'. The *Sunday Times* of London on 14 June 1987 summed up Bavadra's dilemma as he headed back home: 'Fiji's ousted prime minister is left to ponder the meaning of democracy'.

In throwing his weight behind Bavadra's arch political and racial rivals the Governor-General also continued to commit other 'undemocratic acts'. For example, he pardoned Rabuka and his officers for staging a 'bloodless' coup, and accepted the recommendations of the 16-member Constitutional Review Committee that urged the acceptance of a racially-biased Constitution as demanded by the Great Council of Chiefs. The Committee, chaired by a former attorney-general in the Alliance Government, Sir John Falvey, had been charged with 'reviewing the Constitution of Fiji with a view to proposing to the Governor-General amendments which will strengthen the political representation of indigenous Fijians, and, in so doing, bear in mind the best interests of the other peoples in Fiji.'[15] Earlier, the Coalition representatives had refused to serve on the Committee unless the terms of reference were altered to include the interests of all the people of Fiji. In an exchange of letters between the Government House and Bavadra, the deposed Prime Minister had declared:

> As a multi-racial party any coalition will do all within its power to preserve and protect the rights of every citizen of Fiji, irrespective of race, and will not be seen to agree to measures which, wholly or in part, disenfranchise a community or communities. To effectively disenfranchise people born in Fiji, for no reason other than their ethnicity, will not make for the long term of peace and stability of Fiji. On the contrary, it will be sowing the seeds of resentment, disharmony and even confrontation. The world is full of examples. Is it not the very kind of discrimination the Commonwealth says it is fighting against the South African regime?[16]

The *Fiji Times*, reflecting the opinion of the vast majority of hapless Indians, reminded the Fijian people, including the Governor-General, of the consequences:

> The terms infer . . . that whatever happens, the Fijians will be given complete political domination over the non-Fijian majority. . . .
>
> Fijian fears concerning the security of their race in our country are acknowledged. But the greatest error that can now be made by the Fijian people is to fail to accept the deep-seated affection and concern which their non-Fijian citizens have for their welfare and rights. The second greatest error . . . is to believe that majority of non-Fijians will permanently submit . . . to the proposition that on a secondary consideration, quite incidental to the national well-being of this country, the review committee is simply 'to bear in mind the best interests of other peoples in Fiji'.
>
> Realistic Fijians must acknowledge that the majority of the popula-

tion cannot justly or sensibly or lightly be disposed of in such terms. Does the Governor-General think that the answer to our national predicament is to become a watered-down South Africa?[17]

On 17 August 1987 Ratu Penaia received two reports: a Majority Report that echoed the submissions of the Great Council of Chiefs, and a Minority Report setting out the recommendations and opinion of the NFP/FLP Coalition. The committee's proposals that Fiji should become a republic found little support because that would have entailed cutting ties with the Royal Family and the Commonwealth. The Minority Report, signed by four members of the Coalition and two nominees of the Governor-General, called for a return to the 1970 Constitution, as the signatories were satisfied that Fijian interests were adequately represented and protected under that Constitution. Further, they maintained that if the Majority Report's submissions were to be implemented, Fiji Indians would become 'third-class' citizens and be effectively confined to the opposition benches for the rest of their lives.

The Majority Report, signed by 10 members comprising representatives of the Alliance Party, the Great Council of Chiefs and two of the four nominees of the Governor-General, unabashedly demanded that political control remain solely in the hands of the Fijians, in perpetuity. Falvey, a former European Member for the Southern Division in the 1960s, who at that time had declared: 'I am unalterably opposed to any constitutional change which might allow any single racial group immediately, or remotely, to dominate the rest,'[18] now, in 1987, tacitly supported the demands made in the Majority Report.

Proposals contained in the Majority Report included: abolishing the Senate and expanding the House of Representatives from 52 to 71 members, of whom 40 should be Fijians; 22 Indians; eight General Electors and one representative of the island of Rotuma. Fijian members would thus be increased by 18: eight to be appointed by the Great Council of Chiefs; four by the Prime Minister; and six elected from the 14 provinces. The Majority Report also recommended that the Great Council of Chiefs should nominate the Governor-General and a Deputy to act in his absence. If the Great Council of Chiefs made no nomination then the Speaker of the House should act as Governor-General. Tenure of the office of Governor-General should be for a fixed five-year term.

This Report also recommended that the Prime Minister should be a Fijian member in the House, who, in the Governor-General's judgement, was best able to command a majority in the House; and that the four key portfolios of Home Affairs, Fijian Affairs, Foreign Affairs and Finance always be held by Fijians. On the voting system, the Report recommended the abolition of the national roll and national seats; all seats in the House of Representatives to be contested on the communal basis with members being elected only by voters of their own communal group. In addition the Constitution was to spell out, as a major concern to the Fijians: recognition and application of customary law; rights of ownership and use in respect of riverbeds and the foreshore (including swamps, reefs and sandbanks); proprietary rights in relation to minerals; and protection of national heritage.

Bearing all the hallmarks of the demands of the Fijian Nationalist Party, the Majority Report also recommended that Parliament should be authorized to pass laws, in special sectors, positively discriminating against other races for the benefit of Fijians and Rotumans. It, however, recommended that the Queen should remain as Fiji's Head of State.[19]

The Governor-General, having obtained a blueprint for the proposed Constitution, soon found that he was running into uncompromising opposition from the Indians in the form of strikes, boycotts, and bomb blasts. The economy had already taken a heavy toll, noticeably in the two main sources of foreign currency: tourism and sugar. In late June 1987, the currency was devalued by 17.75 per cent and many businessmen and foreign corporations had already smuggled money out of the country. Tourism had been devastated since the 14 May coup, and the sugar crop, mainly in Indian hands, was severely reduced due to a prolonged boycott of the harvest earlier in the year.

In a bid to salvage the country from the brink of economic chaos, and a possible racial war, Bavadra was once again approached to help the Governor-General in the process of 'national reconciliation' and to convince the world that normality had been restored; and, following a series of talks with Ratu Mara, he was finally persuaded to accept the task of forming a caretaker government. Rival parties were to have equal representation in the caretaker government and it would be headed by the Governor-General. In the talks, later known as the Deuba Accord, Bavadra agreed to drop his Supreme Court action against Ratu Penaia, which sought a ruling that Governor-General's dissolution was illegal. The two sides also agreed to the setting up of a new constitutional review committee, comprising three representatives from each side, under a foreign chairman, to examine a 'new form of democracy' for Fiji. The two sides were to take into consideration Fijian demands to strengthen their constitutional, economic and social demands, but the Constitutional Review Committee should provide 'a framework for the multi-racial society in which the rights and interests of all the communities are safeguarded'.[20]

The news brought an immediate protest from the extreme *Taukei* Movement which branded the new deal a 'sell-out' and threatened to use force to secure the constitutional changes advocated by the chiefs. One of the foremost *Taukei* leaders, Ratu Meli Vesikula, announced that the agreement was unacceptable, and later said, 'It is taking the Fijian people back to square one minus. . . . A government of national unity has never given stability in a political climate similar to the one existing in Fiji.'[21] Nevertheless, on Friday 25 September 1987, the two parties went ahead to prepare for the formation of a caretaker government. The formation never took place. At 4 p.m. on the same day Rabuka struck for the second time and resumed control of the country. In a radio broadcast he said that recent developments had made it clear that the objectives of the coup he led in May had not been achieved. He would not tolerate any attempt to deviate from his objectives of giving political control to Fijians. He also disclosed that he had never agreed to the proposed political settlement between the two rival parties; he had told the Governor-General only that he would watch the progress of their discussion.

While the international community and the Queen reacted with shock and sadness, Rabuka remained defiant but in firm control. He indicated that he would declare Fiji a republic, possibly on 10 October, the 17th anniversary of Fiji's independence. Ratu Vesikula who, as former NCO in the Duke of Wellington's Regiment in the British Army, had seen action in Northern Ireland, Cyprus and Malaysia, said that in the light of his experience the military solution was the only option in the current ethnic crisis.[22]

Two days after the second coup, on Sunday 27 September, Rabuka went to Government House to ask the Governor-General for recognition of his military coup, but Ratu Penaia declined, refusing to concede his executive authority as head of Fiji's interim government. 'It will take lions to move me out of here', he said later. In the meeting between the two men Rabuka also offered the Governor-General the presidency in his new republic—an offer that reportedly was refused. Meanwhile, Ratu Penaia reassured the Queen through her Private Secretary that he still remained at his post. The telephone conversation between Ratu Penaia and the Queen's Private Secretary led to an appeal, on the Queen's behalf, to the traditional chiefs in an attempt to win support for Ratu Penaia, in the following terms:

> For her part Her Majesty continues to regard the Governor-General as her representative and the sole authority in Fiji. Anyone who seeks to remove the Governor-General from office would in effect be repudiating his allegiance and loyalty to the Queen. Her Majesty hopes that even now the process of restoring Fiji to constitutional normality might be resumed. Many Fijians hold firm their allegiance to the Crown and to the Governor-General as the Queen's personal representative. The Queen would be deeply saddened if these bonds of mutual loyalty and affection which have so long held the Fijian people and the British monarchy together were to be severed.[23]

This intervention was a decisive factor leading Rabuka to take an abrupt turn. He temporarily shelved his plan to declare Fiji a republic, dismiss the Governor-General, scrap the 1970 Fiji Constitution and install himself as head of an interim government. Instead he entered into another round of talks with the Governor-General in an effort to break the political and constitutional deadlock. Furthermore, the Queen's intervention shifted the focus of attention from the question of Indians' political rights, which her representative had conceded must be trimmed to solve the crisis, to that of whether or not Fiji would become a republic. Regarding the Queen's role *The Guardian* (London) remarked:

> When the crisis began she refused to see the constitutional Prime Minister of Fiji. This may turn out to have been decisive. It was clearly not Dr Bavadra's or his democratically elected government's fate but that of her representative, the Governor-General, that she was concerned about. He put up a fight and she backed him; but the true individual victim of the Fijian putsch is Dr Bavadra, leader of a bi-racial coalition which won an election fair and square.[24]

Others have also analysed the Queen's role in the crisis. Ramesh Thakur and Anthony Wood raised the question as to who advised her and on the basis of what precedents. By her actions, they observed, the Queen was creating precedents for the future in all the realms in which she has a Governor-General. They went on to conclude:

> The Queen not only accepted as valid her representative's endorsement of the coup; she further accepted that, law and convention notwithstanding, he could dispense with a responsible ministry and himself become her adviser. The Queen's role was so passive that she would not intervene even to uphold her own Constitution. It was her representative who had the exclusive right to act as head of state. Nevertheless, the monarch's intervention was apparent and significant. Apart from the statement from the Palace rejecting a meeting with Dr Bavadra, there remain on public record the Queen's words of praise for Sir Penaia, quoted by him the day after he had secretly sworn in Colonel Rabuka.[25]

On 5 October the Governor-General initiated a final round of talks involving himself, Rabuka, Ratu Mara, and Bavadra, in the western township of Lautoka on the issue of a caretaker government under his chairmanship. These talks broke down when Rabuka presented eight demands from the army to be incorporated into the new Constitution, as 'minimum requirements', before handing back executive authority to the Governor-General. In order to help Ratu Penaia 'remain in control of the country' Ratu Mara agreed to these demands but Bavadra rejected them as 'striking at the very roots of democratic process', while the Coalition said it was 'shocked and saddened that they had been accepted by the Alliance'.

The following day Rabuka executed his longstanding threat and, one minute after midnight on 6 October 1987, declared Fiji a republic, effectively severing the country's 113-year links with the Crown and raising the possibility of expulsion from the Commonwealth. While assuring the Indians they had 'nothing to fear', he hinted at the likelihood of the Governor-General becoming the President of the Republic of Fiji. Ra-

buka also appointed an Executive Council of 21 members, with himself
as head and as home affairs and public service minister. The Council included two senior military officers, at least six members of the *Taukei*
Movement, and several members of the Alliance Party. The only Indian
was Mrs Narayan who, though not Fiji-born, was named the newly
created Minister for Indian Affairs. The *Taukei* members included Ratu
Vesikula, who was appointed the new Minister for Fijian Affairs. The
leader of the Fiji Nationalist Party, Sakeasi Butadroka, was also included
in Rabuka's new administration as the Minister for Lands. The appointment of these two men effectively defeated any hopes that the oppression of the Indians would be eased. Rabuka said that the presence of the
Governor-General at Government House did not undermine his regime's
authority, 'It just shows my respect for the person.' But how long would
he be allowed to stay? 'He can stay there forever.' The Governor-
General, backed by Rabuka, soon made a last-ditch attempt to persuade
the Queen to amend the country's Constitution. On 11 October, in an
interview with London's Radio 4 programme, 'The World This Weekend',
he said that the military would step down if changes to safeguard the
rights of the Fijians were made in the Constitution.

Earlier, on 9 October his emissary Ratu Mara arrived in London and
went to the Palace seeking an audience with the Queen. She refused to
see him, referring him to her Private Secretary, Sir William Heseltine.
The Queen and Sir William flew to Vancouver a few hours later for the
Commonwealth summit where the fate of Fiji was soon to be decided.
The Queen's refusal to see Ratu Mara signalled that she would not tolerate a racially biased Constitution for the future rule of Fiji. The last
flicker of hope that the Queen would act decisively having died, led to
speculation that the Governor-General might step down to enable Rabuka to achieve the aim of the coup: power to the chiefs.

On 15 October 1987 Ratu Penaia resigned. In his letter of resignation
to the Queen (who was at the Vancouver Summit as Head of the Commonwealth) Ratu Penaia wrote: 'My endeavours to preserve constitutional government in Fiji have proved in vain, and I can see no alternative way forward.' The Queen, in regretfully accepting the resignation,
expressed her gratitude for his loyal services and admiration for his cou-
rageous efforts to prevent Fiji becoming a republic, and added that she
was sad 'to think that the ending of Fijian allegiance to the Crown
should have been brought about without the people of Fiji being given an
opportunity to express their opinion on the proposal'.[26]

As Fiji took the Governor-General's departure in its stride,
speculation began that Rabuka's next move would be to ask the two high
chiefs, Ratu Penaia and Ratu Mara, to become President and Prime
Minister respectively Ratu Penaia, on the other hand, as he left for his
home on the island of Tavenui for a 'rest', said he would not accept the
presidency. He had earlier indicated that he would decide whether to
become president after seeing the new Constitution which 'must be

acceptable in every way to the people of Fiji and internationally, so that hopefully it would enable Fiji to be readmitted to the Commonwealth. A referendum would be ideal. If a republic was to be set up it should be with the agreement of the people'.[27]

But in a dramatic twist of events Rabuka, later promoted by Ratu Penaia to the rank of Brigadier, announced on 5 December over Radio Fiji that he was surrendering power to the new President of Fiji, Ratu Sir Penaia Ganilau, the former Governor-General of Fiji. He said the country would return to a 'civilian' government on 5 December 1987 headed by Ratu Penaia, 'whom I believe all the people of Fiji trust could assume the burden of leading the restoration to Fiji of normality'. Rabuka said he had never wanted permanent supreme power for himself, and the military had supported him during the two coups to 'prevent what we had seen over the past few years: the gradual erosion of the Fijian way of life with threats to the customs and traditions of the Fijian people'.[28]

The former Governor-General appointed his one-time political ally and leader, Ratu Mara, as Prime Minister of the Republic of Fiji. On 9 December 1987, the new premier, who had been given a free hand to choose his colleagues, announced the formation of a 21-member Cabinet made up of his former Cabinet ministers, four members of the military and some members of the *Taukei* Movement, with Brigadier Rabuka as Minister for Home Affairs to maintain law and order in the country. Rabuka's acceptance of a Cabinet post contrasted with his assertion throughout the coups that he intended to 'go back to the village or perhaps write a book'.

The new Cabinet, comprising 17 Fijians, two Indians and two part-Europeans, saw the departure of some of the 22 Council of Ministers in Rabuka's interim government; they were each given 10 months' salary in compensation. While Ratu Mara spoke of parliamentary democracy, a faction of the *Taukei* charged Rabuka with selling out. Among them were Ratu Vesikula and Butadroka, both Ministers in the previous military administration whom Ratu Mara had ruthlessly dumped. Ratu Vesikula, a minor chief, announced plans to join forces with the Fijian Nationalist Party to represent the 'true aspirations of the Fijian people'. The old Mara-Ganilau combination is 'being rammed down our throats again', declaimed the one-time right-hand man of Brigadier Rabuka who had unceremoniously been left in the cold to 'reclaim his Fijian birthright'. Rabuka retorted that he had appointed a civilian government because its military predecessor was becoming corrupt. 'It was obvious that some of my ministers were using the powers I gave them to achieve their own ends.' He warned the *Taukei* that the army would stand firmly behind Ratu Mara's civilian government.

The role of the Governor-General emerges as the most complex and contentious issue in the whole saga. According to Thakur and Wood he had three possible courses of action: (1) he could have used the prestige of high office to lead a fight for the restoration of democracy and of the ousted government; (2) he could have acted within the conventions of

British constitutional monarchy, finding therein guidance for his actions; or, (3) as he, in fact, did conform to political pressures, precepts and expectations of party and race, use his position to contain excesses of military rule without disavowing the coups' aims.[29]

It does seem that the Governor-General was aware of the imminence of Rabuka's first coup. As a former Deputy Prime Minister he was also aware that Fijian rights were fully protected in the 1970 Constitution, and yet he remained silent on the issue. Instead, he threw in his lot with the Great Council of Chiefs and Rabuka to reduce Indians to 'second-class' citizens. Most importantly, his repeated claims that he was the sole legitimate authority on the islands may have been the factor that prevented the Queen (and possibly, too, many other countries) from acting firmly and promptly against Rabuka. Above all, could the Governor-General have prevented the coup?

The first major sign of Fijian revolt against the Bavadra government took the form of street demonstrations on 23 April 1987. Afterwards, the anti-Bavadra demonstrators handed a petition to the Governor-General in which they declared a vote of no confidence in the NFP/FLP government. The deposed commander of the army, Brigadier Nailatikau, has disclosed that a day before the demonstrations he called together available officers and told them that since the *Taukei* march was to go ahead, they must perform their duty 'if things got out of hand and we were called in'. Earlier, Bavadra, Ratu Penaia and Nailatikau had held a crisis security meeting, as most of the demonstrators were Fijians. As pointed out in the last chapter, the demonstration was noisy but ended peacefully.

What did the Governor-General know about the first coup? When did he know? Firstly, it could be argued that although the Governor-General had constitutional authority, he would be powerless to prevent a coup taking place or to effectively oppose one when it happened. If, however, he had prior knowledge of the imminence of a coup he could at least have alerted the government, or the commander of the army—unless the Governor-General himself was party to the plot. There is evidence that he had been warned of the first coup. What is not known is whether he had alerted the then army commander, Brigadier Nailatikau, before he (Nailatikau) left for Australia in April, shortly after the street demonstrations. The then Prime Minister, Bavadra, was definitely not warned of a possible military coup against his government.

In November 1987 Rabuka disclosed that he had warned the Governor-General that if he 'did not stage a political coup, I would stage a military coup'.[30] According to him:

The *Taukei* Movement emerged—with all its plans for violence, demonstrations and arson. It was at that point that I went to the Governor-General, Ratu Penaia, and asked him if there was something we could do. This was particularly after the *Taukei* had submitted their petition to him expressing displeasure at an Indian-dominated government and urging him to intervene and seek an immediate review of the Constitution. I told him that *if he did not stage a political coup, I would stage a military coup.* I then left.[31] (my emphasis)

Clearly, then, the Governor-General was aware that Rabuka might launch a military coup. Yet, as the Commander-in-Chief of the armed forces, it seems that he neither made any move to alert Rabuka's immediate superiors nor did he dissuade Brigadier Nailatikau from leaving the country. Brigadier Nailatikau claims that he knew nothing of the 14 May coup, but if this was so why did the Governor-General not inform Brigadier Nailatikau so that he could keep Rabuka and other possible coup plotters under surveillance? Or was it simply a lapse of memory on the Governor-General's part? If we are to believe Rabuka, or Brigadier Nailatikau, the Governor-General knew of a possible coup, if he was not actually a co-conspirator. In sum, both the Governor-General and Brigadier Nailatikau's explanations need further qualifications, and the two questions regarding what the Governor-General knew about the first coup, and when he knew it, remain unanswered.

And what of the role of another prominent figure—Ratu Mara? He and Rabuka were 'seen playing golf—separately—at Pacific Harbour Golf and Country Club 40 km west of Suva. Rabuka has denied widespread speculation that Ratu Mara helped plot the coup. According to Ritova and Dean, Rabuka met Ratu Mara and his Samoan guests at the golf course and the latter invited Rabuka for lunch. At lunch there was a wide range of casual talk and local politics, naturally enough, were raised. Rabuka was interested in Ratu Mara's opinion about the way things were heading, and his views on the status of the 1970 Constitution:

We were talking about politics, and I asked how can the Constitution be changed? He [Mara] said the Constitution could not now be changed. The only way to change it—and to use his exact words—'is to throw it out and make a new one, and the likelihood of that is nil'.

Rabuka thinks Ratu Mara was speaking lightly, more in jest then seriousness, for the benefit of his guests,[32] but a week later they were sharing power in Rabuka's interim government.

The Alliance Party/Ratu Mara

A vice-president of the Fiji Labour Party, Simione Durutalo, said Ratu Mara 'has kidnapped democracy and destroyed his own creation, the 1970 Fiji Constitution'. He told *Radio New Zealand* in an interview from Hawaii (where he had fled with his wife and children on the day of the coup), that 'Rabuka is just a pawn. The real man behind the coup is Ratu Sir Kamisese Mara and others in the Alliance Party.' Durutalo, a Fijian, and former University lecturer, said that Ratu Mara during his 17 years in power had 'pretended to the world that he was a multi-racial man and that he was for democracy'.[33]

The leader of the breakaway *Taukei* faction, Ratu Vesikula, said, 'It's more and more the Alliance team back in place. This is the old system being rammed down our throats again in a roundabout way—the backdoor. I would like the indigenous Fijian people to stand united and say, No, enough is enough",'[34] He asserted:

> I see no chance at all of my two ratus [chiefs] here changing their out-look and their life and the running of the country in general ... They were responsible for the 1970 Constitution and putting them back there is tempting fate. What has the old system achieved for the Fijian people? It has achieved the erosion of traditional leadership, ... a lack of patriotism ... disparity between the races in Fiji. It has culmi-nated in two military coups and the possibility of another or some other form of violence.... The Great Council of Chiefs had clearly stated that it will nominate the President, and the Prime Minister would be elected by secret ballot after the general elections. I'm sorry to say this but I feel Rabuka handed power back to a dictator on five December.[35]

In the perspective of history, Ratu Vesikula, himself a chief, must be aware of the historical antecedents of Fijian power. Since 1967 Ratu Mara had been at the helm of both traditional and political leadership of the country, a relic of Fiji's colonial past. Symbolically and in reality Ratu Mara signified the magnitude of power behind chiefly authority. David Routledge, in his study of the struggle for political dominance between the great chiefdoms of pre-colonial Fiji, points out that political leadership had always been in the hands of the great chiefs, and Ratu Mara had ef-fectively combined high traditional status with high political office. In 1987, as a consequence, when only the 'modern' dimension of that leadership emerged in Dr Bavadra, Ratu Mara was unwilling to accept him or afford him the mantle of legitimacy.

It could be argued, therefore, that Rabuka simply handed over to the two high chiefs, Ratu Mara and Ratu Penaia, the power which had tem-porarily slipped out of their hands following the surprise victory of the NFP/FLP Coalition, led by two prominent Fijian commoners, Dr Ba-vadra and Dr Baba. By the end of 1987 the two high chiefs, representing largely the eastern chiefly class, thus, as they had in 1970, found them-selves back in the seats of power. Routledge noted that, at the time of Fiji's independence:

> Successors of the ruling chiefs of early Fiji thus found themselves in power once again giving the appearance of continuity between the pre-1874 and post-1970 political order. The Prime Minister, Ratu Sir Kamisese Tuimacilai Mara bears names that were famous in tradi-tional times. Head of the Vaunirewa, holds the titles of Sau, Tui Nay-

au and Tui Lau and is thus heir to the Fijian paramount line in Lau islands and the Tongan line established by Ma'afu. His wife, Adi Lady Lala, is the Roko Tui Dreketi and *vasulevu* through her mother to the chiefdom of Nadroga. Both, in addition, are direct descendants of the first Cakobau as are Ratu Sir George Cakobau, present Vunivalu of Bau and former Governor-General, and Ratu Sir Penaia Ganilau, kins of the Tui Cakau and present Governor-General. These are merely the most obvious relationships at the highest levels, for intermarriage and the *vasu* ties thus created between chiefdoms are still very much part of the politics of power in Fiji.[36]

The late Dr Rusiate Nayacakalou, in his study of modern and traditional Fijian leadership, warned that 'attempts to displace existing leaders are viewed with suspicion and jealousy and may be met with drastic action'.[37] This may be one of the reasons that prompted Rabuka to react violently, especially as Ratu Penaia, one of the four hereditary chiefs involved, was his own tribal chief. It also reflects the trauma of an indigenous people struggling to encompass tradition within the framework of democracy.

But tradition aside, Ratu Mara's role must be examined in the context of his longstanding position both as a leading politician and as Prime Minister of Fiji.

Unlike Durutalo and Ratu Vesikula, two Fijians prominent in their own society, some have been more charitable in passing judgement on Ratu Mara's involvement in the coup. The Australian journalist, Stuart Inder, of the *Bulletin*, while boasting of securing the first exclusive interview with Ratu Mara shortly after the coup, exonerates him of any serious breach of democratic ideals. As a Pacific reporter for 35 years, who has known Ratu Mara for more than 20 years, Inder remarked that 'my own dismay is even greater than his that a Commonwealth statesman with such a long record of achievement and moderation could be so instantly and savagely condemned abroad without my evidence of his actions'.[38] After a telephone conversation with Ratu Mara on 17 May (the fourth day of the coup) Inder later concluded that 'history will recall the full, extraordinary story of the Fiji coup. It will, I predict, be more generous to Mara than were his fair-weather friends in Canberra and Wellington'.[39] Inder had Prime Minister Lange in mind, who had accused Ratu Mara of treachery under Fiji's Constitution suggesting that Ratu Mara allegedly fomented the rebellion against the Queen.

Firstly, it is in terms of Ratu Mara's own past actions and statements that his role in the current Fijian crisis must be examined. In 1982, in an exclusive interview with Stuart Inder, he alleged that the USSR had funnelled $1 million into the NFP's coffers to oust him from power. He failed to support the charges, claiming that to do so would endanger national security.

When the first coup occurred, in May, Ratu Mara was co-chairing the meeting of the PDU at The Fijian hotel. Although maintaining that he had no prior knowledge of the coup, he told a veteran Fiji journalist, Robert Keith-Reid, while on his way to meet Rabuka on 15 May, that he first heard of the military takeover at 9 a.m. on Thursday (the coup occurred at 10 a.m.), and was shocked and saddened. But after Rabuka had called on him at The Fijian for help he had agreed to serve on the Council of Ministers as Minister for Foreign Affairs, an action he later justified in the following terms:

> I had to do it, because if my house was on fire with my family inside
> ... why should I wait? I must try and rescue them. At our first meet-
> ing, Col Rabuka told us that he was a soldier and did not want to run
> the government ... the sooner he gets back to camp the better it
> would be for all. Col Rabuka then appointed me to look for ways and
> means of bringing about a quick return to normal life. In fact I was his
> *matani vanua* (spokesman) to Government House, until both he and
> the Governor-General agreed that I should advise them, resulting in
> the compromise we now have. I had to do something, because a lot of
> people were saying that I was responsible for bringing about the crisis,
> claiming there were many loopholes in the Constitution. I have now
> done my best in trying to rectify that matter. When Col Rabuka's
> constitutional council decide[s] on something, it will be good for you,
> and the nation as a whole.[40]

Ratu Mara's acceptance of a post in Rabuka's interim government, instead of condemning the racial motivation that lay behind it, cast doubts upon the sincerity of his professed belief in the concept of multiracialism. While the Australian Prime Minister Hawke condemned the coup, his acting Foreign Affairs Minister, Senator Gareth Evans, questioned Ratu Mara's role as a member of the new government. He said Ratu Mara's earlier statements about how shocked he was by the coup appeared to be at variance with his new position. Prime Minister Lange added: 'I believe a word three or four weeks ago from Ratu Mara in support of the constitutional process would have averted all this.'[41] In an editorial the *Sydney Morning Herald* observed that:

> Significantly, Ratu Mara has joined the interim military government —
> a very clear signal that the last thing the traditional Fijian nobility
> wants is a restoration of the Bavadra Government. Even if only a [few]
> ethnic Fijians had foreknowledge of the detailed planning of this
> week's coup, its aftermath suggests that the ethnic Fijian establishment
> had discussed a contingency plan along these lines for years.[42]

The following selected extract from an interview that Ratu Mara gave to a New Zealand television team throws light on some of the questions raised shortly after the coup.

> *Q:* Sir, you were subjected to some very harsh criticism from the

Prime Ministers of Australia and particularly New Zealand. They claim you either could have stopped it or were possibly involved in the coup. What was the story?

A: Well, I was like many of my colleagues who were having a meeting at the Fijian Hotel, on the Democratic Union. We were all quite shocked. I could not believe it at first. I thought the one who communicated with me from the Opposition Office was joking . . . he told me that he was not joking. In fact they are locked up in the Opposition room and (asked) what they should do. I said, 'Well, what were you told to do?' He said, 'We were told to stay here.' I said, 'Well, for God's sake stay there.' I wouldn't know what to do. Then, almost immediately after the announcement of the coup, the radio broadcasts from Australia and New Zealand began to highlight what was happening in Fiji and then the opinions of both leaders whom I thought were quite precipitate in their judgement. They seem to have focused on the role that I have played, in that I have masterminded the coup, and the reason why I did this was in order to get back into power and the reason why I wanted to get back into power was to cover up for corruption. This is all news to me. When I lost the election, I took it as I expected it. It was a fair election. I lost by a small margin, but that was it.

Q: One of the criticisms that Mr Lange made against you was that you failed to say anything or do anything about the Taukei Movement, the marchers and the growing discontent. Do you think in retrospect that you should have done (more) about Apisai Tora and what he was doing?

A: No, Apisai Tora and the other leaders were merely mouthpieces of the crowd, or people who have been meeting, and they were marching against the Constitution that I helped to construct and I couldn't understand why people ask me to say something. It'll be thrown back at my face and I wouldn't have any position to speak on later, if I had made a bid then.[43]

Meanwhile the two principal issues that dominated the meetings of the Great Council of Chiefs were republicanism and the drafting of a new Constitution to give Fijians political control over the Indians. The first raised the question of loyalty to the Queen and the second, the future not only of the Indians, but also of multiracial Fiji which Ratu Mara had been credited with keeping as a 'symbol of hope for the rest of the world'.

Thus Ratu Mara was again confronted with a cruel choice: whether to rest on his past laurels or protect his own position as the hereditary leader of his people. Historically, the Alliance Party and the chiefs who were members, had always rejected the idea of a republic. In the 1982 elections Ratu Mara had skilfully manipulated the Fijian voters, claiming that NFP/WUF's concept of a government based on the Singapore concept would see Fiji become a republic and the Fijian people's link with the Crown severed. In October 1982, when the Queen became the first reigning monarch to open a meeting of the Great Council of Chiefs in the eastern island of Bau, Ratu Mara, as both a Prime Minister and a High Chief, had told her that 'this is an event the memory of which will be treasured by all of us and will be transmitted in many ways to the generations that will follow'. In her speech she told the high chiefs.

> When your forefathers ceded the sovereignty of these islands to the British Crown 108 years ago, they gave it unceremoniously to Queen Victoria. They trusted her to govern righteously and in conformity with native systems of organisation and traditional leadership. I have been delighted to watch your country before and after you gained autonomy in 1970, and I take great pride in coming to you now as Queen of Fiji.[44]

Meanwhile, when, as Princess Elizabeth, the Queen had visited Fiji for the first time, she had echoed similar sentiments but had warned, 'I know that many difficult problems lie ahead, but I am sure that if you approach them as a united people, with the interests of the whole Colony at heart, they will eventually be overcome. I shall follow the future progress of the Colony with keen interest; and shall always pray for the happiness and prosperity of all its inhabitants.'[45]

Thirty years later the problems were now facing the Great Council of Chiefs. Ratu Mara, the most ardent foe of republicanism, had floated the concept of a republic at the meeting of the Great Council of Chiefs in July 1987, which was concerned to achieve Fijian political dominance. He also recommended increasing Fijian representation in the 52-seat House of Representatives by 10 to 32 seats, leaving Indians with 22 and other races with eight seats; later the Great Council of Chiefs introduced a 71-seat single House of Parliament. Ratu Mara, the great champion of multiracialism, ignored the fact that it was disunity among the Fijians, notably the educated urban middle-class Fijians, that had led to a largely Indian government and, for a moment, ended the rule of chiefs.

The seemingly docile and placid Indian community, not the General Electors, were selected as the best instrument to preserve the chiefly political kingdom which was fast disintegrating. In 1976 Ratu Mara, while rejecting a suggestion in the Senate by Senator Inoke Tabua, later a leading *Taukei* member, that 100,000 Fiji Indians should be deported, had said: 'It is now being suggested that there are sections of citizens of Fiji, particularly the Indians, who have not the same rights as any others. I do not see that. If I made a mistake at the conference, please do not support me at this forthcoming election [1977]. I would rather square my conscience with God then to be voted back into Parliament under false pretences. ... If you start removing Indians, the next ones will be the Chinese, the third ones will be the Europeans, and the fourth will be the Lauans.[46]

Ten years later, in 1986, while confronting the forward march of the

Labour Party, he had noted that 'the people of Fiji expect of our Government and our party, a strong progressive government—one truly representative of our multi-ethnic heritage, one in which bitterness, strife and rancour do not find a home. They expect to find in their leaders men (and women) who live above the fog, in public duty, and in private thinking, people whom the spoils of office cannot buy.'[47]

Yet two years later he recommended to the Great Council of Chiefs that it could be bought at the expense of democracy and the 'rights' of Indians, although they had not achieved political domination in 1987. As Robert Norton of Macquarie University, Australia, pointed out:

> They [the Indians] formed half the new Cabinet, and remained a minority in the House of Representatives, as they always would under the present Constitution. The seven Fijian members of the Coalition side held the real power. They could block any attempt by Indians to challenge Fijian privileges—a very unlikely event, for Indians well know the force of Fijian unity on this matter. But even had the Coalition members stood together in such a challenge the Council of Chiefs delegates in the Senate could overrule them. There can be no question that the recent elections did not undermine Fijian political power. Where then is the justification for constitutional change to secure Fijian interests?[48]

In 1976 Ratu Mara and his Alliance Party had rejected the recommendations of the Royal Commission of Inquiry. The following year, after losing the April 1977 elections, Ratu Mara reaffirmed his faith in the Constitution proclaiming that 'I have yet to find a Constitution in the world . . . which would improve on this we have'. But ten years later he was suggesting that the 1970 Fiji Constitution, of which he was the principal architect, be torn apart to fulfil the wishes of the Great Council of Chiefs. He tried to justify his action by laying blame elsewhere: 'I felt that the Constitution was right and I had consulted a constitutional expert, David Butler by name, and his opinion was that the Constitution is right and [if] the Fijians stay united, we would still have power for a long time.'[49]

He went on to state that the 'egg has been broken now. We cannot go back to the Constitution in which we enjoyed peace and stability for a long time and we have to find a Constitution that has to accommodate what has now been shown quite clearly: the wish of the indigenous people'.[50] After the general election in 1982, when the Great Council of Chiefs had called for total Fijian control of the country, one Fijian observer commented that it was directed as much against rebellious commoner Fijians as at non-Fijians. The chiefs, he suggested, were trying to impose 'a culture of silence upon everyone'.[51]

Reacting of the proposals made by the Great Council of Chiefs in 1987, Dr Baba, the former Fijian Minister for Education in Bavadra's government, pointed out that in their submission to the Constitutional

Review Committee the chiefs had proposed that even Fijians would be disenfranchized because Fijian members of Parliament were to be selected through the traditional process of consensus by the provincial councils. Dr Baba said that this was a 'regressive' step, designed to keep the Fijians backward'.[52] While charging that many of the chiefs had not read the Constitution or those sections dealing with Fijian safeguards on land and other related matters, as a member of a profession himself, Dr Baba, calling upon the anti-coup faction among the Fijians, urged 'all Fijians to work towards the restoration of democracy, for it was through democratic opportunities that we were able to be educated'.[53] an obvious reference to the Fijian nobility's contempt of educated Fijian commoners.

It becomes quite apparent that the only way to keep power in chiefly hands is to embark on undemocratic methods to curb the challenge from the Fijian commoners rather than to compete politically against the Fiji Indians. In reply to Ratu Mara, Dr Butler has pointed out that 'if the Fijians had stayed united Bavadra wouldn't have won',[54] a point conceded by Ratu Mara himself: 'I have stated before, we lost by four seats through the division of the Fijians, not simply by the unity of the Indians but through the division of the Fijians. If we have 40 seats and we are *divided* (my emphasis) we will still *lose*.'[55] Why then was there such an urgent need to amend the Constitution at the expense of the Indian community?

In Bavadra's opinion it was to silence such true apostles of Multiracialism as himself, who believed that the Indians and the Fijians are 'one people, one nation'. After being freed from custody he accused Ratu Mara of being behind the coup; he said that in his four weeks in office, he had only just begun to uncover the corruption in the previous administration, making charges that Ratu Mara has consistently denied.

A fortnight after the first coup Ratu Mara had declared publicly that he would resign from politics and not run for election again; Fiji had rejected his leadership and the future of the Alliance Party was for the party members to decide. He was, he said, responsible for the first Constitution, but would have nothing further to do with the new one; even if the Great Council of Chiefs approached him to seek re-election, he would tell them 'please don't try and flog a dead horse, I will not run'.[56]

Eight months later, after making those historical statements, Ratu Mara and his defeated Alliance members joined Rabuka's military bandwagon, without contesting elections, to lead the country. In his address to the nation as the new, unelected, Prime Minister of the Republic of Fiji, Ratu Mara said: 'Fellow citizens, let me assure you that I am not an opportunist.'[57]

What did Ratu Mara know about the first coup? When did he know?

220 'Soldiers in Paradise'

Notes

1. Stan Ritova and Eddie Dean, 1988, p. 44. Captain X has been identified as Isireli Dugu, and his second in command was Captain Savenaca Draunidalo, the ex-husband of Adi Kuini Bavadra, wife of Prime Minister Bavadra.
2. *Islands Business* (Fiji), May 1988. Jone Veisamasama, one of the three key figures at the 19 April 1987 meeting, was killed in July 1988 when a pen pistol he was carrying accidentally triggered.
3. Ritova and Dean, 1988, pp. 49-50.
4. Ibid., p. 50.
5. *Fiji Times*, 31 March 1987, p. 12.
6. *Hansard* (Fiji),14 May 1987.
7. *Fiji Sun*, 15 May 1987.
8. Rabuka and Nailatikau had disagreed in the past. Rabuka, when commanding Fiji's battalion in the Sinai, defied an order from Nailatikau and allowed Major Ratu George Kadavulevu Naulivou to travel to Fiji to attend his father's funeral.
9. Personal conversation, 29 June 1988, London.
10. *Sunday Sun* (Fiji), 13 February 1983, p. 1.
11. Ibid.
12. Ritova and Dean, 1988, pp. 74-76.
13. Ibid., p. 74.
14. *The Bulletin Magazine*, 2 June 1987, p. 21.
15. *Fiji Times*, 4 July 1987, p. 3.
16. Ibid.
17. Ibid., 6 July 1987, p. 6.
18. Quoted in Ahmed Ali, 1977, p. 34.
19. See *Pacific Islands Monthly* (*PIM*), September 1987, pp, 22-25.
20. *Financial Times* (London), 26 September 1987.
21. *The Daily Telegraph* (London), 26 September 1987, p. 32.
22. See *The Dominion Sunday Times*, Wellington, New Zealand, 15 November 1987.
23. *The Independent* (London), 30 September 1987, p. 1.
24. *Editorial*, 7 October 1987.
25. *The World Today*, December 1987, p. 207.
26. *The Daily Telegraph*, 16 October 1987, p. 1.
27. *The Times* (London), 20 October 1987.
28. *PIM*, January 1988.
29. *The World Today*, December 1987, p. 207.
30. *India Today*, 30 November 1987, p. 48.
31. Ibid.
32. Ritova and Dean, 1988, p. 80.
33. *The Sydney Morning Herald* (Australia), 18 May 1987.
34. *Islands Business*, February 1988, p. 10.
35. Ibid., p. 11.
36. David Routledge, 1985, p. 220.
37. R.R. Nayacakalou, 1975.
38. *Islands Business*, June 1987, p. 20.
39. Ibid.
40. *Fiji Times*, 23 May 1987, p. .3.
41. *The Sydney Morning Herald*, 16 May 1987.
42. Ibid.
43. *Commonwealth Today*, September/October 1987, p. 3.
44. *The Daily Telegraph*, 1 October 1982.
45. *Fiji Times*, 16 December 1953.
46. Ibid., 20 September 1976, p. 6.
47. Ibid., 1 July 1986, p. 7.

48. *Islands Business,* July 1987, p. 49.
49. *Fiji Sun,* 28 May 1987, p. 11. David Butler says: 'I only met Ratu Mara once in 1967, and I may have said this—not as a constitutional expert but as a sensible observer.'
50. *Commonwealth Today,* September/October 1987.
51. *Fiji Times,* 8 November 1982.
52. *PIM,* September 1987, p. 23.
53. *Fiji Times,* 22 May 1987, p. 14.
54. David Butler, personal communication.
55. *Commonwealth Today,* September/October 1987, p. 14.
56. *Fiji Sun,* 28 May 1987, p. 11.
57. *PIM,* February 1988, p. 6.

CHAPTER FOURTEEN

THE EXTERNAL DIMENSION

The evidence is circumstantial: there is no 'smoking gun'. But it's legitimate to ask: what did the US know? how soon did it know?; and if it knew, why didn't it tell the Bavadra government?

New Statesman, 28 May 1987.

The Queen cannot, and must not, connive at a constitution drawn up along racist lines. The Commonwealth must be similarly unequivocal when it meets this week in Vancouver. There is no reason to doubt the determination of either party, for racism is the rust that corrodes the ties binding the Commonwealth together.

Observer, 11 October 1987.

The CIA/US Links

'I am concerned', said the Commander-in-Chief of the United States Pacific Command (CINPAC), Admiral Ronald Hays, 'about the growth of the Fiji Labour Party. We will have to keep our eyes on Fiji'.[1] Admiral Hays was reflecting one of the Pentagon's major fears about the future stability of the South Pacific, a pro-Western region.

The Australian Shadow Foreign Minister, John Spender, recalled an American general's comments to him in Hawaii: 'We may not have great gains to make in the region, but we can suffer great losses.' In 1986 the chairman of the US Senate Foreign Relations Committee, Republican Richard Lugar, said he would soon be travelling to Australia, Indonesia, New Zealand, Taiwan and Fiji because 'American foreign policy is at a critical juncture in the Pacific'.[2]

The United States' primary interest in the Pacific region, according to the Department of State, was 'fostering the growth and stability of the region's democratic institutions'. David Laux, Director of Asian Affairs at the National Security Council warned that 'The long range danger of Soviet presence in the Pacific is that they will attempt to create political parties or back political parties that will be divisive and which will eventually lead to the establishment of regimes in the area that are sympathetic to the Soviet Union.'[3] The rise of the Fiji Labour Party and its perceived socialist policies were interpreted as a beginning. An Australian journalist, Bruce Loudon, wrote in April 1987 that 'Coalition win may mean turn to the left':

Socialists? Us? Heavens, no, insists the likeable Dr Bavadra. But all this seems to be a political expediency aimed at winning the election.

The Labour Party is leftist-oriented. It is the first avowedly radical party to gather strength since Fiji became independent. If it won power, albeit in coalition with the NFP, Fiji would, in time, become a very different place. Behind its present benign countenance is a party that is committed to the sort of 'active non-alignment' that would place Fiji alongside the likes of India, Zimbabwe and Cuba, and align it, in the South Pacific, with Vanuatu's Father Walter Lini. That is the worry about the election—that it could end up with victory for a coalition that will see Fiji along a decidedly leftist path. That would clearly be a concern for Australia, in particular, because there can be no minimising the importance of Fiji as a linchpin of Western and democratic interests in the region.[4]

Political observers began to speculate that the destabilization of the Coalition government was a real possibility. Since the main concern of the US was the Coalition's anti-nuclear and non-alignment policies, it was suggested that if Fiji 'is unlikely to be a Grenada, it could be a Chile', referring to the US's role in destabilizing Salvadore Allende's government, and the former US Secretary of State, Henry Kissinger's subsequent secret testimony to the White House, that 'I don't see why we need to stand by and watch a country go communist due to the irresponsibility of its own people'.[5] Dr William Sutherland, Dr Bavadra's permanent secretary, was among those who hinted at a possible coup, and in 1986 warned of the implications of the rise of the FLP on the platform of social reforms.

After any coup, conspiracy theories are liable to proliferate. Who was involved? Who had foreknowledge and at what point? The 14 May coup is no exception. Some circumstantial and some wild stories were published suggesting that various official and unofficial forces from outside Fiji had a hand in Rabuka's coup. Some are undoubtedly false but a few may have some substance. It is worth recording that there is little evidence of direct US involvement in the April elections, but the US did express concern at the Coalition's policies: a US State Department source said the anti-nuclear policy 'concerns us because the proliferation of nuclear-free zones ... without action by the Soviet Union to reduce arms, could affect our ability to deter by limiting the movement of American vessels and other components of our armed forces.'[6] On 23 April 1987, the day on which thousands of Fijians were involved in anti-Indian demonstrations, the US Embassy in Suva denied rumours that the US was behind the marches; and Leslie McBee, the Embassy's public affairs officer, also denied that US officials had been in Fiji the previous weekend.[7]

The rumours gained wider currency when, during a tour of South Pacific countries, Reagan's Ambassador-at-large, General Vernon Walters, made a 'courtesy call' on the Bavadra government and held talks with its Foreign Minister Krishna Datt—just one week before Rabuka seized power.

During his talks with Foreign Minister Datt about Labour's anti-nuclear policies, he stated that the US 'has a duty to protect South Pacific interests', especially from the Libyans. He said there was a Libyan presence in the region and 'I have seen some evidence, but I am not going to go into details. The United States is concerned with anything that might destabilize the area. All these island states are parliamentary democracies that share the same values as we do about peoples, about institutions and about freedom. Anything that threatens them is a concern to us.'[8] He described the Libyans as 'potential mischief makers', and sounded a note of caution about real Soviet motives in the region. In addition to separate meetings with Bavadra and Datt, he met some military officials including, reportedly, Rabuka.

Two days after General Walters left Fiji, the veteran *Sunday Times* (Fiji) columnist, Robert Keith-Reid, warned Bavadra: 'Tim's [Timoci] team is being portrayed by quite a few probing foreign TV [journalists] as being a red hot bunch of nationalising socialistic lefties intent on guiding our national destiny into the hands of the Libyans or somebody like that. If I was Tim I'd play it cool for ... maybe a very long time. You know what Ron Reagan did to Grenada.'[9]

When Rabuka staged his first coup the US was immediately suspected of being in some way involved. Rumours began to circulate of the US as well as the Libyans, Russians and the Iranians having been active in Fiji just prior to the coup. David Weisbrot, a senior lecturer in law at the University of New South Wales, said US involvement in the coup could not be discounted; Joan Coxsedge, a Labour member of the Victorian Parliament, who had accused the Carroll Team of 'propping up' the Alliance Party in the 1982 elections, also alleged that the coup was 'clearly planned by the CIA and pro-US groups in the South Pacific'. In fact, at the time of the coup, Ratu Mara, as we have noted, was at the right-wing PDU meeting, which had been partly funded by the US Republican Party. Among those attending the meeting were Ratu Mara's colleagues in the Australian Liberal Party which had provided $50,000 in 'aid' to the Alliance in 1982 to keep the 'Russians out'.

Some observers were of the opinion that this gathering of the conservatives could not have been a chance meeting. Others claimed that five CIA employees were 'active in Fiji', and that one of them was in Parliament at the time of the coup. On 16 May, *The Sydney Morning Herald*, quoting a Pentagon source, fuelled further speculations of possible CIA involvement, claiming that the Pentagon was delighted by the Fiji coup, and reporting the unofficial Pentagon response: 'We're kinda delighted. All of a sudden our ships couldn't go to Fiji and now all of a sudden they can. We got a little chuckle about the news. But it's a touchy situation. We believe in free elections. Overthrowing governments is not the way to do business.'[10]

Officially, however, in the words of its spokeswoman Ms Philip Oakley, the State Department said that 'The US government is profoundly disturbed whenever a democratically elected government is removed by force. We hope Fiji will return to democratic government as soon as possible'.[11] General Walters was reported to have remarked that any allegation that he had played a role in the coup was 'a fairy story, paranoia from the far side of the moon'. Even the US Secretary of State was drawn into the crisis as new reports alleged that he had given his approval to Rabuka's new military governments.

State Department spokesmn Charles Redman told reporters there was no truth Shultz had communicated US views on 'the new political arrangements in Fiji' to Ratu Mara. 'The Secretary has had no contact with any political leader in Fiji since immediately after the April elections when he sent a note of congratulations to Prime Minister Bavadra and a note of thanks for past co-operation to former Prime Minister Ratu Sir Kamisese Mara', he said. In early October 1987 Ambassador Stapleton Roy, Deputy Secretary for East Asia and Pacific Affairs, appeared before a sub-committee of the Foreign Affairs Committee of the US House of Representatives and rejected allegations of US involvement in the May coup. He also said that General Walters' visit to Suva was approved in advance by the Bavadra government, and that his schedule in Fiji was prepared in co-ordination with Bavadra's Foreign Ministry. Ambassador Roy told the committee:

> The US had no knowledge of either coup before they took place. Had we had advance knowledge we would have strongly and vigorously opposed them. Throughout the recent developments in Fiji our overriding concern has been to preserve and restore parliamentary democracy so that the nation's political institutions could continue to reflect a broadly based consensus.[12]

But suggestions that the US could have played a leading role in toppling the Bavadra government resurfaced when it was claimed that the armed soldiers who stormed Parliament 'were almost certainly Americans'. In an interview with Max Watts of 2SER radio in Sydney, the deposed Deputy Speaker of the House of Representatives, Noor Dean (a criminal lawyer), said he was convinced that the men who arrested him and his colleagues were not Fijian, Joann Wypijewski wrote in *The Nation*. Dean, according to Wypijewski, came to this conclusion after observing the body movement and comportment of US Marines onshore in Sydney. Dean told Wypijewski:

> At least some of them had blackened their hands with what appeared to be shoe polish. They never spoke, but gestured to one another using signals. Rabuka gave orders only in English, even at moments of extreme tension. The 10 hustled their captives into trucks, drove silently with them to army headquarters and there turned over to Fijian army regulars. Then the 10 disappeared.[13]

Wypijewski also quotes Jack Terrell, an expert on the world of mercenaries:

> ... Jack Terrell, a man intimate with the mercenary 'community' (most recently among the *Contras*) and now working as a special investigator in the Philippines for the Washington-based International Center for Development Policy ... told me he believes Rabuka led a squad of mercenaries—at least two of them Americans and two South Africans—acting with a nod from the U.S. government, possibly in the person of Vernon Walters, and brought in on a C-130 SAF Air charter, what he calls 'the Southern Air Transport of South Africa'. Watts has it from four separate sources in Fiji that one of the ten was a Fijian, a Captain Motu; this, says Terrell, is consistent with his theory, since such operations usually included a 'path-finder', or local military person acting as a guide.[14]

The US troops, according to Wypijewski, had landed in Fiji two days before the coup, and a further 50 arrived on 8 June, unloaded unspecified 'equipment' and left six hours later. Wypijewski continues:

> Terrell says for C-130s may have been in Fiji around the time of the coup, and here again Dean is instructive. He told Watts that a U.S. C-130 carrying fifteen black American troops landed unannounced and uncleared at Fiji's Nadi International Airport on May 12, two days before the coup. Watts's sources in Fiji have confirmed this with various civil service workers who requested anonymity. When asked at a June 22 press conference in Sydney to confirm or deny that such a plane had landed in Fiji on May 12, Secretary of Defense Caspar Weinberger offered a foggy disclaimer. Asked the same question on July 30, Pentagon spokesman Commander Chris Baumann said: 'I don't know anything about it. I can't categorically deny it, but I'd love to.'
>
> According to Dean, the plane stayed in Fiji for four days. On June 8, he said, another C-130, carrying about fifty U.S. soldiers, landed at Nausori Airport, eleven miles from Suva, unloaded unspecified 'equipment' and left six hours later. Could these troops have been in Fiji as insurance against a possible backlash? Watts reports an interesting exchange between an Australian attorney out for an evening stroll in Sydney and some U.S. marines who were docked there for two weeks at the beginning of June. The easygoing conversation turned to Fiji, upon which one of the men said, 'I was briefed—we have all been briefed—on Fiji', and another added: 'I am from the Dominican Republic. My country was invaded by American marines, and here I am doing the same thing.' Asked to expand on that, the marine said, 'No, I am forbidden to talk about this.'[15]

The US has refuted these allegations. Richard M. Teare, Deputy Chief of Mission at the US Embassy in Canberra, said 'the article is no more than a web of fabrications, half-truths, unfounded allegations and facts out of context'[16] and pointed out that the US had condemned the coup and had terminated all US assistance programmes to Fiji—actions that no government would take if it had sponsored those who seized power.

In the same article Wypijewski also examines the role of William Paupe, the South Pacific regional director of the US Agency for International Development, and his links with the Alliance MP Tora. In April 1987 Tora, who during the 1977 constitutional crisis had voted for an Indian Prime Minister (Koya) in preference to a Fijian (Captain Maitoga), had led the anti-Bavadra government. Thus Wypijewski asks: 'Where did Tora, who is no aristocrat and whose government salary came to no more than $25,000 a year, get the money to sponsor these [anti-government] activities?'[17]

In June 1987, in Washington, Bavadra had claimed to have information that Paupe had channelled $US 200,000 to Tora for the purpose of fomenting the anti-government demonstrations. Dr Sutherland, Bavadra's permanent secretary, claimed to have stumbled across a file that contained evidence of such a transaction. Paupe denies the allegation; Tora dismisses it as an 'absolute outrageous lie'; and the US Embassy in Fiji has denied all the charges.

The allegations are based on Paupe's earlier activities and the role of USAID in other countries, notably Vietnam and Chile. In Vietnam USAID was accused of acting as cover for CIA operations, and in 1964, it has been claimed elsewhere, the CIA with the co-operation of USAID secretly funnelled up $20 million into Chile to aid Eduardo Frei in his successful bid to defeat Allende for the presidency. Wyjpijewski comments on Paupe:

> He served with AID in Vietnam from 1966 to 1975, a time when the agency trained Vietnamese intelligence and police forces and operated alongside or in concert with the CIA. From 1977 to 1981 he was stationed in South Korea, where AID, through its bankrolling of the AAFLI, played a supporting role in the repression of labor and the obstruction of democratic opposition. His arrival in Fiji coincided with stepped-up US efforts to stifle anti-nuclear sentiment in the Pacific Trade Union Forum, a regional consortium of left/liberal trade unions in which the Fijian labor movement is prominent.[18]

Others have also levelled similar charges at Paupe, who was a former Deputy Assistant of Public Health in the USAID mission during the Vietnam War. James Anthony, an adviser to Bavadra, and the former trade union colleague of Tora, told a news conference in Washington that Paupe had handled $US200,000, describing him as 'a barefoot Ollie North running around the US Embassy in Fiji'.

Paupe, denying that he was CIA operative, said the charge was 'absurd'. The only US aid he had allotted to Tora's home village had been $US25,000 towards replacing a community hall which had been destroyed during a cyclone in 1984. Anthony says he never saw any evidence of such a hall. Asked why he thought Anthony could have made the allegations, Paupe said: 'I can't explain it. I am not a psychiatrist. I don't know what's going on in his head.'[19]

There are several other unexplained matters. Shortly after Rabuka usurped power he had stated that he was only restoring Fiji's pro—Western stance. 'The foreign minister (Krishna Datt) I just ousted is a known frequent visitor to the Soviet Union, and the finance minister (Mahendra Chaudhry) is a friend of the Soviet Union and Libya.'[20] It will be remembered that General Walters had referred to having some evidence of Libyan involvement but that he would not go 'into details'. The New Zealand Prime Minister Lange denied that either New Zealand or Australia had any intelligence information regarding General Walters' activities or discussions in Fiji. The deposed Foreign Minister Datt, whom Rabuka accused of having pro-Soviet sympathies, denies providing General Walters with any information on the subject. Where did General Walters see evidence of Libyan involvement? Who showed him? Rabuka?

On 16 February 1988 the US announced that it was sending an Ambassador to Fiji and starting Congressional talks about restoring about $1.3m in aid, suspended after the two military coups. Ironically, while vigorously applying its famous dictum 'who is not with us is against us' in the Caribbean against two military dictators in Haiti and Panama, Rabuka and his henchmen, led by Ratu Mara, were being welcomed back into the American fold. Shortly after accepting the post of Foreign Affairs Minister in Rabuka's military government, Ratu Mara and a team of military officers went in search of new trading partners, and arms for the RFMF to the South-East Asian countries, and reportedly stopped over at CINPAC headquarters in Hawaii.

In summary, to quote the *New Statesman* of 28 May 1987: 'The evidence is circumstantial: there is no "smoking gun". But it's legitimate to ask: what did the US know? how soon did it know?; and if it knew, why didn't it tell the Bavadra government?'

The Commonwealth

The Fiji Indians and the FLP/NFP Coalition regarded the meeting of the Heads of the Commonwealth in Vancouver in October 1987 as their last hope in the fight against racism. The issue of racism in South Africa was at the top of the Commonwealth Conference agenda when the crisis in Fiji occurred. Since the Commonwealth has given high priority to the struggle to end racist oppression in South Africa, and implicit in the Commonwealth stand is the recognition that apartheid is racism in, and enforced by, law, a flagrant denial of the UN Charter of Human Rights (1948), and of the ethic of human equality and fraternity which is fundamental to the Commonwealth, the official communiqué on Fiji was of extreme importance to the future of its people, especially the Fiji Indians. Developments in Fiji had earlier been equated with apartheid in South Africa, and there were demands for firm action from some quarters. The *Sunday Mirror* (London) wrote on 4 October 1987 that the 'mad colonel must be stopped', and that developments in Fiji 'displayed a revolting display of racism'. Its columnist urged that Rabuka 'must be condemned and regarded with utmost contempt if we are ever to combat the warped idea that one race is automatically superior to another. It is one of the most evil ideas that man has concocted.'

The *Observer* (London) on 11 October urged: 'The Queen cannot, and must not, connive at a constitution drawn up along racist lines. The Commonwealth must be similarly unequivocal when it meets this week in Vancouver. There is no reason to doubt the determination of either party, for racism is the rust that corrodes the ties binding the Commonwealth together.' The Australian shadow spokesman on foreign affairs, John Spender, perhaps summed up the argument when he said that 'if the Commonwealth is to be a viable and living international entity it must be able to provide leadership. If it cannot provide some kind of concerted action towards resolving the Fijian problem, not imposing an answer, it has reached a very sad state in its history.'[21]

When the Commonwealth Conference opened in Vancouver, South Africa and Fiji provided a sore test to the leaders. While the British Prime Minister, Thatcher, refused to act on the call for South African economic sanctions, and spoke in favour of keeping Fiji in the Commonwealth, the Indian Prime Minister Rajiv Gandhi strongly condemned the racism behind the coup, and, in his opening speech, said that 'any counsel of inaction would be a mockery of all that the Commonwealth stands for'. The Fijian minority, he said, had 'taken over the political and human rights of the Indian majority'. Mrs Thatcher pointed out that there were four military governments 'at the moment in the Commonwealth, sitting around that table', thus prompting the New Zealand Prime Minister Lange to remind the members that Fiji was the second country in the world where an individual's political rights will depend on his or her face. 'That's the crude fact about the development in Fiji', he said.

Conference members, while declaring that Fiji was no longer a member of the Commonwealth, in a special statement said that the Commonwealth was ready to offer its assistance towards a resolution of Fiji's problems 'on a basis consistent with the principles that have guided the Commonwealth', and 'could see a reconsideration of Fiji's membership at the next CHOGM conference in 1990'. During the debate Fiji found some friends, notably Malaysia and the Melanesian countries, led by Papua New Guinea. The then Papua New Guinea Prime Minister, Paias Wingti, strongly supported Fiji and made it clear that he would recognize the new regime. In August 1986 he had threatened to withdraw from the Commonwealth over Britain's refusal to apply economic sanctions to

230 The External Dimension

South Africa. A year later he seemed to be opting for 'Melanesian nationalism' rather than condemning the institutionalization of inherent racism on his own doorstep.

In August 1986, the Australian Prime Minister, Bob Hawke, had emphatically stated that 'the purpose of sanctions is precisely to bring home to the South African government that its present posture, a repressive defence of the status quo, entails costs and that a change of course would bring benefits. The object is not to bring South Africa to its knees but to bring it to its senses.'[22] But as far as Fiji was concerned, the Australian Cabinet decided against imposing a range of economic sanctions on the grounds that Fiji was economically already 'close to self-destruction'.

In January 1988 the Australian government lifted the suspension of aid, totalling about $20 million, after the decision by the government to recognize states rather than governments. It was strongly argued that to withhold recognition would be detrimental to Australia's interests in the region. Some thought otherwise. Fiji's deposed Prime Minister Bavadra, in a letter to the Acting Secretary of the Australian Labour party, protested that 'the move will be seen by the majority of Fijians as serving the self-interest of the Australian Labour Government, at the expense of labour principles and values in the region'. The New Zealand government also followed suit with the resumption of aid. The British government went further; it agreed to resume military training for the Fijian military after Mrs Thatcher and Prime Minister Ratu Mara had an hour of 'very friendly' talks at Downing Street in March 1988.

Another element of farce was the role of Fiji itself. Brigadier Rabuka had used the pretext of the indigenous rights to overthrow the Indian-dominated government, but Ratu Mara, on once again becoming Prime Minister, signed an agreement for $8 million of aid from France with the expectations of a further $7.5 million in soft loans. The Fijian navy also held naval exercises with its French counterpart, a country which has systematically denied the right of self-determination to her colonies in the South Pacific, including the indigenous Melanesian Kanaks in New Caledonia.

Meanwhile, Fijian troops still serve with the UN Peac-Keeping Forces in the Middle East, despite the fact that Fiji has flagrantly violated the UN's International Convention on the Elimination of All Forms of Racial Discrimination.

Perhaps the last words belong to Ratu Mara who once declared to the Commonwealth: 'Apartheid is anathema to us. We completely support majority rule in Rhodesia.'[23]

Notes

1. The *Guardian* (London), 15 May 1987, p. 21. See also Admiral Hays' interview with *Fiji* Times, 24 June 1986, p. 8.
2. *Fiji Sun*, 19 August 1986, p. 10.
3. Ibid., 6 October 1986, p. 8.
4. Ibid., 6 April 1987.
5. Seymour Hersh, *New York Times*, 11 September 1974.
6. *Fiji Times*, 23 April 1987.
7. *Fiji Sun*, 24 April 1987.
8. *Fiji Times*, 2 May 1987, p. 3.
9. *Sunday Times* (Fiji), 3 May 1987.
10. *Sydney Morning Herald*, 16 May 1987.
11. Ibid.
12. *Pacific Islands Monthly (PIM)*, December 1987, p. 16.
13. *The Nation*, 15-22 August 1987, p. 118.
14. Ibid.
15. Ibid.
16. *PIM*, January 1988, p. 9.
17. *The Nation*, 15-22 August 1987.
18. Ibid.
19. *Sydney Morning Herald*, 18 June 1987, p. 18.
20. Ibid., 18 May 1987.
21. *The Parliamentarian*, Vol. LXVIV, No. 1, January 1988.
22. Quoted in *Racism in South Africa: The Commonwealth Stand*, Commonwealth Secretariat, Marlborough House, London, 1987.
23. Ibid., June 1979, p. 9.

CHAPTER FIFTEEN

PARADISE LOST

I want them (Fiji Indians) to stay here. It will be a big challenge for us to convert them to Christianity. We either go that way, or they convert us and we all become heathens. Those who do not choose to become Christians can continue to live here, but they will probably find that it is a difficult place to live in.

The Minister for Home Affairs, Brigadier Sitiveni Rabuka, 1988.

Fiji, says the tourist poster, is 'the way the rest of the world should be'. But for the opponents of the military-backed regime, particularly the Fiji Indians, it ought not to be. Shortly after the official statement from the Commonwealth leaders in Vancouver, Dr Bavadra said, 'it will be a time of oppression, a time of isolation and a time of severe economic deprivations'. True to his predictions, grim stories of the torture, rape and harassment of Indians by Fijian soldiers emerged, later corroborated by Amnesty International. According to reports, the Fiji Indians were beaten, forced to stand in sewage pools and subjected to other forms of humilating treatment. A ban was imposed on any form of entertainment, coupled with the imposition of strict Methodist sabbatarianism on Fiji's Hindus and Muslims. The long anticipated day of judgement had finally arrived for the Fiji Indians.

A general review of the trend of events in Fiji's history shows that after its independence in 1970, Fiji remained a collection of peoples of different cultures and sub-cultures, with a Constitution that recognized the existence of different racial/cultural groups. As Spate had said:

Fijians and Indians seemed to me like a young couple, each with admirable qualities but with very differing and to quite an extent incompatible temperaments, forced into a marriage of inconvenience by selfish relatives (the colonial government and early settlers) and locked up in a small house with no chance of divorce. At least barring extremists on both sides, there seems to have been an honest effort to make the best of things.[1]

But Fiji faced its major crisis after independence, and the community became divided on racial lines with the formation of the FNP and the display of Fijian ethnic chauvinism, articulated through the Great Council of Chiefs, which demanded that two-thirds of the seats in the House should be reserved for Fijians; the Prime Minister and the Governor-General should always be Fijians. In the 1960s R.F. Watters had warned that 'little hope remains for Fiji unless all racial groups and especially the

Fijians act now, with vision, resolution and self-sacrifice to subordinate their narrow sectarian interests to the interests of the country as a whole'.[2] Thus in all Fijian leaders' pronouncements the events following the 1987 election was foreshadowed.

The Australian historian, K.L. Gillion, in his study of the history of Indians in Fiji, concludes that their history would show how they 'continued to adapt to the land to which their great grandparents came under such unhappy circumstances. If they were not yet Fijians, they were certainly the Fiji-Indians.'[3] The picture that emerges of the Fiji Indians in the 1980s is that of a community that differs little from its ancestors, destined, like their fellow Indians in South Africa, to rebuild their lives within the Fijian version of apartheid in the South Pacific. While the vast majority of Fijians seem to 'wander between two worlds, one dead, the other powerless to be born',[4] the actions of their present chiefly leaders have demonstrated that they have not abandoned the dream of paramountcy in perpetuity.

The Fiji Indians, unlike their great grandparents, are being marooned in their own homes, sulking and pondering about their future. The following declaration of an Indian politician in 1962 still applies to them today: 'We are Fiji-born people. Personally, I have no home except Fiji. I have no place in India to go back to.'[5]

The Fijian *coup d'etat* of May 1987 has a larger significance now for all the so-called immigrants: how many years should they wait to become 'natives'? The statement of the former Australian Prime Minister, Malcolm Fraser, while commenting on the Australian Bi-Centenary celebrations is worth considering: 'I don't enjoy those Australians who want to go around feeling guilty. When the English came from England they behaved brutally. That's all right, they were Englishmen. Not me, I'm Australian. We should not feel guilty for our sins of 200 years ago.'[6]

For the Fiji Indians the coup that ousted their representatives from Parliament on 14 May 1987, 108 years to the day their ancestors were first introduced to work on the sugar plantations, arrested their progress from plantation to Fiji's Parliament. Their history, however, will record that their own *displacement* from British India prevented the *dispossession* of the Fijian in colonial Fiji. Indeed, ironically, the indentured Indian was uprooted specifically to prevent the disintegration of the Fijian way of life. In 1978, Dr Satendra Nandan, the poet/politician who was among those seized in Parliament on 14 May 1987, had reminded the nation:

> It is interesting to speculate if this peasant labourer had not come to Fiji at a critical time, not only the Fijian way of life but many island communities in the South Pacific would have been disrupted and perhaps permanently dislocated. The planters needed labour, the government wanted economic viability for political stability, and it is anyone's guess what they would have done to achieve this. Thus the displacement of the Indian prevented the dispossession of the Fijian.

234 *Paradise Lost*

This may be the lasting and most significant contribution of the peasants from India. Without this the Fijian might have lost much of his land, and more tragically, his self-respect.[7]

Many Fijians do not realize that what they passionately believe to be their ancient heritage is, in fact, a colonial legacy. As for the future, they have reached that

> ... tide in the affairs of men
> Which, taken at the flood, leads on to fortune;
> Omitted, all the voyage of their life
> Is bound in shallows and in miseries.

It is to be sincerely hoped that they will wake up to the fact that although they were given a Garden of Eden, living on Fiji Islands, that isolation is bad for the individual; it is infinitely worse for a community or a country. Alarm bells are already ringing: a group of Rotumans want to secede from Fiji, some militants are advocating armed struggle, professionals are on the run, and the people in a state of anxiety. The leader of the breakaway *Taukei* Movement, Ratu Meli Vesikula, has said, 'I cannot walk into a room and feel secure. I cannot walk down the street and say I feel secure and I'm sure all the Fijians will feel the same today; the army, the police, the prison officers. They are indigenous Fijians and they'll be looking suspiciously at each other again.'[8] Tribalism, the great swear-word of the Fijians, he warns, will surface again.

In conclusion, the Fijian chiefs still have a choice today—to borrow the late Martin Luther King Junior's warning—non-violent co-existence or violent co-annihilation.

Notes

1. Quoted in Isireli Lasaqa, 1983, p. 209.
2. Ibid.
3. K.L. Gillion, 1977, p. 198.
4. Matthew Arnold, *Stanzas from the Grande Chartreuse*, 1979, p. 301.
5. Quoted in Ahmed Ali, 1977, p. 47.
6. *International Herald Tribune*, 26 January 1988.
7. *Fiji Sun*, 10 June 1978, p. 11.
8. *Islands Business* (Fiji), January 1988.

Postscript 1989: Apartheid in Paradise

... As was to be expected, the coup has polarised Fiji racially. The strength of Fiji's political and economic anatomy lay in multi-racialism. Today, the Indian people are cowed and afraid ... For the Fijian people, no other event in seventeen years of independence has raised their political consciousness so sharply. In six short months, they have been exposed to the best and worst of democracy – its capacity to change those who govern them for new leaders and its very fragility in the face of organized lawlessness. The fact is that the coup makers, in attempting to unite the Fijians against a common enemy, have left them more divided than ever. The division is political: Coalition against Alliance. It is regional: east against west. It is social: chiefs against commoners.
(Dr Timoci Bavadra, in a taped message to the Evatt Foundation Conference on Human Rights in Sydney in mid-November 1988.)

One of the persistent myths, that both coups were necessary to protect and safeguard ethnic Fijian interests, has rapidly evaporated and, as Bavadra maintains, the Fijians are fighting among themselves. Events in Fiji have moved swiftly since 1987. In September 1988, as expected, Ratu Mara's semi-civilian government approved a draft constitution that discriminates politically against the Fijian Indians, and also stifles political opposition from commoner and urbanized Fijian, particularly those in the western division of Fiji, where Bavadra's power base is firmly rooted.

In general, the draft constitution, backed by the Great Council of Chiefs gives Fijians a 19-seat majority in a one-chamber Parliament. Fijian Indians, who comprise 48.6 per cent of the population, will be allocated 22 seats; Fijians, 46.6 per cent of the population, will have 40 seats including four members nominated by the Prime Minister; the General Electors, five per cent of the population will have eight seats and the Rotumans will elect one Rotuman representative to the new 71 member Parliament. Therefore, 48.6 per cent (Indians) of the Fijian population will have 31 per cent of the seats; 46.6 per cent (Fijians) will have 56 per cent of the seats and 5 per cent (General Electors) 11 per cent.

The intended result is thus to maintain the Fijian Indian population in political subjugation.

The draft constitution reserves the offices of President, Prime Minister and Police Commissioner exclusively for Fijians as well as the Chairmanship of the Fiji Public Service Commission and of the Judicial and Legal Services Commission; it also ensures the hegemony of traditional authority over the Fijians. For example, 28 of the 36 Fijian seats are to represent the 14 Fijian provincial councils, and candidates would be selected from the nominees of district councils dominated by chiefs. These 14 provinces, divided during the colonial days for administrative purposes, will now become Fijian constituencies as well; all, with the exception of three provinces, will elect two members each to the new parliament. In terms of population distribution, Fijians in the eastern part of the island will automatically have a disproportionately higher level of political representation. For example, western Fijians are permitted only one seat per 15,673 people compared with one seat per 8,976 in the Tovata provinces, the traditional base of the eastern chiefs. The Great Council of Chiefs would choose the other eight; the Council would also have power of veto on legislation. Of these eight nominees one will have to become commander of the armed forces and, in effect, will automatically become Minister of Defence in Cabinet. The draft constitution virtually enshrines Christianity (Methodism) as the state religion, while most of the majority non-Fijians are Hindus and Muslims. Furthermore, the draft constitution calls for the abolition of racial cross-voting; all voting would be communal and would be confined to non-Fijians.

In another radical departure the draft constitution proposes a narrower definition of Fijian. Fijians who are to elect their own members are to be registered in the *Vola ni Kawa Bula* and a strict test for eligibility is proposed. According to the Coalition's submission to the Constitution Review Committee, this will make it more difficult for Fijians, *vis-à-vis* the other races, to become qualified to elect their members of Parliament through *Vola ni Kawa Bula* membership. Many Fijians who would normally qualify under the present provisions would become ineligible. The requirement for Fijians to vote within their provincial boundaries/ constituencies means that they would have no voice in the elections of members representing the constituencies in which they live. This has serious implications for those Fijians who have left their home villages to reside permanently elsewhere. It would discriminate particularly against urban Fijians who see their interests as inextricably related to opportunities and interests available in urban areas. With the availability of rapid educational advancement and growing economic opportunities, the tendency for Fijians to leave their traditional homes will grow. Not only will this system inhibit initiative and enterprise, but it tends to discourage the development of the party system to which Fijians have become accustomed and which is essential for the development of a healthy, democratic government.

It must be pointed out that the Constitution Review Committee's recommendations, largely articulating the wishes of the Great Council of Chiefs, did not represent the views of all indigenous Fijians. The Commission received more than 800 written and 161 oral submissions. An overwhelming majority of Fiji Indians who made submissions favoured retention of the 1970 Constitution, while the Fiji Muslim League's submission demanded four separate seats for Muslims, but supported the Chiefs' resolutions. The League's President, Sherani, a political colleague of Ratu Mara, was, however, bitterly denounced by a majority of the Muslims. Led by Noor Dean (the deposed Deputy Speaker in the Bavadra Government) the Muslims accused the League of trying to fragment the Indian community. While reminding the Chiefs that there had been five Muslims in the dissolved parliament and six in the previous one, Dean claimed that any attempt to split Indians on religious lines would be ineffective. "We have the same heritage and skin colour even though we differ in ideology and religious beliefs." Muslims refused to be forced into submission and the Commission failed to reach agreement on the question of separate seats in Parliament for Muslims.

The General Electors' submission ranged from seeking no change to the 1970 Constitution to favouring minor changes. In some cases, they made the point that they were over-represented and should have fewer seats in Parliament.

Well over 60 per cent of individual Fijians who made submissions were not in favour of any change to the 1970 Constitution. While some accused the Chiefs of 'still living in the medieval age [and] aggressively championing the cause of discord, strife, decadence, retrogression and possible genocide', over 10,000 Fijians, defying the likely loss of jobs, promotions and scholarships, voluntarily signed the Back to Early May Movement petition. Some emphatically stressed that it was the sacrifice on the part of Fijian Indians that had facilitated the Fijian community's retention of its customary lifestyles without compromising its tradition and culture. The position of the chiefly system and the military and the provincial administration had always depended on the work and taxes largely paid by Fijian Indians and other non-Fijians.

The dominant opinion held by many moderate Fijians on several contentious issues can be best illustrated by quoting Jone Dakuvula, a cousin of Rabuka. While rejecting the racial zero-sum analysis of the two coups he claimed that 'what happened on the 14th of May 1987 must offend any self-respecting intelligent Fijian's sense of decency, justice and generosity'. In pleading for the retention of the 1970 Constitution, Dakuvula called upon 'all intelligent, patriotic, Christian Fijians' to ask themselves whether they deserved to be seen as 'unjust, uncaring racists and fascists'. Accusing the 'colonial' chiefs of keeping the commoner Fijians in political subjugation and an economic morass, Dakuvula personally challenged Rabuka on Fijian unity, specifically for his remarks during the two coups that 'I want all the Fijian people to be on one side. The whole thing is a solidarity of the Fijians and then we can compete'. In Dakuvula's words:

> This reactionary utopian notion has no basis in history or current realities. We Fijians have never been united at any time, either at the village level or national level. The various confederations of competing and warring *vanuas,* now roughly reflected in the provinces, outline these divisions. Any experienced village chief will tell Colonel Rabuka that all Fijian villages are riven with competing divisions along family, *tokatoka, mataqali* and other lines.

Furthermore, Dakuvula maintained that any chief who claimed to command his villagers' loyalty and unity at all times these days was 'a liar'. He said Rabuka need look no further than the position and history of his *mataqali,* or the factional political divisions within the military 'to have his utopian notion mugged by reality'. One main reason why the Great Council of Chiefs is obsessed with Fijian unity at the national political level is that many chiefs can no longer rely on the villagers for co-operation. In his itemized criticisms of the coups, Dakuvula also attacked the Taukei Movement, which the moderates had accused of being representative of elements who could realize their ambitions to take over institutions of power outside the state. He singled out one of the leading Taukeist spokesman, Ratu Meli Vesikula, who had remarked in 1987:

> We are preserving the Indian people from a possible bloodbath by relocating a sense of balance. They can't leave us for dead socially, they can't leave us for dead economically, and then think they can take over the political leadership of this country without Fijians fighting back.

Dakuvula, while neatly echoing the sentiments of the moderate Fijians, prophesied:

> Fijian political unity is an illusion, a chimera that can never be achieved, let alone forced upon the people. What the Taukei Movement and the Great Council of Chiefs proposal will achieve is the exact opposite of what they desire: it will result in provincialism, parochialism, unhealthy rivalries, patronage, corruption and the discrediting of the chiefly system.[2]

This passage neatly sums up the state of affairs within the Fijian community. One of the most dramatic developments has been Vesikula's defection into the Bavadra camp. Vesikula, who, through long hours of prayer, came to realize the un-Christian nature inherent in the two coups and the draft constitution, now agrees that the draft's proposals would sow the seeds of violence, and is convinced there can be no racial peace except under a genuine non-racial meritocracy. Perhaps more important and surprising is Vesikula's belated admission of Ratu Mara's alleged role in the first coup; in a signed affidavit to the Queen he alleges that Ratu Mara was involved in the planning and execution of Rabuka's first coup in May 1987. Vesikula's departure has also split the Taukei Movement, whose President, Adi Litia Cakobau, daughter of the paramount Chief of Fiji, Ratu George Cakobau, formally denounced Vesikula for attempting to subvert the chiefs' wishes. In January 1988, however, three members of the splinter movement unsuccessfully attempted to kidnap Ganilau and replace him as President with Adi Litia's father, Ratu George Cakobau.

The potential tribal and clan power struggle came to a head when the ageing Cakobau[3] declared that he, and not the Queen, as Ratu Mara had claimed in London, held the title 'Tui Viti', and that he had no plans to abdicate. In retaliation, and amid charges of corruption and tribalism, Cakobau's son, one of the original Taukeists, was unceremoniously suspended as Assistant Roko Tui by the Taukei-infiltrated Fijian Affairs Board: the Fijian tribe had finally split, brawling publicly. But the worst spectacle of in-fighting was among the ministers of the Methodist Church, which claims the loyalty of 70 per cent of Fijians. The pro-coup and fundamentalist Methodists (who favour a total ban on Sunday trading and sports), led by the Reverend Manasa Lasaro, are quarrelling among themselves and have attracted the condemnation of Fijians of other Christian denominations, including the Fijian Indians.

These sad intra-tribal rivalries have also opened a fundamental debate among the Fijians: who is a Fijian? All Fijians know, from their primary school history books, that the first Fijians to arrive in the country were led by the Chief Lutunasobasoba, who landed with his people on the west coast of Viti Levu, at Vuda, the home village of Bavadra. These 'voyaging' people were mainly Melanesian, but successive and, at times, bloody invasions of Polynesian Tongans introduced a hybrid Melanesian/ Polynesian Fijian culture and tradition. Shortly after the coup, in fact, the *Fiji Sun* opened the debate by asking on what fixed racial criteria could a 'Fijian' be defined. The Reverend Akuila Yabaki (who had compared the two coups to Hitler's Nazism in Germany) argued that there was no such thing as a 'pure' Fijian; intermarriage between Fijians, Samoans, Tongans, and Europeans resulted in the different peoples sharing cross-cultural influences. Dakuvula had asked: 'What is so special about us descendants of the many waves of early settler groups in Fiji that our political rights to be the government must be greater and secured unaccountably, compared to descendants of later settlers?' He cautioned that Fiji could not achieve national reconciliation and an honourable return to parliamentary democracy on the basis of leaving the majority of Fiji's citizens with a sense of being wronged and unjustly treated by a minority who had neither an electoral nor moral mandate to make such changes. Dakuvula further argued that the people did not want an apartheid-type regime because the Fijian Indians were no longer foreigners, but part of the Fijian polity. Why should the Indo-Fijians accept diminution of their political rights in their own country; the country of their birth?

The Fijian Indians have a history of fighting for their rights. As far back as 1946 their leaders had plainly warned:

We have lived in this country, as sugar in milk, and we shall always live just the same as we have done in the past. It has never been our desire to dominate over anybody, but let it be remembered that we will not tolerate any domination from others.

In recent months several Fijian Indians, defying death threats, have come forward to represent the voice and will of the silent majority. Among a handful of remarkable individuals is Mahendra Chaudhry, the former Finance Minister in the deposed Bavadra government, who, while refusing to emigrate, declared:

We have a fight on our hands and I believe in dealing with it until the matter is resolved one way of the other. I was born here. I am not a foreigner here. I have every right to fight for this country. We are not going to subjugate ourselves to a constitution of this kind, signing away all our rights and agreeing to be slaves.[4]

Mohammed Rafiq Kahan, who had organized an arsenal of weapons to Fiji, and subsequently warded off an extradition bid by the Fijian government, captured the resentment and determination to fight, when he said:

I wanted you to test the guns that we are going to supply to our brothers [Fijian Indians] here because Fiji is making a fool of itself in the world. There are traitors running this country... The [arms] were brought to Fiji for the protection of the Indian people during civil disturbances.[5]

Furthermore, there has been a major shift in strategies, tactics, principles and demands on the part of a hard core of Fijian Indian reactionaries. There are those who are now pressing for full equality and land rights, anchoring their claims on the recent pronouncements of Australian and New Zealand politicians who have defended their own rights to rule over the indigenous peoples in the two respective countries.[6] The more militant and radical Fijian Indians believe that violence is virtually the only answer in the face of the chiefs' intransigence and the international community's indifference. Their leaders are publicly warning that the draft racist constitution would ultimately lead to such violent confrontations as are seen in Sri Lanka. With a huge portion of arms shipped to Fiji still unaccounted for, they told the Constitution Review Committee:

> Racism, which the Government and the draft constitution have elevated to high dogma, is a cancer which will destroy our body politic . . . There is no doubt that . . . it will lead to terrible violence.
> Just because those who had been oppressed have not hit back is no reason to believe that they will forever remain compliant. The time will undoubtedly come when their patience will run out and, refusing to submit to further humiliation and deprivation, they will retaliate.[7]

The situation in Fiji lies somewhere between that of Sri Lanka and that of South Africa, but as Commonwealth Secretary-General Shridath Ramphal[8], himself an offspring of Indo-Guyanese 'coolies', once remarked about the minority whites in South Africa:

> [they] . . . remain blind to the future of their own children as they continue to deny a presence to the majority peoples of these lands. They have sown the winds of racism, yet seem surprised at the harvest. They have left millions no recourse but to exercise their right to rebel, and have made ideologues of an entire generation'.[9]

Fiji has always practised its own version of apartheid: a minority (Fijian) population exercises political control over the majority (Fijian Indians); its people are racially classified, and legally required to state their race on passport application forms; like Africans in South Africa, Fijian Indians have never been allowed to fish freely in Fijian waters, or to live in any part of the country without the state's prior approval. The most fundamental restriction applies to land ownership rights. The 1913 Land Act of South Africa prevents Africans (80 per cent of population) from acquiring land outside their 'reserves' (13 per cent of the country). Similarly, in Fiji, Fijian Indians own only 1.7 per cent of the land, while the Fijian population has inalienable right to over 80 per cent of the land. Crudely put, the Fijian Indians and their indentured peers have always lived on 'bantustans' allocated by the British colonial government and subsequently by the Fijian Chiefs.

Meanwhile, the Commonwealth and the United Nations remain indifferent to the developments in Fiji. Australia and New Zealand abandoned Bavadra in pursuit of their economic and strategic interests. Ramphal says the Commonwealth has little influence on events in Fiji.

The United Nations have accepted the changes in Fiji with minimal demur. Its Secretary-General, on the 25th anniversary of the United Nations Special Committee Against Apartheid in South Africa, said that 'it is an indictment of our times that such an iniquitous policy as apartheid should prevail for so long against current or world opinion', but has failed to respond positively to a call by Bavadra[10] to impose sanctions on Fiji for sponsoring 'an unprecedented scale of racial discrimination and oppression'.[11] Instead, the UN accepted a detachment of Fiji Police, hand-picked by Rabuka, to form part of the UN Transition Assistance Group overseeing the transfer of power to blacks in Namibia, ironically headlined by a London newspaper 'Fijian charm breaks racial barrier'.[12]

The most active participant in dictating the course of political change in Fiji, however, is France, the pariah of the South Pacific. While the world is congratulating France on the 200th anniversary of the Declaration of the Rights of Man and of Citizen, the French are providing thousands of dollars in aid to Fiji to construct security installations, and are supplying helicopters to Rabuka's army to hover over Fijian Indian hamlets suspected of formenting rebellions against the Fijian feudal chiefs.

What of the future? The racialist pronouncements of high-ranking Fijian chiefs suggest their determination to introduce 'apartheid in paradise'. The President, Ratu Penaia Ganilau, echoing the high-priest and architect of racism in South Africa, Dr H. F. Verwoerd, affirmed the primacy of race in Fiji, when he declared:

> We want the Indians and Europeans to continue to run their business but we [native Fijians] must have political dominance at all times . . . The migrant races in the country have complete control – except political leadership . . . [We] will not sacrifice political leadership of [our] country nor at the same time accept the [paramount position] of other races.[13]

Ganilau also defended the enshrinement of Christianity as a state religion, saying it was the wish of the chiefs who ceded Fiji to Great Britain in 1874. He was supported by Ratu Mara who insisted that the draft constitution addressed 'the rights and aspirations' of the Fijian population.

These pronouncements, however, do not represent the majority opinion. As a Maori professor, Ranginui Walker, declared in Auckland in 1987:

> The coup is nothing more than a shameful use by an oligarchy that refuses to recognize and accept the winds of change in Fiji. It would appear from this distance that the Great Council of Chiefs, still living in their traditional ways, have been misled. Their land rights are secure under the [1970] constitution. But because they have not been taught their rights they are readily manipulated and swayed by demagogues'.[14]

To summarize: three scenarios are possible for the forseeable future: 1) an attempt by the Coalition's supporters and coup opponents in the west of the country, comprising the bulk of Fijian Indians and western

Fijians, to secede and form a separate state; 2) the Fijian Indians embarking on a violent campaign of terror and sabotage, and 3) a group of disgruntled army officers seizing power for themselves from Rabuka, Mara, and Ganilau. In fact, in March 1988, a group of army officers in collusion with the splinter Taukei Movement, actually entertained such a possibility. The threat still exists, as Vesikula, himself an ex-British Army major and a chief, had remarked, 'Now that power has been given to the Tovata group, what is there to stop chiefs from other areas to go to the military camp and order their people to lay down their arms and join them?'

Significantly, the one certainty is that Rabuka[15] has opened a Pandora's box of tribal and regional rivalries in the army – and the inevitable possibility of a counter-coup.

But with the chiefs determined to imprison themselves in the racist garb of supremacy and tradition, and their antagonists, the Fijian Indians, threatening violence and vengeance, both sides must be urged to re-examine the findings of the Royal Commission that investigated Fiji's electoral system in 1975. This Commission had strongly advocated extending national seats in order to defeat the politics of communalism. The chiefs, prejudiced by lack of vision, must, on the other hand, in the months and years to come, realize that 'tradition is a guide, not a jailer'[16] in order to save their country from the calamity that confronts them;[17] the Fijian Indians with a history of rebellion on the sugar plantations and burning political ambitions in their hearts are repeating the lines of Richard Lovelace: *Stone walls do not a prison make – Nor iron bars a cage.*

Notes

1. In June 1990, the Great Council of Chiefs approved a slightly modified new Constitution entrenching indigenous Fijians' political supremacy in perpetuity.

2. For a detailed criticism of the two coups, see Dakuvula's article in *Pacific Issues,* No.3, 1987, pp 7-13.

3. Cakobau died on 25 November 1989.

4. Chaudhry, quoted in *Islands Business,* July 1989, p.73, and *The Age* (Australia) 13 February 1989, p.11.

5. Kahan, quoted in Christopher Harder, *The Guns of Lautoka,* New Zealand, 1988, pp 1-2.

6. On Aboriginal land rights treaty (*Bulletin,* 6 September, 1988), the Australian MP, John Howard, commented: 'Land rights is fundamentally wrong, because what land rights inevitably leads to is large-scale alienation of enormous sections of Australia to a very few people. I do not accept the doctrine of hereditary guilt. I acknowledge that, in the past, wrongs were done to Aborigines. But they weren't done by me.' Similarly, the New Zealand Minister of External Relations and Trade, Mike Moore, commenting on race relations in New Zealand had remarked: 'To claim that because someone's ancestors (Europeans) came to

New Zealand 100 years and not 1,000 years ago made them less of a citizen with fewer rights or love of their country was arrogant, simplistic and wrong . . . People from many countries contributed equally to New Zealand's growth and they would not tolerate second class citizenship in a first class country.' (*New Sunday Times*, Malaysia, 1 January 1989).

Some Fijian Indians cite other examples where descendants of immigrants rule or have ruled over the 'indigenous people'.

7. *Sydney Morning Herald* (Australia), 17 January 1989, p.11.

8. In May 1990 Ramphal retired as Commonwealth Secretary-General.

9. Quoted in *Racism in South Africa: The Commonwealth Stand,* Commonwealth Secretariat, Marlborough House, London, 1987.

10. Dr Bavadra died of cancer on 3 November 1989. His widow, Adi Kuini Bavadra, has taken over the leadership of the Fiji Labour Party.

11. Quoted in *Sanctions,* Cape Town, South Africa, 1988/89, p.2.

12. *The Times* (London), 3 July 1989.

13. *Sydney Morning Herald,* 10 November 1988, p.15, and Islands Business, December 1988, p.26.

14. *The New Zealand Listener,* 27 June 1987, p.8.

15. In January 1990, Rabuka, who has promoted himself to major-general, resigned as Home Minister, but remains commander of the Army.

16. Somerset Maugham, *The Summing Up,* Pan, London, 1976, p.150.

17. In May 1990, the Indian embassy was shut down and its diplomats expelled because of India's support for Fijian Indians and for the restoration of democracy in Fiji.

APPENDIX: CHRONOLOGY OF EVENTS: 14 MAY 1987 TO AUGUST 1988

14 May 1987
Lt-Col Rabuka and 10 armed members of RFMF enter Government Buildings, Suva; Prime Minister, Ministers and backbenchers taken to RFMF HQ, Suva; Speaker and Opposition members allowed to leave; Fiji's international telephone and telex links cut; news broken by FM96 radio reporter who witnessed coup from Parliamentary Press Gallery.

Radio Fiji broadcasts take-over in Rabuka's name; announces new government will take over quickly; imminent release of detained members of Bavadra's administration.

Rabuka summons foreign and Commonwealth diplomatic representatives to meeting; Australian and New Zealand High Commissioners refuse to attend.

Rabuka holds press conference; says coup 'pre-emptive' measure to avoid Fijian violence against Bavadra's Indian-dominated government; announces suspension of Constitution; plans for interim Council of Ministers (COM); intention to return Fiji to democratic government under revised Constitution; suspends RFMF Commander Ratu Epeli Nailatikau, RFMF Chief of Staff and Commissioner and Deputy Commissioner of Police.

Governor-General (GG) issues statement, broadcast by Radio FM96, which then told by RFMF not to re-broadcast. Statement said GG 'deeply disturbed by events of this morning' which had 'created unprecedented situation which must not be allowed to continue', that Executive power under Fiji's Constitution 'is vested in Her Majesty the Queen which by law and convention I exercise on her behalf on the advice of the Cabinet. In the temporary absence of Ministers of the Crown I have assumed that authority.' Went on to say he had issued Proclamation of State of Public Emergency and was taking immediate steps to 'restore the lawful situation. I wish to emphasise that the Constitution is the supreme law of Fiji', that it had not been over-ridden and that all public officers 'duly appointed ... remain in office'. As Commander-in-Chief in Fiji he called upon 'all officers and men in the [RFMF] to return to their lawful allegiances in accordance with the Oath of Office and their duty of obedience without delay.' He then commanded the people of Fiji to 'respect and obey the Constitution' for the sake of peace and prosperity.

Chief Justice (CJ) visits GG; GG contacts Buckingham Palace, receives message of encouragement from Queen; Fiji High Commission, Canberra, delivers formal note to DFA advising of coup and requesting recognition.

15 May 1987
Rabuka announces Council of Ministers (COM), which is dominated by ex-Alliance Ministers (including Ratu Mara); is predominantly Fijian, only two Indian and one European members.

Radio Fiji announces COM; COM holds first meeting, reportedly discussed constitutional amendments and press censorship.

Rabuka makes press statement claiming military regime in full control and people of Fiji's acceptance of events; reasserts coup necessary to pre-empt breakdown of law and order; states that countries with whom Fiji has diplomatic relations should recognize new government.

Ministry of Information directs *Fiji Times* and *Fiji Sun* to cease publication; Radio Fiji occupied by RFMF.

Chief Justice summoned by Minister for Justice who tells him: Constitution to be abrogated, the regime will govern by decree; after an interval constitutional conference to be convened. With abrogation, judges' appointments lapse, but they would be reappointed on 17 May under new Oath of Allegiance.

Armed soldiers eject staff of *Fiji Times* and *Fiji Sun* from their offices; foreign journalists questioned by RFMF; both *Fiji Times* and *Fiji Sun* appear normally on 15 May carrying GG's statements and reports of overseas reactions critical of the coup.

Rabuka moves into Prime Minister's Office.

Accompanied by legal adviser and Ratu Mara, Rabuka calls on GG to press his case that Constitution be suspended. GG refuses to accept this, tells Rabuka it is his (GG's) responsibility to take control; asks Rabuka to stand down with his troops so that an Emergency Council could be called; Rabuka agrees to discuss this with COM. (It is unclear when, if at all, on Friday this second COM meeting took place.)

16 May 1987

GG leaves Government House to attend burial ceremony of close relative at Taveuni.

Mainly Indian crowd begins assembling outside detained Prime Minister's residence; is broken up by RFMF.

Rabuka holds press conference accompanied by Peter Stinson (former Alliance Cabinet member, named as COM Finance Minister) and Ahmed Ali (former Alliance Cabinet member, now COM Information Minister). Stinson announces bank closure for all foreign exchange business on 18 May; claims that the $5\frac{1}{2}$ months' foreign currency reserves will enable Fiji resist sanctions threatened by Australian and New Zealand trade unions. Rabuka denies Ratu Mara's or foreign elements' involvement in coup but implies two members of Bavadra's Cabinet have pro-Soviet and pro-Libyan sympathies.

Fiji Times and *Fiji Sun* fail to appear.

Supreme Court Judges and Chief Magistrate meet CJ who informs that GG has refused Rabuka's request to abrogate Constitution; Judiciary agree to continue normally and refuse any directives from military regime; results of meeting transmitted to GG and regime.

Indian shops in Lautoka and Nadi close as gesture of protest.

Bavadra appeals to Australian government for help; British High Commission receive petition in his favour.

17 May 1987

RFMF enter hotel rooms of some foreign journalists; question them and confiscate tapes/notebooks.

RFMF forcibly divide detainees at PM's residence into Indian and Fijian groups; Indians moved elsewhere in Suva where large crowds gather.

About 400, mostly Indians, march from PM's residence to prayer meeting; police break up march, arrest leaders.

GG returns from Taveuni; swears in Rabuka as head of government; this not revealed publicly until 18 May.

CJ urges GG to resist military regime's demands for recognition.

Radio Fiji announces that GG and Rabuka will make important announcement at 22.00 hours; but this fails to materialize.

RFMF remain deployed around government and media buildings; exhibit increasing heavy-handedness.

Two Coalition Senators (one fijian, one Indian) call on British High Commission to express concern at situation and ask about possibility of raising matter of coup at the UN.

18 May 1987

GG issues statements saying: after obtaining advice of CJ and Judiciary he has decided it is impossible for him to recognize military regime; also that regime has recognized his right to exercise executive authority and urged him to remain as GG. This statement prompts widespread relief as it seems crisis may now be resolved. Shortly afterwards statement issued by Ministry of Information reveals Rabuka already sworn in as head of government and GG would swear in COM at 09.00, 19 May.

Increase in tension and military harassment; major shops in Suva open but many businesses remain closed; Indian demonstrators assemble in central Suva.

Bavadra reportedly smuggled message to Australian and New Zealand governments asking for intervention; later confirmed in Canberra and Wellington.

Fiji newspapers refuse to publish under conditions of censorship.

Rabuka issues statement appealing for racial harmony; assures Indians they are 'part of our history and our future'.

19 May 1987
Airport worker at Nadi hijacks Air New Zealand 747, demands release of Bavadra government; asks to be flown to Libya; later overpowered by crew.

COM members arrive at Government House for swearing in; increased tension when GG fails to act on promised swearing in.

Special meeting of Great Council of Chiefs (GCOC) in Suva.

RFMF issue statement in which Rabuka declares: 'The penalty for treason in all Commonwealth countries is death, and if this is to be my destiny I will accept it'; thanks army for support; says he knows he cannot remain part of it.

GG makes statement calming situation; announces that at 08.30 he told Rabuka it was constitutionally impossible for COM to be sworn in; and (1) restated illegality of Rabuka regime; (2) dissolves existing Parliament; (3) establishes Council of Advisers (COA) to assist him (GG) as head of government in day-to-day administration and considers possible amendments to Constitution 'taking into account existing practicalities and social structure of Fiji'; (4) promises new elections in due course; (5) extends prerogative of mercy to all implicated in coup; (6) reiterates rule of law, and administration remain in place as before coup; (7) appeals for calm; that first step taken in return to 'normality'.

All detained Ministers and MPs released; Bavadra says those involved in coup guilty of treason; indicates he will co-operate with GG.

GCOC meeting continues, but needs more time to consider GG's statement; further session 08.30, 20 May.

Unrest reported in West Viti Levu where pine forest and cane field on fire, shops and banks close, few buses running.

Commonwealth Secretary-General publicly renews support for GG and stands ready to help.

20 May 1987
GCOC resumes; reports suggest that majority back military regime.

About 100 Indians assemble in Albert Park (opposite Government Buildings) for prayer and protest meeting; attacked by about 100 Fijian youths, injuring about 30 Indians; about 200 Fijians storm through central Suva, shops/offices close.

Addressing about 1,000 Fijians outside Suva Civic Centre, Rabuka calls for calm; GG summons Rabuka and GCOC Chairman, expresses concern at disturbances in Albert Park and central Suva; issues statement that police, with RFMF, would ensure public safety; Rabuka appeals on radio for calm.

GCOC meeting critical of GG's plan; unprecedented calls for republic; strong anti-Indian feelings expressed. Much discussion of proposed COA's composition; members of COM active in lobbying to preserve their positions. GG attends GCOC, explains his scheme; tells chiefs he will not appoint members to COA until he has received their (chiefs') resolutions.

Office of Commissioner of Northern Labasa burned; three more forest fires reported in Lautoka making 50 since 14 May; Fiji trade unions request Australia and New Zealand unions to impose blockade.

21 May 1987
Continued GCOC meeting again adjourns without conclusions. Reports indicate

discussion tends towards maintaining relations with Crown after speech from Ratu Mara and GG and latter's relay of Queen's message. Indications that compromise will be worked out on GG's package, including membership of COA and examination of Constitution; Rabuka also addresses GCOC.

GG sees Rabuka who is reportedly happy with day's discussion; rumours that Rabuka unwilling to serve with any Coalition members; he appears at Suva Civic Centre and declares 'we have won'.

Uneasy calm in Suva but virtually all schools, shops, businesses stay closed; almost no Indians to be seen; RFMF briefly detain group of sailors from HMNZS Wellington; Suva Court remand in custody 21 Fijian youth charged with violence and theft during disturbances on 20 May; *Fiji Times/Fiji Sun* resume publication uncensored; both exercising caution in reporting.

22 May 1987

GCOC meeting resumed; renewed calls for republic; GG remains firm; resulting compromise endorsed by Ratu Mara and Rabuka. Rabuka summoned by GG before GCOC meeting but tells meeting he had got all he wanted; Ratu Mara announces intention to retire from politics.

GG's compromise formula announced on radio; 19-strong COA to be formed, eight responsible under Rabuka's chairmanship for reviewing Constitution, 10 for day-to-day administration. COA ethnically and politically mixed, but Alliance and Fijian interests predominate; membership includes only three Indian and two Coalition places; most are moderates; Rabuka's more strident COM supporters omitted. Rabuka retains control of RFMF and police; GG confirms amnesty and state of emergency; GG swears in part of COA.

Bavadra's initial public reaction to GG's plan negative, reportedly describes it as 'totally unacceptable' but reserves position on participation. Will not talk to GG when he telephoned.

23 May 1987

GG swears in remaining COA members (excluding Coalition places); Bavadra talks to GG about COA: says feels let down because of poor consultation in light of his pledges of support.

Announces that schools will reopen on 25 May.

Bavadra meets cross-section of Fijian communities in West Viti Levu; their continued support leads him to take hard line on participation in COA. Rumours in Lautoka of reconstituting Bavadra's government as 'legitimate government of Fiji' in the West.

Coalition delegation leave for New Zealand.

Fiji Times/Fiji Sun express sympathy for Bavadra's position; hope he will accept GG's invitation to join COA.

24 May 1987

Bavadra chairs meeting of most Coalition MPs in Ba; subsequent statement describes GG's actions and dissolution of Parliament as 'unconstitutional'; calls upon him to 'immediately restore democratically elected government to office'.

25 May 1987

Most shops/schools open; buses/taxis operating in Suva; Radio Fiji resumes normal broadcasting pattern; Radio Australia/BBC relays, interviews Bavadra.

Three forest fires in Lautoka; attack on Australian expatriate's house in Nadi.

Upsurge in British/Fiji dual nationals renewing UK passports; some Indian families already left for Australia.

Cancellation of, mainly tourist, building projects.

19-member COA holds first meeting, all given portfolios: Rabuka, Home Affairs; Ratu Mara, Foreign Affairs; Coalition places allocated relatively junior positions; economy discussed; help for banks experiencing runs pledged.

Reportedly RFMF still raiding Coalition members' residences in Suva; almost certainly unknown to GG.

26 May 1987
GG tries to arrange meeting with Bavadra; civil disobedience begins in West; schools/shops closed; GG warns emergency power will be used; little support for civil disobedience elsewhere.

Stocks of foodstuffs under pressure; some shops introduce basic rationing; press freedom high; *Fiji Sun* boldly blames military for 'current tyranny of fear'.

Police reportedly collecting private firearms in Labasa; Sugar-Cane Growers Council (SCGC) warn production target (450,000 tonnes) will not be reached due to delayed crushing.

Air Pacific reduces international flights as hotel bookings fall.

Meeting of Bavadra Cabinet members (except those in West) in Suva, Sir Vijay Singh (Chief Executive of SCGC) attends.

27 May 1987
Fiji Times reports Rabuka saying elections cannot take place for 'at least 16 months' because constitutional amendments will take at least a year.

Reverend Mustapha resigns from COA, is unhappy at Ratu Mara's and Rabuka's domination of proceedings and conflict of interest with his pastoral duties.

Announces that Fiji will not send delegation to South Pacific Forum (SPF) meeting in Asia.

Official statement by GG on Radio Fiji rebukes Rabuka for comments on election time-scale, tells him to refrain from making such public comments in interests of general calm.

New Zealand Judges of Fiji's Court of Appeal reportedly written to GG stressing that legal amendment to Constitution only by parliamentary process; if this is not adhered to, all three Judges will resign.

RFMF raid Dr Nandan's (Coalition MP) house, but he absent after tip-off.

Ratu Mara in interview to foreign journalists denies involvement in coup and having any authority to prevent Rabuka's actions; justifies involvement as trying to help 'put the fire out'.

28 May 1987
Press reports GG's rebuke to Rabuka; situation in West increasingly normal after two-day disruption.

Reserve Bank Governor admits helping cover large withdrawals; FS10m injected into commercial sector to maintain liquidity; confirmed there will be no devaluation.

Much normal government work at standstill through lack of political direction and RFMF commandeering official vehicles.

RFMF detain two members of Bavadra government and Sir Vijay Singh; released only after GG's direct intervention; reports that three Bavadra Cabinet members have left Fiji; Permanent Secretary for Health, friend of Bavadra, detained at Nadi on return from overseas.

Spokesman for GG releases statement on constitutional changes, saying it should be made 'quite clear that whatever changes were made would be done within the law and after taking into account the interests of all the people of Fiji'.

29 May 1987
Reports indicate significant RFMF presence in Ministry of Home Affairs.

Bavadra files summons in Civil Division of Supreme Court seeking declaration that GG's dissolution of Parliament is illegal and that he (Bavadra) remains Prime Minister.

Fiji Times carries comment from CJ that there is no legal way to circumvent election of new Parliament before revisions can be made to Constitution.

Daily papers carry corrective comment to major misunderstanding of many Fijians that an Indian-dominated government could override constitutional provisions protecting Fijian land owernship.

June 1987

Bavadra tells GG he is still unwilling to join COA but ready to continue dialogue with GG; GG meets delegation of 50 Indian community/business/union leaders and cane farmers; says RFMF presence solely to protect persons/property; farmers can hold meetings to discuss harvest and will be paid in normal way; confirms that SCGC would organize harvest (not RFMF); GG also visits RFMF detachment in West.

New Zealand Survey Ship Monowai instructed to sail at five-hours' notice following withdrawal of diplomatic clearance.

RFMF open fire on British High Commission landrover at Suva docks; High Commissioner protests to Permanent Secretary at MFA; passes word to GG (in West Viti Levu); landrover released from dock area two hours later.

Fiji Times/Fiji Sun extensive coverage of GG's activities in West Viti Levu but no details of meeting with Bavadra; civil disobedience continues in West; shops closed in Nadi and Lautoka; Suva relatively normal.

RFMF commissions civilians with no previous military experience; some key civil functionaries drafted, e.g., General Managers of FSC and Electricity Authority.

GG meets Fijian and Indian groups in West, with Bavadra's Attorney General (Reddy) and Deputy Prime Minister (Sharma); no details released. GG returns to Suva 3 June.

Civil disobedience continues in West; movement of funds out of country running at F$2m daily (pre-coup F$100-200,000); foreign reserves decline; commercial liquidity of F$13.8m surplus converted into deficit of F$8.2m.

New Zealand waterside unions lift embargo on food and medical supplies; Reddy leaves for Sydney.

1,000 Fijians led by Ratu David Toganivalu and Adi Liti Cakobau (COM) prevent Bavadra and 200 supporters reaching Vunivalu (Paramount Chief); Ratu David says proper channels to approach Vunivalu not adhered to, that Vunivalu old and sick should not be exploited for political purposes. Bavadra delegation retires.

New Zealand lawyer John Cameron (legal adviser to Bavadra) has work permit withdrawn; he appeals.

Police detain executive members of Fiji Trade Union Congress.

Rabuka promoted full Colonel; Nailatikau's appointment simultaneously terminated.

Bavadra leaves Fiji for London.

Three-man Coalition delegation en route to London breaks journey in Bombay and meets Natwar Singh, Minister of State in the Indian Ministry of Foreign Affairs.

FTUC meets to discuss attitude to Australian and New Zealand union bans; divided because of different effects on its members.

GG speaks to nation again: says there is no military regime, he is exercising executive authority; RFMF deployed to protect public interest and should receive cooperation not confrontation; adds there will be no unlawful change to the Constitution but the review would look at strengthening the political rights of indigenous Fijians; all sections of community would be able to express their views; GG has still not decided how review is to be conducted; gives assurance that sections of the Constitution protecting fundamental rights and freedoms, citizenship, the judiciary and the public service will not be reviewed; calls for reopening of schools and gives assurances on payments for cane farmers; calls for a start to the sugar harvest at the 'appropriate time' so that the sugar mills could begin crushing on 18 June; warns of disastrous consequences if the 1987 harvest lost. (Text of this broadcast carried in press on 8 June.)

Reports of continued ill-discipline by some sections of RFMF; unauthorized and forced searches.

Bavadra arrives in London; received by supporters (Action Committee for the

Restoration of Democracy in Fiji); declares his intention to see members of the British government and the Queen; press reports say Queen will not see Bavadra.

GG enacts the Republic Emergency (Maintenance of Supplies and Services) Regulations which give GG, Permanent Secretary, Finance, and Permanent Secretary, Employment and Industrial Relations, wide-ranging powers to secure essential services; powers also contain reversal of normal presumption of innocence.

Fiji Times and *Fiji Sun* express concern. (The Regulations were not, in fact, published until 16 June.)

John Cameron files claim with the Supreme Court on behalf of a client harassed by RFMF, seeking a declaration that State of Emergency and 1987 Emergency Regulations are unconstitutional.

Reverend Raikivi (COA member for Information) denies that the declaration of a republic is imminent.

The Governor of the Fiji Reserve Bank predicts that, in the short term, the economy will contract but from a position of relative strength; also ruled out early devaluation.

Press reports dominated by meeting of SCGC in Nadi and Ba where farmers demand payment of balance due on last year's crop, full price for 1987 crop within five weeks of cane deliveries, and withdrawal of RFMF.

GG broadcasts proposal for a Constitutional Review Committee (CRC) to work for an uncontested election under existing Constitution; then to implement agreed constitutional changes in the context of a Council for National Reconcilation consisting of new Parliament and COA combined; Rabuka again speaks of a republic if GG's scheme fails.

Reports of unsuccessful sabotage attempt on BF oil pipeline, at Nadi airport.

GG hosts Queen's Birthday Garden Party as usual. Bavadra meets Sir William Heseltine in London.

Customary RFMF Queen's Birthday Parade cancelled.

Reports of unsuccessful sabotage attempt on sugar-railway bridge near Nadi. Bavadra leaves London for Washington.

Public holiday to mark Queen's Official Birthday; GG speaks on Radio Fiji, directs preparations for sugar harvest to be ready at all mills by 23 June, crushing to begin at Labasa and Rakiraki on same day; at Lautoka and Ba on 30 June. Tells cane farmers that: army will restrict its presence, compromise arrangements will be made for payments, full force of law will be used against anyone attempting to interfere in harvest.

Lau Provincial Council meets in Suva; considers constitutional reforms going beyond Chapter V (composition of Parliament); calls for 'sovereign Fijian democratic state'; Fijian as national langauge; positive discrimination in the public services, education and employment in favour of Fijians. Council wants 40 of the 52 seats in House of Representatives for Fijians (all but five nominated), ten Indian and two others. Three Rolls would be established without cross-voting; Senate would be replaced by a House of Chiefs; certain key posts (nine Ministers and RFMF Commander) reserved for Fijians.

Coalition MPs meet in Ba, reiterate support for Bavadra, express concern at GG's directives to sugar industry; after meeting Dr Rakka and Navin Patel detained for three hours by RFMF and police because permit for meeting was wrongly dated.

Fiji Sun publishes allegations that Rabuka has bought house in a Suva suburb favoured by wealthy Indians and expatriates, on a 100% mortgage, from prominent Alliance politican. *Fiji Times* carries a centre-spread produced by the RFMF justifying its actions.

Bavadra calls on Lange in Wellington; GG's Emissary calls on Lord Glenarthur at the FCO to explain GG's proposals.

Press/radio reports that RFMF authorized by COA to commandeer 100 privately (Indian) owned lorries in Labasa to move sugar harvested by the Fijian farmers in Seaqaqa to Labasa Mill.

GG, on tour around Labasa, explains proposals for CRC.

The Nadroga Provincial Council considers proposals similar to those put before the Lau Council; reports indicate even more extreme pro-Fijian measures are before Rewa Council.

Baba, the deposed Minister of Education, describes GG's proposals as 'unimpressive, disappointing and ill conceived', 'GG's plan is not on'.

Further emergency decree announced, embodying powers to enter/take possession of land, wharves, jetties, railways, buildings or other property (e.g. crops); can be exercised at relatively low level (Police Inspector, RFMF Captain and above).

Six Coalition supporters arrested after a meeting; released evening of 24 June.

Fiji Times publishes Ratu Mara's interview with New Zealand TV in full including his reference to possibility of a republic; also reports Baba's remarks (23 June) on GG's plans.

GG officially inaugurates sugar crushing at Labasa but very little cane to process.

Bavadra returns to Fiji, met by 1,000 supporters at Nadi; he says: important for him to meet GG but does not wish to negotiate from position of compromise; still considers peaceful solution attainable; does not wish to urge cane growers to harvest; wants to discuss the latest constitutional proposals with supporters before going further.

Rabuka in press interview comments on GG's plan; thinks it could 'achieve the objective I set out to achieve for Fijians and the people of Fiji, if not, there are other options drawn up by RFMF but not discussed with GG.

Commonwealth Secretary-General receives formal request from GG for a list of constitutional advisers from which to choose.

Bavadra calls on GG, makes a number of points: equitable representation of all races contained in 1970 Constitution needs to be reflected in CRC; Coalition would ensure that Constitution will treat all races fairly; GG should begin discussion with Ratu Mara; cane harvest can be speeded up only if RFMF profile reduced; decision on CRC participation would depend on consultation with his colleagues.

Meeting of 23 Coalition MPs in Ba basically reaffirms Bavadra's points to GG on 26 June; also stresses need for Indians to be allowed to meet and discuss their policies unhindered; and for freedom of the media and movement.

Commonwealth Secretary-General replies to GG assuring him of willingness to help provided all principal parties involved in constitutional process.

GG talks to Bavadra and other Coalition members in Lautoka; Bavadra maintains refusal to participate in COA despite offer of further two seats; also says he would like CRC to first examine 1970 Constitution to see if any changes are needed; GG promises to consider this.

Preliminary hearing of Bavadra's summons seeking a declaration that dissolution of Parliament was illegal is held in Chambers; case proper opens on 22/23 July.

RFMF spokesman, commenting on continuing brief detentions, says, 'Due to the current conditions everyone is suspect until proven otherwise.'

Fiji $ is devalued by 17.75%, adding to bleak economic outlook; minimum lending rate and statutory reserve deposit both increased by 1% to 9% and 6% respectively.

FSC chairman announces that, following consultations with GG, all mills will cease crushing until 31 July (Lautoka and Ba had never started); that this is in response to several acts of sabotage and walk-outs by Rakiraki and Labassa; work force claimed that 1,700 tonnes of sugar produced sufficient for local demand for one month; 2,500 FSC employees laid of.

July 1987
RFMF detains three members of Bavadra's deposed government at a Hindu temple in Suva, for about two hours, questioning them about Indian shop closures; widespread shop closures in Suva for first time since early days of coup.

RFMF announces all ranks have agreed to 'voluntary' 25% pay cut.

GG releases composition and terms of reference of CRC; Chairman is Sir John Falvey, former Attorney General.

Bavadra releases text of his letter to GG objecting to CRC composition and terms of reference.

Taukei Movement releases statement saying it would support a republic if that was the only way to satisfy Fijian aspirations.

500 Bavadra supporters meet at Nadi; reportedly decide Coalition should not participate in CRC unless terms and membership amended; also pass resolution calling on cane farmers not to cut crops until political crisis resolved; other resolutions include condemnation of RFMF harassment; support for the 1970 Constitution; establishment of a fighting fund. Some Fijians present stress need for their community to recognize Indians' contribution to Fiji's stability and prosperity.

Fiji Times carries RFMF warning to diplomatic missions about contact with 'pro-Labour people'.

Ratu Mara and a group of senior RFMF officers leave Fiji, no official reason given.

Fiji Times carries letter from Bavadra's spokesman (Naidu) outlining risk of losing Commonwealth membership by becoming republic.

CRC holds first meeting without Coalition representation; Chairman hints at possible changes in terms of reference; *Taukei* contradict this.

Dr Sahu Khan, President of Fiji Law Society and one of GG's nominees, tells of his concern at participating in CRC without Coalition representation.

Bavadra and GG meet to discuss Coalition participating in CRC; GG tells Bavadra Ratu Mara unwilling to meet him because still very 'disturbed' and 'not in the right frame of mind'.

GG, Sir John Falvey, Rabuka, Bole, Reddy and Baba meet to discuss CRC terms of reference; compromise formula agreed for submission to respective supporters.

Fiji Times interview with Rabuka; he says: 'there is no turning back'; he does not rule out republic; Ratu Mara's overseas mission seeking new sources of supply for RFMF.

GG's negotiating group on CRC terms of reference meets again; Rabuka and Bole say the compromise unacceptable; further negotiation produces further compromise formula which clears way for Coalition participation in CRC from 13 July.

About 1,500, nearly all Fijians, attend meeting of Indigenous Fijian Landowners Association (IFLA) at Lautoka; endorse Bavadra's position; support 1970 Constitution; reject idea of republic.

About 300 members of the Fiji Nationalist Party (FNP) meet; support coup and republic; resolve that the UK should pay for/organize removal of all Fiji Indians.

FTUC National Secretary and four other union leaders detained for one hour by RFMF after attending meeting to discuss lifting of Australian and New Zealand union trade bans; GG later demands explanation from police.

Fiji Sun carries letter from Sir Len Usher concerning implications of republicanism; pointing out the unifying effect of the Crown since 1874; and possible threat to Commonwealth membership.

Interim government announces 25% cut in all civil service salaries, without union agreement.

Taukei meet in Suva; adopt hard line toward CRC; speakers adopt aggressive line; even accepting violence might be necessary.

Datt, Bavadra's Foreign Minister, detained by RFMF at barracks (as opposed to police station); released without charge next day.

Coalition supporters meet at Rakiraki. Reddy questions how far GG is in control; asserts coup is continuing with RFMF taking increasing political role. Parliamentary Board decides to participate in CRC in response to GG's alteration of terms of reference.

FSC yield to pressure; agree to reopen Labasa mill from 15 July; would reclose if sufficient cane not available.

GG announces relaxation in regulations concerning public and group meetings.

CRC meets including the Coalition representatives; decides to extend submission date to 24 July, and travel to other centres.

GG meets Bavadra in Suva.

Bavadra's Supreme Court action adjourned indefinitely.

Qantas recommence a full service to Fiji. Tourism revives under 'cut price' stimuli.

FSC and SCGC reach agreement on resuming cane harvest.

Public Service Commission postpones indefinitely implementation of proposed 25% cut in civil service salaries.

GG confirms normal trade union activities can proceed unhindered; expresses regret at detention of senior FTUC figures on 9 July; announces revised offer for sugar-cane farmers agreed by FSC and SCGC. Bavadra supports GG's hope that the harvest will restart.

Permanent Secretary for Fijian Affairs announces that GCOC will meet on 20 July including *all* Fijian members of dissolved House of Representatives.

Fiji Sun reports *Taukei* will arrange march of up to 10,000 people through Suva on 20 July to call upon GNCOC to declare a republic immediately.

Australian and New Zealand waterside unions lift trade boycott with effect from 20 July.

Taukei submission to CRC calls for Constitution in which '*Taukei* culture guides and dominates all facets of life in Fiji'.

GCOC meeting begins.

Ratu Mara visits again South-East Asian countries including Singapore, Indonesia and Korea regarding trade and military assistance.

GCOC submission to CRC agreed, proposing a unicameral Parliament with a Fijian absolute majority and reservation of key portfolios (including Prime Minister) for Fijians.

August 1987

Bavadra's spokesman, Naidu arrested and detained for 15 hours.

Former Police Commissioner, Raman and former Assistant Commissioner arrested (later released) for allegedly plotting against regime.

Solicitor-General and Acting First Parliamentary Counsel (both British OSAS) resign after their advice on limits on GG's powers rejected.

Application by Crown to strike out action by Bavadra refused; no date set for full hearing.

CRC report handed to GG, consisting of Majority Report and dissenting Minority Report by six members (four Coalition nominees'; two GG's).

September 1987

Initial meeting between delegations of Coalition and Alliance chaired by GG to seek an alternative way forward. *Taukei* members stage 'Lovo' on government offices lawn, later attack Richard Naidu.

Coalition agrees to resume talks with Alliance under the GG's chairmanship, provided they are held outside Suva.

Coalition/Alliance resume talks at Hyatt Regency Hotel on Coral Coast. Venue subsequently moves to Deuba.

Some Coalition homes fire-bombed including Naidu's parents'.

Further unrest in central Suva by *Taukei* supporters; youths rampage in city centre; one rioter shot in leg by soldiers.

Mass breakout from Naboro prison outside Suva. Escapees allowed by Security Forces to march on Government House with various demands, including pardons.

Bavadra agrees to drop court case against GG.

Alliance and Coalition parties agree to bipartisan caretaker government with GG as Head (the Deuba Accord). *Taukei* reject agreement.

Second military coup led by Colonel Rabuka (25 September 1987).

Army arrest about 80 politicians, civil servants, judges (including Judge Rooney).

journalists and others. Both daily newspapers and independent radio station closed. Night curfew and restrictions on Sunday activities established.

Bomb explodes in car in Suva; one killed.

The GG rejects invitation from Rabuka to be President of planned Republic and declines to stand down (27 September).

Rabuka tells press conference Fiji will be declared Republic; replacement for the 1970 Constitution being drafted.

Bavadra released from detention to attend a meeting between the GG, Rabuka, Ratu Mara and Bavadra at Government House.

Rabuka declares himself Head of State and no longer recognizes the GG as such (1 October).

Meeting in Lautoka between Army, Alliance and Coalition delegations, chaired by the GG. Coalition team rejects Army's eight 'minimum demands'.

Rabuka declares Fiji a Republic (6 October).

Fiji dollar further devalued by 15.25%. Mara leaves for talks at Buckingham Palace, as emissary of the GG.

Rabuka appoints 21-member Executive Council of Ministers with himself as Head of Government; states elections held within 12 months.

Chief Justice Sir Timoci Tuivaga and seven Supreme Court Judges refused to serve new regime; are dismissed.

GG requests Queen to relieve him of his duties, which she does.

CHOGM at Vancouver declares Fiji's Commonwealth membership lapsed.

Military government names new judges and magistrates, including two European, three Indian and two Fijian judges and seven Indian and three Fijian magistrates.

November 1987

Papua New Guinea (PNG) first country to recognize military government.

Four Supreme Court judges nominated for office; two decline appointment.

Rabuka promoted to Brigadier. Curfew lifted.

FTUC calls on military government to restore full trade union rights, which is done.

Foreign Minister Bole on 'private' visit to Australia and New Zealand.

Visit by Malaysian Foreign Minister Abu Hassan.

Foreign Minister Bole and Trade Minister Bose leave for two-week visit to China and Indonesia (Indonesian visit later cancelled).

December 1987

Rabuka, Ratu Penaia Ganilau and Ratu Mara meet at Government House. Rabuka announces that he is stepping down, dismisses his 22 ministers and appoints Ratu Sir Penaia Ganilau as first President of the Republic of Fiji; Ratu Mara to be Prime Minister.

Ratu Mara sworn in as Prime Minister. *Taukei* Movement express disapproval but deeply divided.

Ratu Mara announces 21-man cabinet, including ten from Rabuka's government and four military officers including Rabuka.

French offer of $14m aid package to Fiji disclosed.

Government approves $42m budget for Financial Year 1988 including 30% cut in government operating expenditure.

Police break up *Taukei* demonstrations in Suva; arrest two members of *Taukei* Movement.

Air New Zealand resumes Fiji service after seven-month suspension.

Bavadra's spokesman, Richard Naidu, has Fiji nationality revoked; given 28 days to leave Fiji.

January 1988

A group of Rotumans try to secede in protest against severing of links with the British Crown; Fijian Army shoots down Union flag on the island.

President Ratu Sir Penaia Ganilau grants immunity from prosecution to soldiers involved in the two coups; assuming full executive authority, formally abolishes Britain's Privy Council as the highest appeal body. Under the new judicial system, a nine-member High Court to replace the old Supreme Court; Court of Appeal maintained; new Supreme Court to replace the Privy Council; former Chief Justice, Sir Timoci Tuivaga, reappointed.

Fijian High Commissioner to London, Sailosi Kepa, recalled to Suva as the new Minister of Justice.

A Gang of Fijian youths armed with war club and sword, believed to be members of breakaway *Taukei* faction, attempt to seize control of Radio Fiji intending to broadcast they are taking control of the government; arrested by police.

Australia announces a reversal of diplomatic procedures to allow Canberra to renew formal relations with Fiji; changes criterion from recognition of governments to recognition of states.

February 1988

Austzalia and New Zealand resume aid to Fiji.

US sends Ambassador to Fiji; starts Congressional talks over restoring aid.

Brigadier Ratu Epeli Nailatikau, ousted army chief, appointed Republic of Fiji's first Ambassador to Great Britain.

Fiji tells foreign journalists they must in future obtain special permission to work there; this regarded overseas as potential censorship.

162 prisoners freed under general amnesty; President grants immunity from prosecution to political offenders charged after the 1987 April election.

March 1988

Prime Minister Ratu Mara visits London hoping to persuade Queen to accept title of Paramount Chief or 'Tui Viti' of the islands, originally held by Queen Victoria.

Warmly received at Downing Street but told his country must have acceptable Constitution before it could return to Commonwealth, and before the Queen would be willing to resume her role as Head of State.

Australia names Robert Cotton as its first Ambassador to Fiji.

Fijian troops and police guard Sigatoka, small Indian settlement 200 miles from Suva, after a group of Fijians go on a rampage, burning houses and vehicles. No one hurt.

April 1988

British Prime Minister, Margaret Thatcher, held hour-long 'very friendly' talks with Ratu Mara at Downing Street; discloses in House of Commons that Britain will again train Fijian military officers at British staff colleges and other establishments.

The Vunivalu of Bau, Paramount Chief Ratu Sir George Cakobau, declares that he, and not the Queen as claimed, holds the title 'Tui Viti', and has no plans to abdicate.

Ratu Sir Penaia Ganilau installed as one of Fiji's three senior chiefs, in a traditional ceremony as head of the Tovata Confederacy, ancient Fijian kingdom extending across four provinces in northern and eastern Fiji.

May 1988

Australian Customs seize 16 tons of arms in Sydney bound for Fiji.

The alleged mastermind behind the shipment, Mohammed Rafiq Kahan, flees from Sydney within hours of the arms discovery.

Fiji police allegedly try to 'gas' 18 protesters, including a British priest, after detaining them for holding illegal demonstration on 14 May, the anniversary of the first of two coups. All later released.

Eight chiefs are charged with sedition for trying to declare Rotuma independent of Fiji.

June 1988
22 people, including Ratu Mara's brother-in-law Ratu Mosese Tuisawau, charged with armed offences following seizure of large quantity of rifles, bayonets and grenades.

Police detain more than 40 Indians including two former Cabinet ministers, who are released later, after several tonnes of weapons are discovered in a series of raids.

Taimud Ahmed, Fiji-Indian aged 37, appears in Sydney court charged with conspiracy relating to 'an intention to engage in a hostile activity in a foreign state'. Mohammed Rafiq Kahan identified in court as plot's alleged mastermind.

Australian Prime Minister Bob Hawke personally intervenes to refuse visa to Rabuka who tries to visit Australia to promote his new biography, *Rabuka: No Other Way.*

Christopher Harder, Canadian lawyer defending five Indians charged with arms smuggling, detained for questioning.

President Ratu Sir Penaia Ganilau formally signs new Internal Security Decree, 1988, giving army power to shoot to kill anyone found with illegal arms who resists arrest. Rabuka, as Minister for Internal Security, has extraordinary range of powers which violate international standards of human rights. Basically he may:

1. Order the detention of any persons for up to two years;
2. Order restriction of movement, freedom of expression, employment, residence or activity;
3. Prohibit the printing, publication, sale, issue, circulation or possession of any written material, and prohibit its communication through word of mouth;
4. Require approval for any form of entertainment or exhibition;
5. Close down schools or educational institutions for up to six months and forbid or restrict the movement of teachers or students;
6. Proclaim any area as a security danger, or control area, whereupon a curfew may be imposed by any police officer above the rank of sergeant;
7. Order the possession or destruction of land and buildings in security areas;
8. Confiscate items of food or other supplies.

A USP lecturer arrested and severely beaten for publishing an article critical of Rabuka's book.

New Zealand Prime Minister David Lange attacks Fiji's draconian emergency regulations.

July 1988
British police detain Mohammed Rafiq Kahan in London in connection with the arms find in Australia and Fiji.

A Fiji Navy patrol sent to three of outer islands to quell reported outbreaks of witchcraft and drunken violence.

August 1988
Security officials detain Mesake Koro, Chief Reporter *Fiji Times*, under the new Internal Security Decree.

The sporadic harassment of Fiji Indians continues in most parts of Fiji.

BIBLIOGRAPHY

Ali, Ahmed (1972) 'The Fiji General Election of 1972', *Journal of Pacific History* (JPH), Vol. 8, pp. 171-180.

Ali, Ahmed (1973) 'The Indians of Fiji: Poverty, Prosperity and Security', *Economic and Political Weekly*, Vol. 8, No. 36.

Ali, Ahmed (1975) 'Fiji: Arrival of Communal Franchise', *Journal of Pacific Studies* (JPS), Vol. 1, No. 1, pp. 20-46.

Ali, Ahmed (1977a) *Fiji: From Colony to Independence 1874-1970*, University of the South Pacific (USP), Suva.

Ali, Ahmed (1977b) 'The Fiji General Election of 1977', *JPH*, Vol. 12, pp. 189-201.

Ali, Ahmed (1977c) 'The Emergence of Muslim Separatism in Fiji', *Plural Societies*, Vol. 8, No. 1, pp. 57-69.

Ali, Ahmed (1980) *Plantation to Politics: Studies on Fiji Indians*, USP, Suva.

Ali, Ahmed (1982) 'Fiji: The Politics of a Plural Society', *Politics in Melanesia*, USP, Suva.

Ali, Ahmed and Alexander Mamak (1979) *Race, Class and Rebellion in the South Pacific*, George Allen and Unwin, Sydney.

Anthony, James and Norman Meller (1963) *Fiji Goes to the Polls: The Crucial Legislative Council of 1963*, East West Centre Press, Honolulu, Hawaii.

Anthony, J. (1969) 'The 1968 Fiji By-Elections', *JPH*, Vol. 1, No. 4, pp. 132-35.

Anthony, J. (1988) 'US Strategic Interests in the Pacific', *Covert Action Information Bulletin*, Washington, No. 29 (Winter), pp. 3-6.

Bogdanor, Vernon and David Butler (eds.) (1983), *Democracy and Elections: Electoral System and Their Political Consequences*, Cambridge University Press (CUP), Cambridge.

Burns, Alan (1963) *Fiji*, Her Majesty's Stationery Office (HMSO), London.

Butler, David (1977) 'Politics and the Constitution: Twenty Questions Left by Remembrance Day', in Howard R. Penniman (ed.), *Australia at the Polls: The National Elections of 1975*, Washington.

Chick, J. (1973) 'Fiji: The General Election of 1972', *Pacific Perspective*, Vol. 1, No. 2, pp. 54-61.

Dean, Eddi and Stan Ritova (1988) *Rabuka: No Other Way*, The Marketing Team International Ltd., Suva.

Derrick, R.A. (1950) *A History of Fiji*, Vol. 1, Suva.

Dorrance, John (1980) *Oceania and the United States: An Analysis of US Interests and Policy in the South Pacific*, National Defense University Research Directorate, Washington.

Durutalo, Simione (1985) 'The Fiji Trade Union Movement at the Crossroads', *JPS*, Vol. 11, Suva.

Fisk, E.K. (1970) *The Political Economy of Independent Fiji*, Australian National University (ANU) Press, Canberra.

Freney, Denis (1977) *The CIA's Australian Connection*, Sydney.

Furnivall, J.S. (1948) *Colonial Policy and Practice: A Comparative Study of Burma and Netherlands East Indies*, CUP, Cambridge.

Gillion, K.L. (1962) *Fiji's Indian Migrants: A History to the End of Indenture in 1920*, Oxford University Press (OUP), Melbourne.

Gillion, K.L. (1977) *The Fiji Indians: Challenge to European Dominance 1920-46*, ANU Press, Canberra.

Grazebrowk, A.W. (1980) 'The Russian Pacific Fleet', *Pacific Defense Reporter*, pp. 15-24.

Herr, Richard (1983) 'Strategy and Security: The Choices are Few', in Ron Crocombe and Ahmed Ali (ed.), *Foreign Forces in Pacific Politics*, USP, Institute of Pacific Studies, Suva, pp. 290-308.

Holsti, K.J., (1974) *International Politics* (2nd edn.), Prentice-Hall International, Inc., London.

Hurst, John (1983) *Hawke, PM*, Angus and Robertson, Australia.

Keith-Lucas, Bryan (1976) 'Pacific Psephology', *Parliamentary Affairs*, Vol. XXIX, No. 3.

Kelly, Paul (1983) *The Dismissal*, Angus and Robertson, Australia.

Kuepper, W.E. et al. (1975) *Ugandan Asians in Great Britain*, Croom Helm, London.

Kux, E. (1970) 'Is Russia a Pacific Power?', *Pacific Community*, April 1970.

Lal, B.V. (1982) 'An Uncertain Journey: The Voyage of the Leonidas', *JPS*, Vol. 8, pp. 55-69.

Lal, B.V. (1983) Girmitiyas: 'The Origins of the Fiji Indians', *JPH*, Canberra.

Lal, B.V. (1985) 'Kunti's Cry: Indentured Women on Fiji Plantations', *The Indian Economic and Social History Review*, Vol. 22, No. 1, pp. 55-71.

Lasaqa, Isireli (1984) *The Fijian People: Before and After Independence 1959-77*, ANU Press, Canberra.

Lewis, W.A. (1965) *Politics in Africa*, London.

Lijphart, Arend (1977) *Democracy in Plural Societies: A Comparative Exploration*, Yale University Press, New Haven.

Macnaught, T.J. (1982) *The Fijian Colonial Experience: A Study of Neo-Traditional Order under British Colonial Rule prior to WWII*, ANU Pacific Research Monograph No. 7.

Mamak, Alexander (1978) *Colour, Culture and Conflict: A Study of Pluralism in Fiji*, Pergamon Press, Sydney.

Mayer, Adrian (1963) *Indians in Fiji*, OUP, London.

Mitrowich, F.R. (1971) 'The Hapless Asians of East Africa', *Plural Societies*, Vol. 2, No. 1 (Spring).

Milne, R.S. (1981) *Politics in Ethnically Bi-polar States: Guyana, Malaysia, Fiji*, The University of British Columbia Press, Vancouver.

Murray, David (1980) 'Fiji', in Georgina Ashworth (ed.), *World Minorities in the Eighties*, Quartermaine House Ltd. and Minority Rights Group, London.

Naipaul, V.S. (1962) *The Middle Passage*, Andre Deutsch, London.

Narayan, Jai (1984) *The Political Economy of Fiji*, South Pacific Review Press, Suva.

Narsey, Wadan (1979) 'Monopoly Capital, White Racism and Superprofits in Fiji: A Case Study of CSR', *JPH*, Vol. 5.

Narsey, Wadan (1985) 'The Wage Freeze and Development Plan Objectives: Contradictions in Fiji Government Policy', *JPS*, Vol. 11.

Nation, John (1978) *Customs of Respect: The Traditional Basis of Fijian Communal Politics*, ANU Development Studies Monograph No. 14.

Nayacakalou, R. (1975) *Leadership in Fiji*, OUP, Melbourne.

Norman, Dorothy (ed.) (1965) *Nehru: The First Sixty Years*, Vol. 1, London.

Norton, Robert (1977) *Race and Politics in Fiji*, University of Queensland Press, St. Lucia.

Norton, Robert (1981) 'The Mediation of Ethnic Conflict: Comparative Implications of the Fiji Case', *Journal of Commonwealth and Comparative Politics*, Vol. 19, pp. 309-28.

Plange, Nik-K (1985) 'Colonial Capitalism and Class Formation in Fiji: A Retrospective overview', *JPS*, Vol. 11.

Premdas, R. (1980) 'Constitutional Challenge: The Rise of Fijian Nationalism', *Pacific Perspective*, Vol. 9, No. 2, pp. 30-44.

Premdas, R. (1980) 'Elections in Fiji: Restoration of the Balance', *JPH*, Vol. 4, No. 4, pp. 197-204.

Premdas, P. (1981) 'Towards a Government of National Unity in Fiji: Political Interests versus Survival of State', *Pacific Perspective*, Vol. 10.

Race, Jeffrey (1972) *War Comes to Long An: Revolutionary Conflict in a Vietnamese Village*, University of California Press, California.

Rakoto, A. (1973) 'Can Custom Be Custom-Built? Cultural Obstacles to Fijian Communal Enterprise', *Pacific Perspective*, Vol. 2, No. 2.

Rokotuivuna, A. (1973) *Fiji: A Developing Australian Colony*, International Development Action, Melbourne.

Roth, G.K. (1953) *Fijian Way of Life*, OUP, Melbourne.

Routledge, David (1985) *Matanitu: The Struggle for Power in Early Fiji*, Suva.

Scarr, D. (ed.) (1983) *Fiji: The Three-Legged Stool—Selected Writings of Ratu Sir Lala Sukuna*, London, companion volume to Scarr's biography of Sukuna, *Ratu Sukuna: Soldier, Statesman, Man of Two Worlds*, London.

Spate, O.H.K. (1959) *The Fijian People: Economic Problems and Prospects*, Suva.

Tinker, Hugh (1974) *A New System of Slavery*, OUP, London.

Tinker, Hugh (1975) 'Indians Abroad: Emigration, Restriction, and Rejection', in Michael Twaddle (ed.), *Expulsions of a Minority: Essays on Ugandan Asians*, Athlone Press, London.

Tinker, Hugh (1976) *Separate and Unequal*, C. Hurst and Company, London.

Vasil, R.K. (1984) *Politics in Bi-Racial Societies: The Third World Experience*, Vikas Publishing House Pvt. Ltd., New Delhi.

Ward, R.G. (1965) *Land Use and Population in Fiji*, London.

Watters, R.F. (1969) *Koro: Economic Development and Social Change in Fiji*, Clarendon Press, Oxford.

Yacoe, C. (1984) 'Reagan's Pacific Isles Policies', *Pacific Magazine*, May/June.

Official Publications

Report of the Commission of Inquiry into the Natural Resource and Population Trend of the Colony of Fiji, 1959 (Suva: Legislative Council of Fiji, Council Paper No. 1, 1960).

Report of the Working Committee Set Up to Review the Agricultural Landlord and Tenant Ordinance No. 23 of 1966 (Parliamentary Paper No. 13, 1975).

Report of the Fiji Constitutional Conference 1970, Cmnd. 4389 (London, HMSO, 1970).

Report of the Royal Commission Appointed for the Purpose of Considering and Making Recommendations as to the Most Appropriate Method of Electing Members to, and Representing the People of Fiji in, the House of Representatives (Parliamentary Paper No. 24, 1975).

Report of the Royal Commission into the 1982 Fiji General Election (Parliamentary Paper No. 74, 1983).

Newspapers and Magazines

FIJI:
Fiji Sun (Daily)
Fiji Times (Daily)
Islands Business News (Monthly)
Pacific Islands (Monthly)

AUSTRALIA:
The Australian
The Bulletin
Melbourne Herald

LONDON:
Daily Telegraph
Financial Times
The Guardian
The Sunday Observer
The Sunday Times
The Times

Index

Verwoerd, H.F., 242
Vesikula, Ratu Meli, 206, 207, 209, 210, 213, 214, 234, 238-9, 242
Victoria, Queen, 7, 142, 217
Vietnam, 227
Viuyasawa, Ratu Keni, 193
Volavola, Ratu Livai, 58
voting: communal, 236; eligibility for, 236

wage freeze, 166, 168, 171
Walker, Charles, 107
Walters, Vernon, 223-6, 228
Watters, R.F., 232
Watts, Max, 225
Weinberger, Caspar, 226
Weiner, Myron, 27
Weisbrot, David, 224
Western Democratic Party, 4

Western United Front (WUF), 69, 71, 72-5, 77, 81, 94, 137, 159, 175, 176
White, Eirene, 8
White, Sir John, 100, 112, 118-19, 132, 134, 149, 163, 164-5
Whitlam, Gough, 56, 60, 115, 151
Wilkinson, Marian, 103, 112, 122, 173
Williams, Eric, 11
Williams, John Brown, 142
Wingti, Paias, 229
Wood, Anthony, 208, 210
World Bank Report, 26
Wypijewski, Joann, 225-7

Yabaki, Rev. Akuila, 239

Zimbabwe, 156